COMPUTING MEANING

Studies in Linguistics and Philosophy

Volume 73

The titles published in this series are listed at the end of this volume.

COMPUTING MEANING

Volume 1

edited by

HARRY BUNT
Tilburg University, The Netherlands

and

REINHARD MUSKENS
Tilburg University, The Netherlands

KLUWER ACADEMIC PUBLISHERS
DORDRECHT / BOSTON / LONDON

A C.I.P. Catalogue record for this book is available from the Library of Congress.

ISBN 1-4020-0290-4
Transferred to Digital Print 2001

Published by Kluwer Academic Publishers,
P.O. Box 17, 3300 AA Dordrecht, The Netherlands.

Sold and distributed in North, Central and South America
by Kluwer Academic Publishers Group,
101 Philip Drive, Norwell, MA 02061, U.S.A.

In all other countries, sold and distributed
by Kluwer Academic Publishers,
P.O. Box 322, 3300 AH Dordrecht, The Netherlands.

Printed on acid-free paper

Printed in the Netherlands.

CONTENTS

HARRY BUNT AND REINHARD MUSKENS

COMPUTATIONAL SEMANTICS

1. INTRODUCTION

Computational semantics is concerned with computing the meanings of linguistic objects such as sentences, text fragments, and dialogue contributions. As such it is the interdisciplinary child of semantics, the study of meaning and its linguistic encoding, and computational linguistics, the discipline that is concerned with computations on linguistic objects.

From one parent computational semantics inherits concepts and techniques that have been developed under the banner of formal (or model-theoretic) semantics. This blend of logic and linguistics applies the methods of logic to the description of meaning. From the other parent the young discipline inherits methods and techniques for parsing sentences, for effective and efficient representation of syntactic structure and logical form, and for reasoning with semantic information. As is often the case with inheritance, blessings are mixed and computational semantics' legacy not only contains useful elements but also many problems and unresolved issues. In fact, many of the well-known problems in semantics such as those relating to handling ambiguity and vagueness, as well as fundamental issues regarding compositionality and context-dependence, re-appear in computational semantics in a form even more compelling than in formal semantics. In this introductory chapter we shall highlight some of the issues and problems we think are most pressing. We shall start with discussing a straightforward way to implement formal semantics in the tradition that started with Montague's work. Then, after a conceptual analysis of the principle of compositionality and a discussion of its role in computational work, the *problem of ambiguity* will be introduced and it will be shown that the straightforward way of taking standard formal semantics as a specification of computer algorithms needs to be amended. An important issue in computational semantics is that of the *context dependency* of language. The task set to computational semanticists is to provide concrete linguistic objects with abstract meanings; as concrete linguistic objects are utterances rather than sentences (types of utterances), computational semantics

H. Bunt and R. Muskens (eds.), Computing Meaning, Volume 1, 1–32.
© 1999 *Kluwer Academic Publishers. Printed in the Netherlands.*

needs to draw in a lot of the work that takes context into account and traditionally goes under the banner of pragmatics. After a discussion of this, and of the need for *underspecified representations* of meaning, which arises out of the ambiguity problem, the chapter closes with an overview of the other chapters in this book.

2. Algorithmic Realisations of Model-Theoretic Semantics

The beginnings of computational semantics can be traced back to the pioneering work of Richard Montague in formal semantics. His work is of direct relevance to computational semantics, due to the detail and precision with which it describes how the expressions of a small 'fragment' of some natural language can be associated with meaning representations in a formal, logical language for which a model-theoretic interpretation is provided.

The association of language with logic is defined in two steps in Montague's work. First, since natural language is ambiguous but logic is not, the expressions of the fragment under consideration (let us call it NL_0) must be 'disambiguated'; each expression may have one or more *readings*. Formally this boils down to defining a 'disambiguation' relation ρ between expressions in NL_0 and expressions in some language $\mathcal{R}$ of readings. In Montague (1973) $\mathcal{R}$ is a collection of 'analysis trees', but we may illustrate the set-up here by letting $\mathcal{R}$ be a collection of Logical Forms in the sense of May (1977). In (1) below, the Logical Forms (1c) and (1d) are readings of (1a), while (1b) corresponds to the constituent structure of (1a). Accordingly we have that $(1a)\rho(1c)$ and that $(1a)\rho(1d)$.

(1) a. Every student caught a fish

    b. $[_S[_{NP}$ every student$]$ $[_{VP}$ caught $[_{NP}$ a fish$]]]$

    c. $[[$every student$]^1$ $[[$a fish$]^2$ $[e_1[$caught $e_2]]]]$

    d. $[[$a fish$]^2$ $[[$every student$]^1$ $[e_1[$caught $e_2]]]]$

    e. $\forall x[S(x) \rightarrow \exists y[F(y) \wedge C(x,y)]]$

    f. $\exists y[F(y) \wedge \forall x[S(x) \rightarrow C(x,y)]]$

An important constraint on the language $\mathcal{R}$ in Montague's set-up is that its elements should be *uniquely readable* and that it should be possible to define a translation *function* τ from $\mathcal{R}$ into some interpreted logical language.[1] In classical Montague Semantics the logic of choice is Intensional Logic (IL), a variant of Russell's and Church's Theory of Types. Here we may illustrate the procedure by using classical logic, assuming that $\tau((1c)) = (1e)$ and that $\tau((1d)) = (1f)$.

Once ρ and τ are defined, we have an interpretation of NL_0, provided that the target of τ really is an interpreted logic. For such logics $\mathcal{L}$ an interpretation function $[\![.]\!]$ is defined which, given a model M and an assignment a, associates with each well-formed expression φ of $\mathcal{L}$ a semantic value $[\![\varphi]\!]^{M,a}$ constructed from the entities in M. Obviously, the compound relation $\rho \circ \tau \circ \lambda\varphi.[\![\varphi]\!]^{M,a}$ associates semantic values with expressions of NL_0. Montague stressed that the intermediate stage of logical representations is inessential: in theory it is possible to map readings of natural language expressions to model-theoretic meanings directly.

Suppose that ρ and τ are defined for some fragment NL_0 and that sentences in NL_0 are thus associated with truth-conditions. Then the following kind of questions are answerable in principle.

1. Does sentence S on its reading r **follow** from sentence S' on reading r'? This boils down to asking whether $\tau(r') \models_{\mathcal{L}} \tau(r)$ (where $\models_{\mathcal{L}}$ is the relation of logical consequence in the logic $\mathcal{L}$).

2. Is sentence S on its reading r **true** in situation s? This boils down to finding a model M which models the relevant aspects of s and to asking whether $M \models \tau(r)$.

This means that notions of *truth* and *logical consequence* are now defined for NL_0, be it that both are given relative to the various possible readings of the expressions involved, a restriction which is not unnatural.

There is some empirical bite to this. People have *intuitions* about the notions of truth and consequence in their native language, even though these intuitions usually leave many cases undecided. True, it is often difficult to elicit clear judgements about the question whether some sentence is true in a given situation or the question whether one sentence follows from another, and even speakers of the same ideolect may not find themselves in agreement about some of these questions. But there are also many cases in which judgements are clear. This means that the entailment relation and the notion of truth that we

---

[1] τ should be functional *modulo* logical equivalence, i.e. if $\tau(\alpha) = A$ and A' is logically equivalent with A, we also write $\tau(\alpha) = A'$.

get from ρ and τ may in fact be contradicted by empirical evidence, if we accept native speaker judgement as such. Montague thought of his work as pertaining purely to mathematics, but in the light of the possibility that a particular choice of ρ and τ may be falsified, we may re-interpret his theory as being empirical and start playing the usual game of conjectures and refutations. By considering larger and larger fragments NL_0, adapting the definitions of ρ and τ, playing with various possibilities for the intermediate language $\mathcal{R}$, and varying the logic $\mathcal{L}$, we may try to obtain better and better approximations to natural language, its truth conditions, and the natural language entailment relation.

Turning to the possibility of realising Montague Grammar algorithmically, we see that for many steps existing technology can be used. Parsing technology provides us with a realisation of the transition from strings to surface structures such as the one from (1a) to (1b). And once we have found logical representations such as the ones in (1e) and (1f), theorem proving technology can be used to provide us with a partial answer to the entailment question discussed in 1. above. Since any logic $\mathcal{L}$ that aspires to translate natural language will be undecidable, we can only hope for a partial answer here, but in practice a lot of reasoning can be automated and many theorem provers (especially those of the tableau variety) also as a bonus provide us with counterexamples to invalid arguments. Evaluation of a sentence on some given model, as in 2., can also be automated, as the excellent educational program *Tarski's World* amply illustrates. A restriction here is that models must be finite (otherwise quantification cannot be decided). In practice, models can take the concrete form of databases. Some of the earliest work in this area are that in the PHLIQA project at Philips Research (see Bronnenberg et al., 1979; Bunt, 1981; Scha, 1983) and that of Konolige (1986).

This leaves us with the transitions from surface structure to Logical Form, e.g. from (1b) to (1c) or (1d), and from Logical Form to $\mathcal{L}$, e.g. from (1c) to (1e). As we are now in the province of computational semantics proper, let us look at these transitions in some detail. Here is a little calculus that performs the first of the tasks mentioned. It uses a *storage* mechanism inspired by that of Cooper (1983) and computes a ternary relation κ between (a) a surface structure, (b) a Logical Form, and (c) the store, which will be a set of superscripted surface structures of category NP here.

(2) (Terminate) $\kappa(A, A, \emptyset)$,   if A is a terminal;

     (Store) $\kappa(NP, e_k, \{NP^k\})$,   where k is fresh;

     (Pass) $\dfrac{\kappa(A, \alpha, s) \quad \kappa(B, \beta, s')}{\kappa([_C AB], [\alpha\beta], s \cup s')}$

     (Retrieve) $\dfrac{\kappa(NP, \nu, s) \quad \kappa(S, \sigma, s' \cup \{NP^k\})}{\kappa(S, [\nu^k \sigma], s \cup s')}$

In the Pass rule, C can be any syntactic category; in the Store and Retrieve rules, NP and S stand for any surface structure of category NP and S, respectively. The idea is that a Logical Form can be obtained from a given surface structure by traversing the latter in a bottom-up manner, putting elements that can raise, such as quantified NPs, in store, and retrieving them later nondeterministically at some S node.[2] Applied to (1), for example, the calculus can be used to derive $\kappa((1b), (1c), \emptyset)$. Rule Store licences the NPs *every student*, with Logical Form e_1 and store $\{[_{NP} \text{ every student}]^1\}$, and *a fish* with logical form e_2 and store $\{[_{NP} \text{ a fish}]^2\}$. Rule Pass can be used to derive the VP *caught a fish* (where *caught* is licensed by rule Terminate) with Logical Form [caught e_2], and can subsequently be used to obtain *every student caught a fish* with Logical Form $[e_1[\text{caught } e_2]]$. Rule Pass also licenses *a fish* and *every student* with Logical Forms [a fish]^2 and [every student]^1, respectively; finally, successive applications of Retrieve result in the derivation of $\kappa([_S[_{NP} \text{ every student}] [_{VP} \text{ caught } [_{NP} \text{ a fish}]]], [[\text{a fish}]^2 [e_1[\text{caught } e_2]]], \{[_{NP} \text{ every student}]^1\})$, and to the desired end result $\kappa([_S[_{NP} \text{ every student}] [_{VP} \text{ caught } [_{NP} \text{ a fish}]]], [[\text{every student}]^1[[\text{a fish}]^2 [e_1[\text{caught } e_2]]]], \emptyset)$.

The calculus in (2) is simple, but it has a nice property. It is perhaps worth noting that in cases such as (3) below, where an NP can raise out of NP, the latter can happen only if the embedded NP is retrieved from store later than the embedding one. This means that it will not be possible to derive forms where *a company* does not c-command its trace.

---

[2] Note that the calculus allows retrieving an NP and immediately storing it by using $\kappa(NP, e_j, \{NP^j\})$ as the left premise in the (Retrieve) rule. This will lead to a structure $[e_j^k \sigma]$, with NP^j stored and σ containing e_k. Further processing would lead to a structure $[NP^j[\cdots[e_j^k[\cdots e_k \cdots]]\cdots]]$, i.e. to a chain. At present structures $[e_j^k \sigma]$ will be left uninterpreted by the (Quantify In) rule discussed below, but the addition of a simple type-lifting rule would render them interpretable.

(3) Every representative of a company saw some samples

Our relation ρ can be defined by letting $\rho(A, \alpha)$ if and only if $\kappa(A, \alpha, \emptyset)$ and it may be observed that this in fact gives a computational realisation of the disambiguation relation, as the calculus above is almost identical to the logic program implementing it.

The stage is now set for translating Logical Forms into logical formulas. One of the central ideas in Montague Grammar is that this can be done by shifting to a *typed* logic with lambda abstraction over variables of arbitrary type. Translations of terminal elements can then be as in the following mini-lexicon.

(4) every $\rightsquigarrow \lambda P' \lambda P \forall x[P'(x) \to P(x)]$ (type $(et)((et)t)$)

a $\rightsquigarrow \lambda Q' \lambda Q \exists y[Q'(y) \wedge Q(y)]$ (type $(et)((et)t)$)

student $\rightsquigarrow S$ (type et)

fish $\rightsquigarrow F$ (type et)

caught $\rightsquigarrow C$ (type $e(et)$)

The mapping τ can be defined as follows.

(5) (Lex) $\tau(\alpha) = A,$ if $\alpha \rightsquigarrow A$;

$\tau(e_k) = x_k,$ (type e)

(App) $\tau([\alpha\beta]) = \begin{cases} \tau(\alpha)(\tau(\beta)), & \text{if } \tau(\alpha)(\tau(\beta)) \text{ is well-typed,} \\ \tau(\beta)(\tau(\alpha)), & \text{if } \tau(\beta)(\tau(\alpha)) \text{ is well-typed,} \\ \text{undefined otherwise;} \end{cases}$

(Q In) $\tau([\nu^k \sigma]) = \begin{cases} \tau(\nu)(\lambda x_k.\tau(\sigma)), & \text{if this is well-typed,} \\ \text{undefined otherwise.} \end{cases}$

Here α, β and ν range over labeled bracketings which do not carry an outermost superscript, so that (App) does not apply when (Q(uantify) In) does. Clearly, maximally one of the first two cases in (Apply) will lead to results on any given input. The reader will note that our previous requirement that $\tau((1c)) = (1e)$ and that $\tau((1d)) = (1f)$ is met.[3]

---

[3] Applying rule Q In twice for processing the Logical Form parts [every student][1] and [a fish][2], and using rule App (plus Lex) to translate the resulting subexpressions, results in the formula $(\lambda P \forall x[S(x) \to P(x)])(\lambda x_1.(\lambda Q \exists y[F(y) \wedge Q(y)])(\lambda x_2.(C(x_2)(x_1))))$, which is a notational variant of (1e).

We are now in the possession of a well-defined disambiguation relation ρ and a well-defined translation function τ, both easily implementable. But there is an obvious inefficiency in the combination of our calculi, since while ρ is computed by recursing over phrase structures, the function τ is computed by recursing again over the output of ρ. It would be nicer to have a calculus that computes $\rho \circ \tau$ in one fell swoop. Here is one.

(6) (Terminate) $\vartheta(A, A', \emptyset)$, if $A \rightsquigarrow A'$ is in the lexicon;

    (Store) $\vartheta(NP, x_k, \{\dot{N}P^k\})$, where k is fresh;

    (Apply) $$\frac{\vartheta(A, A', s) \quad \vartheta(B, B', s')}{\vartheta([_C AB], A'(B'), s \cup s')};$$

$$\frac{\vartheta(A, A', s) \quad \vartheta(B, B', s')}{\vartheta([_C AB], B'(A'), s \cup s')};$$

    (Retrieve) $$\frac{\vartheta(NP, Q, s) \quad \vartheta(S, S', s' \cup \{NP^k\})}{\vartheta(S, Q(\lambda x_k.S'), s \cup s')}$$

Again we have the self-evident side conditions that the second argument of ϑ must remain well-typed. Clearly $\vartheta(A, A', s)$ will be derivable for some labelled bracketing A, term A', and store s if and only if there is a Logical Form α such that $\kappa(A, \alpha, s)$ and $\tau(\alpha) = A'$ are derivable in our previous calculi. Since A and A' are in the relation $\rho \circ \tau$ iff $\vartheta(A, A', \emptyset)$, we have a direct computation of that relation. Intermediate computation of Logical Forms is avoided. The calculus in (6) is very close to Cooper's original mechanism of Quantifier Storage, be it that it stores NP surface structures, not NP meanings. It has perhaps some edge over existing systems of Cooper storage. On the one hand it repairs the difficulty that Cooper's original formulation had with sentences such as (3), which contain an NP that can rise out of NP. On the other hand the calculus keeps the structure of stored elements simple. The mechanism of 'Nested Cooper Storage' in Keller (1986) is closely related to the present proposal, but Keller's 'nested stores' are rather more complex data structures than our sets of labelled bracketings for NPs.

This closes the gap between the output of our parser, which we assumed to be in tree format, and the input of our theorem prover, which we took to be classical logic. The calculus in (6) will work for toy context-free grammars of natural language fragments, but will also scale up to more realistic systems.

At this point it may seem that implementation of semantic theories is plain sailing. In order to automatically get information about entailments in natural language, parse the sentences involved, translate the resulting constituent structures to some logical language using a mechanism such as that in (6), and then use standard theorem proving technology. (Less than standard theorem proving technology will be needed of course if your target logic is less than standard.) The procedure seems simple enough, but in fact it cannot be realised on any realistic scale. The reason is the *pervasive ambiguity of natural language*. This will be explained in section 4 below.

3. COMPOSITIONALITY

3.1. *Compositionality and contextuality*

Montague's work falls squarely within the tradition of semantics following the Principle of *Compositionality*, which says in its most general formulation that *The meaning of a compound expression is a function of the meanings of its parts*. Partee et al. (1990) formulate the principle slightly more restrictively as follows: *The meaning of a compound expression is a function of the meanings of its parts and of the syntactic rule by which they are combined*.

Montague applies the compositionality principle on a rule-to-rule basis, assuming that for each syntactic rule, specifying how an expression can be built from simpler ones, the grammar contains a corresponding semantic rule that says how the meaning of the expression depends on the meanings of the parts.

It should be noted, however, that Compositionality in its most general formulation does not necessarily require a rule-to-rule correspondence between syntax and semantics. The notion of 'part', occurring in the principle, is often understood as 'constituent' in the sense of a substructure that has a significance in a syntactic structural description, but this is an unnecessarily restricted interpretation. A grammar may define the set of well-formed expressions of a language by means of derivation rules without attributing a structural syntactic significance to the elements that are used in the rules (as in some versions of Categorial Grammar); the semantic composition function may then operate on these 'parts' rather than on syntactically significant parts.

Intuitively, it would seem that compositionality is a strong property of the way syntax and semantics are related in a grammar, but this is less obvious when a notion of 'part' is allowed that does not necessarily have a syntactic significance. And even when only syntactically significant parts are allowed, the power of Compositionality is not really clear, since the notion of syntactic part is theory-dependent; different grammatical theories use different kinds of parts. Janssen (1996) has shown that many purported counterexamples to Compositionality in sentence meaning can be handled by introducing new kinds of part, new syntactic constructions, or new kinds of meaning. Similarly, he proves that for any recursively enumerable language L (i.e. any language that can be generated by a Turing machine) and any computable function M that assigns meanings to the expressions of L, it is possible to cast M in a compositional form. This latter result strongly suggests that any grammar for any given natural language can be cast in a compositional form. In other words, if natural languages can be described by grammars at all, then they can be described by compositional grammars.

In view of these results, one may feel that the compositionality principle does not really make a strong claim about the relation between syntax and semantics. We feel that this is indeed so and agree with Janssen in that the principle merely serves a methodological purpose, not strictly an empirical one. But there is a claim that is often felt to be entailed by Compositionality, although in fact it is much stronger. This is the view that the meaning of an expression can only depend on the expression itself and thus entails the negation of Frege's principle of *Contextuality*, which says that *"One should ask for the meaning of a word only in the context of a sentence, and not in isolation."* That Compositionality in fact does not entail the negation of Contextuality (*pace* Janssen (1996)) is easily seen, however, as the first principle literally only constrains the relation between the meanings of complex expressions and the meanings of their parts and is silent about the question where simple expressions derive their meanings from.

Let us consider some examples to show that Compositionality and Contextuality can peacefully coexist. Phenomena such as anaphora and VP deletion involve the dependence of expressions upon other expressions. For example, on the intended reading of (7a) the pronouns *"they"* and *"it"* depend on previous material for their interpretation. *"They"* refers back to the five girls and *it* refers back to the kissing. This means that these words cannot be taken to have meaning in isolation. On the other hand, once the simple expressions in (7a) are provided with their right interpretation, it seems obvious that the meanings of mother categories can be computed from the meanings of their daughters. So in (7a) words do not have meaning in isolation but the meaning of complex expressions are functions of the meanings of their parts. Similarly, the interpretation of *"did"* in (7b) cannot be considered in isolation, as it obviously depends on the previous VP. But once *"did"* is interpreted correctly as *kissed five girls* the meaning of the sentence can be computed in a rule-by-rule way.

(7)   a. John kissed five girls. They liked it.

    b. John first kissed five girls and then Max did

We also want to point out that the question in how far expressions can be considered in isolation, depends on the notion of 'expression' that we are using. Are we talking about the type or the token, the sentence or the utterance? The tokens in (8a) and (8b) are different occurrences of the same sentence.

(8)   a. Where *does* Mary live?

    b. WHERE DOES MARY LIVE

A *sentence* being a linguistic abstraction from utterances, there can be no methodological objection against assuming its meaning to be some sort of abstraction of the meanings of all its possible utterances in different contexts. This gives a certain independence from context, be it an imperfect one. *Utterances* on the other hand, are clearly context-dependent to a large degree. The meaning of an utterance depends not only on the information contained in the utterance itself, but is also strongly dependent on contextual considerations. This consideration is the more pressing in computational semantics as the task of the computational semanticist will often consist in devising algorithms to provide concrete utterances with a precise meaning.

3.2. *Compositionality, bottom-up construction, and bottom-up evaluation*

There are a number of ideas closely related to Compositionality that should carefully be distinguished from the concept itself. We discuss two of them here as they are relevant to the computational perspective on semantics. The first we may call the idea of *Bottom-up Construction*, the second may be dubbed *Bottom-up Evaluation*. In order to explain what Bottom-up Construction is, we have drawn a syntactic tree for the sentence *"John believes Mary kissed Sue"* in (9). In (10) the tree in (9) gets interpreted by means of a system of equations, each equation expressing the value $\sigma(n_i)$ of node n_i, either in terms of some constant (if n_i is a leaf node) or in terms of the values of its daughters.

(9)

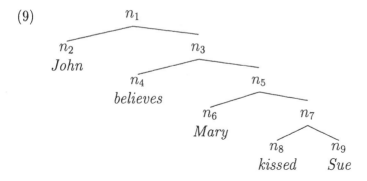

(10) $\begin{aligned}
\sigma(n_2) &= \text{john} \\
\sigma(n_4) &= \text{bel} \\
\sigma(n_6) &= \text{mary} \\
\sigma(n_8) &= \text{kiss} \\
\sigma(n_9) &= \text{sue} \\
\sigma(n_1) &= \sigma(n_3)(\sigma(n_2)) \\
\sigma(n_3) &= \sigma(n_4)(\sigma(n_5)) \\
\sigma(n_5) &= \sigma(n_7)(\sigma(n_6)) \\
\sigma(n_7) &= \sigma(n_8)(\sigma(n_9))
\end{aligned}$

From the equations in (10) the value of $\sigma(n_1)$ can be computed to be $bel(kiss(sue)(mary))(john)$. But note that there are different ways to go about here. A *top-down* construction could first compute $\sigma(n_1) = \sigma(n_3)(\sigma(n_2))$, then $\sigma(n_1) = \sigma(n_4)(\sigma(n_5))(\sigma(n_2))$, then $\sigma(n_1) = \sigma(n_4)(\sigma(n_7)(\sigma(n_6)))(\sigma(n_2))$, etc. But working *bottom-up* we could first derive $\sigma(n_7) = kiss(sue)$, then $\sigma(n_5) = kiss(sue)(mary)$, and so on, until the top is reached. Compositional interpretation schemes often go with bottom-up semantic construction, but it is important to note that this need not be the case. The equations in (10) satisfy the semantic compositionality requirement, but a solution can be found by traversing them in arbitrary order. In Muskens (1995) it is argued that this order-independence of interpretation is computationally useful. Note that the possibility of casting the semantics of (9) in the form of a system of equations that is solvable by means of a series of simple substitutions rests on the absence of variables. Had any of the intermediary representations contained a free variable, at least one substitution would not have been possible. Muskens (1995) discusses a simple technique ('internalising the binding mechanism') which overcomes this difficulty and makes it possible to always represent semantic values by means of systems of equations.

While these considerations show that Compositionality and Bottom-up Construction should be separated at least on a conceptual level, the following quotation from Nerbonne (1995) introduces still another concept, namely that of the order in which terms are *evaluated*.

Compositionality concerns the relation between syntax and semantics — i.e. (static) linguistic structure, not processing. Nonetheless, the compositional view often extends to a natural and popular interpretation, that of bottom-up processing. This is a natural interpretation because compositional semantics specifies the semantics of phrases via functions on the semantics of their daughters. It is natural to evaluate arguments before attempting functions to them (although partial and so-called 'lazy' evaluation schemes certainly exist).

Here the question is not so much in which order a final semantic representation of some expression is computed, but in which order the various parts of that representation are evaluated on a given model. Consider e.g. a disjunction $\varphi \vee \psi$. A strict bottom-up evaluation scheme would (a) compute the value of φ, (b) compute the value of ψ (not necessarily in this order), and then (c) take the maximum of the results. Lazy evaluation, on the other hand, would allow concluding that the value of $\varphi \vee \psi$ is 1 as soon as one of the disjuncts evaluates to 1. There is clearly a computational advantage to be gained here. The input-output behaviour of both evaluation schemes is the same only on the condition that the evaluation of a formula always returns a value. When this is not the case, for instance because information of a presuppositional character can render one subexpression undefined, empirical considerations may bear upon the question which evaluation scheme should be chosen.

Note that a radical interpretation of Bottom-up Evaluation would make it very unattractive from a computational point of view. In (1) we have given the value of (1c) as (1e), but this result was obtained after tacitly performing simplifications on the basis of λ-conversion. Evaluating (1e) on a finite model should be feasible if the model is not too large, although each quantifier essentially requires inspecting all elements of the domain. But Bottom-up Evaluation requires that daughters be evaluated before their mothers are, so it seems to require that the value of *every*, i.e. of $\lambda P' \lambda P \forall x[P'(x) \rightarrow P(x)]$, on the model given be computed before it is combined with the value of *student*, S, and so on. As this needlessly gives a gigantic explosion of the number of computations involved, it must be concluded that Bottom-up Evaluation on a strict interpretation is extremely unattractive. Whether there can be more acceptable weaker interpretations of this evaluation scheme remains to be seen, but it is clear that Bottom-up Evaluation and Compositionality should not be confused.

A technique somewhat similar to lazy evaluation that does result in a compositional process has been applied for computing meanings as early as in 1984 in the TENDUM system (see Bunt et al., 1984), where quantificational ambiguities where treated by postponing disambiguation in a process that constructs the meaning of a noun phrase as a pair ⟨quant', nom'⟩ where quant' represents the semantics of a quantifying phrase and nom' represents the semantics of the head noun with any modifiers. Only when NP meanings are used to compute clause meanings are the quant' and nom' parts combined to form NP meanings of the usual kind. This process is somewhat similar to the use of Cooper storage but is more clearly compositional.

4. THE AMBIGUITY PROBLEM

The design of a process that computes meanings for a nontrivial range of sentences meets one obstacle more than any other: the overwhelming amount of ambiguity and vagueness inherent to natural language. Compositionality tells us that we can combine word meanings into the meanings of phrases, and phrase meanings into the meanings of sentences. But ambiguity and vagueness present problems to this at all points in the process. It presents problems at the lexical level, since most words are ambiguous (as well as vague), so for a start we have to assume a *range* of meanings for every word rather than a single meaning. Disregarding vagueness for the moment, we can hope that these ranges are finite sets, but this isn't entirely certain. Consider the meanings of prepositions like 'at', 'on', 'in'; these words allow an enormous range of semantically different uses, where it often seems rather arbitrary why one preposition should be used rather than another one (as witnessed by the difficulty of chosing the right prepositions in a foreign language). For many words, in particular for many of the most frequently used words, we have to assume large sets of meanings. The combination of words to form phrases, and of phrases to form sentences, gives rise to additional ambiguities: those caused by syntactic ambiguities, such as PP attachment, as well as those that have no syntactic reflection, for instance when scope-bearing expressions are combined to form larger structures. Together these phenomena cause an explosion of the number of alternatives that must be considered by a process that is able to compute all the meanings of a nontrivial sentence. To appreciate the size of this problem, consider the following example.

Suppose (rather modestly!) that every word has 3 meanings. Take a simple sentence, like the present one, of twelve words length. Assume that the sentence is analysed in a strictly binary fashion, as illustrated in the tree diagram (11). For each of the nodes A, B, C, D, E and F there are 9 possible compound meanings to consider. At the next level up, for P, Q and R there are $9 \times 9 = 81$ choices. For node T, we have $81 \times 81 = 6.561$ possibilities, and at the top level we have $81 \times 6.561 = 531.441 \ (= 3^{12})$ possibilities. In other words, a modest degree of lexical ambiguity alone gives rise to half a million meanings for a simple sentence.

(11)

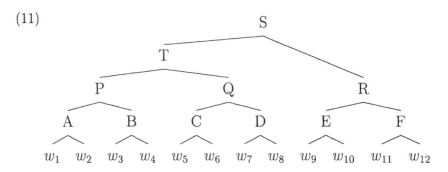

When we add syntactic and purely semantic (phrasal) ambiguity, we get truly astronomical numbers of interpretations. For instance, Hobbs and Shieber (1987) argue that the sentence

(12) Some representatives of every department in most companies saw a few samples of every product

has 42 valid alternative scopings.

More generally, in a sentence with five NPs, like (12), we have, depending on the constraints on scoping implied by the syntactic relations between the NPs, any number between 16 and 120 of alternative NP scopings. Many noun phrases also have a collective / distributive ambiguity, as illustrated by *"We lifted the piano"* vs. *"We ate an apple"*. Clearly, all these forms of ambiguity are independent, so we can have sentences with many lexical ambiguities on top of scope ambiguities and ambiguities of the collective / distributive kind.

The third major source of ambiguity, that of alternative syntactic parses, is again in essence independent of the first two sources. And many other sources of ambiguity can be added, such as intensional versus extensional interpretation, literal versus figurative, metaphorical and idiomatic readings, the count/mass ambiguity (*"Mary had a little lamb"*), and restrictive versus presuppositional interpretation of relative clauses. These are just a few of the many other forms of ambiguity that are always on the lurch.

When we move to the level of discourse structure things get even worse. Not only are there new kinds of ambiguity to account for, as different attachments to discourse structure may be possible (see Gardent and Webber, 1998), but in addition a text consisting of n sentences, which are each m-ways ambiguous, will have m^n readings, as in the case of lexical ambiguities. In general, if a text grows, the number of its readings grows exponentially with it. This, essentially, is why the straightforward pipelined architecture implied in section 2 urgently needs amendment. The architecture essentially is a generate-and-test procedure, but since the number of readings to be generated is exponential in the length of the input, the algorithm is intractable and cannot be carried out, either by language users or by computers.

Clearly, the pervasive phenomenon of ambiguity in natural language makes it extremely difficult to design effective processes for computing the meanings of a nontrivial range of sentences. It is no wonder that the design of such processes has so far not been very succesful. Of course, not all the possibilities we have been considering in the above calculations are actually possible when the sentence is used in a certain context. The particular discourse domain will rule out many lexical meanings and combinations of those, and will also make certain scopings and quantifier interpretations very unlikely. What becomes especially clear, though, is that the number of possibilities to consider is incredibly large, and that a compositional process that would first calculate all logically possible disambiguated sentence meanings, and subsequently use context information to select the intended contextual utterance meaning from those, is not computationally viable.

At this point we may also note a strange aspect of the principle of compositionality that we did not yet consider. It speaks of *"the meaning of a compound expression"*. The use of the singular *the meaning* is common in formulations of the compositionality principle, but clearly has no basis in reality: expressions in natural language hardly ever have one single meaning. Speaking of *the meaning* is reasonable only when applied to *utterances*, where often only one of the many possible meanings of the sentence is contextually possible or relevant. This is why people can use language without constantly dealing with millions of possible meanings. (But as already noted, the meanings of utterances by their very nature do not obey Compositionality.)

5. COMPUTING UTTERANCE MEANING

5.1. *Sentence meaning and utterance meaning*

Research in computational semantics is concerned both with the algorithmics of sentence semantics and with the computation of utterance meaning, the ultimate dream being to be able to effectively compute the meanings of concrete manifestations of language, thereby allowing computers for instance to extract meaning from texts and to interact intelligently in dialogues with a human user.

Utterances, the concrete manifestations of sentences (or phrases, or other linguistic constructs), come with physical properties such as intonation, temporal structure and loudness in the case of a spoken utterance, and lay-out and punctuation marks in the case of a written utterance. These physical properties contribute to the meaning of an utterance. Moreover, an utterance appears in a certain context: it has a speaker, an addressee, a time and a place of occurrence in the case of a spoken utterance, and in the case of a textual utterance it has an author, a reader, and also a temporal and spatial context of occurrence. These and other contextual properties also contribute to the meaning that an utterance has.

For computing utterance meanings, we thus have three sources of information:

1. linguistic information: the semantic information carried by the component words and phrases and by the syntactic composition; anything that goes into the meanings of the sentence that is uttered;
2. physical utterance information: the information carried by the physical properties of the speech signal or the textual form of the utterance;
3. context information: the information that the speaker and hearers have about the domain of discourse; their (knowledge of their) respective goals and purposes; the spatio-temporal properties of

the situation in which the utterance occurs, etc. (see further Bunt, 1999).

Since sentences, in contrast with utterances, are theoretical constructs that have no existence outside linguistic analysis and discussion, the computation of sentence meanings is either of purely theoretical interest, or of potential interest for the computation of utterance meanings. Let us therefore consider the possible contribution of sentence meaning to the computation of utterance meanings.

5.2. *The contribution of sentence meaning to utterance meaning*

The computation of utterance meanings, as indicated above, involves combining linguistic and physical utterance information and context information, whereas computing sentence meanings only takes linguistic utterance information into account.[4] For an utterance u of a sentence S, the sentence meaning of S contributes directly to the computation of the meaning of u only when the processing of the *linguistic* information in u forms a separate stage. Assuming that physical utterance information and context information, being rather different types of information, are taken into account in separate stages as well, the straightforward organization of such a process would be as follows.

(13) 1. Compute the possible readings of S from the linguistic utterance information.
      2. Apply physical utterance information to filter out certain unintended readings of u and to add pragmatic meaning aspects (see below).
      3. Use context information to select the most plausible and relevant reading(s) of u.

Given the astronomical numbers of readings that we have seen to be involved in sentence meaning computation, this is not a computa-

---

[4] Note that the study of sentence meaning in formal semantics keeps context information out of the door by concentrating on isolated sentences, or by taking context into account in an extremely limited fashion, taking for instance a small amount of linguistic context (previous discourse) into consideration for dealing with anaphora, or taking parametric notions of speaker, hearer, time and place into account for the interpretation of indexicals, as in Montague (1968). But computational semantics must consider a much richter notion of context and its pervasive pervasive influence on meaning, which involves reasoning with speaker and hearer beliefs and with a full picture of interactive situations, in order to establish the intended meanings of words and phrases.

tionally feasible approach. To obtain a more efficient process, one idea is to take nonlinguistic information into account at an earlier stage, in order not to generate astronomically many readings in the first place. Concerning the use of physical utterance information, the following approaches can be found:

1. *'Prosody for pragmatics'*: prosodic information is considered as contributing to 'pragmatic' aspects of meaning (recognition of speech act type; topic-focus articulation, etc.). This is typically done after the processing of linguistic utterance information. In this case, physical utterance information is used to enrich the meanings generated from linguistic information, rather than to cut down the number of readings.

2. *'Punctuation for pragmatics'*: similarly for textual utterances, using e.g. end-of-sentence punctuation marks for speech act interpretation and intrasentential punctuation marks for information packaging analysis.

3. *'Preprocessing for punctuation'*: in a stage preceding the syntactic and semantic sentence analysis, punctuation marks are stripped from the utterance, and are interpreted perfunctorily.

4. *'Punctuation as linguistic information'*: punctuation marks are considered as linguistic elements and incorporated in the grammar. In this case (some of) the physical and linguistic utterance information are truly integrated.

Only in the latter case is physical utterance information used in a way that may lead to the generation of a smaller set of readings. This approach is found only rarely and in incomplete ways, since the incorporation of punctuation and layout into grammar formalisms is largely unchartered territory. Note that this approach does not have a separate phase of computing sentence meanings. The other approaches do have a separate phase of sentence meaning construction, and they do not make the organization (13) computationally less unattractive.

Concerning the early use of context information, one obvious possibility is to use knowledge of the domain of discourse to restrict the possible meanings of lexical items. For ambiguity at the phrasal level, a technique that is commonly used in language processing systems is to use domain information to rule out certain combinations of lexical meanings. This can be done by type checking, either interleaved with the construction of sentence meanings or as a filtering step afterwards. Although the use of domain information may help to reduce the number of readings, in general these approaches still result in the generation of large sets of readings, most of which have to be discarded through much more sophisticated ways of using context information, since finding the intended meaning of an utterance is more a matter of taking into account what is contextually coherent, plausible and relevant than of deciding what is semantically possible.

To improve this situation, two approaches seem possible:

— Apply context information interleaved with linguistic information and block the generation of most sentence meanings at an early stage.

— Do not first generate alternative unambiguous possible meanings, but use the linguistic information to generate structures that capture *constraints* on the meanings that an utterance of the sentence may have. Use context information to add further constraints, thereby resolving ambiguities.

The first of these approaches is extremely difficult in practice, since the application of context information involves complex reasoning with pieces of information which during the linguistic information processing are only partly available. This poses problems both for the reasoning involved, and for the organization of interleaved linguistic information processing and reasoning. The second approach has been developed in computational semantics under the name of *underspecified semantic representations*. We consider this approach and its significance for effective utterance meaning computation in the next section.

6. Underspecified Representations

Traditionally, semantic representations are expressions in a logical language that represent 'disambiguated' natural language sentences. An *underspecified* semantic representation of a sentence, or USR, is a formal representation of the semantic information expressed in the sentence, where anything that cannot be resolved on the basis of linguistic information is left unspecified. For example, an underspecified semantic representation may leave the relative scopes of quantifiers or the attachment of modifier phrases unspecified. An USR can thus be regarded as a shorthand for the representations of a number of unambiguous meanings, or alternatively as a specification of the constraints that all unambiguous meanings have to satisfy.

The idea of underspecified semantic representations is often traced back to the 'Quasi-Logical Form' (QLF), a particular form of underspecified representation that was pioneered in the Core Language Engine system (Alshawi, 1992), especially for leavimg quantifier scopes unresolved. For example, the sentence *"Every students owns a book"* would have the QLF (14), which leaves the relative scope of the two quantifiers underspecified:

(14)   [own,   qterm(<t=quant,n=sing,l=every>,X,[student,X]),

        qterm(<t=quant,n=sing,l=a>,Y,[book,Y])]

The use of QLF representations has been well publicized and has been very influential. However, the idea has a longer history. In the seventies the designers of the PHLIQA question answering system developed the idea of building semantic representations that would leave lexical ambiguity and vagueness unresolved by means of metavariables (see Medema et al., 1975; Bronnenberg et al., 1979; Bunt, 1981; Scha, 1983). In the TENDUM dialogue system, semantic representations were constructed leaving various kinds of structural ambiguities underspecified, such as collective/distributive readings, count/mass ambiguities, and modifier attachment ambiguities (see Bunt, 1985). Recently other, more sophisticated forms of underspecified representation have been defined in Discourse Representation Theory (Reyle, 1993), in the DenK project (Kievit, 1998) and in the Verbmobil project (Bos et al., 1994; Copestake et al, 1995).

Underspecified representations have great computational advantages, for two reasons. First, they allow purely linguistic information processing to generate a very small instead of a very large number of representations. Second, they open the possibility of a *monotone process* of utterance meaning computation where context information is used in a constructive way to add constraints to underspecified representations, as opposed to the generate-and-test approach where context information is used to discard large numbers of unambiguous representations.

The use of underspecified representations has advantages not only for dealing with ambiguity, but also for approaching the problem of semantic *vagueness*. Vagueness is distinguished from ambiguity in that the variations in meaning of a word cannot be described by a finite set of well-delineated alternative readings. Vagueness is therefore in fact even more troublesome for effective meaning computation than ambiguity. But once we allow underspecification in semantic representations, we can also allow predicates and other referential terms to be underspecified as to what precisely they refer to, and use contextual information to make this more specific by adding constraints on reference.

A related problem for which underspecified semantic representations may provide a solution, is that of the appropriate degree of precision in referential meaning. Whereas the traditional notion of 'disambiguated sentences' presupposes the possibility of total lack of ambiguity and vagueness, natural language expressions in fact may be considered unambiguous in one context, while requiring more fine-grained disambiguation or 'precisification' in another. In Artificial Intelligence, this issue has been addressed by introducing the notion of 'granularity' in modelling world knowledge (see Hobbs et al., 1987). Indeed, rather than assuming an absolute notion of 'unambiguity', it seems more appropriate to consider ambiguity and vagueness *relative to a certain context*. On this view there is no absolute definition of the set of meanings of a given sentence; meaning itself is a context-dependent notion.

While underspecification in semantic representations does seem to form a powerful concept, its theoretical status, its formal definition, and its possible use in reasoning are still the subject of study and discussion. Concerning their theoretical status, a central issue is whether underspecified representations are to be regarded as merely compact notations, useful as intermediate structures in a disambiguation processes, or whether they have a theoretical significance of their own. One reason to think that they may have a significance of their own is that people sometimes use ambiguous utterances in situations where it would be unnecessary, irrelevant, or even unintended to disambiguate. In such a situation, an underspecified semantic representation would seem to be an adequate description of the end result of a hearer's interpretation process. The following example illustrates this.

Since I have moved to another house a number of boxes with books and papers are still piling up in the hall, waiting to be carried upstairs to my study. In the morning, before going to the office I say to my two sons:

(15) If you carry these boxes upstairs today, I'll give you an ice cream.

When I come home in the evening, my sons confirm: *"We carried the boxes upstairs, dad!"* and so I buy them an ice cream.

The sentence uttered in (15) is multiply ambiguous due to the quantifiers. The boxes may be carried upstairs individually or collectively, both in the way the boys act, and in the way the boxes are acted upon. I, the speaker, don't care whether the boys act collectively or individually (or get the help of the boys next door...), nor do I care whether the boxes are carried one by one or in groups (or whether they are unpacked, and repacked upstairs...). I certainly would not want the boys to spend effort on the disambiguation of my quantifiers, looking for an unambiguous interpretation they should try to satisfy. *There isn't any!* Instead, what I really meant to say was: "If you carry the boxes upstairs *in some way or other,* then I will give you an ice cream", and I would hope that the boys would act on the basis of understanding that 'ambiguous meaning'.

This example shows not only that people can use ambiguous utterances for succesful communication but also that people are able to reason with ambiguous information – which is largely the same thing. When I come home at night and conclude that the boys deserve an ice cream, I combine two ambiguous premises to derive a conclusion:

(16)   The boys have carried the boxes upstairs

If the boys have carried the boxes upstairs,

I will give them an ice cream
_____

I will give them an ice cream

It thus seems possible to apply a rule like Modus Ponens to such ambiguous premises. Moreover, it is hard to imagine that this reasoning process makes use of the possible disambiguations of the premises, the more so since I did not intend the quantification in the *if*-clause in (16) to be disambiguated in the first place.

Whereas (16) suggests that direct inferences are possible with underspecified representations, other examples can be found that suggest the opposite. Questions concerning the interplay between inferencing and disambiguation, and concerning the rules for direct inferencing with ambiguous premises, form a hot issue in computational semantics today (see e.g. van Deemter, 1995; König and Reyle, 1996; Reyle, 1995; Jaspars, 1999).

The observation that it is at least sometimes possible to reason directly with underspecified representations supports the view that such representations have a meaning of their own. This view gets additional suppport from the application of underspecification to vagueness. Consider example (17), uttered by a speaker while giving the hearer a present.

(17) This is something Canadian.

The word *"Canadian"* can in general mean a lot of things, such as made in Canada, acquired in Canada, located in Canada, characteristic of

Canada, symbolizing Canada, controlled by the Canadian government, owned by a Canadian company, having its headquarters in Canada, etc. The situation in which (17) takes place of course rules out some of the possible more specific meanings of *"Canadian"*, but it still leaves many possibilities open – especially if the present is wrapped. Now it would not seem natural for the receiver of (17) to assign one of the possible more specific meanings of the word to *"Canadian"* in this utterance, especially as long as the present is not unwrapped; rather, the receiver may be assumed to assign (17) a vague meaning that may be paraphrased as *"This is something relating to Canada"*. As the present is unwrapped, the receiver may make his interpretation more specific. This process can be modelled by introducing a dummy predicate as a metavariable in an underspecified representation like (18), as suggested by Hobbs et al. (1993).

(18) $This\ x_1 : NN(x_1, \texttt{canada})$

At some stage the dummy predicate NN ('relating to') may be instantiated by a more specific relation supplied by the context. In this example one could imagine the metavariable NN to be replaced by the more specific predicate *Coming-from*; when the speaker provides additional information about the origin of the present, this may be further specied as *Produced-in*, which in turn may be further specified if additional context information becomes available as, for example, *Grown-in*, *Manufactured-in*, or *Designed-in*.

This example suggests that, while NN is a semantically vacuous predicate at one end of a scale of specificity, and other predicates such as *Coming-from* and *Produced-in* are somewhere along this scale in the direction of greater specificity, there would not seem to exist a predicate of greatest possible specificity. Absolute precision in meaning seems to be an illusion, as is also suggested by the phenomenon of 'granularity' that we came across, and so we may have to admit that meaning representations should be considered to *always* be underspecified to some degree...

7. ABOUT THIS BOOK

In the chapter *On Semantic Underspecification*, **Pinkal** provides an overview of the motivations underlying the use of underspecified semantic representations, of what they may be taken to mean, of how they can be used in reasoning, and of their theoretical status. He notes that USRs are motivated not just by their advantage in efficient natural language processing in the face of ambiguity, but also in allowing *robust* processing in the case of incomplete linguistic information, as often happens in speech understanding; moreover, in some cases it may be irrelevant or even undesirable to disambiguate an underspecified representation. Concerning the meaning of underspecified representations, Pinkal argues that the view of an USR as a partial description of logical formulae, or as a disjunction of its possible unambiguous instances, is inadequate, as is the view that an USR is semantically equivalent to the disjunction of the set of unambiguous logical formulae which it describes. In order to understand what an USR means, Pinkal examines various possibilities for defining entailment relations for USRs. He suggests that a cautious interpretation in terms of the possible readings of USRs seems most appropriate: an USR A entails an USR B iff every possible reading of B is classically entailed by every reading of A, but he also argues that the situation is complicated by phenomena of discourse parallelism. He therefore suggests a distinction between two entailment concepts, a 'dynamic' one that takes parallelism constraints into account, and a 'static' one that does not. In view of the interaction that may occur between discourse parallelism phenomena and the possible readings of an USR, Pinkal argues that underspecified representations form a layer of information which may be truth-conditionally irrelevant, but which is indispendable for discourse semantics.

Ramsay, in his chapter *Dynamic and Underspecified Interpretation without Dynamic or Underspecified Logic* addresses the demands on logical formalisms for underspecified meaning representation, as well as the demands that follow from the idea that utterance meanings should be viewed as context-changing operations. He argues, contra Groenendijk & Stokhof (1990, 1991) and many others, that there is no need for a special dynamic logic, and contra Reyle (1993) and many others that there is no need either to develop special logics for underspecification. He argues that very minor extensions to first-order logic are adequate both for accounting for the dynamics of meaning and for dealing with underspecification, by allowing belief sets of various kinds to be represented by propositions and using a constructive interpretation of the underlying logic.

Asher and Fernando are concerned with the utterance meaning disambiguation problem from the perspective of Discourse Representation Theory. In the chapter *Labeled Representations, Underspecification* *and Disambiguation* they discuss the effects of discourse on disambiguating (sub)expressions and, treat the problem of computing those effects formally by imposing a labeling structure over discourse representation structures. This leads to barebones forms of segmented and underspecified DRT. They consider the possibility of marrying SDRT and UDRT, and argue that this can be done, with rather dramatic consequences for discourse interpretation. By allowing underspecification at all levels, they show that the requirements on contextual update seem to reduce, disambiguating only when the gains are worth the computational effort.

Richter and Sailer's chapter proposes a new approach to underspecified semantics in HPSG. They show that a general framework for underspecified semantic representation languages can be reconciled with the traditional logical architecture of HPSG as outlined in (Pollard and Sag, 1994), and as formalized in (King, 1994). As an example of a semantic object language that can be treated within this scenario, an extensional typed logic with lambda abstraction is extended to an underspecified representation language as described in (Bos, 1995), and the resulting language is modeled in HPSG.

Zadrozny tackles the problem of simplicity in grammars via the *minimum description length* principle of Rissanen (1982) and uses this principle to give more bite to the principle of compositionality. Compositionality in itself is empirically vacuous (Zadrozny, 1994) proves a result that he claims entails this vacuity). Informally researchers have always agreed that the functions composing the meanings of complex expressions out of the meanings of their parts should be simple, but up till now no formal characterisation of simplicity was forthcoming. Clearly, the problem of simplicity in linguistic descriptions is deep and important. Zadrozny's idea to use the minimum description length principle here seems to have much wider applications.

Van Genabith and Crouch in their chapter replace the static meaning representation language in the LFG linear logic based glue language semantics approach (Dalrymple et al., 1996; 1997) with a 'dynamic' representation language (Muskens, 1994b; 1996). This move extends the original approach to discourse phenomena and can be combined with an approach to underspecification developed in (Crouch & Genabith, 1996). On the other hand it provides linear logic based approaches to quantifier scope and underspecification for dynamic semantics. QLF and UDRT style interpretations are sketched for a set of linear logic premises thus obtained. The results are briefly compared with some alternative approaches discussed in the literature.

Kyburg and Morreau in their chapter *Vague Utterances and Context Change* are concerned with the semantic representation of vague utterances. They present two context update functions that model the context change required to accomodate utterances containing adjective-noun combinations, like *fat pig* and *tall man*. In these models, the extensions of such expressions are sometimes stretched to suit the purposes of the participants in a dialogue: for example, a borderline fat pig may come to be called a fat pig following an utterance of *We will begin with the fat pig*. In the first model, the context change brought about by such an utterance is defined syntactically, in terms of the sentences representing the prior context. An updated context includes as much of the prior context as is consitent with the sentences conveyed by the utterance. This model is too permissive, though, and so an alternative, semantic model is suggested in which the updated context is instead defined in terms of changes to the *models* that support the context. On this view, an utterance can only bring about a new interpretation for a vague predicate according to which it is more precise.

Cooper's chapter *Using Situations to Reason about the Interpretation of Speech Events* applies the situation-theoretic notion of 'restriction' to account for information about an utterance conceived of as an event (a speech event) and for background information provided by the context. Also using role labels associated with abstracts to link various parts of an utterance with roles in the interpretation, he shows how a Montague-like compositional interpretation process can be obtained. Some problems are pointed out which are in part conceptual and in part technical, having to do with the computation of β-reduced λ-abstracts with restrictions. He then considers the possibilities of achieving the effect of restrictions and role labels with proof-theoretic tools which would allow to employ a simpler situation theory, and also possibly to use techniques similar to those used in type-logical approaches to grammar.

Kaplan and Schubert's chapter is concerned with modeling one of the most important aspects of the context of an utterance: the beliefs of the speaker, including his beliefs about the beliefs of the addressee. One of the problems in modeling beliefs is that of logical omniscience, which can sometimes be finessed in practice: when reasoning about another agent's belief the reasoner only has finite resources himself, so he will only discover some of the many conclusions that a conversational partner supposedly believes according to the traditional possible-worlds models of modal logic. This finessing, called 'simulative inference', has been discovered by AI researchers and has been used since the early 1970s (Moore, 1973). Since agents discover only some of the consequences of their beliefs, as they have limited computational resources, a truthful model of beliefs should include a model of computation, like Konolige's deduction model of belief. Konolige's model allows some unrealistic agents and prohibits some realistic ones, therefore Kaplan and Schubert propose a different one, where the computational mechanism for deriving new beliefs from old ones can be any algorithm guaranteed to use finite amounts of time. Using this model, they characterize the conditions under which it is appropriate to reason about other agents by simulating their inference processes with one's own.

The chapter authored by **Meyer Viol, Kibble, Kempson and Gabbay** considers the use of Hilbert's ϵ-operator as a means to obtain the kind of underspecified representations of scope that are widely felt to be needed in computational semantics. The ϵ-calculus (there is also a dual universal τ-operator) is set up as a labelled deductive system here. Noun phrases are associated with certain 'prototerms,' but determination of the term dependencies in those prototerms is delayed by the parsing process. Terms project certain metavariables which can be instantiated later and these instantiations not only fix scope relations but also anaphoric dependencies. The approach treats noun phrases essentially as (type e) *terms* and the chapter analyses wide scope effects as falling together with anaphora.

In a somewhat related development **Schubert** observes that the so-called 'donkey' anaphora that have played a role in logic since the middle ages are all-pervasive in natural language and that much of the 'common-sense' knowledge needed for ordinary reasoning and language understanding characteristically involves them. Donkey anaphora have played a motivating role in the development of dynamic forms of semantics for natural language, but Schubert moves to a more standard logic by considering a procedure of *Dynamic Skolemization*. This procedure involves (i) introducing a Skolem constant for a given existential quantifier, as is also common in theorem proving, and (ii) stipulating a supplementary condition relating the existential statement under consideration with its skolemized form. The resulting representations are context-independent and admit a standard semantics, while referential connections can be made for instances of functional anaphora that are problematic for dynamic semantics.

Ginzburg in his chapter *Semantically-based Ellipsis Resolution with Syntactic Presuppositions* offers a variety of syntactic, semantic and processing reasons which suggest that the resolution process for 'short answers' in dialogue is problematic for existing approaches to ellipsis resolution. Short answers seem to maintain a limited amount of parallelism with their source: even an unbounded number of dialogue turns away, the short answer must bear the category assigned to the corresponding wh-phrase in the source. Ginzburg offers an account of the resolution process which also attempts to explain this unbounded syntactic dependency. He shows how an interrogative meaning can encode a specification for focus which includes constraints on structural realization. This involves developing the notion of a λ-abstract whose argument roles carry syntactic appropriateness restrictions. It is suggested that such a notion is already in essence presupposed in sign-based grammars such as HPSG, and that, with certain independently motivated modifications, such abstracts have similar semantic expressiveness to abstracts that lack such appropriateness restrictions.

Krahmer and Piwek address the question how Van der Sandt's theory of presupposition projection, which is widely acknowledged to give best coverage of the data, can be combined with a theory of *world knowledge*. The addition of some form of world knowledge to Van der Sandt's theory would obviously further improve its coverage and could make precise some explanations which are now intuitively appealing but informal. The way Krahmer and Piwek go about is to cast the theory, which was originally formulated in Discourse Representation Theory in a *Constructive Type Theory* of the Martin-Löf variety. This is argued to facilitate the interaction between world knowledge and presupposition projection. The approach is illustrated by considering cases of bridging and conditional presupposition.

Stone and Hardt's chapter concerns the interpretation of sloppy anaphora and starts with some intriguing examples that show that the phenomenon is really more general than the usual examples would suggest. Sloppy anaphora involve some constituent of category XP containing a 'sloppy variable' of category YP controlled by an element C1. The interpretation of C1 contributes to the meaning of XP via YP. When an anaphoric element XP′ further in the sentence refers to XP, the role of C1 may have been taken over by a new controller C2. The usual instantiations for XP are NP and VP and commonly only the possibility of NPs is considered for sloppy variables, but Stone and Hardt make it plausible that XP and YP can almost freely be chosen from NP, VP, modality and tense. They obtain an interpretation of sloppy anaphora using a dynamic semantics which allows the storing of dynamic objects. Possible context changes between XP and XP' then account for the possible change in interpretation. Thus a uniform treatment of sloppy identities in various categories is obtained.

In their chapter *Linking Theory and Lexical Ambiguity: the Case of Italian Motion Verbs* **Dini and Di Tomaso** describe an approach to the treatment of locative expressions in romance languages which eliminates one of the possible sources of inefficiency of practical NLP systems, viz. presuppositional ambiguity. They show that, contrary to what is often believed, romance locatives do not have two distinct senses, a static one (location) and a dynamic one (goal). On the contrary, only the static sense needs to be assumed, while the goal interpretation is achieved as the result of the interaction of three independently motivated modules of the grammatical organization, viz. the theory of Aktionsart, Linking Theory, and Control Theory.

Last but not least, **Reinhard's** contribution *A Disambiguation Approach for German Compunds with Deverbal Heads* considers German noun-noun compounds such as *"Mitarbeiterbesprechung"*, *"Kinobegeisterung*, and *"Jugendgefährdung"*. Such compounds are not only extremely frequent in German, they are also ambiguous between various readings. Reinhard focuses on noun-noun compounds with a deverbal head, which have the property that the first constituent either satisfies an argument role of the second or stands in a more or less specifiable modifying relation to it. The goal here is automatic prediction of the correct relationship, so that the meaning of the compound can be computed on the basis of the meanings of its parts. The research was carried out on the basis of a corpus (the *Frankfurter Rundschau*) and a number of generalisations about the argument inheritance behaviour of certain nouns could be made. This gives default interpretations in many cases and the analysis also rules out certain readings. Interestingly, the empirical work done here also refutes some theoretical stipulations about argument inheritance that were made in previous literature.

REFERENCES

Alshawi, H. (1992) *The Core Language Engine*. Cambridge, MA: MIT Press.

Alshawi, H. and R. Crouch (1992) Monotonic semantic interpretation. In *Proceedings 30th Annual Meeting of the Association for Computational Linguistics*, 32–38.

Asher, N. (1993) *Reference to Abstract Objects in Discourse*. Dordrecht: Kluwer.

Bos, J. (1995) Predicate Logic Unplugged. In *Proceedings 10th Amsterdam Colloquium*.

Bos, J.; E. Mastenbroek, S. McGlashan, S. Millies, and M. Pinkal (1994) A compositional DRS-based formalism for NLP-applications. In H. Bunt, R. Muskens and G. Rentier (eds.) *Proceedings International Workshop on Computational Semantics*, Tilburg.

Bronnenberg, W.J.; H.C. Bunt, J. Landsbergen, P. Medema, R. Scha, W.J. Schoenmakers, and E. van Utteren (1979) The question-answering system PHLIQA 1. In L. Bolc (ed.) *Natural communication with computers*. London: MacMillan.

Bunt, H.C. (1981) *The formal semantics of mass terms*. Ph.D. dissertation, University of Amsterdam.

Bunt, H.C. (1985) *Mass terms and model-theoretic semantics*. Cambridge, UK: Cambridge University Press.

Bunt, H.C. (1999) Iterative context specification and dialogue analysis. In: H.C. Bunt and W.J. Black (eds.) *Abduction, Belief and Context in Dialogue. Studies in Computational Pragmatics*. Amsterdam: John Benjamins.

Bunt, H.C. and A. van Horck (eds.) (1996) *Discontinuous Constituency*. Berlin: Mouton de Gruyter.

Bunt, H.C.; R.J. Beun, F. Dols, J. van der Linden, and G.O. thoe Schwartzenberg (1984) The TENDUM dialogue system and its theoretical basis. *IPO Annual Progress Report* 19, 107–112.

Cooper, R. (1983) *Quantification and Syntactic Theory*. Dordrecht: Reidel.

Copestake, A.; D. Flickinger, and I.A. Sag (1995) Minimal Recursion Semantics, An Introduction. Ms. CSLI, Stanford Unviersity. eoan.stanford.edu/ergo/parser.html

Crouch, R. and J. van Genabith (1996) Context change and underspecification in glue language semantics. In Butt, M. and King, T.H, (eds.) *Proceedings of the First LFG Conference*, RANK Xerox Research Center, Grenoble, France, 133–147.

Dalrymple, M.; J. Lamping, F. Pereira, and V. Saraswat (1996) A deductive account of quantification in LFG. In M. Kanazawa, C. Pinon, and H. de Swart (eds.) *Quantifiers, Deduction and Context*. CSLI Publications, No. 57, 33–57.

Dalrymple, M.; J. Lamping, F. Pereira, and V. Saraswat (1997) Quantifiers, anaphora, and intensionality. *Journal of Logic, Language, and Information* 6(3), 219–273.

Declerck, T (1996) Modelling information passing with the LFG workbench. In Butt, M. and T.H. King (eds.) *Proceedings of the First LFG Conference*, RANK Xerox Research Center, Grenoble, France.

Deemter, K. van (1995) Towards a logic of ambiguous expressions. In K. van Deemter and S. Peters (eds.) *Semantic Ambiguity and Underspecification*. Stanford: CSLI Publications, 203–238.

Gardent, C. and B. Webber (1998) Describing discourse semantics. In prep.

Groenendijk, J. and M. Stokhof (1990) Dynamic montague grammar. In Kalman, L. and L. Polos (eds.) *Papers from the Second Symposium on Logic and Language*. Akademiai Kiadoo, Budapest, 3–48.

Groenendijk, J. and M. Stokhof (1991) Dynamic predicate logic. *Linguistics and Philosophy* 14, 39–100.

Hobbs, J.R.; W. Croft, T. Davies, and K. Laws (1987) Commonsense metaphysics and lexical semantics. *Computational Linguistics* 13 (3-4), 241–250.

Hobbs, J.R.; M.E. Stickel, D.E. Appelt, and P. Martin (1993) Interpretation as abduction. *Artificial Intelligence* 63, 69–142.

Hobbs, J.R. and S.M. Shieber (1987) An Algorithm for Generating Quantifier Scopings. *Computational Linguistics* 13 (1-2), 47–63.

Janssen, T.M.V. (1997) Compositionality. In J. van Benthem and A. ter Meulen (eds.) *Handbook of logic and language*. Amsterdam: Elsevier, 417–473.

Jaspars, J.O.M. (1999) Structural Logics for Reasoning with Underspecified Representations. In *Proceedings First International Workshop on Inference in Computational Semantics*, Amsterdam, 69–82

Keller, W. (1996) Nested Cooper storage: The proper reatment of quantification in ordinary noun phrases. In U. Reyle and C. Rohrer (eds.) *Natural Language Parsing amd Linguistic Theory*. Dordrecht: Reidel, 432–437.

Kievit, L.A. (1998) *Context-driven natural language interpretation*. Ph.D. Dissertation, Tilburg University.

King, P.J. (1994) An Expanded Logical Formalism for Head-Driven Phrase Structure Grammar. Arbeitspapiere des SFB 340 59. Universität Tübingen.

König, E. and U. Reyle (1996) A general reasoning scheme for underspecified representations. In Ohlbach, H.-J. and U. Reyle (eds.) *Logic and its Applications. Festschrift for Dov Gabbay*. Dordrecht: Kluwer.

Konolige, K. (1986) *A Deduction Model of Belief*. San Mateo: Morgan Kaufmann.

May, R. (1977) *The grammar of quantification*. Ph.D. dissertation, MIT, 247–270.

Medema, P.; W.J. Bronnenberg, H.C. Bunt, J. Landsbergen, R. Scha, W.J. Schoenmakers, and E. van Utteren (1975) PHLIQA 1: multilevel semantics in question answering. *AJCL Microfiche 32.*

Montague, R. (1968) Pragmatics. Reprinted in Thomason, R, (ed.) (1974) *Formal Philosophy, selected papers of Richard Montague.* Yale University Press, 95–118.

Montague, R. (1973) The proper treatment of quantification in ordinary English. Reprinted in Thomason, R, (ed.) (1974) *Formal Philosophy, selected papers of Richard Montague.* Yale University Press, 247–270.

Muskens, R. (1994) A compositional discourse representation theory. In Dekker, P. and M. Stokhof (eds.) *Proceedings 9th Amsterdam Colloquium.* ILLC, Amsterdam, 467–486.

Muskens, R. (1995) Order-independence and underspecification. In *Dyana-2 Deliverable R2.2.C Ellipsis, Underspecification, Events and More in Dynamic Semantics.* ILLC, University of Amsterdam.

Muskens, R. (1996) Combining montague semantics and discourse representation theory. *Linguistics and Philosophy* 19, 143–186.

Moore, R.C. (1973) D-script: A computational theory of descriptions. In *Proc. 3rd International Joint Conference on Artificial intelligence,* 223–229.

Nerbonne, J. (1995) Compositional Semantics - Linguistics and Processing. In S. Lappin (ed.) *Handbook of Contemporary Semantic Theory.* London: Blackwell, 459–482.

Partee, B., A. ter Meulen and R. Wall. (1990) *Mathematical methods in linguistics.* Dordrecht: Kluwer.

Pinkal, M. (1996) Radical underspecification. In Dekker, P. and M. Stokhof (eds.) *Proceedings of the Tenth Amsterdam Colloquium.* ILLC, University of Amsterdam.

Pollard, C., and I. Sag. (1994) *Head-Driven Phrase Structure Grammar.* University of Chicago Press.

Reyle, U. (1993) Dealing with ambiguities by underspecification: Construction, representation and deduction. *Journal of Semantics* 10, 123–179.

Reyle, U. (1995) On reasoning with ambiguities. In *Proc. Seventh Conference of the European Chapter of the Association for Computational Linguistics,* 1–8.

Scha, R.J.H. (1983) *Logical foundations for question answering.* Ph.D. dissertation, University of Groningen.

Rissanen, J. (1983) A universal prior for integers and estimation by minimum description length. *Annals of Statistics* 11, 416–431.

Zadrozny, W. (1994) From compositional to systematic semantics. *Linguistics and Philosophy* 17 (4), 329–342.

MANFRED PINKAL

ON SEMANTIC UNDERSPECIFICATION

1. UNDERSPECIFICATION PHENOMENA

Scope, especially quantifier scope, is the first and best investigated phenomenon in the field of underspecification research. The use of logic representation languages in natural language semantics often requires a choice between alternative scopings in the interpretation process, where this choice seems to be premature or unnecessarily fine-grained. An example is (1a), which can be assigned either (1b) or (1c) as logical representation, although in many cases the relative scope of universal and existential operator may be unclear, or irrelevant, or both.

(1) a. Two foreign languages are spoken by every linguist.

b. $\exists^2 x(foreign\_language(x) \wedge \forall y(linguist(y) \rightarrow spoken\_by(x,y)))$

c. $\forall y(linguist(y) \rightarrow \exists^2 x(foreign\_language(x) \wedge spoken\_by(x,y)))$

The basic idea behind the technique of underspecification is to represent the semantic information connected with a semantically underdetermined utterance A by a partial description of logical structure, rather than enumerating the possible completely specified interpretation alternatives for A. Pioneering research on structural underspecification has been performed at SRI Cambridge. The QLF formalism described in (Alshawi and Crouch, 1992) provides an underspecified treatment of scope as well as certain aspects of referential ambiguity, ellipsis, and focus-background structure.[1]

Another important source for the interest in underspecification is lexical semantics. Example (2) is a representative for a large field of ambiguity phenomena, which are conventionally classified as lexical ambiguities, but differ from trivial cases like the homonyms *bank* or *pen* in several important ways.

---

[1] Earlier, but less influential research on underspecification was performed in the PHLIQA project at Philips Research Labs, where it seems that the concept of 'meta-variables' was actually discovered; see e.g. Bronnenberg et al. (1979); Landsbergen & Scha (1979); Bunt (1984; 1985).

H. Bunt and R. Muskens (eds.), Computing Meaning, Volume 1, 33–55.
© 1999 *Kluwer Academic Publishers. Printed in the Netherlands.*

(2) John began the book

Rather than locating the source of ambiguity of sentence (2) in the verb *begin*, which would require an infinite number of readings for the different kinds of complements the verb can take (*begin to read begin to write begin to paint begin to eat*, ...), James Pustejovsky assumes that the different readings of *begin*+non-event-complement constructions are generated in a systematic way, in his theory of 'Generative Lexicon' (Pustejovsky 1991; 1995). The process is triggered by the type conflict between the verb and its argument, which requires that the two objects be semantically related in an — initially underspecified — way. Specific information about this relation can be retrieved from special lexical information about the argument, e.g., that the typical way of using a book is reading its content (stored in the *qualia structure* of the lexical entry).

A third range of phenomena, which might turn out to be the most important application field for the technique of semantic underspecification, but has only just started to attract the attention of semanticists, is spoken-language understanding. Spoken utterances are often incomplete, and they may be incompletely or wrongly recognized by the human hearer or by a speech recognition system. In (3), a standard example taken from the Verbmobil project is given (for Verbmobil see Wahlster, 1993).

(3) (a) [$_S$ *Treffen wir uns*] [$_{NPdat}$ *den nächsten zwei Wochen*]
    (b) Shall we meet — the next two weeks

Since the speech recognition module was not able to identify the preposition in as part of the input utterance, the parser is not able to identify the last part of the input as an adjunct of the sentence. It passes a sequence of two unrelated analyses to the semantics module, which in turn is unable to combine the corresponding semantic representations directly. It can guess, however, that the two pieces stand in some kind of (underspecified) semantic relation, that the second is a PP modifier of the first (because emission of a preposition is probable), and that it is the special case of a temporal modifier (according to the semantic sort of the head noun). For a first approach to semantic processing with incomplete input see (Worm, 1997).

2. UNDERSPECIFICATION TECHNIQUES

A number of related formalisms for scope underspecification have been proposed during the last years (e.g., (Reyle, 1993; Bos, 1996; Muskens, 1997; Pinkal, 1996; Copestake, Flckinger and Sag, 1997; Egg and Lebeth, 96)). These proposals differ in the choice of the underlying semantic formalism, they differ to some extent in their expressiveness, and they differ in the theoretical status they assign to the respective formalisms. I will not discuss the approaches individually, but rather try to indicate the basic common ideas and intentions, by giving a semi-formal outline of a simple underspecification formalism.

I will use the familiar language of extensional type theory as underlying representation language, for the sake of simplicity (in fact, I will use only the FOL fragment, in my examples). In order to allow partial descriptions of logical formulas, the representation language is augmented by meta-variables X, Y, Z, X_1, X_2, ... (called *labels*, *holes*, or *handles* in the respective formalisms). Meta-variables range over expressions of the representation language, or, to be more precise, occurrences of such expressions. It is convenient to conceive of logical representations as trees, whose leaves are annotated with non-logical constants and variables, and whose non-terminal nodes are annotated with semantic operators (e.g., implication, abstraction with variable x, functional application).[2] This allows to investigate underspecification formalisms in the well-understood framework of tree logic. In particular, meta-variables can be conceived of as referring to nodes, and constraints between meta-variables as partial tree descriptions. Underspecification formalisms usually provide a small inventory of basic constraint types, in addition to equality. These are dominance or subordination constraints $X \triangleleft^* Y$, where $\triangleleft^*$ is a two-place partial-ordering relation between occurrences of expressions (nodes), and constraints $X : A$ stating that part X of the representation under discussion is of form A, where A is a (partially specified) representation language expression. In (4), I give a scope-underspecified representation of (1a) in terms of tree constraints, as an example. X_0 is the designated meta-variable referring to the top node, i.e., the described structure as a whole.

---

[2] For that purpose, we need an explicit operator symbol for function application (e.g., @). I employ the usual notation here (i.e., $a(b)$ instead of $a@b$). For better readability, I will in general use a notation which is as close as possible to logical standard notation (and also close to the notation of most underspecification frameworks).

$$\{X_1 : \exists^2 x(foreign\_language(x) \land X_3),$$
(4) $X_2 : \forall y(linguist(y) \to X_4), X_5 : spoken\_by(x, y),$
    $X_0 \vartriangleleft^* X_1, X_0 \vartriangleleft^* X_2, X_3 \vartriangleleft^* X_5, X_4 \vartriangleleft^* X_5\}$

The constraint set (4) is compatible with (the tree representations of) both (1b) and (1c). It specifies which quantifiers occur and which argument positions they bind, but underspecifies scope order. Actually, (4) is still compatible with an infinite number of logical terms, since it does not constrain the occurrence of additional material in the formula. Nevertheless, it provides a specification of the set consisting just of (1b) and (1c), since these formulae are the only minimal structures satisfying all constraints.

A mechanism for semantic construction which takes a syntactic analysis of sentence (1a) and generates the constraint set (4) from it, can be set up in a simple and straightforward way.[3] If later on context or subsequent discourse provide the additional information that *two languages* outscope *every linguist*, the corresponding constraint $X_3 \vartriangleleft^* X_2$ can be added to (4). The resulting constraint set does not contain (1b) as a minimal solution, which leaves (1c) as the unique reading for (1a). The example demonstrates that disambiguation can be postponed to the point where a maximum of relevant information is available.

Underspecification formalisms also provide a framework for the modeling of lexical reinterpretation cases: In example (2), the type conflict between *begin* and *book* blocks immediate application of the first to the second. We can read off the sentence, however, that the denotation of *the book* must occur somewhere inside the second argument of *begin*. This piece of safe knowledge can, in a first step, be expressed by the constraint set (5).

(5) $\{X_0 : begin(john, X_1), X_2 : the\_book, X_1 \vartriangleleft^* X_2\}$

The second step consists in filling in the space between X_1 and X_2. This can be done by adding, e.g., $X_1 : reading\_of(X_2)$, or $X_1 : writing\_of(X_2)$, using additional semantic information contained in the qualia structure of the lexical entry of the argument, or world knowledge, and determining the contextually most appropriate alternative.

Let us look at the analysis of incomplete input next. In example (3), the input consists of a saturated sentence and a noun phrase,

---

[3] Two related versions of the construction algorithm are given in (Muskens, 1997) and (Pinkal, 1996), respectively.

which cannot be directly related to each other. Given evidence (e.g., prosodic information, external conditions on the dialogue) that the semantic representations for both fragments are part of the same sentence representation, the constraint set (6) can be established.

(6) $\{X_1 : meet(we), X_2 : the\_next\_two\_weeks,$
$\quad X_0 \triangleleft^* X_1, X_0 \triangleleft^* X_2\}$

In a second step, heuristic rules are applied, leading to the combination of X_2 with an underspecified temporal relation (a meta-variable which might be instantiated to *during, after immediately after*, etc., given further context information), and applying the result to X_1. This can be formally expressed by adding the constraints $X_3 = T\_rel(X_2)$ and $X_0 = X_3(X_1)$ to (6), where T_rel is a meta-variable ranging over temporal relations.[4]

The examples should have illustrated one basic advantage of the underspecification technique: Whenever it is impossible to identify one unambiguous meaning representation at some stage in the interpretation process — due to insufficient disambiguation information, type inconsistencies between semantic objects, or incomplete input — we can encode the available safe information in a constraint set, thus specifying the range of possible readings. Later, we can try to obtain more information to narrow down the meaning potential, which is represented by a monotonic extension of the constraint set. To be sure, underspecification techniques by themselves do only a modest part of the job. The hard task of gaining the missing information needed for a satisfactory interpretation can only be done by problem-specific machinery, e.g., by modeling the reinterpretation process along the lines of the 'generative lexicon', or by developing heuristic completion and combination for fragmentary input, as intended in the *Robust Semantic Processing* module of the Verbmobil system (see Worm, 1997; Wahlster, 1993). Underspecification formalisms do, however, provide a general framework to express semantic information with some degree of specificity, and to model its continuous increase in the interpretation process in a natural and efficient way.

I would like to conclude this section with two remarks about the underspecification formalism, one concerning its theoretical status, and

---

[4] More correctly, possible instantiations of T_rel should have the form $\lambda t\, \lambda e.R(e, t)$, where a Davidsonian analysis of verbs and modifiers is assumed, and R ranges over relations of temporal location. Here, as throughout the chapter, I will ignore details of semantic analysis, unless they are relevant for the aims of the chapter.

the other one its expressive power. The underspecification formalism has been introduced above in a pretty informal way, as a mixture of logical representations and meta-elements (in fact, this is the way in which most underspecification formalisms present themselves). In principle, a tree-logical account of underspecification has to make a strict distinction between the meta-level description language, and the logical representation language, whose structures are described (henceforth *object language* or OL in short). Object-language expressions (conceived of as trees) serve as models for the description language. Meta-language terms denote OL expressions, constraints are satisfied or dissatisfied by OL expressions. Since meta-language names for OL symbols can be the respective symbols themselves, the separation of levels does not require any major notational changes. The constraint sets given above can be understood as pure meta-language constructs.

Underspecification formalisms with dominance constraints are an expressive means to describe partial meaning information, but they are not expressive enough to describe all kinds of partial information that occur in natural language utterances. In particular, a problem arises when underspecification and discourse parallelism interact. Like underspecification, parallelism is a pervasive phenomenon in natural language. It occurs, e.g., in question-answer pairs, enumerations, contrastive constructions and corrections. There, it imposes strong semantic constraints requiring that the interpretations of the two utterances in a parallel construction are similar (ideally, identical), except for one pair (or several pairs) of contrasting constituents. This has been long recognized in lexical ambiguity and made use of in the well-known *zeugma test*.

(7) John owns a pen, and so does Bill.

Due to parallelism, the choice of a reading for *pen* in the first clause determines its reading in the second clause (mixed readings are impossible or at least pragmatically marked). A similar kind of interaction takes place in the case of scope ambiguities. The first detailed account of parallelism and scope interaction is given in Ivan Sag's work on ellipsis (Sag, 1976). The classical example was contributed by Hirschbuehler (1982), a variant of which is given in (8).

(8) Two European languages are spoken by every linguist, and two Asian ones are, too.

The first clause of sentence (8) is two-ways ambiguous, and so is the second one. If we represent the underspecified semantics of both clauses by means of dominance constraints (as I did for sentence (1a) in (4)), the resulting constraint set will specify four (minimal) readings for (8). However, there are only two intuitively available readings: Due to parallelism *every linguist* must take either wide scope or narrow scope, in both clauses.

Reyle (1996) proposes a co-indexing technique for modeling covariance induced by parallelism. This technique works fine for the simple case of homonymy, but is difficult to handle in structurally complex cases of underspecification like (8). Pinkal (1996) proposed context unification as a unified framework for scope underspecification and parallelism.

In the Saarbrücken CHORUS project, we decided for another solution, which yields roughly the same expressive power, but is preferable in computational respects: the constraint language is extended by parallelism constraints, which come in two different forms. There is a two-place equality relation $X \sim Y$ stating structural equality between the trees dominated by X and Y. This equality relation is not sufficient to cover the standard cases of parallelism in natural language, since parallel constructions usually contain a pair of contrasting elements in corresponding positions of the respective representations, which are exempt from the parallelism requirement. Therefore, a second type of more complex constraints is employed, which we call 'equality-upto constraints', and which we write as $X/U \sim Y/V$. $\sim$ is a four-place relation stating that the semantic representations of source and target clause are equal, except for the positions taken in by the contrasting elements (the representations of the NPs *two European languages* and *two Asian languages*, in the case of example (8)). Adding the appropriate equality-upto constraint to the scope-underspecified description of the first clause of (8) (which is structurally the same as (4)) yields a constraint set specifying just the two correct interpretations for (8)) (Niehren, Pinkal, and Ruhrberg, 1997a; Niehren, Pinkal, and Ruhrberg, 1997b). I will not comment any further on linguistic aspects of the interaction of underspecification and parallelism, but have to come back to the topic in connection with the question of the appropriate direct, truth-conditional interpretation of underspecified representations.

3. WHAT IS UNDERSPECIFICATION GOOD FOR?

Underspecification improves efficiency, as the examples in the last section have illustrated: Working with fully specified logical representations requires either enumeration and separate processing of numerous interpretation alternatives, or early decision for one possible reading, which may necessitate subsequent revisions, and these tend to be expensive and difficult to control. Working with partial meaning descriptions allows to model semantic analysis (construction and resolution processes) in terms of monotonic extension of a constraint set, which in the optimal case results in the description of a unique logical formula, and in any case improves efficiency by allowing late disambiguation. This is the standard argument in favor of underspecification techniques, and it is a convincing one in view of the pervasive ambiguity and semantic openness of natural language.

However, underspecification opens interesting perspectives for efficient and natural semantic processing also in the case where all needed information is in principle available, and independent from the problem of ambiguity. A variety of different interaction modes between semantics and other linguistic levels can be realized, while the standards of a logic-based representation language are maintained. For underspecification enables semantic processing in a phase of the analysis, where the information is not yet completely there, but still in the process of being generated by other components. Thus, incremental architectures (spanning the levels of speech recognition, syntax, semantic analysis and reasoning), as well as concurrent processing modes on different levels of granularity become possible.

Underspecification moreover facilitates robust processing. Conventional, syntax- and logic-based processing is reliable and precise where it succeeds, but is highly fragile, at the same time: if the conditions of complete and consistent input information are not met, this causes complete failure. 'Flat' heuristic or statistical understanding systems always come up with a result. The results however are unreliable and horribly bad at times. A basic obstacle for combining deep and flat techniques in a sensible way has been the lack of a common semantic framework that allows logic-based, but partial and approximate meaning representation.[5]

As already illustrated in Sect. 2, the underspecification framework

---

[5] The Verbmobil 'research prototype' is to my knowledge the first system which combines the advantages of 'deep' and 'flat' techniques, employing a deep linguistic analysis module and several flat parsers at the same time. If deep analysis is successful (within a given time limit), its result is preferred. Otherwise, one of the alternative flat analyses is selected. Since the different modules work in isolation, the method still leads to sub-optimal results.

allows to represent the information retrieved from fragmentary input by standard techniques of semantic construction, and to model the effect of heuristic rules employed to improve the fragmentary results. The Robust Semantic Processing module that is developed in the second phase of the Verbmobil project, is supposed to make use of these properties, in several respects: to combine heuristic and conventional processing methods, to combine the output of deep and flat parsers, and to process the parsers' output incrementally.

So far, I have pointed out the improvement of efficiency in the process of analysis gained by using underspecification techniques, as well as the improvement of robustness with respect to the variation and quality of the input for semantic analysis. In the remainder of the chapter I will deal with what possibly is the strongest motivation for an underspecification approach: the fact that humans are, and systems should be able to make use of underspecified output of the semantic analysis, without making reference to the single fully specified meaning alternatives. Ideally, the process of interpretation (semantic construction and resolution) reduces the set of possible readings to a singleton. In many cases, however, there is not enough information available and also no need to arrive at a unique reading. Humans seem to have no difficulties in making sense out of the utterance in these cases, and it seems that they exploit the underspecified information in a direct way, without taking the different possible readings into account. Take sentence (9) as an example.

(9) Many linguists and computer scientists in three Saarbrücken institutes work on certain problems of computational semantics.

If you hear an utterance of (9) at an international workshop, it is highly improbable that you definitely decide on one of its numerous readings. (Are there many researchers who are either linguists and computer scientists, or are there many linguists, as well as many computer scientists? Do they work on the same problems, or on different problems? Jointly or individually?). But nevertheless you might conclude that it is worth looking at the home page of Saarbrücken's Computational Linguistics department or of the German Research Center for AI (DFKI). This means that you have drawn inferences from underspecified semantic information. Providing natural language systems with this kind of reasoning abilities would lead to another considerable gain in efficiency: systems working on NL input would get around the alternative of either achieving a complete disambiguation (which may be very expensive and completely irrelevant, at the same time), or of performing classical deduction procedures on a large number of interpretation alternatives, in parallel.

The question of how efficient methods for direct deduction might be realized will be addressed in Sect. 5. In advance, it must be discussed what kind of inferences should be drawn at all, from partial meaning information. What is the appropriate entailment concept, that direct deduction is supposed to meet? What do partial meaning descriptions really mean, after all?

4. WHAT DO UNDERSPECIFIED REPRESENTATIONS MEAN?

Let us sort out a couple of simple but inappropriate answers right at the beginning. First, one could assume that the problem is already solved, since underspecification constraints as expressions of a tree-description language already have a perfect denotational interpretation, in terms of trees standing for logical structures. This is the wrong level of semantics however: (9) is an example of reasoning about the world, not about properties of logical structure. Accordingly, we have to care about a denotational semantics in terms of models that represent the state of the world, rather than object language terms. Entailments on the term-semantic level are 'structure-preserving', e.g., of the general form: If a structure has property F, it has property G as well. Entailments on the level under consideration should be truth-preserving. The interesting instances will be those which do not preserve structure, i.e., which lead from (partial) descriptions of logical formulae to (partial) descriptions of different formulae, e.g., in the inference indicated in (10) (scope ambiguity being indicated by the prefixes in set notation).

$$(10) \quad \frac{\{\forall x : researcher, \exists^2 y : language\}(speak(x, y))}{\{\forall x : linguist, \exists^2 y : language\}(speak(x, y))}$$

Direct interpretation should refer to the level of the truth-conditional semantics used for the interpretation of the object language. The tricky question is how the object language interpretation concept and in particular the concept of truth can be adapted to descriptions which are compatible with more than one object-language expression.

There is a popular and intuitively appealing answer to this latter question: Just interpret ambiguity as object-level disjunction. Faced with an utterance of sentence (1a), you are on the safe side if you take its meaning information to be the disjunction of its readings, which incidentally is identical with the narrow scope existential reading. Similarly, if you hear (11), and know already that Mary went to the savings-bank, it would be not constructive to question its truth on the basis of the falsehood of the other interpretation alternative.

(11) Mary left for the bank

According to Gricean maxims, the hearer should interpret an ambiguous utterance cooperatively, and this pragmatic requirement again is nicely met by the disjunctive interpretation, since it is the widest possible one. However, there is a problem with the argument, despite of its apparent plausibility. It works only in the case of plain, affirmative statements. If you are asked one of the questions (12a) or (12b), the answer *yes* might be misleading in spite of the fact that the corresponding assertions are true under one reading, namely in the case that the speaker had the other reading in mind.

(12) a. Is it true that two languages are spoken by every linguist?

   b. Did Mary leave for the bank?

Similarly, the disjunctive interpretation is inappropriate, if the ambiguity is embedded in a negation, as in (13a) and (13b).

(13) a. It is simply wrong that two languages are spoken by every linguist

   b. Mary didn't leave for the bank

In these cases, disjunctive interpretation amounts to the conjunction of the negation of the two readings, by de Morgan's Law. This is the strongest possible interpretation, risky under the aspect of information acquisition, and maximally uncooperative as a policy of conversational behavior. Thus, the apparent semantic appropriateness of the disjunctive analysis seems to be due to some special pragmatic effects.

Before completely abandoning the option of a disjunctive interpretation, we have to inspect another way of relating underspecification to object-language disjunction. We could assume that an underspecified representation as a whole is semantically equivalent to the disjunction of the set of logical formulae which it describes. This amounts to giving disjunction always widest possible scope. De Morgan does not apply here: If A has the set of readings $\{A_1, A_2\}$, $\neg A$ has readings $\{\neg A_1, \neg A_2\}$, and accordingly, the interpretation of A and $\neg A$ would be taken to be equivalent to $A_1 \vee A_2$ and $\neg A_1 \vee \neg A_2$ (rather than $\neg(A_1 \vee A_2)$), respectively. Unfortunately, there is a different problem with this approach. Take BANK$_1$ and BANK$_1$ as shortcuts for the *'savings-bank'* and the *'river bank'* reading of sentence (14a), respectively.

(14) a. This is a bank

  b. This isn't a bank

Then, (14a) would be represented as BANK$_1$ $\vee$ BANK$_2$, and (14b) as $\neg$BANK$_1$ $\vee$ $\neg$BANK$_2$. Since no object can fall under both readings of *bank*, the two readings of (14a) are mutually exclusive, i.e., both BANK$_1$ $\rightarrow$ $\neg$BANK$_2$ and BANK$_2$ $\rightarrow$ $\neg$BANK$_1$ hold. On these premises, (14a), which is equivalent to BANK$_1$ $\vee$ BANK$_2$, entails as $\neg$BANK$_1$ $\vee$ $\neg$BANK$_2$, which again is equivalent to (14b). This means that any ambiguous expression with mutually incompatible readings entails its negation — a conclusion which is hardly intuitively desirable. The problem is that the entailment concept resulting from the wide-scope disjunctive interpretation is much too weak. To prove $A \models B$, it would be sufficient to show that if A is true under one reading, there is one arbitrary true reading of B.[6]

Interpretation of ambiguity via object-language disjunction is tempting, but definitely inappropriate. In the case of the *bank* example, the result of the wide-scope disjunctive interpretation is particularly unintuitive, since one has to switch the readings systematically, when proceeding from premise to conclusion. This seems to indicate the necessity to make the interpretation for ambiguous expressions context-sensitive, viz., dependent on previous choices of a disambiguation. One way of implementing this dependence is by means of a formal notion of context, defined as a function from ambiguous expressions to possible readings. Interpretation and entailment concept then can be defined in the spirit of the super-valuation technique, which has been proposed for the semantic analysis of vague expressions earlier already (Fine, 1975; Pinkal, 1995). An underspecified formula A is true, if $k(A)$ is true for every possible context k, false, if $k(A)$ is false for every possible context k, and of undefined truth-value otherwise. Entailment is

---

[6] This is the $\exists\exists$-variant in van Deemter's classification of alternative ambiguous entailment concepts (van Deemter, 1996).

not defined on the basis of the global truth-value assignment, but by inspecting the semantic relation between the involved underspecified formulas context-wise. A entails B, if and only if for every context k: If $k(A)$ is (classically) true, then $k(A)$ is (classically) true. With respect to the problem case under discussion, the context-based definition of entailment clearly shows much better behavior. Since the choice of a reading in (14a) fixes the context for the interpretation of (14b), there is no possibility for (14a) and (14b) to become true at the same time. Thus, (14b) not only does not follow from (14a), but it turns out to be inconsistent with it — in nice accordance with classical logic.

Again, there are basic problems concerning the intuitive adequacy of this proposal. Fixing a reading for an ambiguous expression once and for all in a sentence or discourse would not allow to provide sensible interpretations for sentences like (15a) or (15b).

(15) a. The bank is close to the bank (of the river)

 b. The pen is in the pen

As Reyle argues in (Reyle, 1996), even $A \models A$ is only justified under certain assumptions about the pragmatic relation between the two occurrences of A. If a speaker or system has added an underspecified representation to its knowledge base, based on an utterance of (12b), without being able to resolve the ambiguity, and is asked the question (13b), respectively, later, it cannot safely give an affirmative answer, since the reading intended by the informant may be a different one than the reading intended by the person asking the question. All this seems to suggest a much more cautious entailment concept which requires for $A \models B$ to hold that every possible reading of B be classically entailed by every reading of A: The truth of any disambiguation of the premise must guarantee truth of all disambiguations of the conclusion to cover all possible cases of resolution.

This cautious entailment (van Deemter's $\exists\forall$ -variant) can clearly serve as a safe semantic basis for direct deduction. However, a semantics which assumes free choice for all local disambiguation possibilities is not sufficient to account for the obvious interdependence of disambiguation decisions in (16a) and (16b).

(16) a. This is a bank, but it isn't a bank.

 b. This is a bank. So, this is a bank.

Sentence (16a), to say the very least, has a strong tendency to be judged a contradiction, and likewise, there is a strong intuitive tendency to consider (16b) a valid entailment, despite the ambiguity involved. Thus, it seems that the interpretation of underspecification has to take into account some kind or degree of covariation, though not in the obligatory way required by super-valuation semantics. Van Deemter (1996) proposes to employ a notion of coherence: According to his proposal, more uniform interpretations are preferred to less uniform ones among the set of consistent disambiguations of a discourse (everything else being equal). The degree of coherence or uniformity of an interpretation is computed, roughly speaking, by counting occurrences of ambiguous expressions which are assigned identical readings. However, van Deemter's proposal does not provide a real solution. In whichever way the coherence measure applies to the above examples, it will not explain the difference between (15a)/(15b) on the one hand, and (16a)/(16b) on the other hand.[7].

The systematic difference between (15a) and (15b) on the one side, and (16a) and (16b) on the other side is that the latter are instances of the phenomenon of discourse parallelism. As I have pointed out already in connection with the zeugma test and the Hirschbuehler sentence in Sect. 2, parallelism imposes a constraint on semantic interpretation which forces parallel elements to have equal logical representations. Parallel constructions belong to the hard core of semantically relevant covariance cases. If we disregard possible other sources for obligatory covariance (it may well be that there aren't any), a straightforward solution to the direct interpretation problem is at hand. We assume that the cautious semantics considering all possible disambiguations is basically the correct one. Given equality constraints (in one or the other form, cf. Sect. 2), this does not automatically amount to independent choice of readings in all cases, but only within the limits imposed by the constraints. Let us look at the examples. There are no limits on the choice of readings for the occurrences of *bank* in sentence (15a), since the constraint set (17a) describing its meaning potential covers all possible combinations of readings BANK_1 and BANK_2.

---

[7] Pragmatics seems to be the appropriate level for coherence phenomena. Coherence-based decisions for interpretation are be guided by rather weak preferences (corresponding to the Gricean maxims of manner), which in turn are based on a variety of complex factors of textual and conceptual organization, rather than on a simple count criterion. Accordingly, van Deemter's attempt to treat coherence on the level of semantics, leads to a highly non-standard logic for ambiguous expressions.

(17) a. $\{close\_to(X_1, X_2), X_1 \in \{\text{BANK}_1, \text{BANK}_2\},$
$X_2 \in \{\text{BANK}_1, \text{BANK}_2\}\}$

b. $\{X_0 : X_2 \wedge \neg X_3, X_2 : X_4(a), X_3 : X_5(a),$
$X_4 \in \{\text{BANK}_1, \text{BANK}_2\}, X_5 \in \{\text{BANK}_1, = \text{BANK}_2\}, X_2 \sim X_3\}$

On the other hand, the parallelism between the clauses of (16a) introduces the equality constraint $X_2 \sim X_3$ into the description (17b), which rules out different instantiations of X_4 and X_5, and therefore admits only the two inconsistent readings of (16a).[8]

Let us consider next, how the approach can be extended to the entailment relation. If just the logical relation between a set of meaning descriptions σ and a meaning description A has to be judged upon, as in Reyle's data-base query example, all different combinations of local disambiguations must be considered. In these cases, the cautious ($\exists\forall$) entailment concept seems to be the correct one. If we state soundness of (16b), however, we do not just speak about the logical relation between its two clauses, but rather state that the discourse consisting of these sentences forms a conclusive argument. Since the first and second clause stand in the relation of discourse parallelism which induces an equality constraint, the choice of the reading for *bank* in the conclusion of (16b) must be the same as in the premise, and thus truth of the conclusion is guaranteed by truth of the premise. These considerations suggest that a distinction between two entailment concepts must be made, which is conceptually related to the distinction between static and dynamic entailment in dynamic semantics (cf. Groenendijk and Stokhof, 1991). *'Dynamic entailment'* for underspecified representations takes constraints, in particular parallelism constraints, resulting from discourse semantic relations between premises and conclusion, into account, *'static entailment'* doesn't.[9].

---

[8] I have used the *'bank '* symbol for expressions of two different object language types, in the two examples, to keep the notation simple. In (17a), BANK$_1$ and BANK$_1$ are in fact predicates occurring in the scope of the definite article, in a full, Montague-style quantificational analysis. Also, I have not said anything about the way the parallelism between the first and the second, negated clause of (16a) is precisely to be stated, and how it maps to the equality constraint in (17b). The solution is somewhat complex and not relevant for the argument.

[9] If we want to give a formal definition of the dynamic, discourse-related entailment concept, we face a technical difficulty: Since there may be covariance between premises and conclusion, we cannot define it by strengthening

5. REASONING WITH UNDERSPECIFIED REPRESENTATIONS

Providing a direct semantics for underspecified representations is one problem, designing sound and complete calculi for direct deduction is a different one.[10] It is yet another question, however, how to build efficient software systems for reasoning with underspecified information. No answer to this question exists to date, nor even more or less concrete ideas of how such an answer could look like. This is not too surprising because the problem of direct deduction on underspecified representations contains standard deduction for the corresponding object language as a sub-problem. Since the latter should have at least the expressiveness of FOL, a general and tractable method for direct deduction is a priori impossible. Unfortunately, it seems that we have to make use of the full machinery of heuristics and control mechanisms developed for theorem proving to make progress with the hard (in fact, AI-hard) problem of direct deduction for underspecified expressions. In this section, I would like to indicate whata viable pragmatic alternative to this discouraging perspective might look like.

The inspection of practically relevant examples for direct deduction shows that many of those cases which appear as intuitive and natural belong to a special sub-class, viz., arguments which start from underspecified premises and yield completely specified conclusions. This sub-class of inferences is particularly useful, since it renders representations which may be further processed using standard reasoning techniques. Instead of working at a general solution of the problem of direct deduction, one could aim at dividing the problem into an easier task of providing special inference mechanisms for (hopefully) quick and easy extraction of safe knowledge, and the task of reasoning with the result of the extraction, which is a hard, but not problem-specific task, and thus can be left to standard theorem-provers.

Let us take sentence (1a) as an example, again. Since its narrow-scope existential reading is entailed by the stronger wide-scope one, the

---

the cautious static entailment concept with additional conditions, but have to provide a possibility of context-wise evaluation again. We can do this by making technical use of the super-valuation approach mentioned above. Since the description language uses different meta-variables for different occurrences, there is no a priori covariance between different occurrences of an expression. If required, covariance can be explicitly brought about by equality constraints which reduce the set of admissible contexts.

[10] Solutions for several calculi have been proposed. I will not comment on them, however; here (see (Reyle, 1993; van Eijck, 1996)).

former can be inferred from the underspecified representation of (1a) as safe information. The deduction rule could be roughly formulated in the following way: If a pattern like (18) occurs in a constraint set (stating that a universal and an existential quantifier apply to one nuclear expression without specifying a relative scope ordering), add constraint $X_4 \lhd^* X_2$, (which amounts to a specification of the $\exists\forall$-reading).

(18) $\{X_1 = \exists x(X_3), X_2 = \forall y(X_4), X_0 \lhd^* X_1, X_0 \lhd^* X_2,$
$X_3 \lhd^* X_5, X_4 \lhd^* X_5\}$

Note that the rule does not make reference to fully specified OL readings, but rather works directly on the constraint set. This is not too impressive in the example under discussion, but becomes quite helpful in cases where dozens or hundreds of possible readings are around.[11] Another special, not too exciting, but useful type of direct deduction concerns cases of equivalent scope readings. Scope differences sometimes do and sometimes do not affect truth conditions. Examples (19a) and (19b) are cases where relative scope of the quantifiers does not matter.

(19) a. Some linguists speak a foreign language

b. Every linguistics students knows every professor of linguistics.

A method that detects possible candidate pairs for scope equivalence by directly inspecting the semantic description would be obviously useful, since it allows to eliminate spurious scope ambiguities without enumerating and inspecting the disambiguations.

There is a very simple method to arrive at a fully specified object-language representation that denotes the maximum of safe information in an underspecified meaning description, given that there are finitely many readings. Just generate all readings, and connect them by object-language disjunction. The solution is theoretically incontestable: The disjunction denotes safe information, since its truth is guaranteed by the truth of any of the readings, and clearly it is also the maximum of safe information we can get. With respect to practical application,

---

[11] It should be mentioned that the solution is not as easy as I have sketched here, since a prerequisite for the applicability of the rule is that both quantifiers must occur in a positive context, and no different operators can possibly intervene between the two. I just want to give an idea of the special kind of rules I have in mind, and thus I will not go deeper into the problems, here.

it isn't a particularly attractive solution. It involves the schematic
enumeration of all specific readings, again. This is unnecessary in many
scope underspecification cases because they allow a compact treatment,
as shown above, and it hardly leads to useful information in those
cases which do not allow that compact treatment like *bank* and *pen*.
The policy I have in mind is rather the following one: Do not aim at
completeness, but pick out certain sub-problems of direct deduction
(like the identification of weakest scope order, or equivalent scopings).
Apply these special techniques of direct deduction whenever they are
applicable. Otherwise, perform a (partial) disambiguation step, and try
again to apply direct deduction rules to the result. If direct deduction
works well for a given constraint set, a lot of processing time can
be saved. Otherwise, there is a flexible transition to the conventional
technique of working on disambiguations.[12] Apparently, also humans
do not use one method of reasoning with underspecified information
exclusively, but interleave direct reasoning, partial disambiguation, and
maybe a number of other techniques. In earlier work (Pinkal, 1995),
I have argued for a classification of ambiguity phenomena, the main
distinctive criterion being the need or tendency for disambiguation.

6. On the Status of Underspecified Representations

My comments on direct deduction may have left the impression that
underspecification techniques have a rather limited range, once the task
of sentence-internal semantic composition is done: If an underspecified
representation occurs, we either proceed to the specific kernel information shared by its different readings, or retract to disambiguations.
Thus one could assume the following general pattern for semantic processing: First, sentence meaning is computed using partial descriptions
(for which they are undoubtedly useful). Then, these descriptions are
replaced by fully specified logical representations, in one or the other
way, which are the only available and necessary data structures for
further processing steps in the understanding process.

This view is not completely correct, for several reasons, however. On
the one hand, the approach proposed in the last section was meant to

---

[12] To be more precise, this can either mean: make a case distinctions and
work on the resulting cases in parallel, or: pick a preferred alternative, and if
you run into a deadlock, revise your decision. Cf. Poesio (1996), who argues
that the latter kind of reasoning is basic to human processing of underspecified
information.

provide an easy and viable method to exploit underspecified information. There was no claim of completeness involved. Examples like (10) indicate that there might well be useful and natural inference patterns leading from underspecified representations to underspecified representations. On the other hand, there is a specific argument in favor of a more global role of underspecification coming from discourse semantics. Look at (20), which is an example for the interaction between scope and anaphoric binding by virtue of accessibility constraints (cf. Kamp and Reyle, 1993).

(20) Two languages are spoken by every linguist. One of them is English.

If we had replaced the underspecified representation of the first clause of the text in (20) by the $\forall\exists$-reading, the wide-scope existential reading required by the anaphoric subject of the second clause would not be available any more. Another kind of evidence for the relevance of underspecification for discourse structure is provided by the discourse semantic phenomenon of parallelism. In cases of equivalent scope readings as (19a) or (19b) of Sect. 5, one can proceed from the scope neutral description to one arbitrary representation with fixed scope, without losing any truth-conditionally relevant information. However, even in this case the underspecified representation cannot be just dispensed with.

(21) At least one computer science student knows every professor of computer science, too.

Let an utterance of (20) be followed by (21), in which the scope order is crucial for truth conditions. As pointed out in Sect. 2, parallelism requires the corresponding quantifiers of the two sentences to be in the same scope relation. Taking one of the possible equivalent scope orders as the representation of (20), the truth conditions of (21) are fixed in a purely accidental way.

Apparently, there is a layer of information which may be truth-conditionally irrelevant, but is indispensable for discourse-semantics. This reminds of the situation in DRT: Translation of DRSes to formulas of predicate logic preserves the truth conditions, but the discourse-semantic semantic layer of the anaphoric potential is lost. In the same way, replacement of an underspecified representation by the safe kernel leads to loss of semantic information which is relevant for discourse-semantic purposes. Rather than drawing the borderline between underspecification techniques and standard semantic frameworks at the sentence boundary, we may assume a global two-layer model for semantic processing. On the one hand, an underspecified description providing the potential for disambiguation or precisification must be available at any point of the discourse. On the other hand, we can at any point extract specific safe information, and try to do further inferencing on it by conventional means. Thus, the special techniques of direct reasoning proposed in the last section do not amount to replacing the latter, but mediating between the language-oriented level of semantic representation and the non-linguistic information processing level.

I think that this view of the role of underspecification in semantic information processing opens a perspective to tractable, and hopefully efficient solutions for some of the basic tasks in natural language understanding. Let me finally ask whether it could also serve as the basis of an adequate cognitive model of meaning processing. There is a very basic difficulty for giving a general answer to this question. We cannot be sure whether the methods we have available in semantics – be it on the level of logical representation languages or description language constraints – provide access to all dimensions, or even the most relevant ones of the mental encoding of meaning. In fact, there are strong intuitions that certain kinds of semantic information which can only be spelled out in a rather complex way using available techniques, have a rather simple and compact mental representation. One of these cases is ambiguity of quantifier scope. Maybe there is a completely different way of encoding the semantics of sentences with several scope-bearing elements, from which both kernel information and potential of precise readings follow. Another example are ontologically multi-layered common nouns (like *newspaper* and *university*), whose peculiar meaning structure James Pustejovsky tries to capture with the *dotted pairs* of his *Generative Lexicon*. I would refrain from claiming cognitive adequacy for any of the presently available approaches to semantic underspecification. Maybe, even the notion of underspecification itself is inappropriate because it suggests that there is a significant lack of information, where in certain cases at least, it might be the specific representational framework which disallows a direct unambiguous encoding.

However, I do not see any alternative framework which supports the basic kind of processes needed for understanding natural language-efficient semantic construction, context-sensitive meaning assignment, and inference. Thus, underspecification techniques are the best we have to date, although they might eventually turn out to be deeply inadequate.

7. Concluding Remarks

What I have said in this chapter, was mostly programmatic in character. Thus, I addressed things to be done and speculated about the general direction to take in order get these things done, but did not become too specific about details, as it is typically the case with programmatic papers. However, this one has the slight advantage that the program it presents is mainly intended as a program for a special project, the CHORUS project run at Saarbrücken University,[13] rather than a program for the community in general. The principal aim of the project is a unified and tractable method for the representation and processing of all kinds of partial meaning information which have been exemplified in Sect. 1. Subgoals are the design of a constraint language for partial meaning representation (as indicated in Sect. 2); the investigation of methods for semantic analysis with partial input information (as indicated in Sect. 3); the development of direct deduction techniques, as indicated in Sect. 5, and of the theoretical background outlined in Sect. 4. I hope we will be able to present results of this research in the near future.

ACKNOWLEDGEMENTS

The ideas and opinions presented in this chapter have grown in the environment of the CHORUS project and its immediate sister projects in the Sonderforschungsbereich 378. I am indebted to all colleagues working in this group and visitors to the group, in particular to Markus Egg, Jan van Eijck, Jan Jaspars, Michael Kohlhase, Alexander Koller, Reinhard Muskens, Joachim Niehren, and Peter Ruhrberg.

REFERENCES

Alshawi, H. and Crouch, R. (1992) Monotonic semantic interpretation. In *Proceedings of the 30th ACL*, 32–39.

Bos, J. (1996) Predicate logic unplugged. In P. Dekker and M. Stokhof, editors, *Proceedings of the 10th Amsterdam Colloquium*, Amsterdam. ILLC.

---

[13] CHORUS (Semantic Processing using Concurrent Constraints) is part of the SFB (Special Research Division) 378 'ressource adaptive Cognitive Processes' funded by the German Science Foundation.

Bronnenberg, W.J., Bunt, H.C., Landsbergen, J., Scha, R., Schoenmakers, W.J. and Utteren, E. van (1979) The question answering system PHLIQA 1. In L. Bolc (ed.) *Natural communication with computers.* MacMillan, London.

Bunt, H.C. (1984) The resolution of quantificational ambiguity in the TENDUM system. *Proc. COLING'84,* Stanford University, 130 – 133.

Bunt, H.C. (1985) *Mass terms and model-theoretic semantics.* Cambridge University Press.

Copestake, A., Flickinger, D. and Sag, I. (1997) Minimal recursion semantics. An introduction. CSLI, Stanford University.

Deemter, K. van (1996) Towards a logic of ambiguous expressions. In K. van Deemter and S. Peters, editors, *Semantic ambiguity and underspecification,* pages 203–237. CSLI Publications, Stanford.

Eijck, J. van (1996) The logic of ambiguation. In The FraCas Consortium, editor, *Building the Framework, FraCas Deliverable 15.*

Egg, M. and Lebeth, K (1996) Semantic interpretation in HPSG. Paper presented at the 3rd Conference on HPSG, Marseilles.

Fine, K. (1975) Vagueness, truth, and logic. *Synthese,* 30:265–300.

Groenendijk, J. and Stokhof, M. (1991) Dynamic predicate logic. *Linguistics & Philosophy,* 14:39–100.

Hirschbühler, P. (1982) VP deletion and across the board quantifier scope. In *Proceedings of NELS 12.*

Kamp, H, and Reyle, U. (1993) *From Discourse to Logic.* Kluwer, Dordrecht.

Landsbergen, J. and Scha, R. (1979) Formal languages for semantic representation. In. S. All'en and J. Petöfi (eds.) *Aspects of automatized text processing.* Buske, Hamburg.

Muskens, R. (1997) Order-independence and underspecification. Proceedings of the Workshops in Prague (Feb 1995) and Bad Teinach (May 1995), Vol. 2: Comments and Replies, 155-166, Arbeitspapier des IMS, Universität Stuttgart.

Niehren, J. Pinkal, M. and Ruhrberg, P. (1997) On equality up-to constraints over finite trees, context unification and one-step rewriting. In *Proceedings of CADE'97.*

Niehren, J., Pinkal, M. and Ruhrberg, P. (1997) A uniform approach to underspecification and parallelism. In *Proceedings of ACL'97,* 410–417, Madrid, Spain.

Pinkal, M. (1995) *Logic and Lexicon.* Kluwer, Dordrecht.

Pinkal, M. (1996) Radical underspecification. In P. Dekker and M. Stokhof, editors, *Proceedings of the 10th Amsterdam Colloquium,* 587–606, Amsterdam, ILLC.

Poesio, M. (1996) Semantic ambiguity and perceived ambiguity. In *Semantic Ambiguity and Underspecification.* CSLI-Publications, Stanford, CA. ·

Pustejovsky, J. (1991) The generative lexicon. *Computational Linguistics,* 17:409–441.

Pustejovsky, J. (1995) *The generative lexicon*. MIT Press, Cambridge.

Reyle, U. (1993) Dealing with ambiguities by underspecification: construction, representation, and deduction. *Journal of Semantics*, 10:123–179.

Reyle, U. (1996) Co-indexing labeled DRSs to represent and reason with ambiguities. In Deemter, K. van and S. Peters, S. eds, *Semantic ambiguity and underspecification*, 239–268. CSLI Publications, Stanford, CA.

Sag, I. (1976) *Deletion and logical form*. PhD thesis, MIT, Cambridge, MA..

Wahlster, W. (1993) Verbmobil: Translation of face-to-face dialogues. In *Proceedings of the 3rd European Conference on Speech Communication and Technology*, pages 29–38, Berlin, Germany.

Worm, K. (1997) Robuste semantische Verarbeitung. Verbmobil-Report 200, Universität des Saarlandes, Saarbrücken, December 1997. Available from http://www.dfki.de/verbmobil/.

ALLAN RAMSAY

DYNAMIC AND UNDERSPECIFIED INTERPRETATION WITHOUT DYNAMIC OR UNDERSPECIFIED LOGIC

1. WHY STICK TO DOXASTIC LOGIC?

Most people these days accept the idea that meanings of natural language utterances have a dynamic, context-changing character. You produce an utterance in a context. Your hearer processes this utterance with respect to the context, doing things like anchoring referring expressions, choosing among alternative readings, and perhaps reasoning about why you might have said this, and thus updates his or her view of the world. The notion goes back at least to (Gazdar, 1979), and has been taken up within such theories as situation semantics (Barwise and Perry, 1983), file change semantics (Heim, 1983), discourse representation theory (DRT) (Kamp, 1984; Kamp and Reyle, 1993) and dynamic predicate logic (DPL) (Groenendijk and Stockhof, 1991). A striking property of all these theories apart from (Gazdar, 1979) is that in order to accommodate the idea that meanings are dynamic they provide extensions to classical logic.

It is also widely recognised that the possibility that a single sentence may have numerous readings, arising from lexical and structural ambiguity and from the fact that natural language does not seem to constrain quantifier scope very tightly, is extremely problematic for computational semantics. There seem to be three main reactions to this problem: (i) throw up your hands in despair and hope someone else will solve it, (ii) enumerate the interpretations, possibly in some tightly packed notation, and try to choose between them e.g. by seeing which ones are consistent (Wedekind, 1996), or (iii) extend the logic so that you can reason with, or at least give truth values to, underspecified representations (Reyle, 1993; Alshawi, 1992).

It is well-known that changing the expressive power of your representation language changes, at least in the worst case, the computational tractability of your problem. Sometimes you will decide to live with that. You may find that the extra expressive power of some richer formalism enables you to say things so much more neatly that you feel

H. Bunt and R. Muskens (eds.), Computing Meaning, Volume 1, 57–72.

you have made an aesthetic gain, or you may know that although you
are using the expressive power of the richer formalism you are in fact
inhabiting a fragment with the same computational properties as the
original (e.g. although it may convenient to use the notation of first-
order logic to describe simple type hierarchies, the fragment you are
using actually has linear computational complexity).

I also believe that changing the expressive power of the representation language makes a huge difference to the ontology of your theory.
If Occam's razor says that you should not multiply entities unnecessarily, then multiplying the *kinds* of entities in your theory is an
even greater sin. The aim of the present paper is to return to a notion
which is present in (Gazdar, 1979), namely that you can account for the
context-changing nature of meanings by appeal to an orthodox doxastic
logic.

Why should this be preferable to introducing a dynamic logic? After
all, in moving to a doxastic logic I am going beyond simple first-order
logic, so I also am violating my sharpened Occam's razor.

The key here is that you need doxastic logic, or at any rate a mechanism for reasoning about beliefs, in all sorts of other places. You need
it in linguistics if you want to consider not just what something means
in a given context but also why someone might say it in that context,
you need it in theories of education where you have to think about how
teachers reason about what their students know and what they ought
to know, you need it in everyday life to reason about who to ask for
information that you want, you need it all over the place. So although
it may not be immediately obvious that this is the best way to deal
with the dynamic aspects of meaning and with underspecification, I am
certainly not introducing a representation scheme whose sole purpose
is to account for these phenomena. I am taking something which is
already needed for various tasks and seeing whether I can make it do
these ones as well.

What sort of doxastic logic am I going to use? The vast majority
of work in AI has followed Hintikka's observation that some properties
of knowledge, and to a lesser extent belief, look a bit like properties
of modal logics (Hintikka, 1962). There has been a great deal of work
following up this suggestion, both for general reasoning about knowledge, belief and action (e.g. Moore, 1984) and for reasoning about
knowledge and belief in the context of various kinds of linguistic action
(e.g. Appelt, 1985; Cohen and Levesque, 1980; Cohen et al., 1990). I am
not keen on this approach. In particular, the fact that *any* semantics
for *any* modal notion requires the sets of sentences to which one has

a particular attitude to be complete and consistent undermines the applicability of such notions to belief. Belief sets are never complete and are often inconsistent. As such, it seems thoroughly inappropriate to treat belief as a modality, and to try to ground it in terms of sets of possible worlds (and all AI applications of this idea use the possible worlds semantics as the basis of the inference technique, by grounding inference in reifications of the accessibility relationship).

I am therefore going to use a simple, and I think appealing, alternative. I shall take it that when someone says that they believe something, they mean that they have access to a body of evidence from which it can be derived. Where they get their evidence from, what sorts of derivation they are prepared to perform, will vary from person to person — I might, for instance, trust your evidence but not accept your reasoning processes. I shall therefore denote the fact that agent A believes proposition P by

$$private([A]) \rightarrow P$$

where $X \rightarrow Y$ is implication as understood in constructive logic.

In other words, the base beliefs of some individual A can be taken to be a single, probably rather large, proposition called $private([A])$. Then if A is capable of justifying P on the basis of $private([A])$ then they are at least capable of saying that they believe it. If you want to reflect the fact that different people employ different inference rules, e.g. by setting resource limits, then any of the techniques used in resource logics such as linear logic (Girard, 1987) or labelled deduction (Gabbay, 1989) will suffice.

This view of belief has most of the properties you would want. You can cope with scope phenomena, so that you can distinguish between

$$private([ralph]) \rightarrow \exists X \, spy(X)$$

and

$$\exists X private([ralph]) \rightarrow spy(X)$$

You can cope with nesting of beliefs by allowing $private([A, B, C])$ to denote what A believes that B believes that C believes. And, crucially for the application of this notion of belief to underspecification, interpreting $P \rightarrow Q$ *constructively* means that you can distinguish between $private([A]) \rightarrow (P \vee Q)$ and $(private([A]) \rightarrow P) \vee (private([A]) \rightarrow Q)$. This would not have been the case with a classical interpretation of $\rightarrow$, since

$$(P \to (Q \lor R)) \equiv ((P \to Q) \lor (P \to R))$$

is classically valid.

This logic is clearly reminiscent of Konolige's treatment of belief (Konolige, 1986), and is also closely in tune with later work by Hintikka (Hintikka and Kulas, 1985). I do not want to get into a detailed comparison of these views of belief here. In the remainder of this paper I am simply going to use this notion to tackle the relevant problems in semantics.

2. ANCHORS AS CLAIMS ABOUT PUBLIC KNOWLEDGE

We turn now to the first of the semantic notions that need to be dealt with: the fact that meanings function as context-change operators. The key point here is that if I say to you something like

(1) Allan Ramsay is a well-known portrait painter.

then I am inviting you to (i) identify someone who we both know as Allan Ramsay and (ii) extend your view of the world (your discourse model, your view of the common ground, ...) with the fact that this person is a well-known portrait painter. The invitation to do these two things *is* the meaning of this utterance. Whether you are prepared to accept this invitation is another matter, but the moves that are open to you are predicated on your recognising what I am inviting you to do.

Now if the only person who you think we are both aware of who is called Allan Ramsay is in fact me then what you will do about part (i) of the invitation will differ from what an art historian would do. Note that even if you *are* an art historian, you might well interpret this as a sentence about me if you have grounds for believing that I don't know about the portrait painter, or even if you think that I am unaware of your vocation and hence that I might not think that you know about him.

I am therefore going to follow (Gazdar, 1979) in viewing what he called pre-suppositions, which include the anchoring effects of referring expressions, as statements about the speaker's view of the common ground. I will denote this by $public([S], [S, H])$ — the huge conjoined set of propositions which the speaker S believes are shared with the hearer H. In particular, I am going to assume that part of the content of an NP like *"the man"* is that, as far as the speaker is concerned, there is exactly one individual X for which the information that is shared with the hearer supports the claim that X is a man:

$$\exists! X (public([S], [S, H]) \rightarrow man(X))$$

I am obviously ignoring recency and salience effects here, but the general principle is clear: if I talk to you about *"the man"* I must think that we both have some particular man in mind.

But that's not all that S will do with this NP. He or she will also tell you something about this man. They might, for instance, say *"The man died"*. Note that for this sentence to be acceptable H has to accept S's view that the common ground supports a proof that there is exactly one (salient) man. I suggest that the following is a suitable formal paraphrase of this sentence:

$$\exists A :: A < now$$
$$\exists! B public(s, [s, h]) \rightarrow man(B)$$
$$\wedge \exists C at(A, C) \wedge \theta(C, agent, B)$$
$$\wedge event(C) \wedge type(C, die)$$

This paraphrase is obtained by analysing the sentence as described in (Ramsay and Schäler, 1995; Ramsay, 1996). All that we need to do is to interpret *"the"* as

$$\lambda A(\lambda B(\exists! C public(s, [s, h]) \rightarrow A.C \wedge B.C))$$

and then follow standard compositional techniques.

Rather like the work reported in (Konrad et al., 1996), this system enables you to obtain different semantic analyses by setting and unsetting switches — useful for teaching and for exposition. I shall reconsider the arguments in (Ramsay, 1996) shortly, and in order to do so I will reset some of the switches that produce a more complex analysis of tense and aspect, but as far as the main argument of the current paper is concerned I shall use the settings that produce the simple treatment of these phenomena in the above paraphrase.

What does this paraphrase say? It amounts to a claim by the speaker that for exactly one item B the common ground supports the claim that B is a man, plus a further claim that B died. In other words, it invites the hearer to accept these two claims. In order to do so, he or she will have to see whether their own view of the common ground either supports an appropriate chain of reasoning, or whether they are prepared to 'accommodate' this claim and accept the result even if they can't actually justify it from the common ground. This typically happens if the claim is unsurprising, so that you will accommmodate the presuppositions of

(2) The driver of the bus I came to work on must have been drunk.

but not those of

(3) The driver of the bus my monkey went to work on must have been drunk.

because although your view of the common ground does not support the claim that I came to work on a bus and that there was a driver of that bus, it is unsurprising. Not so for (3).

In (Ramsay, 1996) I argued that the way to account for the different temporal properties of

(4) A man is sleeping.

and

(5) A man is hiccupping.

is by allowing both sentences to talk about sets of events, and using the meaning postulates associated with the particular verbs and with the progressive marker to sort out the cardinality of this set. Thus, turning some of the appropriate switches back on, the interpretations of (4) and (5) are

$\exists A man(A)$
$\quad \wedge \ \exists B prog(now, B)$
$\quad\quad \wedge \ \forall C :: \{B.C\}$
$\quad\quad\quad\quad \theta(C, agent, A) \wedge event(C) \wedge type(C, sleep)$

$\exists A man(A)$
$\quad \wedge \ \exists B prog(now, B)$
$\quad\quad \wedge \ \forall C :: \{B.C\}$
$\quad\quad\quad\quad \theta(C, agent, A) \wedge event(C) \wedge type(C, hiccup)$

The first of these says that the relation $prog$ holds between the instant now and some set B, where every member C of B is an event of type *sleep* whose agent is the man A, and likewise for the second. Leaving aside whether it is a good idea to ascribe the role of agent to the subject of either of these verbs, the paraphrases as given say nothing about the size of the set C. We need to back such paraphrases up with meaning postulates which spell out what we know about the terms that appear in them. The crucial ones for present purposes are:

$$\forall A \forall B prog(B, A)$$
$$\rightarrow \exists C :: \{A.C\} \forall D :: \{start(D, C)\} D < B$$
$$\wedge \exists E :: \{A.E\} \forall F :: \{end(F, E)\} B \leq F$$

$$\forall A extended(A)$$
$$\rightarrow \forall B start(B, A)$$
$$\rightarrow \forall C end(C, A)$$
$$\rightarrow \exists D(B < D \wedge D < C)$$

$$\forall A instantaneous(A)$$
$$\rightarrow \forall B start(B, A)$$
$$\rightarrow \forall C(end(C, A) \rightarrow B = C)$$

The first of these says that if *prog* holds between an instant T and a set E then at least one member $Y1$ of E started before T and at least one $Y2$ ended at or after T. There is nothing here to say whether $Y1$ and $Y2$ are the same or different, but general properties of sets say that a non-empty set has either one member or more than one member.

The other two simply say that if E is an extended event then there is some instant between its start and end, whereas if it is instantaneous then its start and end are identical. The meaning postulates for *"sleep"* and *"hiccup"* will include ones that say that sleeping events are extended whereas hiccupping is (conceptually) instantaneous.

If someone utters either (4) or (5) to you, they are inviting you to accept these paraphrases *and* their consequences. Before you do so, you should at least check that these are reasonable. One way to do this is by building a model in which the paraphrase and everything else you know is true.

Now building models is, in general, quite a hard thing to do. Fortunately (Manthey and Bry, 1988) provide a theorem prover which can be adapted very neatly to this task. In essence, Manthey and Bry's original theorem prover attempts to derive a proof of a goal A from assumptions Δ by enumerating the potential models of $\{\neg A\} \cup \Delta$ and showing that none of them are reasonable. In (Ramsay, 1995) I have shown how to extend this theorem prover to cope with intensionality and abstraction, and I have recently further extended it to handle equality. I can therefore use it, slightly backwards, to enumerate the potential models of $\{[\![(4)]\!], \mathrm{MP_{prog}}, \mathrm{MP_{extended}}, \mathrm{MP_{instantaneous}}\}$. In other words, I can use it to see what the world would be like if (4) (or (5)) and the meaning postulates were all true. It takes very little time at all to show from first principles that (4) and the meaning postulates have a model where there is a single event, and a bit less than two seconds to show that in any model of (5) and the meaning postulates there must be at least two hiccups, i.e. that (5) must have an iterative interpretation but (4) need not[1].

Suppose we take the same line with respect to sentences containing referring expressions. If H is to accept what S says then it must at least be compatible with everything else H believes, including H's background knowledge (which in turn includes the meaning postulates for the terms which underly the utterance) and in particular H's view of the common ground. If S believes that the common ground supports some conclusion but H does not then something has gone wrong. So given the above paraphrase of *"The man died"*, one thing H will want to do is verify that $\exists! B(public(s, [s, h]) \rightarrow man(B))$ is a reasonable claim. As far as S is concerned, there is exactly one B for which the common ground supports the claim that $man(B)$. But if the common ground is actually common then H's view of it should also support this claim.

I tackle this in two stages. Proving that some body of evidence supports a proof that there is something which satisfies some property is a routine activity, and the task can be performed perfectly well by the theorem prover. Proving that there is only one such item is much much harder. The problem is that the existence proof is monotonic — if $\Delta \vdash \exists x P$ then $\Delta \cup \Gamma \vdash \exists x P$ — whereas the uniqueness proof is not, since Γ may provide evidence that there is another item which satisfies P, and then indeed subsequent information may show that these two were the same after all. I therefore deal with the existence part of the claim by obtaining a proof and the uniqueness part by showing that there is at least one model where there is only one such item. The nature of the theorem prover is such that it can be equally easily used to obtain proofs by eliminating possible models or to obtain models. So given a proposition $public(h, [s, h])$ which constitutes a picture of H's

---

[1] The range of aspectual markers and their associated meaning postulates will vary across languages, but the flexibility provided by this approach remains useful.

view of the common ground, I deal with *"The man died"* by showing that for some B this proposition supports a proof of $man(B)$ and is compatible with there being no other men.

The inner workings of the theorem prover involve, as usual, various stages of normalisation. In particular, existential quantifiers are eliminated by Skolemisation, so that by the time the proofs that there is a man, and that there may just be one, are completed there will be a unique Skolem constant which denotes that man, say $sk17$. So once H has decided to accept this part of the utterance, the update step consists of adding

$$\exists A :: \{A < now\}$$
$$\exists Bat(A, B) \wedge \theta(B, agent, sk17) \wedge event(B) \wedge type(B, die)$$

to $public(h, [s, h])$. And if the conversation proceeds without any hiccups then S will presume that H has done this, and hence will add this proposition to $public(h, [s, h])$, thus keeping the two views in step.

This is fine for basic referring expressions. How does it relate to the subtler cases that led, for instance, to the development of DRT? Consider first the paraphrase of

(6) If a farmer owns a donkey he beats it.

as

$$\exists Aat(now, A)$$
$$\wedge \ \exists Bdonkey(B)$$
$$\wedge \ \exists Cfarmer(C)$$
$$\wedge \ \exists Dat(now, D)$$
$$\wedge \ theta(D, object, B) \wedge theta(D, agent, C)$$
$$\wedge \ event(D) \wedge type(D, own)$$
$$\rightarrow \ \exists!Epublic(s, [s, h]) \rightarrow neuter(E)$$
$$\wedge \ \exists!Fpublic(s, [s, h]) \rightarrow masculine(F)$$
$$\wedge \ \exists Gat(now, G)$$
$$\wedge \ theta(G, object, E)$$
$$\wedge \ theta(G, agent, F)$$
$$\wedge \ event(G) \wedge type(G, beat)$$

Given our constructive view of implication, this says that if the proposition that a farmer owns a donkey is added to what S knows then he or she will be able to prove

$\exists! Apublic(s, [s, h]) \rightarrow neuter(A)$
$\quad \wedge \; \exists! Bpublic(s, [s, h]) \rightarrow masculine(B)$
$\quad\quad \wedge \; \exists Cat(now, C)$
$\quad\quad\quad \wedge \; \theta(C, object, A) \wedge \theta(C, agent, B)$
$\quad\quad\quad \wedge \; event(C) \wedge type(C, beat)$

Consider the first bit of this, which corresponds to the interpretation of *"it"*. This bit says under the specified circumstances there would be exactly one object for which S would be able to prove that the common ground supported the claim that it was neuter. What are the specified circumstances? That the existence of a farmer, the existence of a donkey, and a relation between them have been added to what S knows. If they were added publicly, for instance if H had said *"Well Pedro owns a donkey"*, then clearly the common ground would support such an argument, since the existence of a (sex-unspecified) donkey would have been conceded. Likewise, the concession that there is a farmer yields the material required for justifying the claim $\exists! F((public(s, [s, h]) \rightarrow masculine(F))$. There is thus nothing mysterious about the fact that a referring expression in the consequent of a conditional sentence can pick up its referent from the antecedent. The conditional as a whole commits the speaker to being able to justify the conclusion if supplied with evidence for the antecedent. If you supply evidence for the antecedent of (6) then you have, immediately, supplied the evidence the speaker needs to back up the claims $\exists! E, (public(s, [s, h]) \rightarrow neuter(E)$ and $\exists! F((public(s, [s, h]) \rightarrow masculine(F))$.

A similar well-known puzzle concerns the interpretation of sentences like

(7) Each man kills the thing he loves.

The formal paraphrase of this is

$\forall A :: \{man(A)\}$
$\quad \exists! Bpublic(s, [s, h]) \rightarrow thing(B)$
$\quad\quad \wedge \; \exists! Cpublic(s, [s, h]) \rightarrow masculine(C)$
$\quad\quad\quad \wedge \; \exists Dat(now, D)$
$\quad\quad\quad\quad \wedge \; \theta(D, object, B) \wedge \theta(D, agent, C)$
$\quad\quad\quad\quad \wedge \; event(D) \wedge type(D, love)$
$\quad\quad \wedge \; \exists Eat(now, E)$
$\quad\quad\quad \wedge \; \theta(E, object, B) \wedge \theta(E, agent, A)$
$\quad\quad\quad \wedge \; event(E) \wedge type(E, kill)$

This says that S believes that given a particular man there would be a unique entity B such that the common ground would support the following two claims: (i) that B was a thing (very informative!), and (ii) that there was a unique entity C such that the common ground supported a proof that C was masculine and that C loved B. Clearly, if S is supplied with a man then showing that the common ground supports a proof that there is a man is straightforward. The other parts depend on the common-sense knowledge that each man loves one thing.

Again the constructive interpretation of the logic, so that universal statements and implications are commitments to provide justifications under appropriate circumstances, does nearly all the work for us. Taking a constructive view of the basic logical operators, and allowing propositions to stand for 'what the speaker believes' and 'what the speaker believes is in the common ground', we have a treatment of reference which handles all the simple and problematic cases with virtually no extension of the expressive power of first-order. The task of doing the required reasoning automatically is as easy as you will get for any kind of epistemic reasoning: not easy, but manageable.

3. UNDERSPECIFICATION OR AMBIGUITY?

Can we deal with underspecification within the same framework? I shall concentrate on the ambiguities that arise from lexical and structural ambiguity, though I believe that the treatment outlined here will also cover the intrinsic underspecification of scope by structure. Again the key observation is that underspecification arises from the hearer's uncertainty about what the speaker has actually committed him or herself to. So when we get an attachment ambiguity, as in

(8) I saw a man in the park

or a lexical ambiguity such as

(9) I left it in the bank

the problem is not that the *speaker* doesn't know whether it was a man in a park or a seeing event in park, or whether it was the edge of a river or a financial institution. The speaker is not, except in pathological cases, in any doubt. The problem is that the *hearer* doesn't know.

Now any chart parser will obtain the two analyses of (8) by packing the descriptions of the VPs *(saw (a (man in the park)))* and *((saw a man) (in the park))*. The task for semantics is to work out (i) how to pack the shared aspects of the interpretations, which are rather more substantial than the shared aspects of the syntactic analyses, and (ii) what they signify when you have done it.

I will tackle (ii) first. It seems throughly inappropriate to treat underspecification as simple disjunction. (9) does not mean the same as *"I left it either by the river's edge or by the place where I keep my money"*. What the hearer has to do is decide that the speaker is committed to one of two things: that either *private([s])* → "by the river's edge" or *private([s])* → "by the financial institution". So what I want to do is to pack the shared parts of the two interpretations, and to leave the differences as a disjunction with respect to the speaker's commitment. Thus I would like to obtain (and do obtain) the following interpretation of (8):

$$
\begin{aligned}
&\exists A :: \{A < now\} \\
&\quad \exists B at(A, B) \\
&\qquad \wedge\ \exists! C public(s, [s, h]) \rightarrow speaker(C) \\
&\qquad\quad \wedge\ \exists D man(D) \\
&\qquad\qquad \wedge\ \theta(B, object, D) \wedge \theta(B, agent, C) \\
&\qquad\qquad \wedge\ event(B) \wedge\ type(B, see) \\
&\qquad\qquad \wedge\ \exists! E public(s, [s, h]) \rightarrow park(E) \\
&\qquad\qquad\quad \wedge\ private([s]) \rightarrow in(B, E) \\
&\qquad\qquad\qquad \vee\ private([s]) \rightarrow in(D, E)
\end{aligned}
$$

The difference between the two interpretations has been isolated away in the bottom corner, where it is unclear whether it is B, the seeing event, or E, the man, which the speaker claims is in the park. You can do any reasoning you want with the rest of the paraphrase. You can infer that the speaker saw some man, and that he is telling you something about some park which you can both identify. But if you want to know whether it was the man that was in the park or the seeing you are going to have to do some more work. Note that this means I am *not* taking (8) to be underspecified. As far as the speaker is concerned, (8) is fine, and has a single, clear meaning. The problem is that the hearer does not know what that meaning is. In other words, as far as the hearer is concerned (8) is *ambiguous*. The purpose of constructing a paraphrase like the one given above is to isolate the ambiguity so that (i) the hearer can make some use of this utterance even without

sorting out whether it is the man or the seeing that is in the park, and
(ii) the problem is localised so that if the hearer does need to sort it
out the relevant factors can easily be identified.

Quarantining off the underspecified parts of the two interpretations
and packing the remainder is fiddly but not difficult or computationally
expensive. You have spot that the potential for sharing information
exists, but if you are building your semantics compositionally and using
a chart to pack structures with the same syntactic properties than
spotting situations where it can be done is a trivial matter. You may
then want to convert the potentially shared material to some normal
form, since otherwise trivial differences may block you. For instance,
you may find that one of the interpretations looks like $(A \wedge (B \wedge C'))$
and the other like $((A \wedge B) \wedge C')$. You do not want the potential for
combining A and B to be blocked by the bracketing, which merely
reflects the order in which the syntactic constituents were found. This
kind of normal forming is also trivial, though anyone who has ever
written a theorem prover will know that it can be intricate without actually being challenging or interesting. And once you have appropriate
items in a common format, finding the places where they differ is also
straightforward.

It is thus easy to take a parse forest and construct a packed semantic
representation of the kind given above. It is even easier if the difference
is purely lexical, as in (9):

$$\exists A :: \{A < now\}$$
$$\exists! B \, public(s, [s, h]) \to neuter(B)$$
$$\wedge \; \exists! C \, public(s, [s, h]) \to speaker(C)$$
$$\wedge \; \exists D \, at(A, D)$$
$$\wedge \; \theta(D, object, B)$$
$$\wedge \; \theta(D, agent, C)$$
$$\wedge \; event(D) \wedge type(D, leave)$$
$$\wedge \; \exists! E \, in(D, E)$$
$$\wedge \; public(s, [s, h])$$
$$\to private([s]) \to bank2(E)$$
$$\vee \; private([s]) \to bank1(E)$$

The divergent part here says that there is exactly one item E for which
the common ground will tell you either that S believes E to be a river
bank or that he or she believes it to be a financial institution — in other
words, that the common ground ought to suffice not just to identify E
but also to choose between the two alternatives.

The same approach should work if the underspecification concerns quantifier scope, though you cannot use the packing implied by the chart to spot when to apply it. The important thing is that by dealing with underspecification this way I can get (i) a single representation of the information that is *not* underspecified and (ii) an intuitively appealing treatment of the underspecified parts without any extension of the underlying logic beyond the simple, non-modal, treatment of belief given above.

4. CONCLUSIONS

I have shown that it is possible to use a very minor extension of first-order logic to give formal paraphrases of natural language sentences which are dynamic and/or underspecified. All you need, on this account, is to allow belief sets of various kinds to be represented by propositions, and to use a constructive interpretation of the underlying logic. The resulting paraphrases are amenable to standard theorem proving techniques: the mechanism provided by (Manthey and Bry, 1988) and refined in (Ramsay, 1991; Ramsay, 1995) is particularly suitable, given the explicit manner in which it attempts to enumerate models.

The discussion of ambiguous sentences in Section 3 showed how to give a compact representation in which the problematic parts are isolated and are clearly marked as being things that speaker has expressed opinions about. I have not had space to say anything about how you might decide which opinions the speaker actually held — how you might resolve the ambiguity rather than just identifying and isolating it. The most promising way to use this kind of representation for disambiguating examples like (8) and (9) is to assume that only a very strange speaker would claim that the common ground supported something impossible. So if you try to construct a model of a sentence such as

(10) I saw a man with black hair.

you will explore various options. These are models of what the speaker is claiming, and hence should include anything which is explicitly marked as a claim by the speaker. Clearly any model of the speaker's beliefs which includes things which obviously contradict other background facts will be rejected, and hence you will not get a model where the speaker used black hair to see someone. This approach to ambiguity resolution mirrors the ideas described in (Wedekind, 1996), which I believe is the right way to go.

REFERENCES

Alshawi, H., editor (1992) *The Core Language Engine*. Bradford Books/MIT Press, Cambridge, Mass.

Appelt, D. (1985) *Planning English Sentences*. Cambridge University Press, Cambridge.

Barwise, J. and Perry, J. (1983) *Situations and Attitudes*. Bradford Books, Cambridge, MA.

Cohen, P. R. and Levesque, H. (1980) Speech acts and the recognition of shared plans. In *Proceedings, Canadian Society for Computational Studies of Intelligence*, pages 263–270.

Cohen, P. R., Morgan, J., and Pollack, M. E. (1990) *Intentions in Communication*. Bradford Books, Cambridge, Mass.

Gabbay, D. M. (1989) Labelled deductive systems. Technical report, Dept. of Computing, Imperial College.

Gazdar, G. (1979) *Pragmatics: Implicature, Presupposition and Logical Form*. Academic Press, New York.

Girard, J. Y. (1987) Linear logic. *Theoretical Computer Science*, 50:1–102.

Groenendijk, J. and Stockhof, M. (1991) Dynamic predicate logic. *Linguistics and Philosophy*, 14:39–100.

Heim, I. (1983) File change semantics and the familiarity theory of definiteness. In Baur, R., editor, *Meaning, Use and the Interpretation of Language*, pages 164–189, Berlin. Walter de Gruyter.

Hintikka, J. (1962) *Knowledge and Belief: an Introduction to the Two Notions*. Cornell University Press, New York.

Hintikka, J. and Kulas, J. (1985) *Anaphora and Definite Descriptions: Two Applications of Game Theoretic Semantics*. D. Reidel, Dordrecht.

Kamp, H. (1984) A theory of truth and semantic representation. In Groenendijk, J., Janssen, J., and Stokhof, M., editors, *Formal Methods in the Study of Language*, pages 277–322, Dordrecht. Foris Publications.

Kamp, H. and Reyle, U. (1993) *From discourse to logic: introduction to model theoretic semantics of natural language*. Kluwer Academic Press, Dordrecht.

Konolige, K. (1986) *A Deduction Model of Belief*. Pitman, London.

Konrad, K., Maier, H., Milward, D., and Pinkal, M. (1996) An education and research tool for computational semantics. In *Proceedings of the 16th International Conference on Computational Linguistics (COLING-96)*, pages 1098–1102, Copenhagen.

Manthey, R. and Bry, F. (1988) Satchmo: a theorem prover in Prolog. In *CADE-88*.

Moore, R. C. (1984) A formal theory of knowledge and action. In Hobbs, J. and Moore, R., editors, *Formal Theories of the Commonsense World*, pages 319–358, New Jersey. Ablex Pub. Corp.

Ramsay, A. M. (1991) Generating relevant models. *Journal of Automated Reasoning*, 7:359–368.

Ramsay, A. M. (1995) A theorem prover for an intensional logic. *Journal of Automated Reasoning*, 14:237–255.

Ramsay, A. M. (1996) Aspect and aktionsart: fighting or cooperating? In *Proceedings of the 16th International Conference on Computational Linguistics (COLING-96)*, pages 889–894, Copenhagen.

Ramsay, A. M. and Schäler, R. (1995) Case and word order in English and German. In *Recent Advances in Natural Language Processing*, Tzigov Chark.

Reyle, U. (1993) Dealing with ambiguities by underspecification: construction, representation and deduction. *Journal of Semantics*, pages 123–179.

Wedekind, J. (1996) On inference-based procedures for lexical disambiguation. In *Proceedings of the 16th International Conference on Computational Linguistics (COLING-96)*, pages 980–985, Copenhagen.

NICOLAS ASHER AND TIM FERNANDO

LABELED REPRESENTATIONS, UNDERSPECIFICATION AND DISAMBIGUATION

1. INTRODUCTION

From a formal semantic perspective, interpreting natural language utterances can be broken down into two tasks:

(I) Constructing logical forms or semantic representations of the utterances

and

(II) Manipulating well-formed semantic representations.

Assuming semantic representations are drawn from a formal language, the problem (I) of *formalization* must be addressed before reasoning (II) with*in* a formal system can commence. In *Discourse Representation Theory* (DRT; Kamp and Reyle, 1993), the point is simply that a *Discourse Representation Structure* (DRS) must be associated with a natural language statement before one can speak of model-theoretic interpretations that lie behind the manipulations in (II), constituting the reason for bothering with (I).

Experience has shown that picking out a formal semantic representation faithful to a natural language statement is extremely difficult, resulting in pressure to blur the distinction between (I) and (II). The interest in *ambiguous* and *underspecified* semantic representations arose, at least in part, out of a desire to reduce the distance between natural language utterances and semantic representations. Of course, this leads to a gap between on the one hand, ambiguous and underspecified representations, and, on the other hand, unambiguous and fully specified representations (required to make sense of ambiguity and underspecification). The present paper is an attempt to combine two extensions of DRT, *Underspecified Discourse Representation Theory* (UDRT; Reyle, 1993) and *Segmented Discourse Representation Theory* (SDRT; Asher, 1993; Lascarides and Asher, 1993), which concentrate on two complementary aspects of this gap: the first, on representing ambiguity; the

H. Bunt and R. Muskens (eds.), Computing Meaning, Volume 1, 73–94.

second, on doing away with it. An example of an ambiguous expression excluded from (Kamp and Reyle, 1993) is $x =?$, described by Asher (1993) (following DRT folklore) as 'an incomplete condition' that 'anaphora resolution will make complete' (p. 73).[1] It is to complete such conditions (by supporting anaphora resolution and various other processes involved in discourse interpretation) that a system of *discourse relations* and *segmented discourse representation structures* (SDRSs) is introduced in SDRT. As shown in (Asher, 1996), this extension can be presented perspicuously through a labeling system, similar to that used in UDRT for scope ambiguities. The present paper extends the use of labels to different levels (viz., word, sentence, discourse), with the intuition that the colon : between the label l and the expression e in $l : e$ serves as a 'fence' for keeping the uncomputable content of e from spoiling the computational demands on disambiguation. Exactly what we mean by this will occupy much of the paper. At the end, we sketch some ideas on how to deal with ambiguity with a mix of 'wait and see' and non-monotonic strategies.

2. From Truth Conditions to Information Packaging

To motivate our approach, we begin by recalling a formal distinction drawn in DRT between *conditions* and *discourse representation structures* (DRSs). Call a pair $s = (M, f)$ consisting of a first-order model M and a function f from some (possibly empty) set of variables to the universe of M a *model-embedding pair*. A condition φ can be thought of as an ordinary 'static' (truth-conditional) formula, interpreted, relative to a fixed set MEP of model-embedding pairs, as the set $[\![\varphi]\!] \subseteq MEP$ of model-embedding pairs at which it is *true* (à la Tarski):

$$[\![\varphi]\!] = \{s \in MEP \mid \varphi \text{ is true at } s\} .$$

By contrast, a DRS is a pair (U, C) consisting of finite sets U and C of discourse referents (or variables) and of conditions respectively, which is 'dynamic' insofar as its meaning is taken to be a binary relation $[\![U, C]\!] \subseteq MEP \times MEP$ on model-embedding pairs, specifying its

---

[1] The string $x =?$ should *not* be confused with the perfectly unambiguous random assignment $x :=?$, employed in (Groenendijk and Stokhof, 1991) to assign an indeterminate value to a variable introduced by an indefinite, or with the corresponding DRS $(\{x\}, \emptyset)$.

input/output behavior:

$$[\![U,C]\!] = \{(s,s') \in \textit{MEP} \times \textit{MEP} \mid \text{on input } s, (U,C) \text{ can output } s'\} \, .$$

As the set C of conditions in a DRS (U,C) can be conjoined[2] into a single condition φ_C so that $[\![U,C]\!] = [\![U,\{\varphi_C\}]\!]$, and as $[\![\emptyset,\{\varphi_C\}]\!] = \{(s,s) \mid s \in [\![\varphi_C]\!]\}$, the difference between conditions and DRSs is that a DRS may have a non-empty set of discourse referents (i.e., U need not be $\emptyset$).

The set U of discourse referents in a DRS (U,C) makes a genuine difference in discourse interpretation inasmuch as it yields clues concerning the structure of the information conveyed by the discourse (represented by (U,C)). In particular, U provides information about the entities talked about in the discourse. These in turn supply possible referents for anaphora resolution. Clearly, however, U need not encode sufficient information either to make a choice, in cases such as (1) where more than one candidate presents itself, or to construct the required referent, in say bridging examples like (2).

(1) Ernest has a brother. He feeds him.

(2) Ernest has a bike. The seat is bent out of shape.

One might turn to the set C of conditions for help — but again without any guarantee of finding it. At least two problems plague a truth-conditional approach to discourse interpretation:

(P1) the prohibitive costs of extracting truth-conditional information

and

(P2) the coarseness of grain of what can be extracted truth-conditionally.

By (P1), we have in mind, for instance, the undecidability of first-order logic, rendering consistency checks (such as that required by the might construct of Groenendijk, Stokhof and Veltman, 1996) hopeless (non-r.e.). As for (P2), the difficulty is that the information typically encoded into C is, if abstracted from all matters but truth, not quite fine enough, even when supplemented with U; an example is anaphora resolution in

---

[2] If necessary (following the strict conventions of DRT, according to which logical connectives are defined on DRSs) by first turning a condition φ into a DRS $(\emptyset, \{\varphi\})$.

(3), for which we take it that the reading where *he* refers to Ernest is to be preferred to that where *he* refers to Ernest's brother (even though the first sentence establishes no semantic difference between Ernest and his brother).

(3) Ernest has a brother. He also has a pigeon.

To overcome obstacles (P1) and (P2), we will magnify, rather than minimize, the distinction between DRSs and conditions, by enriching the set U of discourse referents in a DRS (U, C) with more structure. Insofar as truth occupies a privileged place in semantics, it makes sense to dedicate C solely to truth conditions, consigning to our enrichment of U other matters, which may nonetheless bear on C, through a subsequent process of discourse interpretation. In particular, the aforementioned expressions $x =?$ (which are not among the conditions or DRSs assigned an unambiguous semantics via $[\![\cdot]\!]$) can be collected to pick out a set $U_? \subseteq U$ of discourse referents x requiring anaphora resolution; and the set U can then be expanded into the structure $\langle U, U_? \rangle$. Of course, in practice, it may be convenient to write $x =?$ among the other conditions in C (in the lower portion of the box). But even then, we ought not to forget that quite unlike conditions in C, the expression $x =?$ is merely a signal to some anaphora resolution module for attention, to be discarded as soon as it has spawned a genuine (if not true) condition. But as we have already mentioned, anaphora resolution may require much more than just U and C, suggesting that the structure $\langle U, U_? \rangle$ be enriched further. Without spelling out just now what that is, let us write P for that enrichment, the idea being that P describes information packaging, to complement the information content kept in C.

Having passed from the DRS (U, C) to the pair (P, C), let us next relate the information packaging/content dichotomy to ambiguity. If any consensus has developed at all about formalizing ambiguity, it is the necessity of locating the uncertainty characteristic of ambiguity at a meta-level, removed from the object level where unambiguous expressions lie. Inasmuch as the conditions in C are unambiguous, it is natural to equate that meta-level with P, and to think of $x =?$ as an ambiguous expression subject to a form of disambiguation called anaphora resolution.[3] The meta/object-level division between P and C is complex and involves rules not only for

---

[3] Various tools for anaphora resolution like *centering* (Grosz, Joshi and Weinstein, 1995) or the salience ordering on discourse referents in (Asher and

(a) discriminating between information packaging (P) and information content (C),

but also for

(b) communication between P and C.

The motivation for item (a) comes from the problem (P2) of coarseness of grain in C, and, also, in no small measure, from the costs, (P1), of retrieving information from C, which is, in addition, crucial for item (b). The idea, put in operational terms, is that the process of discourse interpretation should have immediate unrestricted two-way access to P, but not to C, for which it must, in view of (P1), submit itself to a rigorous border control regime. By 'two-way access to P', we mean that the discourse interpretation process should not only be able to feed information into P (thereby updating it, as well as C), but also request information from P. But then if the discourse interpretation process is to be, in some sense, 'effectively computable,' then so too must the logic for P. Hence, another reason for separating out P from C is that it would be wishful thinking to expect the logic for C to be effectively computable. By contrast, insofar as information packaging must necessarily be, in some sense, finite (if only because of the infeasibility of unpacking something infinite, let alone the problem of storing an infinite amount of packaging material), it is more plausible to assume that the logic for P would be more tractable. What makes the entire business rather delicate, however, is that it is not at all clear that discourse interpretation can get by without occasionally requesting information from C. Consider, for instance, the connection argued in (van der Sandt, 1992) between anaphora resolution and presupposition projection. In effect, van der Sandt (1992) supplements quasi-conditions like $x =$? with restrictions of the kind in (Barwise and Cooper, 1993) that must somehow be accommodated within (the representation that defines) C. This poses considerable computational challenges through its unrestricted use of a logic for C (including consistency checks).

As an initial step to addressing this problem (something one of us has done elsewhere), our notational system exposes it. More specifically, our proposal for item (b) amounts to a labeling system, similar to that

---

Wada, 1989) would also exploit the meta-level P. Hardt (1996) formulates centering in dynamic semantics by picking out a distinguished variable (or discourse referent) to serve as the *discourse center*. The discourse center is subject to re-assignment, yielding conditions [sic] that, in contrast to those in C, may well be retracted in the normal course of a discourse. This difference is another reason for locating the notion of a center not in C, but in P.

used in (Reyle, 1993), with the crucial additional idea of employing the
colon : in $l : e$ as a fence separating the label l (belonging to P) from
the expression e (belonging to C) which (in contrast to l) is potentially
arbitrarily complex. As the expressions e in (Reyle, 1993) are treated
only as pieces of syntactic material, our use of : is essentially different.[4]
On the other hand, it does share with (Reyle, 1993) the aim of dealing
with ambiguity in a computationally effective manner — an aim that
requires integrating different levels of structure.

3. BETWEEN DISCOURSE MACRO-STRUCTURE AND MICRO-STRUCTURE

It is one thing to isolate an instance of ambiguity within a word (as
in the case of lexical ambiguity) or say, a sentence (as in the case of
quantifier scope ambiguity); it is quite another matter to resolve that
ambiguity. The former suggests that the problem is a local one; whereas
experience with the latter teaches us that the solution often involves
a more global consideration of the discourse. Consider the discourse
(4) below, from Asher and Lascarides (1995), where the intervening
sentence (4b) makes all the difference in disambiguating *bar*.

(4) a. The judge asked where the defendant was.

   b. The barrister apologised, and said he was at the pub across
      the street.

   c. The court bailiff found him slumped underneath the <u>bar</u>.

To account for (4), we must recognize that a discourse is, as argued
in (Grosz and Sidner, 1986), composed of *segments*, and so we must
determine

---

[4] Another body of work that should be mentioned is that of *Labelled Deductive Systems*, where *"metalevel aspects of inference are brought into the proof system as elements of the labelling algebra..., but retain their separate identity. The slogan is that of 'bringing semantics into the syntax.'"* (p. 247, Gabbay and Kempson, 1996) The present approach differs in that labels are brought in as aids to *constructing* logical forms, rather than as semantic entities (be they possible worlds in modal logic, or proofs in some type system) against which fully constructed logical forms are to be *evaluated*. We hope to be able to say more about the distinction between semantic construction and semantic evaluation elsewhere.

(T1) what those boundaries are

and

(T2) how the segments are joined.

In SDRT, the tasks (T1) and (T2) are intertwined within a hierarchical structure of *segmented DRSs*, defined inductively from DRSs through *discourse relations* modeled after Hobbs (1985), Polanyi (1985) and Thompson and Mann (1987). Under the perspective within which we have been proceeding, taking DRSs as atomic forms of discourse segments is perhaps natural enough — assuming that these atomic forms can, in fact, be decomposed at a lower (e.g., intra-sentential) level. What may require more motivation is the choice of discourse relations that join segments so as to form larger segments. Here we will steer clear of this controversy, and concentrate (in a neutral vein) on more abstract matters.

The proposal that there is some structure to a multi-sentence discourse that must, if the discourse is to be interpreted, be uncovered (along the lines suggested by (T1) and (T2)) is essentially no different from what is by now the widely held view that some form of syntactic analysis of a sentence is a prerequisite to interpreting that sentence. The only difference is the step up in scale from a sentence to a piece of discourse, plus the possibility that the larger discourse structure may not only presuppose structure at the lower (intra-sentential) level, but, in fact, determine what that structure is. Given this two-way interaction between macro- and micro-levels, one might be tempted to do away altogether with the separation into levels. But just as we have (in the previous section) been at pains to maintain a distinction between P and C (even though discourse interpretation may require both), let us insist on differentiating between macro- and micro-levels (noting parenthetically that the division between macro- and micro-levels is orthogonal to that between object- and meta-levels, underlying C and P, respectively). The next three sections flesh out the preceding ideas in more precise terms.

4. LABELED REPRESENTATIONS AND LINKS (WITHOUT HOLES)

To pick out a specific occurrence of an expression e, one might, as in (Reyle, 1993), introduce a label l and, applying it to that occurrence, write $l : e$. In order to carry this out for an occurrence of e within a larger expression, it is useful to consider how expressions are generated. An expression, such as the formula $(\forall x)(x = y \lor f(x) < z)$ from predicate logic, is the product of *constructors*, such as $\forall$, x, $=$, y, $\lor$, f, $<$ and z, each of which is assigned an *arity* indicating the number of arguments it takes. For example, x, y and z each have arity 0 (taking, as they do, no argument), while $\forall$ has arity 2 (one for a variable, and another for a formula), as do $=$, $\lor$ and $<$ (though these require different *sorts* of arguments, which we will, for the sake of simplicity, ignore[5]). Now, to accommodate labels l within an expression e, we can simply increase the arity of each constructor by 1, using that additional argument place for a label (which can remain implicit in case that occurrence is of no interest). In UDRT and in (Bos, 1996), the other ('genuine') arguments of a constructor are often left as 'holes' representing scope ambiguity, the idea being that disambiguation consists, as Bos (1996) puts it, of 'plugging' these holes with labels. We will attend to holes in the next section, but keep things in this section whole in order to describe another application of labeling, for which holes need not enter (at least not immediately).

The application we have in mind is discourse macro-structure, of the kind described in the preceding section. Without spelling out what exactly discourse segments and discourse relations are, suffice it to say that a discourse relation is a constructor that takes n discourse segments as arguments. For instance, in (Asher, 1993), $n = 2$ and

(i) a discourse segment is either a DRS or a *segmented DRS* (SDRS), which, like a DRS, is a pair $(\mathcal{U}, \mathcal{C})$ of sets consisting of a finite set $\mathcal{U}$ of discourse segments, and a finite set $\mathcal{C}$ of SDRS conditions on $\mathcal{U}$, where

(ii) an *SDRS condition on* $\mathcal{U}$ is an expression obtained by applying a discourse relation to discourse segments from $\mathcal{U}$.

We will exploit the parallel between an SDRS and discourse micro-structure given by a DRS (U, C) with a view towards effective disambiguation (unhindered, to the extent possible, by the problems (P1) and (P2) noted in Section 2). The step from (U, C) to $(\mathcal{U}, \mathcal{C})$ will be reformulated as one from (U, C) to (P, C), where P represents information packaging (that can come at either the macro- or micro-level). Towards that end, observe that a discourse relation R holds between discourse

---

[5] A sorted version would take an arity to be a sequence of sorts indicating the sort required at each argument place. (E.g., $\forall$ has arity (*variable,formula*).) This complicates the notation, but can otherwise be incorporated in a straightforward way to what follows.

segments $x_1, \ldots, x_n$ *relative to some context* y, which itself constitutes a discourse segment. More concretely, for instance, the sentence *John pushed him* can be said to 'explain' *Max fell* within the discourse (5), analyzed in (Lascarides and Asher, 1993), but (presumably) not within (6).

(5) Max fell. John pushed him.

(6) Max fell. He got up. John pushed him.

That is, a discourse relation R is more properly conceived as having arity not n, but rather $n+1$, as it would under a labeling system, where $R(x_1, \ldots, x_n)$ is transformed to $y : R(x_1, \ldots, x_n)$. To bring this observation out into the notation, it is natural to define discourse relations not on SDRSs directly, but rather on instances, or labels, of them as in (Asher, 1996).[6] Hence, the elements in the set $\mathcal{U}$ forming an SDRS $(\mathcal{U}, \mathcal{C})$ can be regarded simply (and more generally) as labels. As a concrete example, the SDRS $(\mathcal{U}, \mathcal{C})$ for (5) is given by $\mathcal{U} = \{\pi_0, \pi_1, \pi_2\}$, $\mathcal{C} = \{Explanation(\pi_1, \pi_2, \pi_0)\}$, with labels π_1 and π_2 to be linked (as described below) to DRSs for the clauses *Max fell* and *John pushed him*, respectively. (The label π_0 is introduced to allow more complicated SDRSs to be built from $(\mathcal{U}, \mathcal{C})$.)

To integrate the labeling across both macro- and micro-levels of discourse structure, we will formulate the notion of labeled representation as a relational structure (in the sense of predicate logic). The idea is, given some set of constructors, to associate with a constructor f of arity n an $(n + 1)$-ary relation symbol R_f, so that for a constructor e with arity 0,

$$l : e \quad \text{becomes} \quad R_e(l)$$

and a constructor f of arity 2,

$$l : f(e, e') \quad \text{becomes} \quad R_f(l_e, l_{e'}, l)$$

---

[6] In (Asher, 1993) and other previous work, the contextual nature of the semantics of discourse relations was captured by the fact that each DRS generated as part of an SDRS had a distinct set of discourse referents. Accordingly, it was perfectly consistent to maintain that the relation *Explanation* held between the two DRSs in the SDRS for (5) but not between the two (different) DRSs generated by the same sentences in (6). The label notation is an improvement in that it allows one to ignore details about the DRS construction procedure.

where l_e labels the occurrence of e in $l : f(e, e')$ and $l_{e'}$ does the same for e'. For the record,

Definition. Given a set Σ of constructors f with specified arities $n_f \in \{0, 1, \ldots\}$, a *labeled Σ-representation* is a pair $\langle U, I \rangle$ where

(L1) U is a non-empty set

(L2) I is an (interpretation) function with domain Σ, such that for every $f \in \Sigma$ of arity n, $I(f)$ is an $(n+1)$-ary relation on U (i.e., $I(f) \subseteq U^{n+1}$)

and (take a deep breath)

(L3) the binary relation $Succ$ on U is well-founded, where (by definition) $Succ$ consists of exactly the pairs $(l, l') \in U \times U$ such that for some $f \in \Sigma$ of positive arity $n > 0$, and some $(n-1)$-tuple $l_1, \ldots, l_{n-1}$ from U,
$(l, l_1, \ldots, l_{n-1}, l') \in I(f)$ or $(l_1, l, l_2 \ldots, l_{n-1}, l') \in I(f)$ or $\cdots$ or $(l_1, \ldots, l_{n-1}, l, l') \in I(f)$.

In item (L3), the binary relation $Succ$ is what is sometimes referred to in the literature as a 'successor' or immediate dominance relation, the transitive closure of which is subordination. To see why it should be well-founded, let us define the notion that an element $l \in U$ *labels* a Σ-expression e (built recursively from the constructors in Σ) by induction on e as follows.

If e is an atomic expression — i.e., a constructor in Σ of arity 0 — then l labels e iff $l \in I(e)$. For the inductive step, l labels $f(e_1, \ldots, e_n)$ iff $(l_1, \ldots, l_n, l) \in I(f)$ for some $l_1, \ldots, l_n \in U$ such that l_1 labels e_1 and $\ldots$ and l_n labels e_n.

Returning to (L3), observe that $Succ$ traces the inductive generation of an expression, and must thus be well-founded, provided that

(a) for every $l \in U$, l cannot be re-used as a label within the same occurrence of an expression

and

(b) for some fixed number i, every $l \in U$ can label at most i occurrences of expressions.[7]

---

[7] To the extent that a label merely signifies an occurrence, it is natural to require that a label apply to at most one occurrence (i.e., $i = 1$). Recall, however, that for applications to discourse macro-structure, a label also serves as a 'context,' relative to which a discourse relation joins certain discourse segments.

Part (a) is implied already by (L3), whereas (b) will follow from some finiteness assumptions that will be imposed in Section 6. For now, let us isolate a notion that will prove useful for relating labeled Σ-representations induced by discourse micro- and macro-structure, respectively. Given a labeled Σ-representation $\langle U, I \rangle$, and the binary relation $Succ$ defined on U as in (L3) above, call an element $l \in U$ *atomic* if there is *no* $l' \in U$ for which $Succ(l', l)$. That is, $l \in U$ is atomic precisely if l is minimal relative to subordination.

Next, let us associate labeled Σ-representations with discourse micro- and macro-structure by choosing $\Sigma_\circ$ and Σ° respectively as follows.

Micro-structure$_\circ$. Let $\Sigma_\circ$ be a set of constructors, yielding (as expressions) discourse referents and conditions. More precisely, the constructors in $\Sigma_\circ$ of arity 0 are discourse referents. Constructors in $\Sigma_\circ$ of arity > 0 return conditions, when applied to either conditions or discourse referents. That is, constructors of arity > 0 include not only atomic relation symbols, but also logical connectives, quantifiers, etc.[8]

Macro-structure$^\circ$. Constructors in Σ° of arity 0 are discourse segments; constructors of arity > 0 are discourse relations.

Beyond the fact that discourse segments have arity 0, and discourse relations have certain positive arities, the precise nature of discourse segments and discourse relations can, for the purpose of inducing a notion of labeled Σ°-representation, be left open. The force or 'semantic content' of these (syntactic) constructors can be brought out elsewhere, through, for example, the following link with micro-structure. Given

a labeled $\Sigma_\circ$-representation $\langle U_\circ, I_\circ \rangle$ (for micro-structure), the atomic elements of which form the set $A_\circ$

and

a labeled Σ°-representation $\langle U^\circ, I^\circ \rangle$ (for macro-structure), the atomic elements of which form the set A°,

let $\in_U$ and $\in_C$ be two relations $\in_U \subseteq A_\circ \times A^\circ$ and $\in_C \subseteq (U_\circ - A_\circ) \times A^\circ$, supporting the intuition that for every $u \in A_\circ$ and $k \in A^\circ$,

---

[8] Recall that we have been ignoring sorting of expressions to simplify the notation. There is also the complication that in DRT, the logical connectives and quantifiers operate not on conditions but on DRSs. It is easy enough, however, to get the constructors in the form mentioned above, by defining, for example, the operations on conditions φ according to the effects of the DRT operations on the DRSs $(\emptyset, \{\varphi\})$; similarly, when discourse referents as well as conditions are involved.

$u \in_U k$ iff u labels a discourse referent in the

(universe of the) DRS labeled by k

and for every $c \in U_o - A_o$,

$c \in_U k$ iff c labels a condition in the DRS labeled by k .

That is, $\in_U$ and $\in_C$ associate with every atomic element $k \in A^\circ$ (of macro-structure) the DRS (U_k, C_k), where

$$U_k = \{f \in \Sigma_o : (\exists u \in A_o) \ u \in_U k \text{ and } u \in I_o(f)\}$$
$$C_k = \{\varphi : (\exists c \in U_o) \ c \in_C k \text{ and } c \text{ labels } \varphi \text{ (relative to}$$
$$\langle U_o, I_o \rangle)\}$$

Clearly, a relation $\in_U$ can be hardwired as a relation between constructors in Σ_o of arity 0 (i.e., discourse referents) and constructors in Σ° of arity 0 (i.e., discourse segments) by encoding a set of discourse referents into the notion of a discourse segment (as in the case of a DRS). On the other hand, the relation $\in_C$ cannot be hardwired (in the same way) as a relation between constructors in Σ_o of positive arity, and constructors in Σ° of arity 0, since a constructor in Σ_o of positive arity does not constitute a (completed) condition, requiring, as it were, a labeled Σ_o-representation for completion.

Turning to the non-atomic elements of U°, an $l \in U^\circ - A^\circ$ has discourse macro-structure given by I°, and inherits the micro-structure of its atomic constituents (i.e., the atomic elements related to it by subordination). As described in Section 6, the discourse relations connecting discourse segments may impose certain constraints on the micro-structure of those discourse segments. Focussing for now on macro-structure, let us mention a simple 'connectedness' constraint on $\langle U^\circ, I^\circ \rangle$ amounting to a very primitive notion of *coherence*; namely, that there is a label $Top \in U^\circ$ such that for every $l \in U^\circ - \{Top\}$, (l, Top) is in the transitive closure of the binary relation $Succ$ mentioned in (L3) above — i.e., every $l \in U^\circ - \{Top\}$ is subordinate to Top. Note that by (L3), there is at most one such label Top.

Collecting together notions from this section, let us define a Σ_o, Σ°-*packet* $\hat{P}$ to be a 5-tuple specifying a particular choice of

$$\langle U_o, I_o \rangle, \ \langle U^\circ, I^\circ \rangle, \ \in_U, \ \in_C, \ Top \ .$$

We will often drop the parameters Σ_o, Σ° (when they can be ignored in the background), and speak simply of packets.

5. DISCOURSE INTERPRETATION AND UNDERSPECIFICATION

What, one might ask, have we gained by reformulating (in the previous section) the step from discourse micro-structure (U, C) to macro-structure $(\mathcal{U}, \mathcal{C})$ as one from (U, C) to $(\hat{P}, C)$? The process of discourse interpretation can, as in DRT, be conceived as an *updating of discourse contexts*, which, as every programmer knows, requires some coding or representation if the process is to be realized computationally. Now, the point behind spelling out a notion of a labeled representation is to lay down a solid basis for integrating SDRT and UDRT. But to actually carry out such an integration, we will need to bore holes into our labeled representations.

Let us explain. The notion of a *discourse context* given in (Asher, 1996) specifies a particular packet $\hat{P}$, as well as (i) an element $Current \in U^\circ$ that labels the last discourse segment analyzed, and (ii) a certain function (we will get to in the next section) assigning discourse segments *main eventualities*. But confining our attention at present to packets $\hat{P}$, a crucial question to ponder is

(Q) should the initial discourse context in a discourse interpretation process, in fact, *single out a particular* packet $\hat{P}$, and, even if it did, should the output of a discourse interpretation process also specify exactly one packet?

Notice that we have smuggled into (Q) the presupposition of a definite output. Both the uniqueness and existence of an output might very well be challenged, under an approach to ambiguity based on non-determinism. Be that as it may, the widespread interest in underspecification suggests that the answer *"no"* to both parts of (Q) is worth exploring.

The idea behind underspecified representations is simply to leave things out. We have gone through great lengths to formulate labeled $\Sigma_\circ$-representations as relational structures so that, for instance, the first-order language of these relational structures can be used to describe families of labeled $\Sigma_\circ$-representations. Writing R_f for the $(n + 1)$-ary relation symbol induced by a constructor f in $\Sigma_\circ$ of arity n, and adding a binary relation symbol $\leq$ for the reflexive-transitive closure of the relation $Succ$ mentioned in (L3), the generalization of UDRT in (Bos, 1996) is obtained by considering atomic formulas of the form $R_f(x_1, \ldots, x_n, l)$ and $x \leq y$, where holes are nothing more than variables (at this meta-level of packaging). Other forms of ambiguity (e.g., lexical) can be captured if the constructors can be replaced by variables, as in higher-order logic. SDRT invites similar investigations of labeled Σ°-representations, separate from or in conjunction with labeled Σ_o-representations via fixed or varying choices of links $\in_U$ and $\in_C$. Doubts (such as that expressed in Wilson, 1996) that discourse relations of the sort used in SDRT must be identified in order to interpret a discourse suggest that perhaps R_f ought, at least in some cases, to be left underspecified (i.e., as a hole). An essential consideration that must be brought into the picture is, as Wilson (1996) argues, 'processing effort.' It is precisely that issue which the next section tries to address, in formal terms.

6. FINITELY PACKAGING INFINITE CONTENT

Having been concerned, in Sections 4 and 5, almost exclusively with information packaging, let us now peek at the content inside. But as we will be interested in just how much effort that takes, let us define a labeled Σ-representation $\langle U, I \rangle$ to be a *finitely labeled Σ-representation* if, in addition to (L1), (L2), and (L3), it meets the following requirement (reflecting the finiteness of discourse)

(L4) U is finite, and $I(f) \neq \emptyset$ for at most finitely many f's in Σ.

Henceforth, all labeled Σ-representations (in particular, those in packets $\hat{P}$) will be assumed to be finitely labeled Σ-representations. It follows that a packet is a perfectly finite object that can readily be Gödel-numbered, and fed to a computer.

Writing Φ for the collection of conditions, let us assume also that we are given some notion $\vdash \subseteq Power(\Phi) \times \Phi$ of logical entailment on these conditions (by virtue of which the conditions can be said to have content[9]). Now, fix a packet $\hat{P}$. Recall from Section 4 that every atomic element k of the macro-structure $\langle U^\circ, I^\circ \rangle$ is assigned a set $C_k \subseteq \Phi$ of conditions. The key to the content encoded by a packet $\hat{P}$ is the relation $:\vdash$ between such elements k and conditions φ, defined by

$$k :\vdash \varphi \quad \text{iff} \quad C_k \vdash \varphi.$$

---

[9] 'Content' here can be understood in the model-theoretic terms mentioned in Section 2, assuming $\vdash$ is connected to that by a completeness theorem, as in first-order logic.

The relation $:_\vdash$ can be extended to arbitrary (non-atomic) elements in the macro-structure $\langle U^\circ, I^\circ \rangle$, including Top, for which

$$Top :_\vdash \varphi \quad \text{iff} \quad (\bigcup_{k \in A^\circ} C_k) \vdash \varphi$$

The computational costs of $:_\vdash$ can be traced to $\vdash$, for which the best we can hope for is that it be recursively enumerable (as in the case of first-order logic). It is for this reason that we have described the relation : earlier as a 'fence' for keeping discourse interpretation computationally effective.

As we have also mentioned, however, the pressure to jump the fence can be irresistible when theorizing about discourse without regard for computation. It may be necessary in any case to construct discourse representations of the sort that incorporate discourse macrostructure, a point made by numerous researchers in the area of discourse interpretation. But just how should one access the information in the conditions? To determine a range of temporal relations, Lascarides and Asher (1993) make do with the trivial 'inspection' notion $:_I$ of inference relation, given by

$$k :_I \varphi \quad \text{iff} \quad \varphi \in C_k \ ,$$

together with a function Ev picking out the *main eventuality* $Ev(k)$ associated with the label k. The idea, in general, is to enrich a packet with some finite structure $\mathcal{E}$ around the image of Ev, approximating the worlds picked out by $\{\varphi \in \Phi \mid Top :_\vdash \varphi\}$ (according to the model-theoretic interpretation of conditions mentioned in Section 2 above). An additional feature of SDRT is the use of a non-monotonic logic to determine discourse relations between discourse segments, and (for instance) the temporal relations between the eventualities. The non-monotonicity here reflects a human tendency to disambiguate discourse without necessarily incontrovertible evidence. But the computational cost of nonmonotonically inferring the appropriate SDRS is high even in the best of cases, involving only $:_I$ and quantification over the afore-mentioned finite structure, and hopeless in the more realistic case, where the use of $:_\vdash$ is less restricted. But the use of a non-monotonic logic is not limited to SDRT; many other researchers in AI working on discourse make an appeal to some sort of nonmonotonicity. But, typically (for instance see Hobbs's work on abduction), they set : to full first order logic, which results in an intractable notion of validity. To get computational results with a computationally intractable notion, they then must make intensive use of heuristics—which, we think, leads to a different, and not altogether clear definition of the validity concept associated with :. We take it to be a central concern of theoretical research on underspecification, interpretation and disambiguation to make clear exactly what logic is associated with :.

In addition to making nonmonotonic leaps in discourse interpretation, however, humans also live with ambiguity. Indeed, part of the interest in underspecification is the possibility of filling in holes monotonically as the discourse progresses. To what degreee can the nonmonotonicity in SDRT be reduced through underspecification? Without attempting to settle this question now once and for all, let us try to be more precise about what we mean by a discourse context. An *idealized discourse context* Ω is a tuple consisting of a (finite) packet $\hat{P}$, a label *Current* $\in U^\circ$ (pointing to the last discourse segment analyzed), a function *Ev* with domain U°, and possibly some additional finite structure built around the image of *Ev*.

To turn an idealized discourse context Ω into a *discourse context*, two ingredients are needed:

(a) a finite set $U_?$ of *pieces* of Ω (to be treated as holes)

and

(b) a set Γ of *constraints* on Ω (specifying requirements on how to fill the holes in $U_?$).

By 'pieces' of Ω, we mean not only

(I) labels $l \in U_\circ \cup U^\circ$ in the packet specified by Ω

but also

(II) constructors $f \in \Sigma_\circ \cup \Sigma^\circ$ (buried) in the domain of $I_\circ$ and of I°.

Confining our attention first to micro-structure, scope ambiguities represented in UDRT and in (Bos, 1996) can be captured by

(a) including among $U_?$ labels from $U_\circ$ (as allowed under (I)), and
(b) encoding into Γ the requirement that such holes be filled (in a bijective manner, if we wish) from some set of pieces of Ω disjoint from $U_?$, in accordance with certain subordination constraints (expressed through an auxiliary symbol $\leq$).[10]

---

[10] The reader familiar with the *underspecified representations* $\langle H, L, C \rangle$ of (Bos, 1996) should be able to extract such triples as special instances of the notion of a discourse context above, noting the formal (but otherwise inessential) difference that holes are treated (for the sake of convenience) as labels above.

In addition, cases of lexical and pronominal ambiguity can be represented by

(a) throwing into $U_?$ constructors from Σ_o (as allowed under (II)),

although for these cases,

(b) it is not at all clear that Γ should require that such holes be plugged with material from Ω.

That is to say, a crucial difference between the structural ambiguities represented in UDRT and the lexical and pronominal ambiguities disambiguated in SDRT is that in the latter, specifying the material with which to plug the holes can be highly non-trivial (as illustrated by bridging phenomena). In particular, it is doubtful whether Γ should require that those holes be filled by pieces in Ω.

At the discourse macro-level, pieces in item (I) specify *where* to attach a discourse segment, while pieces in item (II) specify *what* discourse relation to link discourse segments with. In SDRT, Γ would constrain all labels in $U^o - \{Top\}$ to be subordinate to *Top*, and relate the main eventualities of discourse segments linked by particular discourse relations according to the rules set out, for instance, in (Lascarides and Asher, 1993).

By including into $U_?$ discourse macro-items from (I) and (II), we allow for the possibility of underspecifying the structure of discourse, according to considerations centering around 'processing effort'. For instance, suppose we have a discourse segment K (possibly underspecified) and a label l that is to be incorporated into some (initial) discourse context. One option — a 'lazy' and trivially monotonic one — is to simply add the label l to $U_?$ and any other underspecified elements in K to $U_?$. The other elements in K are simply added to the appropriate sets in the packet given by the context.

Another option is to resolve some of the underspecification by using various bits of the SDRS update procedure of (Asher, 1993; 1996; forthcoming). As we have already mentioned, the update procedure is nonmonotonic. It uses various sources of information to fill in or plug the holes in the underspecified representation. One source of information is the lexicon. Another with which we have been particularly

---

By introducing discourse structure into the representations, traces of syntax of the kind left, for example, in the notion of a plugging (present in the revised semantics of URs in Definition 8 of Bos, 1996) can be analyzed semantically, yielding a fully compositional interpretation of ambiguous expressions, relative to some (possibly partial) notions of disambiguation (Fernando, 1997).

concerned here is the information contained in the conditions C of our representations. We have sought, for the sake of computational efficiency, to limit access to C and its associated notion of logical consequence. In fact, however, we might have to generalize this strategy if our update procedure is to have access, say, to the information in interpreters' stores of world knowledge. For instance, it might be sufficient, as SDRT's approach to temporal anaphora suggests, to exploit causal and inheritance relationships between event types. Access to this information is governed by another sort of 'fence' between information packaging and the contents of beliefs. We forego exploration of this here, but we note that such limited access is essential if the process of plugging holes proposed by theories like SDRT is to be computationally feasible at all. For the plugging of holes in these theories exploits a nonmonotonic notion of consequence which in turn requires consistency tests. The consistency tests must be limited to formulae of a language for which validity is decidable, if the process is to be computationally feasible. And this means that we cannot use all information in the conditions of a packet or in the agent's world knowledge since this information requires for its expression at least a first order language. We will assume then in what follows that our process of plugging holes, whatever it is in detail, must remain decidable.

This suggests that we may not wish to plug all the holes in an underspecified representation at once. In fact it may not be computationally feasible to plug all the holes given the information at hand in the underspecified representation and the background context. Which underspecified elements we want to resolve will depend, as relevance theorists have pointed out, on how much computational cost we think is associated with the resolution and the amount of information the interpreter hopes to gain from the computation. Sperber and Wilson (1986) define a bit of information to be relevant just in case the cognitive effects from processing this information are worth the cost of processing it. More precisely, they define a scale of relevant information:

> The greater the cognitive effects achieved by processing some information, the greater the relevance.

> The smaller the effort needed to achieve those effects, the greater the relevance.

We borrow Sperber and Wilson's definition of relevance to define a notion of a relevant computation. Which way of tackling ambiguity an interpreter chooses will be governed by considerations of relevance:

The resolution of underspecified elements is relevant if and only if the interpretive effects of doing so will be worth the cost of the calculation.

Here are some examples that flesh out this relevance based approach to reasoning with underspecified representations. For instance, the presence of a clue word or conditions in the look-up may make it almost effortless to compute the discourse relation through which to attach the new label l. On the other hand, although it may be quite expensive to compute the discourse relation, the resolution of other underspecifications — both lexical and pronominal — may depend on this computation (see Asher and Lascarides, 1995). In this case too, it might seem appropriate for the interpreter to calculate the discourse relation. If, however, the other underspecified elements do not rely on a choice of discourse relation, the interpreter might leave the choice of R unresolved (if the computation of R is itself not trivial). Similarly, computing an attachment site might, in some cases, be very easy (especially if there is only one possible site), but, in other cases, quite expensive. In the latter case, it might behoove the interpreter to take the 'lazy' way out.

A skeptic might ask, why not always be lazy? Why should we take risks? Is the strategy of filling in underspecified elements nonmontonically ever relevant in the sense we have just described? To such a lazy skeptic, we offer the following two responses.

First, we can show that being lazy sometimes demonstrably fails to get the intended message in cases where jumping to conclusions does get the intended message (or at least more of it). A case in point is the SDRT reasoning that underlies the temporal relation between the eventualities in (5). But there are many other examples, not only having to do with temporal anaphora but with other forms of anaphora, lexical ambiguity and presupposition. So if the goal of interpretation is to recover the intended message, then sometimes nonmonotonic reasoning such as that used in SDRT to plug holes in underspecified representations is unavoidable.

Second, there is also a trade-off between the complexity of the SDRT-like reasoning that fills in the holes of the underspecified representation and the computational costs of reasoning with underspecified representations themselves. While the cost of the reasoning that fills in the holes may be high, there are two mitigating factors that might lead us to pursue the strategy of filling in the holes in an underspecified representation.

(a) *Where* a hole can occur in the representation is *linguistically* constrained. A hole isn't just *any* missing bit of information that we might want; linguistic theory, in particular, syntax and lexical compositional semantic principles, determine where the holes in an underspecified representation will occur. Hence, there may be specialized logics for ':', intermediate between the trivial, inspection notion $:_I$ and $\vdash$ that suffice to fill holes, once certain linguistic constraints on those holes are specified.[11]

(b) A decidable method for filling in holes such as that given by $:_I$ together with the nonmonotonic formalism used in SDRT and then reasoning with fully specified, first-order formulas in the usual way is less complex than reasoning with underspecified representations based on quantification over their completions (i.e., disambiguations) inasmuch as checking one disambiguation is easier than worrying about many.

7. CONCLUSION

There is a striking logical contrast in disambiguation between the adventurous non-monotonicity in SDRT and the cautious stillness of U-DRT. This is, no doubt, due in no small measure to the very different directions in which SDRT and UDRT have been pushed — SDRT towards the semantics/pragmatics interface, and UDRT towards computational work. We have tried above to outline a level of representations at which such a connection might be established. Marrying SDRT with UDRT has dramatic consequences for discourse interpretation. By allowing underspecification at all levels, we can reduce the requirements

---

[11] One of the underlying motivations of SDRT is that such decidable methods can be found for various forms of semantic underspecification. In this the SDRT perspective is decidedly different from Hobbs's abductive approach to discourse interpretation. For Hobbs, discourse interpretation is the open ended task of inferring abductively all the 'relevant information' for a full understanding of the text, which typically will bring in all sorts of world knowledge about the entities being mentioned in the discourse. It is not limited to filling in linguistically specified holes in an underspecified representation, which, as we noted above, is the task SDRT's nonmonotonic reasoning component sets itself. Hobbs fuses the task of determining a fully specified representation with the task of reasoning with the (fully specified) representation itself and integrating it with one's beliefs.

on contextual update, disambiguating only when we think the gains are worth the computational effort.

REFERENCES

Asher, N. (1993) *Reference to Abstract Objects in Discourse.* Kluwer, Dordrecht.

Asher, N. (1996) Mathematical treatments of discourse contexts. In P. Dekker and M. Stokhof, editors, *Proc. Tenth Amsterdam Colloquium.* ILLC, University of Amsterdam.

Asher, N. (fortc.) Logical foundations of discourse interpretation. In J. M. Larrazabal, editor, *Logic Colloqium '96.*

Asher, N. and A. Lascarides (1995) Lexical disambiguation in a discourse context. *J. Semantics*, 12, 1995.

Asher, N. and H. Wada (1989) A computational account of syntactic, semantic and discourse principles for anaphora resolution. *J. Semantics*, 6, 1989.

Barwise, J. and R. Cooper (1993) Extended Kamp notation: a graphical notation for situation theory. In P. Aczel, et al., editors, *Situation Theory and Its Applications*, volume 3. CSLI, Stanford.

Bos, J. (1996) Predicate logic unplugged. In P. Dekker and M. Stokhof, editors, *Proc. Tenth Amsterdam Colloquium.* ILLC, University of Amsterdam.

Fernando, T. (1997) Ambiguity under changing contexts. *Linguistics and Philosophy*, 20, 1997.

Gabbay, D. and R. Kempson (1996) Language and Proof Theory. *J. Logic, Language and Information*, 5, 1996.

Groenendijk, J. and M. Stokhof (1991) Dynamic predicate logic. *Linguistics and Philosophy*, 14, 1991.

Groenendijk, J., M. Stokhof, and F. Veltman (1996) This might be it. In J. Seligman and D. Westerståhl, editors, *Logic, Language and Computation*, volume 1. CSLI Lecture Notes Number 58, Stanford.

Grosz, B., A. Joshi, and S. Weinstein (1995) Centering: a framework for modeling the local coherence of discourse. *Computational Linguistics*, 21(2), 1995.

Grosz, B. and C. Sidner (1986) Attention, intentions, and the structure of discourse. *Computational Linguistics*, 12(3), 1986.

Hardt, D. (1996) Centering in dynamic semantics. In *Proceedings COLING-96.*

Hobbs, J.R. (1985) On the coherence and structure of discourse. Technical Report 85-37, Center for the Study of Language and Information, Stanford.

Kamp, H. and U. Reyle (1993) *From Discourse to Logic.* Kluwer, Dordrecht.

Lascarides, A. and N. Asher (1993) Temporal interpretation, discourse relations and commonsense entailment. *Linguistics and Philosophy*, 16(5), 1993.

Polanyi, L. (1985) A theory of discourse structure and discourse coherence. In P.D. Kroeberger et al., editors, *General Session, 21st Regional Meeting of the Chicago Linguistics Society*.

Reyle, U. (1993) Dealing with ambiguities by underspecification: construction, representation and deduction. *J. Semantics*, 10(2), 1993.

Sandt, R.A. van der (1992) Presupposition projection as anaphora resolution. *J. Semantics*, 9(4), 1992.

Sperber, D. and D. Wilson (1986) *Relevance: Communication and Cognition*. Blackwell, Oxford.

Thompson, S. and W. Mann (1987) Rhetorical structure theory: a framework for the analysis of texts. In *IPRA Papers in Pragmatics*, volume 1. 1987.

Wilson, D. Truth, coherence, relevance: recent approaches to pragmatics. Invited talk, ITALLC 96, London, July 1996.

FRANK RICHTER AND MANFRED SAILER

UNDERSPECIFIED SEMANTICS IN HPSG

1. INTRODUCTION

Theories of semantic underspecification assign semantically ambiguous sentences a unique semantic representation. In computational applications of natural language processing, the need for a compact representation arises in order to avoid potentially highly disjunctive specifications of different readings which scope ambiguities may introduce. Typical instances of ambiguities treated by underspecification are scope ambiguities of adjectives in NPs with respect to PPs as illustrated in (1a), and different possible scopings of a quantifier with respect to some other scope-bearing element in sentences like (1b) (cf. Pinkal, 1995; Reyle, 1993).

(1) a. a former professor in Tübingen
   former(in-Tübingen(professor))
   in-Tübingen(former(professor))

   b. every professor didn't answer
   every-professor(not(answer))
   not(every-professor(answer))

While HPSG is frequently used for the implementation of natural language fragments (Frank, 1994; Keller, 1994; Hinrichs et al., 1997; Verlinden, 1999), the main focus of research in the HPSG framework has been on syntactic phenomena; and the semantic concepts traditionally appealed to have been borrowed from situation semantics (Pollard and Sag, 1987; Pollard and Sag, 1994). Since HPSG is widely used as a basis for computational implementations, the question arises if a general framework for semantic underspecification can be integrated with it. Such a framework is presented in (Bos, 1995), which defines a general formalism for semantic representation languages that can be applied to semantic object languages such as predicate logic, dynamic predicate logic, and discourse representation theory. If the envisaged

95

H. Bunt and R. Muskens (eds.), Computing Meaning, Volume 1, 95–112.
© 1999 Kluwer Academic Publishers. Printed in the Netherlands.

integration is possible, a number of semantic theories would become available to HPSG linguists.

In the following sections, we show how Bos's semantic representation language can be defined in HPSG. As a concrete example of an object language, we choose Ty2 (Gallin, 1975), which is one of the standard formal languages in natural language semantics.

2. SYNTAX AND SEMANTICS IN HPSG

According to (Pollard and Sag, 1994) and (King, 1994), a grammar in the HPSG formalism consists of a signature and a theory, which is a set of descriptions. In the signature, the sort hierarchy, attribute names, and appropriateness function are defined. For example, in the grammar presented in (Pollard and Sag, 1994), *verb* is a maximally specific subsort of *head*, VFORM is an attribute, and the appropriateness function on ⟨*verb*,VFORM⟩ yields the sort *vform* as its value. The maximally specific sorts in the sort hierarchy are sometimes called species. The signature fixes an epistemic system for the linguistic universe, and generates a set of descriptions which is closed under negation, conjunction and disjunction. We call the descriptions which comprise a theory the constraints of that theory. Usually, they are stated as implications. Prominent examples are the Head Feature Principle and the Subcategorization Principle. Every object in the linguistic universe must satisfy every description in the theory, and the linguistically intended model contains instances of all objects that are permitted by the theory. In a sense, the intended model is the largest possible model of the grammar. When we talk about objects denoted by the grammar, we implicitly refer to objects in such an exhaustive model.

Given that the HPSG formalism uses a logic of descriptions, a natural place for underspecification is the logical description language. Whereas objects in the model of the grammar must be totally well-typed and sort resolved, i.e., of a maximally specific sort containing all possible sub-objects, descriptions are usually partial. Typical instances of descriptive underspecification are the use of sorts which are not maximally specific and the use of relations. Sorts which are not maximally specific denote the set of objects whose species are subsumed by them in the sort hierarchy; and there may be several n-tuples which satisfy an n-ary relation.

In HPSG, syntax and semantics are treated on the same level of representation, and both are subject to the same set of constraints.

(Nerbonne, 1992) and (Frank and Reyle, 1995) exploit the uniform logical architecture of the grammar for a treatment of scope ambiguities in the description language. The idea is to specify the grammar in such a way that, while there is exactly one syntactic structure for a given sign, there can be multiple semantic structures which each correspond to one reading of the sentence. One should notice that, in this approach, every concrete object in the denotation of the grammar has a semantic structure which unambiguously determines a unique reading for that object.

Our own approach to semantic underspecification differs from those described in two respects. First, we provide a general framework which allows for the integration of several logical languages into underspecified semantic representation languages. (Nerbonne, 1992) and (Frank and Reyle, 1995) are only concerned with one logical language, namely a language for generalized quantifiers and DRT, respectively. Second, we do not locate semantic underspecification in the description language. Rather, a sentence with multiple readings receives a unique syntactic and unique semantic structure. In other words, there is only one object in the grammar that represents this sentence. This, in turn, means that the semantic representation itself is vague, and its interpretation is a set of readings rather than a single reading.

One advantage of this approach is that it is possible to draw on the literature on underspecified semantic representation languages (cf. Pinkal, 1995; Bos, 1995; Reyle, 1993, among others). Second, in a computational application, the number of HPSG structures to be computed for ambiguous sentences is reduced to one. For this idea to work, it is essential that sentences subject to semantic underspecification indeed have a single syntactic structure. In traditional approaches, this is usually not the case. For example, in most theories, (1a) above receives distinct syntactic analyses for the two readings given. In HPSG, the clear differentiation between phonological word order and syntactic structure (phenogrammatical structure and tectogrammatical structure, respectively; cf. Dowty, 1996) in linearization grammars provides the theoretical background for a syntactic analysis that is essentially underspecified (Kathol, 1995). As we will see in example (15) below, in a linearization grammar, the syntactic tree position of adjuncts and complements can be fixed independently of word order. Constraints that take the actual phonological word order into account can then be used to derive a semantic representation appropriate for a given syntactic structure and word order. If word order permits, we obtain an underspecified semantic structure.

In the following sections, we restructure the CONTENT value of HPSG signs. It will be shown that our new *content* objects can be mapped to an underspecified semantic representation language· as defined in (Bos, 1995). We are able, thus, to establish a direct link between grammars in HPSG and a general metalanguage for semantic underspecification.

3. AN UNPLUGGED SEMANTICS FOR HPSG

In this section, we briefly summarize the proposal made in (Bos, 1995) for an underspecified semantic representation. We then show that this proposal can be cast in terms of an HPSG signature. Finally, a mapping from the objects in the model of an HPSG theory to underspecified semantic representations is defined.

(Bos, 1995) defines an underspecified semantic representation in the following way: Given some formal language, $\mathcal{L}$, a set of *labels*, and a set of metavariables called *holes*, $\mathcal{L}$ is extended to a language, $\mathcal{L}U$, that allows for metavariables in its syntax. A *labeled formula* is an element of $\mathcal{L}U$ together with a label. A *constraint* is of the form $k \leq k'$, where k and k' are taken from the union of the set of holes and the set of labels. An *underspecified representation* (UR) is a triple $\langle H, L, C \rangle$ that consists of a set of holes, a set of labeled formulae, and a set of constraints.

(Bos, 1995) is only interested in certain kinds of URs, namely URs that have a top element under $\leq$ with respect to a bijection from H to L. Such a bijection is called a *possible plugging*. The interpretation of a UR is the set of interpretations of the top-labeled formula of L under each possible plugging.

For our purposes, we do not introduce labeled formulae. Instead, we use formulae of $\mathcal{L}U$ directly. To stay close to Bos's terminology, however, we will sometimes refer to formulae of $\mathcal{L}U$ as labels. In (2), we formally define some notions that we will need later.

(2) a. Let *Hole* be the set of metavariables.

   b. Let *Meta* be the set of all formulae of $\mathcal{L}U$ (each element of *Hole* is in *Meta*). For each $H \subseteq Hole$, $Meta_H$ is the subset of $Meta \setminus Hole$ which contains no metavariables that are not in H.

   c. Let *Constr* be the set of constraints such that, for each $k, k' \in Meta$, $k \leq k' \in Constr$. For each $M \subseteq Meta$, $Constr_M$ is the set of constraints that only contains formulae from M.

d. Let $\mathcal{UR}$ be the set of all triples $\langle H, L, C \rangle$ such that $H \subseteq Hole$, $L \subseteq Meta_H$, $C \subseteq Constr_{H \cup L}$.[1]

The semantics of elements of $\mathcal{UR}$ is defined exactly as in (Bos, 1995), and as described above.

Having defined the semantic representation we are aiming for, we can now define an HPSG signature and a mapping, SR, from objects licensed by that signature to the union of the sets defined in (2). For the moment, we ignore those parts of the definitions of SR which depend on peculiar characteristics of $\mathcal{L}$. In the next section, a specific formal language will be substituted for $\mathcal{L}$, and the definition of SR will be completed.

We add a sort, *meta*, with subsorts *hole* and *label*, to the HPSG sort hierarchy. SR maps each finite, acyclic object of sort *meta* to an element of *Meta* in such a way that each *hole* object is mapped to an element of *Hole*, and each *label* object is mapped to a formula of the language, $\mathcal{LU}$.

Secondly, we introduce a sort, *constr(aint)*, in order to capture the subordination constraints of (Bos, 1995). The attributes A1 and A2 are appropriate to *constr* objects and yield objects of sort *meta* as values. The representation function, SR, maps each finite, acyclic object of the sort *constr* to a member of *Constr*, such that, for each such object u, of sort *constr*, with u_1 as its A1 value and u_2 as its A2 value, $SR(u) = SR(u_1) \leq SR(u_2)$.

Finally, we introduce a sort, *underspecified-representation* (*ur*), which corresponds to Bos's URs. Three list-valued attributes, HOLES, LABELS and CONSTRAINTS, are appropriate to *ur*. The values of these attributes correspond to the sets H, L and C, respectively. In addition, we use the auxiliary attributes MAIN and TOP to make global information locally available.[2] *ur* objects replace the traditional *content* objects of HPSG. The appropriateness conditions for the sort *underspecified-representation* are given in (3).

---

[1] In our HPSG formalization, lists are used to represent sets of holes (metavariables) and constraints. Since, in our semantic representations, we are only concerned with finite sets, nothing hinges on this difference.

[2] Compare with the use of the relations **main** and **top** in (Bos et al., 1996).

(3) *u(nderspecified-)r(epresentation)*

	HOLES	*list(hole)*
	LABELS	*list(label)*
	CONSTR(AINTS)	*list(constr)*
	MAIN	*label*
	TOP	*hole*

For the definition of SR on *ur* objects, an auxiliary representation function, LR, from *list* objects to lists is needed:

For each finite, acyclic object u of sort *list*:
  if u is of sort *elist*, then $LR(u) = \langle\ \rangle$,
  if u is of sort *nelist* with u_1 as its FIRST value and u_2 as its REST value, then $LR(u) = \langle SR(u_1)|LR(u_2)\rangle$.

Using LR, we let SR map each finite, acyclic object of sort *ur* to a member of $\mathcal{UR}$ such that, for each object u of sort *ur*, with h as its HOLES value, l as its LABELS value, and c as its CONSTR value,

$$SR(u) = \langle LR(h), LR(l), LR(c)\rangle.$$

For each *ur* object u, $SR(u) \in \mathcal{UR}$. The linguistic theory must ensure that each theoretically relevant *sign* object in the model[3] has a finite, acyclic CONTENT value, u.

4. Ty2 AS AN UNPLUGGED SEMANTIC LANGUAGE

In this section, a concrete semantic object language is substituted for $\mathcal{L}$. As an example of an unplugged language, $\mathcal{LU}$, we adopt a version of the language Ty2 as presented in (Groenendijk and Stokhof , 1982). Ty2 is an extensional typed logic with lambda abstraction. We write *Type* for the set of types which can be constructed from the basic types, e, t, s. We extend Ty2 to include holes, i.e., metavariables. The extended language will be referred to as Ty2U. In (4), the set of well-formed expressions of Ty2U is defined.

(4) For each set *Var* of variable symbols, for each set *Const* of constant symbols, and for each set *Hole* of metavariable symbols, Ty2U is the smallest set such that,

---

[3] In the present framework, saturated phrases which only have a finite number of constituents are theoretically relevant signs.

- for each $x \in Var \cup Const \cup Hole$, and for each $\tau \in Type$, $x_\tau \in \text{Ty2U}$,
- for each $\phi_{\langle \tau, \tau' \rangle}, \psi_\tau \in \text{Ty2U}$, $(\phi_{\langle \tau, \tau' \rangle} \psi_\tau)_{\tau'} \in \text{Ty2U}$,
- for each $v \in Var$, for each $\tau \in Type$, and for each $\phi_{\tau'} \in \text{Ty2U}$, $(\lambda v_\tau . \phi_{\tau'})_{\langle \tau, \tau' \rangle} \in \text{Ty2U}$,
- for each $\phi_t, \psi_t \in \text{Ty2U}$, $(\neg \phi_t)_t, (\phi_t \wedge \psi_t)_t, (\phi_t \vee \psi_t)_t$, $(\phi_t \rightarrow \psi_t)_t \in \text{Ty2U}$,
- for each $v \in Var$, for each $\tau \in Type$, and for each $\phi_t \in \text{Ty2U}$, $(\exists v_\tau . \phi_t)_t, (\forall v_\tau . \phi_t)_t \in \text{Ty2U}$.

We assume that the set of constants, $Const$, is finite, and each constant symbol is assigned a specific semantic type. For this purpose, we use a function, T, from $Const$ to $Type$. We then define Ty2U_T as that subset of Ty2U in which, for each $c \in Const$, each occurrence of an expression of the form c_τ is such that $\tau = T(c)$.

As Ty2U is a typed language, we must include semantic types in the HPSG signature. This is done with the sort hierarchy in Fig. 1.

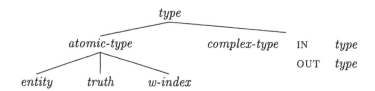

Figure 1. Sort hierarchy for semantic types

We can now refine the sort hierarchy of *meta* given in the last section. The attribute TYPE is defined on *meta*; *hole* is a species; and the species below *label* mimic variables, constants, application, abstraction, logical constants and quantifiers. In Fig. 5, the sort hierarchy below *meta* is expressed by indentation.

The logical types of the subsorts of *meta* are constrained in the usual way by the descriptions in Fig. 3 on page 103. [4]

---

[4] In Fig. 3, we use the syntax of (King, 1994). Attributes are written in small capitals; sorts, in italics. A path consists of the colon (:) and a sequence of attributes. $\pi \sim \sigma$ means that path π is defined, and has a value of sort σ. $\pi \approx$

meta	TYPE	type
	hole	
	label	

var(iable)
const(ant)
    $const_1$

    ...

    $const_n$

appl(ication)	FUNC(TOR)	meta
	ARG(UMENT)	meta
abstr(action)	VAR	variable
	ARG	meta
neg(ation)	ARG	meta
l(ogical)-const(ant)	AGR1	meta
	ARG2	meta

    dis(junction)
    con(junction)
    imp(lication)

| quant(ifiers) | VAR | variable |
| | SCOPE | meta |

    universal
    existential

Figure 2.   The sort hierarchy below *meta*

For each species below *const*, there is a constraint that fixes its semantic type. In (5), such a constraint is given for a non-logical constant
species of type $\langle s, \langle e, t \rangle \rangle$, like *sleep*, which we assume to be the species
$const_{127}$.

(5) $:\sim const_{127}$ $\rightarrow$:TYPE IN$\sim$*w-index*

                  $\wedge$:TYPE OUT IN$\sim$*entity*

                  $\wedge$:TYPE OUT OUT$\sim$*truth*

π' means that paths π and π' are defined, and have identical values. The logical
constants, $\wedge$, $\vee$, $\rightarrow$ and $\neg$, receive a classical set-theoretic interpretation.

$:\sim appl \quad \rightarrow \quad$:FUNC TYPE IN $\approx$:ARG TYPE

$\qquad\qquad\qquad\quad \wedge$:FUNC TYPE OUT $\approx$:TYPE

$:\sim abstr \quad \rightarrow \quad$:TYPE IN $\approx$:VAR TYPE

$\qquad\qquad\qquad\quad \wedge$:TYPE OUT $\approx$:ARG TYPE

$:\sim neg \quad \rightarrow \quad$:ARG TYPE$\sim truth$

$\qquad\qquad\qquad\quad \wedge$:TYPE$\sim truth$

$:\sim l\text{-}const \quad \rightarrow \quad$:ARG1 TYPE$\sim truth$

$\qquad\qquad\qquad\quad \wedge$:ARG2 TYPE$\sim truth$

$\qquad\qquad\qquad\quad \wedge$:TYPE$\sim truth$

$:\sim quant \quad \rightarrow \quad$:SCOPE TYPE$\sim truth$

$\qquad\qquad\qquad\quad \wedge$:TYPE$\sim truth$

Figure 3.   Type restrictions

We can now give the final definitions of the function SR. The definition in (6) treats the mapping of *type* objects into *Type*. This mapping is needed in (7) to state the mapping from the set of *meta* objects into the set of Ty2U expressions.

(6) For each finite, acyclic object u of sort *type*:

if u is of sort *entity*, then $SR(u) = e$,

if u is of sort *truth*, then $SR(u) = t$,

if u is of sort *w-index*, then $SR(u) = s$,

if u is of sort *complex-type*, with u_1 as its IN value and u_2 as its OUT value, then $SR(u) = \langle SR(u_1), SR(u_2) \rangle$.

When we map a *meta* object to a Ty2U expression, we must take care of the variables, metavariables and constants which occur in Ty2U expressions. For this purpose, we parameterize SR with respect to three functions, V, H and C.

V is a bijection from the set of *var* objects to $Var \times Type$, such that, for each object u of sort *var*, with u' as its TYPE value, if $V(u) = v_\tau$, then $SR(u') = \tau$. H is a bijection from the set of *hole* objects to $Hole \times Type$, such that, for each object u of sort *hole*, with u' as its

TYPE value, if $H(u) = h_\tau$, then $SR(u') = \tau$. C is a bijection from the set of species below *const* to $Const \times Type$, such that, for each species $const_i$ below *const*, and for each u of sort $const_i$ with u' as its TYPE value, if $C(const_i) = c_\tau$, then $SR(u') = \tau = T(c)$.

(7) Given the functions T, V, H, C, for each object u of sort *meta* with TYPE value t:

if u is of sort *var*, then $SR(u) = V(u)$,

if u is of sort *hole*, then $SR(u) = H(u)$,

for each c_i that is a species below *const*, if u is of sort $const_i$, then $SR(u) = C(const_i)$,

if u is of sort *appl* with u_1 as its FUNC value and u_2 as its ARG value, then $SR(u) = (SR(u_1)SR(u_2))_{SR(t)}$,

and analogously for the other subsorts of *label*.

With definition (7), the mapping from the semantic representation of an HPSG sign, i.e., from the *ur* object under its CONTENT attribute to Ty2U, is complete. One should note the following interesting correspondences between *ur* objects and elements of $\mathcal{UR}$, and between elements of $\mathcal{UR}$ and descriptions of *ur* objects:

- The equivalence class of *ur* objects whose SR values are identical can be characterized purely in terms of properties inherent to these objects.
- For each UR $\in \mathcal{UR}$, there exists an HPSG description which denotes exactly those *ur* objects which are mapped to UR by SR under some bijections V, H and C.

Figure 4 illustrates how the semantic interpretation proceeds: We augmented an HPSG grammar, Γ, with a signature and descriptions that concern the shape of the CONTENT value of signs. Under HPSG's interpretation function, D (King, 1994), the constraints of Γ pertaining to the semantics of signs denote a set of *ur* objects in the model of Γ. Every *ur* object of the equivalence class [ur-object$_{\text{HPSG}}$] is mapped to the same Ty2U expression. This is guaranteed by the definitions of SR above. Since the semantic representation of HPSG signs is now mapped to Ty2U expressions, we can rely on the definitions of (Bos, 1995) for the correct interpretation of these formulae.

In the next section, we illustrate our treatment of semantic underspecification with two linguistic examples.

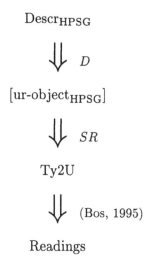

$\text{Descr}_{\text{HPSG}}$

$\Downarrow D$

$[\text{ur-object}_{\text{HPSG}}]$

$\Downarrow SR$

Ty2U

$\Downarrow$ (Bos, 1995)

Readings

Figure 4.   Steps of Semantic Interpretation

5. URs in HPSG Semantics

In this section, we consider the German translations of the examples given in the introduction. In (8), example (1a) is repeated in German. The readings of the NP in (8) are given below the example. Syntactically, we assume a single representation of the NP, where — independent of the reading — the PP is realized higher up in the tree than the rest of the NP.[5]

(8) (jeder) ehemalige Professor in Tübingen
    former(in-Tübingen(professor))
    in-Tübingen(former(professor))

In (9), we give the semantic part of the lexical entries used in (8). Because each Ty2U expression can be translated into an HPSG description, we can use formulae of Ty2U as a shorthand notation inside AVMs. We use the non-logical constant $\mathbf{prec}'_{\langle s, \langle s, t \rangle \rangle}$ which holds between two indices, w_1 and w_2, if w_1 precedes w_2 in time.[6]

---

[5] See (Richter and Sailer, 1996) for a proposal that satisfies this requirement.

[6] By convention, w_i will always stand for a variable of type s; x_i, for a variable of type e; and h_i, for a hole of any type.

(9) *ehemalige:*

$$
\begin{bmatrix}
ur \\
\text{HOLES} & \langle h_0, h_2 \rangle \\
\text{LABELS} & \langle \boxed{3} \lambda w_3 \lambda x_3 . \exists w_4 [\text{prec}'(w_4, w_3) \wedge h_2(w_4)(x_3)] \rangle \\
\text{CONSTR} & \langle \, \rangle \\
\text{MAIN} & \boxed{3} \\
\text{TOP} & h_0
\end{bmatrix}
$$

Professor:

$$
\begin{bmatrix}
ur \\
\text{HOLES} & \langle h_0 \rangle \\
\text{LABELS} & \langle \boxed{1} \lambda w_1 \lambda x_1 . \text{prof}'(w_1)(x_1) \rangle \\
\text{CONSTR} & \langle \boxed{1} \leq h_0 \rangle \\
\text{MAIN} & \boxed{1} \\
\text{TOP} & h_0
\end{bmatrix}
$$

in Tübingen:

$$
\begin{bmatrix}
ur \\
\text{HOLES} & \langle h_0, h_1 \rangle \\
\text{LABELS} & \langle \boxed{2} \lambda w_2 \lambda x_2 . h_1(w_2)(x_2) \wedge \text{in-Tübingen}'(w_2)(x_2) \rangle \\
\text{CONSTR} & \langle \, \rangle \\
\text{MAIN} & \boxed{2} \\
\text{TOP} & h_0
\end{bmatrix}
$$

With these lexical entries in hand, we can define a SEMANTICS PRINCIPLE (SP) that constrains the CONTENT value of a phrase according to the CONTENT values of the daughters and the kind of construction. The parts of the SP needed for the examples in this section are given in (10). For simplicity, we assume strictly binary branching structures.

(10) SEMANTICS PRINCIPLE: In each phrase:

1. the values of the HOLES and the LABELS attributes are the concatenations of their respective values on the daughters,
2. the value of the MAIN attribute is identical to its value on the head daughter.
3. the value of the TOP attribute is identical to its value on both daughters.
4. the value of the CONSTR attribute is a list, l, which contains exactly the following elements:

   a) each member of the CONSTR values of the daughters is in l,
   b) in a *head-adjunct-phrase*, where x is the MAIN value of the non-head daughter, t is the TOP value and m the MAIN value of the head daughter, $x \leq t$ and $m \leq x$ are in l,

c) in a *head-complement-phrase* with a verbal head and quantified NP as complement, where m and t are the MAIN and TOP values of the head, q is the MAIN value of the non-head, and n is the hole that corresponds to the nucleus of the non-head, $q \leq t$ and $m \leq n$ are in l,

d) in a *phrase* with a quantifier as head and a nominal projection as non-head, where r is the hole that corresponds to the restriction of the quantifier, and m is the MAIN value of the nominal projection, $m \leq r$ is in l.

Using the lexical entries in (9) and the SP in (10), we obtain a CONTENT value for the NP in (8) that can be described by (11).

$$
(11) \quad
\begin{bmatrix}
ur \\
\text{HOLES} \quad \langle h_0, h_1, h_2 \rangle \\
\text{LABELS} \quad \langle \boxed{1}, \boxed{2}, \boxed{3} \rangle \\
\text{CONSTR} \quad \langle \boxed{1} \leq h_0, \boxed{1} \leq \boxed{2}, \boxed{1} \leq \boxed{3}, \boxed{2} \leq h_0, \boxed{3} \leq h_0 \rangle \\
\text{MAIN} \quad \boxed{1} \\
\text{TOP} \quad h_0
\end{bmatrix}
$$

The possible readings of the *ur* object described in (11) are expressed by the possible pluggings of its semantic representation. There are exactly two such pluggings:

(12) a. $P_1 = \{SR(h_0) = SR(\boxed{2}), SR(h_1) = SR(\boxed{3}),$
$SR(h_2) = SR(\boxed{1})\}$

in-Tübingen(former(professor))

b. $P_2 = \{SR(h_0) = SR(\boxed{3}), SR(h_1) = SR(\boxed{1}),$
$SR(h_2) = SR(\boxed{2})\}$

former(in-Tübingen(professor))

We can now look at an example which involves interaction between a quantifier and an adjunct that has scope over the finite verb, like the sentence in (1b). In (13) the German translations of the two readings are given.

(13) a. daß nicht jeder Professor antwortet

b. daß jeder Professor nicht antwortet

The semantic parts of the relevant lexical entries are given in (14). In addition, we use the lexical entry for *Professor* from (9).

(14) *nicht:*

$$
\begin{bmatrix}
ur \\
\text{HOLES} & \langle h_0, h_8 \rangle \\
\text{LABELS} & \langle \boxed{8}\lambda w_5.\neg h_8(w_5) \rangle \\
\text{CONSTR} & \langle \; \rangle \\
\text{MAIN} & \boxed{8} \\
\text{TOP} & h_0
\end{bmatrix}
$$

jeder:

$$
\begin{bmatrix}
ur \\
\text{HOLES} & \langle h_0, h_5, h_6, h_7 \rangle \\
\text{LABELS} & \langle \boxed{6}\lambda w_3 \forall x_2.h_5(w_3)(x_2) \rightarrow h_6(w_3), \boxed{7}\lambda w_4.h_7(w_4)(x_2) \rangle \\
\text{CONSTR} & \langle \boxed{7} \leq h_6 \rangle \\
\text{MAIN} & \boxed{6} \\
\text{TOP} & h_0
\end{bmatrix}
$$

antwortet:

$$
\begin{bmatrix}
ur \\
\text{HOLES} & \langle h_0, h_4 \rangle \\
\text{LABELS} & \langle \boxed{4}\exists w_1.h_4(w_1), \boxed{5}\lambda w_2 \lambda x_1.\text{antwort}'(w_2)(x_1) \rangle \\
\text{CONSTR} & \langle h_0 \leq \boxed{4}, \boxed{4} \leq h_0, \boxed{5} \leq \boxed{4} \rangle \\
\text{MAIN} & \boxed{5} \\
\text{TOP} & h_0
\end{bmatrix}
$$

(15)

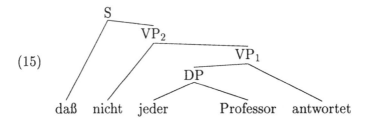

As a consequence of the Semantics Principle, the structure whose syntactic tree is depicted in (15)[7] must have several $\leq$-constraints on its CONSTR list. At the DP node, case (4d) applies: h_5 is the restriction hole of the quantifier; and $\boxed{1}$ is the MAIN value of the noun; thus $\boxed{1} \leq h_5$ is on the CONSTR list.

At the VP_1 node, case (4c) applies: $\boxed{5}$ is the MAIN value of the head; h_0 is its TOP value; $\boxed{6}$ is the MAIN value of the complement; and h_6 is

---

[7] The reader should bear in mind that a linearization grammar is presupposed. The description in (15), therefore, does not determine the phonological linear precedence relation between *nicht* and *jeder Professor*, i.e., (15) describes both sentences in (13).

the nucleus hole of the complement; $5 \leq h_6$ and $6 \leq h_0$ are, therefore, on the CONSTR list.

At the VP_2 node, case (4b) applies: 5 is the MAIN value of the head; h_0 is its TOP value; and 8 is the MAIN value of the adjunct. $5 \leq 8$ and $8 \leq h_0$ are, thus, on the CONSTR list.

The lexical entries contribute the following additional constraints: $7 \leq h_6$ (*jeder*), $1 \leq h_0$ (*Professor*), $h_0 \leq 4$, $4 \leq h_0$, and $5 \leq 4$ (*antwortet*).

Due to the constraints introduced by the lexical entries and by the SP, there are only two possible pluggings for sentence (15). They are given in (16).

(16) a. $P_1 = \{SR(h_0) = SR(4), SR(h_4) = SR(8),$
$\qquad SR(h_5) = SR(1), SR(h_6) = SR(7),$
$\qquad SR(h_7) = SR(5), SR(h_8) = SR(6)\}$

$\exists w. \neg (\forall x [\mathbf{professor'}(w)(x) \rightarrow \mathbf{antwort'}(w)(x)])$

   b. $P_2 = \{SR(h_0) = SR(4), SR(h_4) = SR(6),$
$\qquad SR(h_5) = SR(1), SR(h_6) = SR(8),$
$\qquad SR(h_7) = SR(5), SR(h_8) = SR(7)\}$

$\exists w \forall x. [\mathbf{professor'}(w)(x) \rightarrow \neg(\mathbf{antwort'}(w)(x))]$

It has been observed (Jacobs, 1988; Beck, 1996) that, in German, the relative order of a quantified NP and a negation particle determines their relative scope. The two possible word orders for the syntactic structure in (15), thus, determine the reading. Sentence (13a), therefore, only has the reading implied by plugging P_1; and (13b) has the reading expressed by P_2. To capture the relevant generalization, we add the following clause to part 4 of the SP:

(17) 4. (e) in a sentence with MAIN value m, and PHON value P, for each two dominated scope-bearing constituents C_1 and C_2 with MAIN values c_1 and c_2 and PHON values P_1 and P_2, if there are *meta* objects m_1 and m_2 in c_1 and c_2, such that $m \leq m_1$ and $m \leq m_2$ are in l and P_1 precedes P_2 in P, then $c_2 \leq m_1$ is in l.

Adding (17) to the SP in (10) will give us the desired result for the sentences in (13). In these sentences, the negation, *nicht*, as well as the quantifier, *jeder*, are to be considered as scope-bearing in the sense of (4e) of the SP. The MAIN value of the sentence is 4. In the

CONSTR list of the sentence, there are, *inter alia*, $\boxed{4} \leq \boxed{8}$, where $\boxed{8}$ is the MAIN value of *nicht*; and $\boxed{4} \leq h_6$, where h_6 is a component of $\boxed{6}$, which is the MAIN value of *jeder*. In (13a), *nicht* phonologically precedes *jeder*, thus $\boxed{6} \leq \boxed{8}$ is part of the overall CONSTR list. In (13b), *jeder* phonologically precedes *nicht*. (4e) enforces the constraint $\boxed{8} \leq h_6$ on the CONSTR list. It can be confirmed that only P_1 is compatible with the constraint $\boxed{6} \leq \boxed{8}$, and that only P_2 is compatible with the constraint $\boxed{8} \leq h_6$.

For languages like English, where word order is not as directly linked to scope as in German, (17) would not be a part of the SP. Thus the corresponding English sentence, (1b), is, in fact, ambiguous.

The two examples considered in this section illustrate that the proposed semantics for HPSG can treat ambiguities for nominal modifiers, quantifiers, and scope-bearing adverbials. Word order can, furthermore, be used to constrain the number of possible readings.

6. CONCLUSION

Adopting the formalization of HPSG in (King, 1994), we argued that the appropriate location for semantic representations in HPSG is in the denotation of the grammar rather than at the level of descriptions. We summarized the work of (Bos, 1995), which proposes a general framework for extending different object languages to semantic metalanguages, and showed that his approach can be captured in HPSG. For this purpose, we replaced the traditional CONTENT value of HPSG by *underspecified-representation* objects which can be mapped to expressions of a semantic metalanguage constructed from Ty2. Finally, we showed that ambiguities arising from quantifiers and nominal modifiers can be treated in the proposed underspecified HPSG semantics.

The suggested treatment of semantic underspecification offers an interesting perspective on the unified account of syntax and semantics in HPSG. Since, in principle, HPSG is computationally tractable (cf. Goetz & Meurers, 1995), an integral computational treatment of syntactic and semantic representation should be possible.

Bos (1995) shows that its treatment of underspecification can be applied to dynamic predicate logic and DRT. We expect that these logics can be substituted for Ty2 in our approach to underspecified representations for HPSG. In this respect, the present proposal is more general than other approaches to underspecified semantics in HPSG (e.g. Frank & Reyle, 1995; Nerbonne, 1992), which presuppose a specific semantic object language.

ACKNOWLEDGEMENTS

For detailed comments on an earlier version of this chapter, we wish to thank Adam Przepiórkowski. Tilman Höhle and Paul King helped us shape our ideas about underspecified semantics and how semantic underspecification can be treated in HPSG, although they might not agree with our particular solution. Gerald Penn not only kindly corrected our English but suggested substantial improvements.

REFERENCES

Beck, S. (1996) *Wh-constructions and transparent logical form*. Doctoral dissertation, Universität Tübingen.

Bos, J. (1995) Predicate logic unplugged. In *Proceedings of the 10th Amsterdam Colloquium*.

Bos, J., B. Gambäck, Chr. Lieske, Y. Mori, M. Pinkal, and K. Worm (1996) Compositional semantics in Verbmobil. In *Proceedings of COLING '96*.

Dowty, D. (1996) Toward a minimalist theory of syntactic structure. In H. Bunt and A. van Horck (eds.) *Discontinuous Constituency*. Mouton de Gruyter, Berlin, 11–62.

Frank, A. (1994) Verb Second by lexical rule or by underspecification. Arbeitsberichte des SFB 340 43. Universität Stuttgart.

Frank, A., and U. Reyle (1995) Principle based semantics for HPSG. In *Proceedings of the Seventh Conference of the European Chapter of the Association for Computational Linguistics*, 9 – 16. Association for Computational Linguistics.

Gallin, D (1975) *Intensional and higher order modal logic*. North Holland, Amsterdam.

Götz, T., and D. Meurers (1995) Compiling HPSG type constraints into definite clause programs. In *ACL '95*.

Groenendijk, J., and M. Stokhof (1982) 1982. Semantic analysis of wh-complements. *Linguistics and Philosophy* 5:175 –233.

Hinrichs, E., D. Meurers, F. Richter, M. Sailer, and H. Winhart (1997) Ein HPSG-Fragment des Deutschen, Teil 1: Theorie. Arbeitspapiere des SFB 340, nr. 95. Universität Tübingen.

Jacobs, J. (1988) Probleme der freien Wortstellung im Deutschen. *Sprache und Pragmatik* 5:8–37.

Kathol, A. (1995) *Linearization-based German syntax.* Doctoral dissertation, Ohio State University.

Keller, F. (1994) Extraposition in HPSG. Verbmobil Report 30. Institute for Logic and Linguistics, IBM Scientific Center, Heidelberg.

King, P. J (1994) An expanded logical formalism for Head-Driven Phrase Structure Grammar. Arbeitspapiere des SFB 340 59. Universität Tübingen.

Nerbonne, J. (1992) Constraint-based semantics. In *Proceedings of the 8th Amsterdam Colloquium,* ed. P. Dekker and M. Stokhof, 425–444. Institute for Logic, Language and Information.

Pinkal, M. (1995) Radical underspecification. In *Proceedings of the 10th Amsterdam Colloquium,* 587 – 606.

Pollard, C., and I. Sag (1987) *Information based syntax and semantics. Vol.1: Fundamentals.* CSLI Lecture Notes 13.

Pollard, C., and I. Sag (1994) *Head-Driven Phrase Structure Grammar.* University of Chicago Press.

Reyle, U. (1993) Dealing with ambiguities by underspecification: construction, representation and deduction. *Journal of Semantics* 10(2):123–179.

Richter, F., and M. Sailer (1996) Syntax für eine unterspezifizierte Semantik: PP-Anbindung in einem deutschen HPSG-Fragment. In *Präpositionalsemantik und PP-Anbindung,* ed. S. Mehl, A. Mertens, and M. Schulz. 39–47. Gerhard-Mercator-Universität Duisburg.

Verlinden, M. (1999) A constraint-based grammar for dialogue utterances. Doctoral dissertation, Tilburg University.

WLODEK ZADROZNY

MINIMUM DESCRIPTION LENGTH AND COMPOSITIONALITY

1. INTRODUCTION

In (Zadrozny, 1994) we have shown that the standard definition of compositionality is formally vacuous; that is, any semantics can be easily encoded as a compositional semantics. We have also shown that when compositional semantics is required to be 'systematic', it is possible to introduce a non-vacuous concept of compositionality. However, a technical definition of systematicity was not given in that paper; only examples of systematic and non-systematic semantics were presented. As a result, although our paper clarified the concept of compositionality, it did not solve the problem of the systematic assignment of meanings. In other words, we have shown that the concept of compositionality is vacuous, but we have not replaced it with a better definition; a definition that would both be mathematically correct and would satisfy the common intuitions that there are parts of grammars which seem to have compositional semantics, and others, like idioms, that do not. We present such a non-vacuous definition of compositionality in this chapter.

Compositionality has been defined as the property that the meaning of a whole is a *function* of the meaning of its parts (cf. e.g. Keenan & Faltz, 1995, pp. 24-25). A slightly less general definition, e.g. the one given by Partee et al. (1990), postulates the existence of a homomorphism from syntax to semantics. Although intuitively clear, these definitions are not restrictive enough. The fact that any semantics can be encoded as a compositional semantics has some strange consequences. We can find, for example, an assignment of meanings to phonems, or even the letters of the alphabet (as the cabalists wanted), and assure that the normal, intuitive, meaning of any sentence is a function of the meanings of the phonems or letters from which that sentence is composed (cf. Zadrozny, 1994).

To address these kind of problems we have several options. We can:

H. Bunt and R. Muskens (eds.), Computing Meaning, Volume 1, 113–128.

(a) Avoid admitting that there is a problem (e.g. by claiming that compositionality was never intended to be expressible in mathematical
terms);

(b) Add additional constraints on the shape or behavior of meaning
functions (e.g. that they are 'polynomial', preserve entailment,
etc.);

(c) Re-analyze the concept of compositionality, and the associated
intuitions. That is, that the meaning of a sentence is derived in a
systematic way from the meanings of the parts; that the meanings
of the parts have some intuitive simplicity associated with them;
and that compositionality is a gradeable property, i.e. one way of
building compositional semantics might be better than another.

We will follow course (c). The emphasis will be on simplicity, but the
development of ideas will be formal. (The mathematics will be relatively
simple). The bottom line will be that compositional semantics can
be defined as the simplest semantics that obeys the compositionality
principle.

2. BASIC CONCEPTS AND NOTATIONS

In this section we discuss the issues in representing linguistic information, i.e. the relationship between languages and their models. The first
and the simplest case to discuss is when natural language is treated as
set of words; then the simplest formal model of a natural language
corpus can be the corpus itself. A more complicated model would be a
grammar generating the sentences of the corpus; this model is better
because it is more compact.

A more interesting case arises when some semantics for the corpus
is given. Then, representations become less obvious, and more complicated. Thus to keep the complexity of our presentation under control,
we will discuss only very simple cases of natural language constructions.
This should be enough to show how to define and build compositional
semantics for small language fragments.

Although our methods do not depend on the size and shape of the
corpora, we would like to point out that computing compositional semantics for a large and real corpus of natural language sentences would
require a separate research project, and certainly goes beyond the the
aims of this chapter.

The following issues will now be discussed: (1) representing corpora of sentences using grammars; (2) representing meaning functions; (3) the size and expressive power of representations.

2.1. *Notation and essential concepts*

Sentences, grammars, and meanings
A *corpus* is an unordered set (bag) of sentences; a *sentence* is a sequence of symbols from some alphabet.

A *class* is a set of sequences of symbols from the alphabet. In our notation, $\{a|b|ac\}$ denotes a class consisting of a, b, and ac.

The *length* of an expression is the number of its symbols. To make our computations simpler, we will assume that all symbols of the alphabet are atomic, and hence of length 1; same for variables. Parentheses, commas, and most of the other notational devices $\{, \}, |, ", "$ ... also all have length 1; but we will not count semicolons which we will occasionally use as a typographical device standing for "end of line". In several cases, we will give the length (in parentheses) together with an expression, e.g. $\{a|b|ac\}$ (8).

We define a (finite state) grammar *rule* as a sequence of classes. E.g. the rule $\{a|b\}\{c|d\}$ describes all the combinations ac, ad, bc, bd. We will go beyond finite state grammars when we discuss compositional semantics, and we introduce an extension of this notation then.

The reader should always remember that, *mathematically*, a *function* is defined as a set of pairs [*argument, value*]. Thus, a function does not have to be given by a formula. A formula is not a function, although it might define one: e.g. a description of one entity, like energy, depending on another, e.g. velocity, is typically given as a formula, which defines a function (a set of pairs).

A *meaning function* is a (possibly partial) function that maps sentences (and their parts) into (a representation of) their meanings; typically, some set-theoretic objects like lists of features or functions. A meaning function μ is *compositional* if for all elements in its domain:

$$\mu(s.t) = \mu(s) \oplus \mu(t)$$

We are restricting our interest to two argument functions: . denotes the concatenation of symbols, and $\oplus$ is a function of two arguments. However, the same concept can be defined if expressions are put together by other, not necessarily binary, operations. In literature, $\oplus$ is often taken as a composition of functions; but in this chapter it will mostly be used as an operator for constructing a list, where some new attributes are added to $\mu(s)$ and $\mu(t)$. This has the advantage of being both conceptually simpler (no need for type raising), and closer to the practice of computational linguistics.

Minimum description length

The *minimum description length (MDL) principle* was proposed by Rissanen (1982). It states that the best theory to explain a set of data is the one which minimizes the sum of

 — the length, in bits, of the description of the theory, and
 — the length, in bits, of data when encoded with the help of the theory.

In our case, the data is the language we want to describe, and the the encoding theory is its grammar (which includes the lexicon). The MDL principle justifies the intuition that a more compact grammatical description is better. At issue is what is the best encoding. To address it, we will be simply comparing classes of encodings. The formal side of the argument will be kept to the minimum; and the mathematics will be simple — counting symbols[1]. Counting symbols instead of bits does not change the line of MDL arguments, given an alternative formulation of the MDL principle: (p. 310 of Li & Vitanyi, 1993):

"Given a hypothesis space **H**, we want to select the hypothesis H such that the length of the shortest encoding of D [i.e. the data] together with the hypothesis H is minimal. In different applications, the hypothesis H can be about different things. For example, decision trees, finite automata, Boolean formulas, or polynomials."

The important aspect of the MDL method has to do with the fact that this complexity measure is invariant with respect to the representation language (because of the invariance of the Kolmogorov complexity on which it is based). The existence of such invariant complexity measures is not obvious; for example, Herbert Simon wrote:

"How complex or simple a structure is depends critically upon the way in which we describe it. Most of the complex structures found in the world are enormously redundant, and we can use this redundancy to simplify their description. But to use it, to achieve this simplification, we must find the right representation". (Simon, 1981; p. 228)

---

[1] We assume that the corpus contains no errors (noise), so we do not have to worry about defining prior distributions.

2.2. *Encoding a corpus of sentences*

Assume that we are given a text in an unknown language (containing lower and uppercase letters and numbers):

$$X a0 + Y c1 + X b0 + X c0 + Y a0 + Y b0$$

(We use the pluses to separate utterances, so there is no order implied.) We are interested in building a grammar describing the text. For a short text, the simplest grammar might in fact be the grammar consisting of the list of all valid sentences:

$$\{X a0 | Y c1 | X b0 | X c0 | Y a0 | Y b0\}$$

This grammar has only 25 symbols. However, if a new corpus is presented

$$Z a0 + W c0 + Z b0 + Z c0 + W a0 + W b0$$

The listing grammar would have 49 symbols, and a shorter grammar, with only 39 symbols, could be found:

$$\{X|Y|Z|W\}\{a|b\}\{0\} \quad (17)$$
$$\{Y\}\{c\}\{1\} \quad\quad\quad (9)$$
$$\{X|Z|W\}\{c\}\{0\} \quad\;\; (13)$$

2.3. *How to encode semantics?*

We will now examine a similar example that includes some simple semantics.

Consider a set of nouns n_i, $i \in 1..99$ and a set of verbs v_j, $j \in 1..9$. Let v_0 be *kick* and n_0 be *bucket*; and all other noun-verb combinations are intended to have normal, 'compositional' meanings. If our corpus were to be the 10×100 table consisting of all verb-noun combinations:

$$v_0 n_0 + v_1 n_0 + \;...\; + v_j n_i + ...$$

we could quickly use the previous example to write a simple finite state grammar that describes the corpus: $\{v_0|v_1|...\}\{n_0|n_1...\}$ $(21 + 201)$ But in this subsection we are supposed to introduce some semantics. Thus, let our corpus consist of all those 1,000 sentences together with their meanings, which, to keep things as simple as possible, will be simplified to two attributes. Also, for the reason of simplicity, we assume that only *"kick the bucket"* has an idiomatic meaning, and all other entries are assigned the meaning consisting of the two attribute expression $[[action, v_j], [object, n_i]]$. Hence, our corpus will look as follows:

> *kick bucket action die object nil*
> v_1 *bucket action* v_1 *object bucket*
> ...
> v_j n_i *action* v_j *object* n_i
> ...

Now, notice that this corpus cannot be encoded by means of a short finite state grammar, because of the dependence of the meanings (i.e. the pair $[action, ..., object, ...]$) on the first two elements of each sentence. We will have to extend our grammar formalism to address this dependence (Section 3).

2.4. *On meaning functions*

Even though we cannot encode the corpus by a short, finite state grammar, we can easily provide for it a compositional semantics. To avoid the complications of type raising, we will build a homomorphic mapping from syntax to semantics. To do it, it is enough to build meaning functions in a manner ensuring that the meaning of each $v_j n_i$ is composed from the meaning of v_j and the meaning of n_i. Since our corpus is simple, these meaning functions are simple, too: For the verbs the meaning function is given by the table:

$$[v_0, [verb, v_0]]; \ [v_1, [verb, v_1]] \ ... \ [v_9, [verb, v_9]] \quad (90)$$

For the nouns:

$$[n_0, [noun, n_0]]; \ [n_1, [noun, n_1]] \ ... \ [n_{99}, [noun, n_{99}]] \quad (900)$$

We have represented both meaning functions as tables of symbols. Since this chapter deals with sizes of objects, we compute them for the meaning functions: the size of the first function is $90 = 10 \times 9$, and for the second one it is $900 = 100 \times 9$. Therefore, the meaning function for the whole corpus could be represented as a table with 1,000 entries:

$$[[[verb, v_9], [noun, n_{99}]], [[action, v_9], [object, n_{99}]]]$$
$$...$$
$$[[[verb, v_j], [noun, n_i]], [[action, v_j], [object, n_i]]]$$
$$...$$
$$[[[verb, v_1], [noun, bucket]], [[action, v_1], [object, bucket]]]$$
$$[[[verb, kick], [noun, bucket]], [[action, die], [object, nil]]]$$

and the size of this table is 29×1000. Finally, the total size of the tables that describe the compositional interpretation of the corpus is $29000 + 900 + 90$, i.e. roughly $30,000$. Notice that if we had more verbs and nouns, the tables describing the meaning functions would be even larger.[2]

Also, note that we have not counted the cost of encoding the positions of elements of the table, which would be the *log* of the total number of symbols in the table. This simplifying assumption does not change anything in the strength of our arguments (as larger tables have longer encodings).

3. COMPOSITIONAL SEMANTICS THROUGH THE MINIMUM DESCRIPTION LENGTH PRINCIPLE

In this section we first extend our notation to deal with semantic grammars. Then we apply the minimum description length principle to construct a compact representation of our example corpus. This experience will motivate our new, non-vacuous definition of the notion of *compositional semantics* given in Section 4.

3.1. *Representations*

We have seen that it is impossible to efficiently encode our semantic corpus using a finite state grammar. Therefore, we have to make our representation of grammars more expressive (at the price of a slightly bigger interpreter). Namely, we will allow a simple form of unification.

Example. Assume we do not want $\{a|b\}\{a|b|d\}$ to generate ab. We can do it by changing the notation:

$$X = \{a|b\}$$
$$\{X\}\{X|d\}$$

The intention is simple: first, we define a class variable (X) for the class consisting of elements a and b; then we generate all strings using the rule with variable X: XX and Xd; and finally we substitute for X all its possible values, which produces aa, ad, bb and bd.

---

[2] The reader familiar with (Zadrozny, 1994) should notice that the meaning functions obtained by the solution lemma also consist of tables of element-value pairs. It is easy to see that for the corpus we are encoding the solution lemma produces the same meaning functions.

More generally, let us assume that we have an alphabet $a_1, a_2, ...$, and a set of (class) variables $X_1, X_2, ...$ A *grammar term*, denoted by t_i, is either a sequence of symbols from the alphabet or a class variable. By a *grammar rule* we will understand one of the three expressions

$$X_m = \{X_j\} \ ... \ \{X_n\}$$
$$X_m = \{t_i|...|t_k\}$$
$$X_m = X_l$$

A *grammar* is a collection of grammar rules. The language generated by the grammar is defined as above.

Thus, new classes are obtained from elements of the alphabet by either the *merge* operation, which on two classes X and Y produces a new class C_{XY} consisting of the set theoretic union of the two: $C_{XY} = \{X|Y\}$; or by concatenating elements of two or more classes. We permit renaming of classes, because we want to be able to express constructions like $Noun_{person}$ *know* $Noun_{person}$:

$$N1 = Noun_{person}$$
$$N2 = Noun_{person}$$
$$\{N1\}\{know\}\{N2\}$$

3.2. *An MDL algorithm for encoding semantic corpora*

In (Grunwald, 1996) a greedy algorithm for clustering elements into classes is presented. The algorithm is trying[3] to minimize the description length of grammars according to the MDL principle. This algorithm would not work properly on our semantic corpus, because Grunwald's representation language is not expressive enough. However, the representation of grammars we introduced above allows us to use the same algorithm with only minor changes.

The basic steps of the greedy MDL algorithm are as follows:

1. Assign separate class $\{w\}$ to each different word (symbol) in the corpus. Substitute the class for each word in the corpus. This is the initial grammar G.
2. Compute the total description length (DL) of the corpus. (I.e. the sum of the DL of the corpus given G and the DL of G).
3. Compute for all pairs of classes in G the difference in in DL that would result from a merge of these two classes.

---

[3] There is no guarantee that the algorithm will produce the minimum length description.

4. Compute for all pairs of classes C_i, C_j in G the difference in in DL that would result from a construction of a new class given by the concatenation rules

$$X = \{C_i\}\{C_j\}$$

5. If there is one or more operations that result in a smaller new DL, perform the operation that produces the smallest new DL, and go to Step 2.
6. Else Stop

3.3. *Applying the MDL algorithm to encode a semantic corpus*

We will now show how the algorithm applies to our corpus of 1,000 sentences. By **Step 1**, the initial grammar G_0 looks as follows:

Initial grammar G_0:

$$\{kick\} \{bucket\} \{action\}\{die\}\{object\}\{nil\}$$
$$\{v_1\}\{bucket\}\{action\}\{v_1\}\{object\}\{bucket\}$$

...

$$\{v_j\}\{n_i\}\{action\}\{v_j\}\{object\}\{n_i\}$$

...

Step 2. Computing the total length: The grammar describes the corpus. The size is of the initial grammar is 18,000 symbols (not counting the encoding of the positions of beginnings of each rule). For all the grammars obtained by the steps of the algorithm, the total length will be the size of the grammar plus the size of the machine that generates languages from grammars. But since the size of this machine is constant, we can remove it from our considerations.

Step 3. Merging. Consider the merge operation for two nouns, and the new class $N_{kl} = \{n_k|n_l\}$ (7), $k, l > 0$. The resulting new description of the corpus is shorter since it removes 20 entries with n_k, n_l of total length 360, and adds two entries of total length 25

$$\{v_i\}\{N_{kl}\}\{action\}\{v_i\}\{object\}\{N_{kl}\}$$
$$N_{kl} = \{n_k|n_l\}$$

However, the merge operation for two verbs produces a better grammar. The new class $V_{kl} = \{v_k|v_l\}$ (7), $k, l > 0$. removes 200 entries with v_k, v_l of total length 3600, and adds one entry of length 25

$$\{V_{kl}\}\{n_j\}\{action\}\{V_{kl}\}\{object\}\{n_j\}$$
$$V_{kl} = \{v_k|v_l\}$$

Notice that merging another verb with *kick* would save only 199 rules, so it will not be done in the initial stages of the application of the algorithm.

Step 4. The reader may check that this step would not reduce the size of the grammar. (This is due to the corpus being so simple, and without substructures worth encoding).

Step 5. The successive merges of v_i's ($i > 0$) will produce the following grammar:

Grammar $G_{V(1)}$:

$$V(1) = \{v_1| \ ... \ |v_9\} \tag{21}$$
$$\{V(1)\}\{n_0\}\{action\}\{V(1)\}\{object\}\{n_0\} \tag{18}$$
$$\{V(1)\}\{n_1\}\{action\}\{V(1)\}\{object\}\{n_1\} \tag{18}$$
$$... \tag{18}$$
$$\{V(1)\}\{n_{99}\}\{action\}\{V(1)\}\{object\}\{n_{99}\} \tag{18}$$
$$\{v_0\}\{n_0\}\{action\}\{v_0\}\{object\}\{nil\} \tag{18}$$
$$\{v_0\}\{n_1\}\{action\}\{v_0\}\{object\}\{n_1\} \tag{18}$$
$$... \tag{18}$$
$$\{v_0\}\{n_{99}\}\{action\}\{v_0\}\{object\}\{n_{99}\} \tag{18}$$

What happens next depends on whether our algorithm is very greedy; namely, whether we insist that all instances of the merging classes are replaced by the result of the merge. If that is the case, we cannot do the merge $V(0) = \{V(1)|v_0\}$, and we will do the merge of the nouns. These merges will produce

Grammar $G_{V(1)N(1)}$:

$$V(1) = \{v_1| \ ... \ |v_9\} \tag{21}$$
$$N(1) = \{n_1| \ ... \ |n_{99}\} \tag{201}$$
$$\{V(1)\}\{n_0\}\{action\}\{V(1)\}\{object\}\{n_0\} \tag{18}$$
$$\{V(1)\}\{N(1)\}\{action\}\{V(1)\}\{object\}\{N(1)\} \tag{18}$$
$$\{v_0\}\{n_0\}\{action\}\{v_0\}\{object\}\{nil\} \tag{18}$$
$$\{v_0\}\{N(1)\}\{action\}\{v_0\}\{object\}\{N(1)\} \tag{18}$$

This is our final grammar (**Step 6**) (if the algorithm is very greedy). We can see that it is much smaller than the original grammar — its total length is less than 300 symbols (vs. 18,000); but it assumes an existence of a language generator. Interestingly, the grammar resembles the compositional semantics, as usually given. The rule with $V(1)$ and $N(1)$ describes the compositional part of the corpus; the rule with v_0 and n_0 – the idiomatic; other rules are in between.

3.4.   *Variations on the MDL algorithm*

A similar result is obtained when we do not insist that all instances of merging classes are replaced by the result of the merge. Starting with the grammar

Grammar $G_{V(1)}$:

$$V(1) = \{v_1|\ ...\ |v_9\} \tag{21}$$
$$\{V(1)\}\{n_0\}\{action\}\{V(1)\}\{object\}\{n_0\} \tag{18}$$
$$\{V(1)\}\{n_1\}\{action\}\{V(1)\}\{object\}\{n_1\} \tag{18}$$

$$...$$

$$\{V(1)\}\{n_{99}\}\{action\}\{V(1)\}\{object\}\{n_{99}\} \tag{18}$$
$$\{v_0\}\{n_0\}\{action\}\{v_0\}\{object\}\{nil\} \tag{18}$$
$$\{v_0\}\{n_1\}\{action\}\{v_0\}\{object\}\{n_1\} \tag{18}$$
$$... \tag{18}$$
$$\{v_0\}\{n_{99}\}\{action\}\{v_0\}\{object\}\{n_{99}\} \tag{18}$$

We can see that the merge $V(0) = \{v_0|V(1)\}$ will decrease the size of the grammar by 99 rules and result in:

Grammar $G_{V(0)}$:

$$V(1) = \{v_1|\ ...\ |v_9\} \tag{21}$$
$$V(0) = \{v_0|V(1)\} \tag{7}$$
$$\{V(1)\}\{n_0\}\{action\}\{V(1)\}\{object\}\{n_0\} \tag{18}$$
$$\{V(0)\}\{n_1\}\{action\}\{V(0)\}\{object\}\{n_1\} \tag{18}$$

$$...$$

$$\{V(0)\}\{n_{99}\}\{action\}\{V(0)\}\{object\}\{n_{99}\} \tag{18}$$
$$\{v_0\}\{n_0\}\{action\}\{v_0\}\{object\}\{nil\} \tag{18}$$

The successive merging of nouns will then produce

Grammar $G_{V(0)N(1)}$:

$$V(0) = \{v_0|V(1)\} \tag{7}$$
$$V(1) = \{v_1|\ ...\ |v_9\} \tag{21}$$
$$N(1) = \{n_1|\ ...\ |n_{99}\} \tag{201}$$
$$\{V(0)\}\{N(1)\}\{action\}\{V(0)\}\{object\}\{N(1)\} \tag{18}$$
$$\{V(1)\}\{n_0\}\{action\}\{V(1)\}\{object\}\{n_0\} \tag{18}$$
$$\{v_0\}\{n_0\}\{action\}\{v_0\}\{object\}\{nil\} \tag{18}$$

If, however we do not do the $V(0) = \{v_0|V(1)\}$ merge, and proceed with the merging of the nouns (e.g. if there were reasons to modify the algorithm), we get:

Grammar $G_{V(1)N(0)}$:

$$V(1) = \{v_1| \ ... \ |v_9\} \qquad\qquad (21)$$
$$N(1) = \{n_1| \ ... \ |n_{99}\} \qquad\qquad (201)$$
$$N(0) = \{n_0|N(1)\} \qquad\qquad (7)$$
$$\{V(1)\}\{N(0)\}\{action\}\{V(1)\}\{object\}\{N(0)\} \quad (18)$$
$$\{v_0\}\{N(1)\}\{action\}\{v_0\}\{object\}\{N(1)\} \qquad (18)$$
$$\{v_0\}\{n_0\}\{action\}\{v_0\}\{object\}\{nil\} \qquad (18)$$

Finally, if we allow some overgeneralization, we can replace the above grammars with an even shorter grammar:

Grammar $G_{V(0)N(0)}$:

$$V = \{v_0| \ ... \ |v_9\} \qquad\qquad (23)$$
$$N = \{n_0| \ ... \ |n_{99}\} \qquad\qquad (203)$$
$$\{V\}\{N\}\{action\}\{V\}\{object\}\{N\} \qquad (18)$$
$$\{v_0\}\{n_0\}\{action\}\{v_0\}\{object\}\{nil\} \quad (18)$$

Here, clearly v_0 is the idiomatic element. However, both idiomatic and non-idiomatic reading of *kick bucket* is allowed. (In the previously defined grammars, we can also see the distinction between the idiomatic and non-idiomatic elements).

4. A NON-VACUOUS DEFINITION OF COMPOSITIONALITY

The fact that that the MDL principle can produce an object resembling a compositional semantics is crucial. It allows us to argue for a non-vacuous definition of compositionality.

Assume that we have a corpus S of sentences and their parts, given either as a set or generated by a grammar. Let sentences and their parts be collections of symbols put together by some operations; in the simplest and most important case, by concatenation ".".

Definition. A meaning function μ is a *compositional semantics* for the set S if its domain is contained in S, and **a**. it satisfies the postulate of compositionality: for all s, t in its domain:

$$\mu(s.t) = \mu(s) \oplus \mu(t)$$

b. it is the shortest, in the sense of the Minimum Description Length principle, such an encoding. **c**. it is maximal, i.e. there is no μ' with a larger domain that satisfies both **a** and **b**.

To see better what this definition entails, let us consider our semantic corpus again. The set S consists of the 10 verbs and 100 nouns and all noun-verb combinations. The compositional function μ assigns to each word its category e.g. $[n_{17}, noun]$. The question is how to define the operator $\oplus$. Because of the idiom, it cannot be a total function; hence we have to exclude from the domain of $\oplus$ the pair $[[v_0, verb], [n_0, noun]]$. The shortest description of $\oplus$ can be given by translating the grammar of Section 3.2. First, map non-idiomatic verbs and nouns into pairs $\mu(v_i) = [v_i, verb_{nonid}]$, $\mu(n_j) = [n_j, noun_{nonid}]$, $i, j > 0$. Then, put

$$\oplus([[v, verb_{nonid}], [n, noun_{nonid}]]) = [action.v, object.n]$$

Thus defined μ and $\oplus$ correspond to the grammar obtained by the algorithm of Section 3.2 and to the tables of Section 2. This correspondence is not exact, because functions μ and $\oplus$ encode only the systematic, compositional part of the corpus. (But please note this clear distinction between the idiomatic and the compositional parts of the lexicon and the corpus).

However this description of the two functions is not maximal. We obtain the maximal compositional semantics for S by extending the above defined mapping to all nouns $\mu(n_j) = [n_j, noun]$, $j \geq 0$, and extending the domain of $\oplus$

$$\oplus([[v, verb_{nonid}], [n, noun]]) = [action.v, object.n]$$

It is easily checked that this is the shortest (in the sense of the MDL) and maximal assignment of meaning to the elements of set S.[4] Please compare this mapping with $G_{V(1)N(0)}$, and also note that now we have a formal basis for saying that (for this corpus) it is the verb *kick*, and not the noun *bucket*, that is idiomatic.

What are the advantages of defining compositionality using the Minimum Description Length principle? 1. It brings us back to the original definition of compositionality, but makes it non-vacuous. 2. It encodes the postulate that the meaning functions should be simple. 3. It allows us to distinguish between compositional and non-compositional semantics by means of systematicity, i.e. the minimality of encodings, as e.g. Hirst (1987) wanted. 4. It does not make a reference to non-intrinsic properties of meaning functions (like being a polynomial). 5. It works for different models of language understanding: pipeline (syntax, semantics, pragmatics), construction grammars (cf. Fillmore

---

[4] We are assuming that we have to assign the noun and verb categories to the lexical symbols of the corpus.

et al., 1988), and even semantic grammars. 6. It allows us to compare different meaning functions with respect to how compositional they are — we can measure the size of their domains and the length of the encodings. Finally, this definition might even satisfy those philosophers of language who regard compositionality not as a formal property but as an unattainable ideal worth striving for. This hope is based on the fact that, given an appropriately rich model of language, its minimum description length is, in general, non-computable, and can only be approximated but never exactly computed.

5. DISCUSSION AND CONCLUSIONS

5.1. *Lambdas, approximations, and the minimum description length*

Assuming that we have a λ-expressions interpreter (e.g. a lisp program), we could describe the meaning functions of Section 3 as:

$$\lambda X.[noun, X]$$
$$\lambda Y.[verb, Y]$$
$$\lambda [verb, Y][noun, X].[[action, Y], [object, X]]$$
$$\lambda [verb, kick][noun, bucket].[[action, die], [object, nil]]$$

The approximate total size of this description is $size(\lambda - interpreter)$ + 66 (the above definitions) + 110 (to describe the domains of the first two functions).

Clearly, the last lambda expression corresponds to an idiomatic meaning. But note that this definition assigns also the non-idiomatic meaning to *"kick bucket"*. Thus, although much simpler, it does not exactly correspond to the original meaning function. It does however correspond to grammar $G_{V(0)N(0)}$ of the previous section. Also, representations that ignore exceptions are more often found in the literature. This point may be worth pursuing: Savitch argues that approximate representation in a more expressive language can be more compact (Savitch, 1993). For approximate representations that overgeneralize, the idiomaticity of an expression can be defined as the existence of a more specific definition of its meaning.

5.2. *Bridging linguistic and probabilistic approaches to natural language*

The relationship between linguistics principles and the MDL method is not completely surprising. We used the MDL principle in (Zadrozny, 1995) to argue for a construction-based approach to language understanding (cf. Fillmore et al., 1988). After setting up a formal model based on linguistic and computational evidence, we applied the MDL principle to prove that construction-based representations are at least an order of magnitude more compact that the corresponding lexicalized representations of the same linguistic data. The argument presented there suggests that in building compositional semantics we might be better off when the language is build by means of reach combinatorics (constructions), than by the concatenation of lexical items. However, this hypothesis remains to be proved.

It is known that the most important rules of statistical reasoning, the maximum likelihood method, the maximum entropy method, the Bayes rule and the minimum description length, are all closely related (cf. pp. 275-321 of Li & Vitanyi, 1993). From the material of Sections 3 and 4 we can see that compositionality is closely related to the MDL principle; thus, it is possible to imagine bringing together linguistic and statistical methods for natural language understanding. For example, starting with semantic classes of (Dixon, 1991) continue derivation of semantic model for a large corpus using the method of Section 3 with the computational implementation along the lines of (Brown et al., 1992).

5.3. *Conclusion*

We have redefined the linguistic concept of compositionality as the simplest maximal description of data that satisfies the postulate that the meaning of the whole is a function of the meaning of its parts. By justifying compositionality by the minimum description length principle, we have placed the intuitive idea that the meaning of a sentence is a combination of the meanings of its constituents on a firm mathematical foundation.

This new, non-vacuous definition of compositionality is intuitive and allows us to distinguish between compositional and non-compositional semantics, and between idiomatic and non-idiomatic expressions. It is not ad hoc, since it does not make any references to non-intrinsic properties of meaning functions (like being a polynomial). It works for different models of language understanding. Moreover, it allows us to compare different meaning functions with respect to how compositional they are.

Finally, because of the close relationship between the minimum description length principle and probability, the approach proposed in this chapter should bridge logic-based and statistics-based approaches to language understanding.

REFERENCES

Brown, P.F., V.J. Della Pietra, P.V. deSouza, J.C. Lai and R.L. Mercer (1992) Class-based n-gram Models of Natural Language. *Computational Linguistics* 18(4):467-480.

Dixon, R.M.W. (1991) *A New Approach to English Grammar on Semantic Principles*. Clarendon Press, Oxford

Fillmore, C.J., P. Kay, and M.C. O'Connor (1988) Regularity and idiomaticity in grammatical constructions. *Language*, 64(3):501-538.

Grunwald, P. (1996) A Minimum Description Length Approach to Grammar Inference. In S. Wermter et al., editors, *Symbolic, Connectionist and Statistical Approach to Learning for Natural Language Processing*, pages 203-216, Springer, Berlin.

Hirst, G. (1987) *Semantic interpretation and the resolution of ambiguity*. Cambridge University Press, Cambridge, Great Britain.

Keenan, E.L. and L.M. Faltz (1985) *Boolean Semantics for Natural Language*. D Reidel, Dordrecht, Holland.

Li, M., and P. Vitanyi (1993) *An Introduction to Kolmogorv Complexity and Its Applications*. Springer, New York.

Partee, B.H., A. ter Meulen, and R.E. Wall (1990) *Mathematical Methods in Lingusitics*. Kluwer, Dordrecht, The Netherlands.

Savitch, W.J. (1993) Why it might pay to assume that languages are infinite. *Annals of Mathematics and Artificial Intelligence*, 8(1,2):17-26.

Rissanen, J. (1982) A universal prior for integers and estimation by minimum description length. *Annals of Statistics*, 11:416-431.

Simon, H.A. (1981) *The Sciences of the Artificial*. MIT Press, Cambridge, MA.

Zadrozny, W. (1994) From compositional to systematic semantics. *Linguistics and Philosophy* 17(4):329-342.

Zadrozny, W. (1995) The Compactnes of Construction Grammars. IBM Research, T.J. Watson Research Center; Report RC 20003 (88493).

JOSEF VAN GENABITH AND RICHARD CROUCH

HOW TO GLUE A DONKEY TO AN F-STRUCTURE: PORTING A 'DYNAMIC' MEANING REPRESENTATION LANGUAGE INTO LFG'S LINEAR LOGIC GLUE-LANGUAGE SEMANTICS

1. INTRODUCTION

In the present chapter we port a 'dynamic'[1] meaning representation language (Muskens, 1994b; Muskens, 1994a; Muskens, 1996) into the meaning representation slots in the linear logic based glue language semantics developed by (Dalrymple et al., 1993b; Dalrymple et al., 1993a; Dalrymple et al., 1995b; Dalrymple et al., 1997; Dalrymple et al., 1996). In the original proposals the meaning representation language slots are occupied by expressions in a standard, static higher order logic with generalized quantifiers. The revised approach extends the original approach to discourse phenomena and can be combined with the approach to underspecification developed in (Crouch & Genabith, 1996). On the other hand it makes available linear logic based approaches to quantifier scope and underspecification to dynamic semantics. The chapter is structured as follows: first, we give brief introductions to the original LFG glue language semantics and the new 'dynamic' meaning representation language CDRT; we then port the latter into the former; finally we compare the results with some approaches discussed in the literature and sketch QLF (Alshawi & Crouch, 1992) and UDRS (Reyle, 1995) style interpretations for sets of linear logic premises obtained.

2. A LINEAR LOGIC BASED GLUE LANGUAGE SEMANTICS FOR LFG

Lexical-Functional Grammar (LFG) (Kaplan & Bresnan, 1982; Dalrymple et al., 1995a) is a member of the family of early unification based grammar formalisms. It has a number of attractive features

---

[1] The quotes around 'dynamic' are explained on p. 135.

H. Bunt and R. Muskens (eds.), Computing Meaning, Volume 1, 129–148.
© 1999 Kluwer Academic Publishers. Printed in the Netherlands.

which have ensured continued popularity among computational and theoretical linguists alike.

In a series of papers (Dalrymple et al., 1993b; Dalrymple et al., 1993a; Dalrymple et al., 1995b; Dalrymple et al., 1997; Dalrymple et al., 1996) show how a fragment of linear logic can be used in an LFG-setting as a 'glue language' to deductively piece together the meanings of individual words and constituents in a sentence. The premises for the deduction are meaning constructors obtained from the lexical entries of the words in the sentence. These show how meanings assigned to various constituents (or rather, nodes in semantic projections from f-structure) can be combined to build meaning assignments for other constituents.

For example, a sentence such as "John likes Mary" would have the following three lexical premises

John $= subj \rightsquigarrow j$

Mary $= obj \rightsquigarrow m$

likes $= \forall X, Y.\ (subj \rightsquigarrow X \otimes obj \rightsquigarrow Y) \multimap s \rightsquigarrow like(X, Y)$

Here, $\rightsquigarrow$ is an uninterpreted binary relation assigning expressions in an object level meaning language to constituents. Thus $subj \rightsquigarrow j$ assigns a constant j as the meaning of the (mnemonically named) constituent $subj$, which is the subject noun phrase of the sentence. The symbols $\multimap$ and $\otimes$ are the linear logic connectives for implication and (multiplicative) conjunction. The lexical premise for the word "likes" states that if you can show that $subj$ is assigned some meaning X, and obj some meaning Y, then the meaning of the sentence (constituent s) is $like(X, Y)$.[2] The conclusion of the glue language deduction needs to be a single meaning assignment to the sentence constituent, derived from all the lexical premises. By instantiating $j \leftarrow X$ and $m \leftarrow Y$, one can readily derive

$$\text{John, likes, Mary} \vdash s \rightsquigarrow like(j, m)$$

The resource sensitivity of linear logic, plus the demand that we derive a single meaning assignment to the sentence, ensures that each lexical premise is used once and exactly once in the derivation. This is because,

---

[2] Universal quantifiers in linear logic behave more like *any* than *every*. Thus $\forall X, Y.\ (subj \rightsquigarrow X \otimes obj \rightsquigarrow Y) \multimap s \rightsquigarrow like(X, Y)$ means that you can pick any meaning you like for the subject and the object, but you can only pick one.

unlike classical or intuitionistic logic, linear logic does not support inferences of the form: "$A \otimes (A \multimap B)$, therefore $A \otimes B$". Both A and the $A \multimap B$ are consumed in performing modus ponens to conclude B, leaving no A (or $A \multimap B$) to be reconjoined with the inferred B. This consumption of premises ensures that they cannot be used more than once.[3]

Similarly, inferences of the form "$A \otimes C \otimes (A \multimap B)$ therefore B" are also invalid. Because the conjunct C has not been consumed, it *must* be conjoined with the B obtained through modus ponens. Therefore, if we are to derive a single meaning assignment to the sentence, each lexical premise must be used at least once.

For sentences containing quantified noun phrases (Dalrymple et al., 1997; Dalrymple et al., 1996), the same set of lexical premises can be used to produce distinct derivations, assigning different sentential meanings corresponding to different quantifier scopings. In a sense the set of lexical premises can be seen as giving a (fully) underspecified representation of scope. Skipping the intermediate steps, a derivation combining the lexical premises for a determiner *every* and a noun *player* results in a conclusion:

$$\forall Scope, S. \ (\forall x. \ np \rightsquigarrow x \multimap Scope \rightsquigarrow S(x))$$
$$\multimap Scope \rightsquigarrow every(player, S)$$

In this meaning constructor np is the node in the semantic projection corresponding to the noun phrase; $Scope$ is a variable ranging over nodes in the semantic projection that might form the scope of the noun phrase; S is a variable ranging over meaning language expressions. Paraphrasing this constructor, it says: take any constituent $Scope$ that you might choose as the scope of the noun phrase. Then, if by assuming that the noun phrase np has a meaning x you can produce a meaning $S(x)$ for $Scope$, then (effectively discharging this assumption) you can produce a meaning $every(player, S)$ for $Scope$.

To illustrate how a glue language can assign alternate meanings to a quantified sentence (accounting for scope ambiguities) we will consider the example

Every coach picked a player

---

[3] By introducing the linear logic modality !, which allows free repetition of premises, (Dalrymple et al., 1995b) allow controlled reuse of premises in the analysis of VP conjunction.

The semantic projection of this sentence contains a number of nodes (for ease of exposition, we have given the nodes mnemonic names, but no significance attaches to the node names):

- *s*: the projection of the verb *pick*, the verb phrase and the sentence as a whole
- *subj*: the projection of the subject noun phrase *every coach*
- *subj.var*: the projection of the subject determiner, *every*
- *subj.restr*: the projection of the subject noun, *coach*
- *obj*: the projection of the object noun phrase *a player*
- *obj.var*: the projection of the object determiner, *a*
- *obj.restr*: the projection of the object noun, *player*

The lexical meaning constructors (i.e. lexical premises) derived from the semantic projection are (note that in building the projection, variables over nodes in the general lexical entries will have been instantiated to refer to specific nodes in the projection)

$$
\begin{aligned}
&\text{every}: \quad \forall Scope, R, S.\ (\forall x.\ subj.var \rightsquigarrow \\
&\qquad\qquad\qquad x \multimap subj.restr \rightsquigarrow R(x)) \otimes \\
&\qquad\qquad\qquad (\forall x.\ subj \rightsquigarrow x \multimap Scope \rightsquigarrow S(x)) \\
&\qquad\qquad \multimap Scope \rightsquigarrow every(R, S) \\
&\text{a}: \quad\quad\ \forall Scope, R, S.\ (\forall y.\ obj.var \rightsquigarrow \\
&\qquad\qquad\qquad y \multimap obj.restr \rightsquigarrow R(y)) \otimes \\
&\qquad\qquad\qquad (\forall y.\ obj \rightsquigarrow y \multimap Scope \rightsquigarrow S(y)) \\
&\qquad\qquad \multimap Scope \rightsquigarrow a(R, S) \\
&\text{picked}: \quad \forall X, Y.\ (subj \rightsquigarrow X \otimes obj \rightsquigarrow Y) \multimap s \rightsquigarrow pick(X, Y) \\
&\text{coach}: \quad \forall X.\ (subj.var \rightsquigarrow X \multimap subj.restr \rightsquigarrow coach(X)) \\
&\text{player}: \quad \forall Y.\ (obj.var \rightsquigarrow Y \multimap obj.restr \rightsquigarrow player(Y))
\end{aligned}
$$

In these meaning constructors, the variable *Scope* ranges over nodes in the semantic projection, upper case X, Y, R, S are higher-order variables ranging over meanings, and the lower case x is a first order variable.

We can derive the following meaning constructor for the subject NP:

every, coach $\vdash$
$\forall Scope, S.\ (\forall x.\ subj \rightsquigarrow x \multimap Scope \rightsquigarrow S(x))$
$\qquad \multimap Scope \rightsquigarrow every(coach, S)$

with modus ponens (MP) and the substitutions $\langle X \leftarrow x,\ R \leftarrow coach \rangle$.

For the object NP, we derive

a, player ⊢
$\forall Scope, S.\ (\forall y.\ obj \rightsquigarrow y \multimap Scope \rightsquigarrow S(y))$
        $\multimap Scope \rightsquigarrow a(player, S)$

with MP and the substitutions $\langle Y \leftarrow y,\ R \leftarrow player \rangle$
    Using the Currying equivalences

$$(A \otimes B) \multimap C \dashv\vdash A \multimap (B \multimap C) \dashv\vdash B \multimap (A \multimap C)$$

we can rewrite the lexical premise associated with pick as

$$\text{pick}_1 :\ \forall X.\ (subj \rightsquigarrow X \multimap \forall Y.\ (obj \rightsquigarrow Y \multimap s \rightsquigarrow pick(X,Y)))$$
$$\text{pick}_2 :\ \forall Y.\ (obj \rightsquigarrow Y \multimap \forall X.\ (subj \rightsquigarrow X \multimap s \rightsquigarrow pick(X,Y)))$$

Using a consequence of the transitivity of linear implication (TI)

$$\frac{A \multimap (B \multimap C) \quad (B \multimap C) \multimap D}{A \multimap D}$$

we can combine the object NP with pick_1 to give

pick_1, a, player ⊢
$\forall X.\ (subj \rightsquigarrow X \multimap s \rightsquigarrow a(player, \lambda v.pick(X,v))$

with the substitutions $\langle Y \leftarrow y, Scope \leftarrow s,\ S \leftarrow \lambda v.pick(X,v) \rangle$.
    The result is then combined with the subject NP under MP to yield
the narrow scope reading of the indefinite object NP:

every, coach, pick_1, a, player ⊢
$s \rightsquigarrow every(coach, \lambda u.a(player, \lambda v.pick(u,v)))$

with the substitutions $\langle S \leftarrow \lambda u.a(player, \lambda v.pick(u,v)),\ X \leftarrow x,\ Scope \leftarrow s \rangle$.
    An alternative derivation sequence first combines the subject NP
with pick_2 and then the result with the object NP and results in the
specific reading of the indefinite NP:

every, coach ,pick_2 ,a, player ⊢
$s \rightsquigarrow a(player, \lambda v.every(coach, \lambda u.pick(u,v)))$

The linear logic based deductive approach to quantifier scope is
attractive for a number of reasons. Here we mention but one: unlike

many alternative approaches such as Cooper-storage, the linear logic glue language approach to quantification can be shown (Dalrymple et al., 1997; Dalrymple et al., 1996) to respect general well-formedness constraints on possible scopings such as the 'free-variable' constraint (e.g. resulting from the interaction of quantification and bound variable anaphora) without further stipulation, and solely on the basis of propositional structure of the linear logic premises. To give an example, this rules out a wide scope reading of the complex indefinite object NP in *"Every player dismissed a rumour about himself"* because of an undischarged dependence on the subject NP.

In order to identify the substitutions required in the linear logic derivations a version of higher order unification is needed. In general higher order unification is undecidable, but, as (Dalrymple et al., 1997) point out the instances of higher order unification required are all of the form $P(x) = t$ or $f(X) = t$ where t is a closed term.[4] These instances fall within the $l\lambda$ fragment of (Miller, 1990) which is covered by a decidable extension of first-order unification.

3. Compositional DRT: CDRT

The 'dynamic' meaning representation language we want to employ in the revised glue language premises is Reinhard Muskens' compositional version CDRT (Muskens, 1994b; Muskens, 1994a; Muskens, 1996) of Discourse Representation Theory (DRT) (Kamp, 1981; Kamp & Reyle, 1993).[5]

The motivation underlying CDRT is twofold: first, it provides a compositional reformulation of standard DRT and second, it is based on a sorted version of standard 'static' type theory. The idea is to graft and manipulate DRSs as expressions in a host language whose mathematics is well understood rather then to develop a special purpose dynamic 'designer' logic. In order to do this we need to be able to

---

[4] P and X are essentially existential variables, i.e. variables which are instantiated to some other term derived elsewhere in a proof; f and x are essentially universal variables, i.e. variables that stand for arbitrary terms.

[5] Other choices would be λ-DRT (Kohlhase et al., 1996; Bos et al., 1994; Asher, 1993), Dynamic Montague Grammar (Groenendijk & Stokhof, 1990), Dynamic Type Theory (Chierchia, 1991) or the compositional version of DRT due to (van Eijck & Kamp, 1997). As far as we can see similar stories could be told for each of those.

talk about updates (the objects of prime concern in dynamic semantics) in the host language. Consider the following explicitly relational[6]
formulation of the standard DRT semantics. Given a DRS $\langle U, C \rangle =$
$\langle \{x_1 \ldots x_n\}, \{\gamma_1, \ldots, \gamma_m\}\rangle$:

$$
\begin{array}{lll}
\text{(i)} & [\![\langle U, C \rangle]\!] & := & \{\langle i, o \rangle | i[U]o \text{ and } o \in \bigcap_{i=1}^{m} [\![\gamma_i]\!] \in C\} \\
\text{(ii)} & [\![x_l = x_k]\!] & := & \{i | [\![x_l]\!]^i = [\![x_k]\!]^i\} \\
\text{(iii)} & [\![P(x_1 .. x_n)]\!] & := & \{i | \langle [\![x_1]\!]^i, \ldots, [\![x_n]\!]^i \rangle \in \Im(P)\} \\
\text{(vi)} & [\![\neg K]\!] & := & \{i | \neg \exists o \langle i, o \rangle \in [\![K]\!]\} \\
\text{(v)} & [\![K_1 \vee K_2]\!] & := & \{i | \exists o (\langle i, o \rangle \in [\![K_1]\!] \text{ or } \langle i, o \rangle \in [\![K_2]\!])\} \\
\text{(vi)} & [\![K_1 \Rightarrow K_2]\!] & := & \{i | \forall o (\langle i, o \rangle \in [\![K_1]\!] \rightarrow \exists k \langle o, k \rangle \in [\![K_2]\!])\}
\end{array}
$$

DRS are interpreted as transitions (i.e. relations) between input i
and output o assignments (put differently, a DRS updates an input
assignment into an output assignment); DRS conditions are interpreted
as tests (i.e. sets of assignments). The relational semantics is one of the
key ingredients of Dynamic Predicate Logic (DPL) (Groenendijk &
Stokhof, 1991). To use the DPL terminology: conditions are externally
static (i.e. they do not pass on updated assignments); some conditions
are internally dynamic (e.g. $\Rightarrow$ passes on the output assignments of its
antecedent DRS as input assignments to its consequent DRS). In order
to obtain a compositional syntax/semantics interface on the sentential
and subsentential level we could introduce a sequencing operation ';'
(dynamic conjunction in DPL) and lambdas. The sequencing operation
is interpreted as relational composition:

$$[\![K_1; K_2]\!] := \{\langle i, o \rangle | \exists m (\langle i, m \rangle \in [\![K_1]\!] \wedge \langle m, o \rangle \in [\![K_2]\!])\}$$

The lambdas we get via encoding the relational formulation of DRSs
in a sorted version of type thory. In order to do this we need to be able
to talk about assignments (also referred to as states). In type theory,
DRSs would be unpacked as functions of type $s(st)$, i.e. functions from
states into functions from states to truth values (thus shifting from the
relational to the functional perspective). The states provide the encoding of assignments. In the same fashion DRS conditions are encoded
as functions of type st (i.e. functions from states to truth values). To
be sure, the host logic (type theory) is static but the terms encoding
the DRS language capture the desired dynamic effects. This is why we
quote the *dynamic* as in 'dynamic' meaning representation language.

---

[6] This is not much more than a notational variation of the semantics in
(Kamp & Reyle, 1996).

This can be made precise as follows: Muskens' CDRT is based on three-sorted type logic TY_3. In addition to the basic types e for individuals and t for truth values we have a type π for 'pigeon-holes' or registers and a type s for states. A register is a location that can hold exactly one object. Registers are the denotations of discourse referents represented by constants u of type π. States are lists of registers with their associated values. At a particular state i the value associated with a discourse referent u is the object in the register denoted by u. Fix a model. V is a fixed non-logical constant of type $\pi(se)$ and $V(u)(i)$ denotes the value associated with discourse referent u in state i. The expression

$$i[u_1 \ldots u_n]j$$

is short for the term

$$\forall v(((u_1 \neq v) \wedge \ldots \wedge (u_n \neq v)) \rightarrow V(v)(i) = V(v)(j))$$

which states that states i and j differ at most with respect to the values associated with the registers denoted by the discourse referents $u_1 \ldots u_n$. The following three axioms ensure that we have enough states at our disposal to guarantee that each register can hold each individual object (AX_1); that states are the same if they agree on the values of the registers (AX_2) and that different discourse referents refer to different registers (AX_3):

AX_1 $\forall i \forall u \forall x \exists j(i[u]j \wedge V(u)(j) = x)$
AX_2 $\forall i \forall j(i[\ ]j \rightarrow i = j)$
AX_3 $u \neq u'$ for different discourse referents u and u'

DRSs $\langle U, C \rangle = \langle \{x_1 \ldots x_n\}, \{\gamma_1, \ldots, \gamma_m\} \rangle$ and DRS conditions can now be coded in TY_3 as follows:

(i)	$(\langle U, C \rangle)^\diamond$	:=	$\lambda i \lambda o.i[U]o \wedge \gamma_1(o) \wedge \ldots \wedge \gamma_m(o)$
(ii)	$(x_l = x_k)^\diamond$	:=	$\lambda i.V(u_l)(i) = V(u_k)(i)$
(iii)	$(P(x_1, \ldots, x_n))^\diamond$	:=	$\lambda i.P(V(u_1)(i), \ldots, V(u_n)(i))$
(vi)	$(\neg K)^\diamond$	:=	$\lambda i.\neg \exists o\ K^\diamond(i)(o)$
(v)	$(K_1 \vee K_2)^\diamond$	:=	$\lambda i.\exists o(K_1^\diamond(i)(o) \vee K_2^\diamond(i)(o))$
(vi)	$(K_1 \Rightarrow K_2)^\diamond$	:=	$\lambda i.\forall m(K_1^\diamond(i)(m) \rightarrow \exists o\ K_2^\diamond(m)(o))$

Sequencing becomes

$$(K_1; K_2)^\diamond := \lambda i \lambda o \exists m (K_1^\diamond(i)(m) \wedge K_2^\diamond(m)(o))$$

TY_3 expressions are cumbersome to manipulate in full glory. In order to guard against writer's cramp some abbreviations are used in the simulation of the language of DRT in the system outlined above. For some fixed i of type s and for discourse referents u and individual terms t we stipulate:

$$u^\circ = V(u)(i) \text{ and } t^\circ = t$$

In the case of simple DRS conditions of type st with R of type $\underbrace{e(\ldots(e\,t)\ldots)}_{n}$ and τ a discourse referent or an individual variable we write

$$R\tau_1 \ldots \tau_n \quad \text{for} \quad \lambda i. R\tau_1^\circ \ldots \tau_n^\circ$$
$$\tau_1 \doteq \tau_2 \quad \text{for} \quad \lambda i. \tau_1^\circ = \tau_2^\circ$$

For complex DRS conditions of type st with K, K' DRSs of type $s(st)$ we write

$$\neg K \quad \text{for} \quad \lambda i. \neg \exists j K(i)(j)$$
$$K \Rightarrow K' \quad \text{for} \quad \lambda i. \forall j (K(i)(j) \to \exists k \ K'(j)(k))$$

DRSs are of type $s(st)$ and we write

$$[u_1 \ldots u_n | \gamma_1 \ldots \gamma_m] \quad \text{for} \quad \lambda i \lambda j. i[u_1 \ldots u_n]j \wedge \gamma_1(j) \wedge \ldots \wedge \gamma_m(j)$$

To give a simple example, $[u|player(u)\ smile(u)]$ is short for the term

$$\lambda i. \lambda j. (\forall v (u \neq v) \to V(v)(i) = V(v)(j))$$
$$\wedge player(V(u)(j)) \wedge smile(V(u)(j))$$

Sequencing of DRS is represented as ';' and we write

$$K; K' \quad \text{for} \quad \lambda i \lambda j \exists k (K(i)(k) \wedge K'(k)(j))$$

Given these definitions the following (nonsymmetric) merging lemma (ML) allows us to merge certain DRSs:

$$\text{ML:} \quad AX_{1,2,3} \models [\vec{u}|\vec{\gamma}]; [\vec{u}'|\vec{\gamma}'] = [\vec{u}\ \vec{u}'|\vec{\gamma}\ \vec{\gamma}']$$
$$\text{where } \vec{u}' \text{ does not occur in } \vec{\gamma}$$

4. CDRT AS A MEANING LANGUAGE IN GLUE LANGUAGE SEMANTICS

The abbreviations introduced above have taken us back to a notation close to standard DRT. We have, however, gained something important along the way: first, we have an encoding of DRT in a sorted version of standard type theory and second, we have the lambdas from the type theory. We are now in a position to formulate a compositional syntax/semantics interface for a DRT semantics. A categorial grammar fragment with corresponding meaning representation translations in the DRT simulation in the TY_3 based system outlined above is given in (Muskens, 1994a):

$every^n$	$(s/(n\backslash s))/cn$	$\lambda R \lambda S.[\|([u_n\|]; R(u_n)) \Rightarrow S(u_n)]$
	$((s/n)\backslash s))/cn$	
a^n	$(s/(n\backslash s))/cn$	$\lambda R \lambda S.[u_n\|]; R(u_n); S(u_n)$
	$((s/n)\backslash s))/cn$	
$picked$	$(n\backslash s)/n$	$\lambda x \lambda y[\|pick(x,y)]$
$coach$	cn	$\lambda x[\|coach(x)]$
$player$	cn	$\lambda x[\|player(x)]$

Categorial grammar and linear logic are close relatives. Categorial grammars constitute a fragment of non-commutative linear logic. The glue language approach is slightly more flexible: it is based on a fragment of commutative linear logic in order to handle e.g. quantifier scope. In the glue language approach, combination possibilities are constrained by the structure of the meaning constructors and the nodes in the semantic projections. The interplay between the two allows tight or looser couplings between semantic derivations and syntactic derivations, as desired. Apart from these differences, the proximity between them makes it reasonably straightforward to port the categorial grammar semantic component into the meaning representation language slots in Dalrymple et al.'s linear logic premises. Systematically unpack the λ-prefixes in Muskens' translations as universally quantified variables in antecedents of implicative ' $\multimap$ ' linear logic premises in the glue language meaning constructors:

$$\text{every}^1 : \; \forall Scope, R, S. \; (\forall x. \; subj.var \rightsquigarrow$$
$$x \multimap subj.restr \rightsquigarrow R(x)) \otimes$$
$$(\forall x. \; subj \rightsquigarrow x \multimap Scope \rightsquigarrow S(x))$$
$$\multimap Scope \rightsquigarrow [|([u_1|]; R(u_1)) \Rightarrow S(u_1)]$$

$$\text{a}^2 : \quad \forall Scope, R, S. \; (\forall x. \; obj.var \rightsquigarrow$$
$$x \multimap obj.restr \rightsquigarrow R(x)) \otimes$$
$$(\forall x. \; obj \rightsquigarrow x \multimap Scope \rightsquigarrow S(x))$$
$$\multimap Scope \rightsquigarrow [u_2|]; R(u_2); S(u_2)$$

picked : $\forall X, Y. \; (subj \rightsquigarrow X \otimes obj \rightsquigarrow Y) \multimap s \rightsquigarrow [|pick(X,Y)]$

coach : $\forall X. \; (subj.var \rightsquigarrow X \multimap subj.restr \rightsquigarrow [|coach(X)|])$

player : $\forall X. \; (obj.var \rightsquigarrow X \multimap obj.restr \rightsquigarrow [|player(X)|])$

The lexical premises are instantiated to the f-structure (and associated semantic projection) of our example sentence. Note that the dual category assignments to determiners in the categorial grammar fragment are no longer required in the linear logic based framework. In a sense, the corresponding f-structure provides a single, scopally underspecified syntactic representation. R and S are variables of type $\pi(s(st))$ and x and X variables of type π. The instantiated DRS fragments in the meaning representation slots in the lexical meaning constructors are abbreviations of TY_3 expressions of type $s(st)$, with states abstracted over. To give an example, the meaning constructor for *player* is short for

$$\text{player} : \; \forall X. \; (obj.var \rightsquigarrow X$$
$$\multimap obj.restr \rightsquigarrow \lambda i. \lambda j. i = j \wedge player(V(X)(j)))$$

The TY_3 type system is very basic (it is flat and does not have polymorphism). Provided term unification respects type assignment in TY_3, the higher order term matching task reduces to the one in described in (Dalrymple et al., 1997). In particular, the higher order term matching is still decidable.[7] The derivations of the meaning representations in the new meaning representation language are then simple variations of the derivations in Sect. 2 above plus some optional applications of the merge lemma ML.

Briefly, for the subject NP:

$\text{every}^1, \text{coach} \vdash$

---

[7] P.c. Fernando Pereira.

$\forall Scope, S.\ (\forall x.\ subj \rightsquigarrow x \multimap Scope \rightsquigarrow S(x))$
   $\multimap Scope \rightsquigarrow [|([u_1|]; [|coach(u_1)|]) \Rightarrow S(u_1)]$

with the substitutions $\langle X \leftarrow x,\ R \leftarrow \lambda x.[|coach(x)|]\rangle$. The semantic representation of the scope node is reduced to $[|([u_1|coach(u_1)|]) \Rightarrow S(u_1)]$ by application of ML.

For the object NP:

a^2, player $\vdash$
$\forall Scope, S.\ (\forall x.\ obj \rightsquigarrow x \multimap Scope \rightsquigarrow S(x))$
   $\multimap Scope \rightsquigarrow [u_2|]; [|player(u_2)|]; S(u_2)$

with the substitutions $\langle X \leftarrow x,\ R \leftarrow \lambda x.[|player(x)|]\rangle$. ML reduces the semantic representation of the scope node to $[u_2|player(u_2)|]; S(u_2)$.

The Currying equivalences yield

$pick_1 : \forall X(subj \rightsquigarrow X \multimap \forall Y(obj \rightsquigarrow Y \multimap s \rightsquigarrow [|pick(X,Y)|]))$·
$pick_2 : \forall Y(obj \rightsquigarrow Y \multimap \forall X(subj \rightsquigarrow X \multimap s \rightsquigarrow [|pick(X,Y)|]))$

Using transitivity of linear implication (TI) we may first combine the object NP with $pick_1$

$picked_1$,a^2,player $\vdash$
$\forall X(subj \rightsquigarrow X \multimap s \rightsquigarrow [u_2|player(u_2)|]; [|pick(X,u_2)|]$

with the substitutions $\langle Y \leftarrow x,\ Scope \leftarrow s,\ S \leftarrow \lambda x.[|pick(X,x)|]\rangle$. Application of ML yields $[u_2|player(u_2)\ pick(X,u_2)|]$ as reduced semantic representation for the s node

The result is combined with the subject NP to yield the narrow scope reading of the indefinite NP:

every^1, coach, $picked_1$, a^2, player $\vdash$
$s \rightsquigarrow [|([u_1|coach(u_1)|]) \Rightarrow [u_2|player(u_2)\ pick(u_1,u_2)|]]$

with the substitutions $\langle S \leftarrow \lambda x.[u_2|player(u_2)\ pick(x,u_2)|],\ X \leftarrow x,\ Scope \leftarrow s\rangle$.

Again the alternative derivation sequence first combines the subject NP with $pick_2$ and then this with the object NP, and results in the specific reading of the indefinite NP:

every^1, coach, $pick_2$, a^2, player $\vdash$
$s \rightsquigarrow [u_2|player(u_2), [u_1|coach(u_1)|] \Rightarrow [|pick(u_1,u_2)|]]$

We will briefly illustrate the dynamics of the resulting system (which is inherited from the dynamics of the meaning representation language) with the following simple two sentence discourse:

Exactly one[1] representative arrived. She[1] was late.

where the anaphoric dependencies are indicated in terms of superscripts for antecedents and corresponding subscripts for corefering pronouns. In simple extensional type theory the determiner *"exactly one"* would be associated with a term such as

$$\lambda P \lambda Q \exists x (P(x) \wedge Q(x) \wedge \forall y([P(y) \wedge Q(y)] \rightarrow x = y))$$

In CDRT this translates to the following meaning constructor:

exactly one[1]:

$$\forall Scope, R, S. \ (\forall x. \ subj.var \rightsquigarrow x \multimap subj.restr \rightsquigarrow R(x)) \otimes$$
$$(\forall x.subj \rightsquigarrow x \multimap Scope \rightsquigarrow S(x))$$
$$\multimap Scope \rightsquigarrow [u_1|]; R(u_1); S(u_1);$$
$$[|([u_i|]; R(u_i); S(u_i)) \Rightarrow [|u_1 = u_i]]$$

where u_i is new

With this we derive

Exactly one[1],representative,arrived $\vdash$
$s_1 \rightsquigarrow [u_1|representative(u_1) \ arrive(u_1)]$
$\qquad [u_2|representative(u_2) arrive(u_2)] \Rightarrow [|u_1 = u_2]]$

and this provides the context against which the continuation of the discourse is interpreted. The pronoun *"she"* in the second sentence contributes the following NP-type lexical premise:

$$she_1 : \ \forall Scope, S. \ (\forall x.subj_2 \rightsquigarrow x \multimap Scope \rightsquigarrow S(x))$$
$$\multimap Scope \rightsquigarrow S(u_1)$$

Note that the premise is instantiated to the anaphorically resolved f- and s-structure associated with the second sentence in the discourse. Like other compositional dynamic semantics, but unlike classical DRT, CDRT requires anaphorically resolved syntactic input representations.

On this view, anaphora resolution is not part of semantics 'proper' but rather delegated to some other (syntactic or pragmatic) component of the grammar. For our present purposes this means that the CDRT glue language based approach has to be complemented with e.g. a syntactic approach to anaphora resolution in LFG as in (Dalrymple, 1993). With this the semantic contribution of the second sentence is computed as

$$she_1, \ was, \ late \vdash s_2 \leadsto [|late(u_1)]$$

The first and the second sentence are combined in terms of a sequencing operation induced by the lexical premise associated with the full stop '.':

$$`.' : \ \forall P, Q. \ (s_1 \leadsto P \otimes s_2 \leadsto Q) \multimap dis \leadsto P; Q$$

where dis, s_1 and s_2 are the semantic projections of the entire discourse, the first sentence and the second sentence respectively.[8] Again the lexical premise given above is instantiated to the f- and s-structure associated with the sample discourse. With this we get

Exactly one[1], representative, arrived, ., she$_1$, was, late $\vdash$
$dis \leadsto [u_1|representative(u_1) \ arrive(u_1)$
$\quad\quad [u_2|representative(u_1)arrive(u_2)] \Rightarrow [|u_1 = u_2] \ late(u_1)]$

which can easily be see to be equivalent to the following DRS in the familiar box notation:

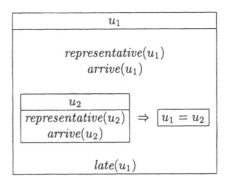

Just like (Dalrymple et al., 1997)'s original approach our modified approach allows us to compute all scope possibilities. In a sense a set of

---

[8] This can easily be formulated recursively to allow for discourses of arbitrarily many sentences.

linear logic premises can be looked upon as a fully underspecified representation, where the linear logic derivations rule out dangling variable occurrences and cases of vacuous quantification. (Crouch & Genabith, 1996) present an approach to scope underspecification in glue language semantics, which allows full specification as well as partial or complete underspecification of scope (as in QLF (Alshawi & Crouch, 1992) and UDRT (Reyle, 1993; Reyle, 1995; König & Reyle, 1996)). Ordering constraints on f-structure nodes are added to the lexical premises, e.g. *subj* $\succ$ *obj*, expressing that for some given syntactic structure the subject NP has wide scope over the object NP. The constraint, roughly speaking, forces the glue language derivation to consume the object meaning constructor before the subject constructor. (To be more accurate, the scope ordering constraints reflect certain properties in the topology of glue language derivations when carried out in a natural deduction system for linear logic, as provided by (Troelstra, 1992)). The point to note is that this approach carries over unchanged when moving from a static meaning language to a 'dynamic' one.

5. Conclusions

Let us briefly take stock: we have imported a 'dynamic' meaning representation language (CDRT) into the the meaning representation language slots in (Dalrymple et al., 1993b; Dalrymple et al., 1993a; Dalrymple et al., 1995b; Dalrymple et al., 1997; Dalrymple et al., 1996)'s linear logic based glue language semantics. The fact that the transplant is based on a simple extension of ordinary type theory is responsible for the fact that there are not too many allergic reactions in the host. In many respects, CDRT was picked with care to suit the task at hand. As far as we can see, however, the strategy employed is quite general and should be adaptable to a number of dynamic semantic theories which from the point of view of CDRT may look more like special purpose designer logics (e.g. λ-DRT (Kohlhase et al., 1996; Bos et al., 1994; Asher, 1993), Dynamic Montague Grammar (Groenendijk & Stokhof, 1990), Dynamic Type Theory (Chierchia, 1991) or the compositional version of DRT due to (van Eijck & Kamp, 1997)).

This makes developments in dynamic semantics available to linear logic based LFG semantics. And in the other direction, it makes the glue language treatment of scope available to dynamic semantics, improving on earlier approaches such as Cooper storage in that the 'free variable' constraint does not need to be stipulated, but simply follows from the propositional structure of the linear logic premises.

It has to be remarked that the approach to providing LFG with a dynamic semantics component outlined here is by no means the only one. The most direct approach is probably the one presented in (Genabith & Crouch, 1996a; Genabith & Crouch, 1996b; Genabith & Crouch, 1997) where LFG f-structures are either directly or indirectly interpreted as QLFs (Alshawi & Crouch, 1992) or UDRSs (Reyle, 1993; Reyle, 1995; König & Reyle, 1996). On this approach f-structures inherit an underspecified and a dynamic semantics from QLFs or UDRSs. To some extent this approach might be limited by the fact that what is interpreted are f-structures which first and foremost are abstract syntactic representations and it is at least conceivable that they may not provide the most suitable representations for semantic phenomena in all cases.

A completely different approach is presented in (Crouch & Genabith, 1996). Here the machinery of linear logic itself is used to model context management (i.e. interpretation against and update of context) directly (i.e. without the use of a dynamic meaning representation language). The approach is presented in terms of a LFG framework but is of a general nature and independent of a particular grammar formalism. Two further approaches are the ones by (Muskens, 1995) (see also (Pinkal, 1996) for an extension not tied to LFG) and (Declerck, 1996). (Muskens, 1995) gives an LFG-style annotated CF-PSG where (in addition to f-structure annotations) phrase structure rules are annotated with what are called l-descriptions and s-descriptions. l-descriptions determine the structure of logical form expressions and allow to partially determine scope possibilities (in terms of dominance constraints) while s-descriptions determine the composition of semantic representations in the generalized l-trees. f-, l- and s-descriptions are stated as sets of simultaneous constraints (specifications of dominance relations and equality statements) on the various representations and a good representation is a solution to those constraints. (Declerck, 1996) differs from the other underspecified approaches cited here in that he outlines how a fully specified Dynamic Predicate Logic (Groenendijk & Stokhof, 1991) semantics can be integrated into LFG in terms of LFGs projection architecture.

As with (Dalrymple et al., 1997; Dalrymple et al., 1996)'s original approach, our modified approach allows us to compute all scope possibilities. In a weak sense, then, a set of linear logic premises can be looked upon as an underspecified representation. For an approach that allows us to fully or partially underspecify or to completely specify scope (as in QLF or UDRT) in glue language derivations see (Crouch & Genabith, 1996). The approach carries over to the modified glue language semantics outlined here. If a set of linear logic premises is regarded as an underspecified representation then the linear logic deductions mapping this set into fully specified (i.e. disambiguated) meaning representations do (part of) the job of the 'interpretation' clauses in QLF and the disambiguation operation in UDRT.

In other words the linear logic deductions would be instrumental in *defining* the *semantics* of an underspecified representation construed as a set of linear logic premises, rather than being *executed* during the construction of an (unambiguous) semantic representation of some phrase under consideration. Note that this does not yet commit the resulting semantics to a QLF or a UDRT style semantics. Indeed, a QLF style (Alshawi & Crouch, 1992) supervaluation semantics for a set of linear logic premises Δ is obtained as follows:

$$\llbracket \Delta \rrbracket = \begin{cases} 1 & \text{iff for } \textit{all } c \text{ such that } c \in \{c | \Delta \vdash c\}, \ \llbracket c \rrbracket = 1 \\ 0 & \text{iff for } \textit{all } c \text{ such that } c \in \{c | \Delta \vdash c\}, \ \llbracket c \rrbracket = 0 \\ \textit{undefined} & \text{otherwise} \end{cases}$$

where $\vdash$ is the linear logic consequence relation (plus scope constraints as in (Crouch & Genabith, 1996), if required). The different UDRT semantics (Reyle, 1993; Reyle, 1995), on the other hand, are defined classically and take their cue from the definition of the UDRS consequence relations.[9] The most recent version (Reyle, 1995) is

$$\forall \delta (\Gamma^\delta \vdash_{u_n} \gamma^\delta)$$

which reads: a UDRS γ follows from the UDRS premises Γ just in case that if δ_i is a disambiguation of Γ, the corresponding disambiguation δ_i of γ follows, for all δ_i. In other words, if the same ambiguous structure appears in both premise and conclusion, disambiguation proceeds in parallel. The definition implies that a goal UDRS γ is interpreted conjunctively, i.e. $\llbracket \gamma \rrbracket = 1$ iff for all disambiguations δ: $\llbracket \gamma^\delta \rrbracket = 1$, $\llbracket \gamma \rrbracket = 0$ otherwise. In the world of linear logic premises Δ, this translates as

$$\llbracket \Delta \rrbracket = \begin{cases} 1 & \text{iff for } \textit{all } c \text{ such that } c \in \{c | \Delta \vdash c\}, \ \llbracket c \rrbracket = 1 \\ 0 & \text{otherwise} \end{cases}$$

---

[9] We will use $\vdash_{u_n}$ for the *new* consequence relation in (Reyle, 1995) and $\vdash_{u_o}$ for the *original* UDRS consequence relation in (Reyle, 1993).

Plugging two different semantics into the same system facilitates comparison. Here we just note that the original UDRT semantics (Reyle, 1993) and the more recent (Reyle, 1995) each cover two different corners of the QLF semantics (Alshawi & Crouch, 1992) (either *definite truth* or *definite falsity*). To see this note that (Reyle, 1993) takes its cue from

$$\forall \delta \exists \delta' (\Gamma^\delta \vdash_{u_o} \gamma^{\delta'})$$

which results in a disjunctive interpretation of a goal UDRS. Applying this to a set of linear logic premises Δ, we get

$$[\![\Delta]\!] = \begin{cases} 1 & \text{iff there } exists \text{ a } c \text{ such that } c \in \{c | \Delta \vdash c\}, \\ & [\![c]\!] = 1 \\ 0 & \text{otherwise} \end{cases}$$

ACKNOWLEDGEMENTS

We would like to thank Fernando Pereira, Jochen Dörre, Tim Fernando, Massimo Poesio, James Power, Carl Vogel and the anonymous reviewers for helpful suggestions and discussions.

REFERENCES

Alshawi, H. and Crouch, R. (1992) Monotonic semantic interpretation. In *Proceedings 30th Annual Meeting of the Association for Computational Linguistics*. 32–38.

Asher, N. (1993) *Reference to Abstract Objects in Discourse*. Kluwer, Dordrecht, Dordrecht.

Bos, J.; Mastenbroek, E.; McGlashan, S.; Millies, S.; and Pinkal, M. (1994) A compositional DRS-based formalism for NLP-applications. In *International Workshop on Computational Semantics*, Tilburg.

Chierchia, G. (1991) Anaphora and dynamic binding. *Linguistics and Philosophy* 15(2):111–183.

Crouch, R. and Genabith, J. van (1996) Context change and underspecification in glue language semantics. In Butt, M. and King, T.H., editors, *Proceedings of the First LFG Conference*, RANK Xerox Research Center, Grenoble, France. 133–147.

Dalrymple, M.; Hinrichs, A.; Lamping, J.; and Saraswat, V. (1993a) The resource logic of complex predicate interpretation. In *Proceedings of the 1993 Republic of China Computational Linguistics Conference (ROCLING)*. Also Xerox Technical Report ISTL-NLTT-1993-08-03.

Dalrymple, M.; Lamping, J.; and Saraswat, V. (1993b) Lfg semantics via constraints. In *Proceedings of the 6th Meeting of the European ACL (EACL)*, Utrecht.

Dalrymple, M.; Kaplan, R.M.; Maxwell, J.T.; and Zaenen, A., editors (1995a) *Formal Issues in Lexical-Functional Grammar*. CSLI lecture notes; no.47. CSLI Publications.

Dalrymple, M.; Kehler, A.; Lamping, J.; and Saraswat, V. (1995b) The semantics of resource sharing in lexical-functional grammar. In *Proceedings of the Seventh Meeting of the European ACL (EACL)*. 31–38.

Dalrymple, M.; Lamping, J.; Pereira, F.C.N; and Saraswat, V. (1996) A deductive account of quantification in LFG. In Kanazawa, M.; Pinon, C.; and Swart, H.de, editors, *Quantifiers, Deduction and Context*. CSLI Publications, No. 57. 33–57.

Dalrymple, M.; Lamping, J.; Pereira, F.C.N; and Saraswat, V. (1997) Quantifiers, anaphora, and intensionality. *Journal of Logic, Language, and Information* 6(3):219–273.

Dalrymple, M. (1993) *The Syntax of Anaphoric Binding*. CSLI Lecture Notes. CSLI, Stanford, CA.

Declerck, T (1996) Modelling information passing with the LFG workbench. In Butt, M. and King, T.H., editors, *Proceedings of the First LFG Conference*, RANK Xerox Research Center, Grenoble, France.

Eijck, J. van and Kamp, H. (1997) Representing discourse in context. In Benthem, J. van and Meulen, A.ter, editors, *Handbook of Logic and Language*. Elsevier, Amsterdam. 179–237.

Genabith, J. van and Crouch, R. (1996a) Direct and underspecified interpretations of LFG f-structures. In *COLING 96, Copenhagen, Denmark*. 262–267.

Genabith, J. van and Crouch, R. (1996b) F-structures, qlfs and udrss. In Butt, M. and King, T.H., editors, *Proceedings of the First LFG Conference*, RANK Xerox Research Center, Grenoble, France. 190–205.

Genabith, J. van and Crouch, R. (1997) On interpreting f-structures as udrss. In *ACL-EACL-97, Madrid, Spain*. 402–409.

Groenendijk, J. and Stokhof, M. (1990) Dynamic montague grammar. In Kalman, L. and Polos, L., editors, *Papers from the Second Symposium on Logic and Language*. Akademiai Kiadoo, Budapest. 3–48.

Groenendijk, J. and Stokhof, M. (1991) Dynamic predicate logic. *Linguistics and Philosophy* 14:39–100.

Kamp, H. and Reyle, U. (1993) *From Discourse to Logic*. Kluwer, Dordrecht.

Kamp, H. and Reyle, U. (1996)   A calculus for first order discourse representation structures. *Journal of Logic, Language, and Information* 5(3–4):297–348.

Kamp, H. (1981)   A theory of truth and semantic representation. In Groenendijk, J. and editors, *Formal Methods in the Study of Language*. Mathematisch Centrum, Amsterdam.

Kaplan, R.M. and Bresnan, J. (1982) Lexical functional grammar. In Bresnan, J., editor (1982, *The mental representation of grammatical relations*. MIT Press, Cambridge Mass. 173–281.

Kohlhase, M.; Kuschert, S.; and Pinkal, M. (1996) A type-theoretic semantics for λ-DRT. In Dekker, P. and Stokhof, M., editors, *Proceedings of the Tenth Amsterdam Colloquium*. ILLC, University of Amsterdam.

König, E. and Reyle, U. (1996) A general reasoning scheme for underspecified representations. In Ohlbach, H.-J. and Reyle, U., editors, *Logic and its Applications. Festschrift for Dov Gabbay*. Kluwer.

Miller, D.A. (1990) A logic programming language with lambda abstraction, function variables and simple unification. In Schroeder-Heister, P., editor, *Extensions of Logic Programming*. Springer.

Muskens, R. (1994a) Categorial grammar and discourse representation theory. In *COLING 94, Kyoto, Japan*. 508–514.

Muskens, R. (1994b)   A compositional discourse representation theory. In *Proceedings 9th Amsterdam Colloquium*. ILLC, Amsterdam. 467–486.

Muskens, R. (1995) Order-independence and underspecification. In *Dyana-2 Deliverable R2.2.C "Ellipsis, Underspecification, Events and More in Dynamic Semantics"*. ILLC, University of Amsterdam.

Muskens, R. (1996) Combining montague semantics and discourse representation theory. *Linguistics and Philosophy* 19:143–186.

Pinkal, M. (1996) Radical underspecification. In *Proceedings of the Tenth Amsterdam Colloquium*. ILLC, University of Amsterdam.

Reyle, U. (1993) Dealing with ambiguities by underspecification: Construction, representation and deduction. *Journal of Semantics* 10:123–179.

Reyle, U. (1995) On reasoning with ambiguities. In *Seventh Conference of the European Chapter of the Association for Computational Linguistics — Proceedings of the Conference*, Dublin. ACL. 1–8.

Troelstra, A.S. (1992) *Lecture Notes on Linear Logic*. CSLI Lecture Notes, 29. CSLI, Stanford, CA.

ALICE KYBURG AND MICHAEL MORREAU

VAGUE UTTERANCES AND CONTEXT CHANGE

As a dialogue proceeds, utterances will be interpreted relative to a body of assumed common beliefs and suppositions. In keeping with a computational view of mind we shall suppose that these shared common beliefs and suppositions are represented in some way in the interpreter as the sentences of some language. Let a set of sentences representing common beliefs and suppositions be called a *context*. Utterances will be interpreted relative to contexts, but contexts, in turn, will change as a result of utterances. In the simplest case a context will *grow*. That is what will happen when an utterance in no way conflicts with the prior context. The resulting context will include the prior context together with representations of what is conveyed by the utterance.

Things are not always this simple, though. Consider the possibilities for reference using vague definite descriptions. A farmer owns two pigs: the first is a very skinny pig; the second is a much rounder pig, almost, but not quite, a fat pig. Now a veterinarian, who has come to give the pigs shots, says, "*We will begin with the fat pig.*" The farmer could protest that really neither pig is a fat one and both of them know it. Even so, he understands that the veterinarian is referring to the fatter of the two pigs.

The farmer's understanding can be accounted for if we assume that by using the vague definite description "*the fat pig*", the veterinarian suggests a new, more inclusive usage for the expression "*fat pig*"; the farmer for his part, seeing the utility of this new usage for distinguishing between his pigs, and recognizing that such distinguishing will serve their common purposes, adopts the usage. It is as if for the purposes of the conversation the participants agree to represent one of the pigs as fat, so that the definite description will denote. Such *accommodation* of usage will bring about an evolution of the senses of vague expressions in the course of a dialogue.[1] It will lead to context changes that are not simple growth, since representations of common beliefs that were true before a change in usage will in general not be true afterwards. Such context changes we shall call *context shifts*.

It counts in favor of the notion that usage changes during dialogue

---

[1] We borrow this term from David Lewis (1979).

H. Bunt and R. Muskens (eds.), Computing Meaning, Volume 1, 149–166.

that the farmer himself may come to refer to the larger animal with the description *"the fat pig"*. That a change in usage is involved is further suggested by the contrast between this case and another one. Suppose the veterinarian, wrongly thinking that the larger of the two pigs belongs to a neighbour, had said *"We will begin with the neighbour's pig."* This utterance could hardly be thought to suggest a new usage for *"neighbour's pig"*. The farmer would not himself start calling this the neighbour's pig; he would not defer to a new, more inclusive usage of *"neighbour's pig"* on which even his own pig is so called. He might instead put the veterinarian straight, using this expression in its unchanged sense to point out that this is *not* the neighbour's pig.

Accommodation of usage contributes greatly to the expressive power of natural language. Because the extension of *"fat pig"* can be 'stretched' to cover the not-quite-fat pig we do not need another, more inclusive expression to cover the animal in question; similarly, since a home handyman can adjust a crescent wrench to fit some particular nut he does not need another special wrench of just the right size. Accommodation enables us to get by with a relatively small, general purpose lexicon.

In this chapter we shall sketch a model of the accommodation of the usage vague definite descriptions. It is, in the sense of David Marr (1982) a 'computational' model: we shall present a context-update function that models accommodation, but our object is not in the first place to present an algorithm that a language-understanding device might use. Rather, our object is to present a function we think such an algorithm ought to compute. With this goal in mind, we put to one side questions concerning the computational complexity of the accommodation function.

Our account of accommodation combines ideas from three domains: supervaluational accounts of vagueness, theories of conveyed meanings, and theories of belief revision. Supervaluational accounts of vagueness were suggested in the mid 1970s by Kit Fine (1975) and Hans Kamp (1975). From these we borrow an interpretation of vague language. By a theory of conveyed meanings we mean a specification of the literal meanings, presuppositions, and conversational implicatures that are conveyed by utterances. Pieces of such a theory can be found in the work of Paul Grice (1967), and in subsequent work by Lauri Karttunen and Stanley Peters (1979), Gerald Gazdar (1979a, 1979b), and Irene

Heim (1983), among others.[2] We shall not present such an account, but our discussion shall take place against the background of some such theory, the existence of which we presuppose. Finally, one well-known account of belief revision is that of Carlos Alchourrón et al. (1985). The context-update function that we shall propose derives directly from it.

In the next section, we shall describe a language for representing expressions of English and define a partial interpretation for it. In Sect. 3, we shall briefly discuss conveyed meanings. With this background in place, in Sects. 4 and 5, we shall propose a model of context change on which, as we shall demonstrate in Sect. 6, uttering a vague definite description can lead to a context shift. In Sect. 7, we shall discuss several examples that point toward elaborations of our model.

1. VAGUE LANGUAGE

It will facilitate the coming discussion to introduce a formal language in which to represent expressions of English. The language we have chosen to illustrate our approach is in comparison with English very limited in its expressive power, but it has the advantage for our purpose of its simplicity and familiarity: $\mathcal{L}$ is a language of first-order predicate logic augmented with the sentential operator I, read "It is indeterminate whether". $\mathcal{L}$ has individual constant symbols including *Arnold* and *Babe*, and individual variable symbols $x, y, \ldots$; 1-place predicates including *pig*, *fat-pig*, *skinny-pig*, and *curly-tail*; and 2-place predicates including *tail*, *at-least-as-fat-as*, and *fatter*. Some of these expressions – they include *fat-pig*, *skinny-pig*, and *curly-tail* – are designated *vague*. The others – including *tail*, *at-least-as-fat-as*, and *fatter* – are *non-vague*.[3] The formulas of $\mathcal{L}$ are defined with the usual recursion over the logical symbols.

To illustrate, the intended interpretation of *fat-pig(Arnold)* is that Arnold is a fat pig. The intended interpretations of *at-least-as-fat-as(Arnold,Babe)* and *fatter(Arnold,Babe)* are that Arnold is at least as fat as Babe, and that Arnold is fatter than Babe. Finally, the intended interpretation of $I\,(fat\text{-}pig(Arnold))$ is that there is no matter of fact

---

[2] For a survey see (Levinson, 1983) and for more recent work (Beaver, 1997).

[3] We simplify in two ways. First, we consider only the vagueness of predicates, putting to one side questions relating to the vagueness of names and quantifiers. Second, we consider only some predicates to be vague while just about all of them seem to be, to a greater or lesser extent.

about whether Arnold is a fat pig, which is to say that Arnold is a borderline fat pig.

Notice that we have not included in $\mathcal{L}$ representations of vague adjectives like *"fat"*, which can be used to form vague composite expressions like *"fat pig"*. We will treat such composite expressions as if they were semantically simple. A compositional treatment within this partial semantic framework is given by Hans Kamp and Barbara Partee (1995), who interpret adjectives as functions mapping the semantic values of the nouns they combine with onto the semantic values of the resulting adjective-noun combinations. The semantic value of the noun can be thought of as picking out a 'comparison class' relative to which the adjective is interpreted.

That the compositional semantics of adjective-noun combinations has been left to one side underlines something distinctive in our approach. We claim that accommodation of the kind that concerns us here can be accounted for without bringing in comparison classes. It has been put to us that, on the contrary, the compositional analysis of adjective-noun combinations is *just* where the mechanism of this accommodation is to be found. Those that hold this view seem to prefer an alternative treatment suggested by the notion that the semantic value of such an expression depends on a comparison class. Instead of thinking of accommodation as extension-stretching, the alternative is to think of it as the adoption, when interpreting an adjective-noun combination, of a comparison class other than that picked out by the noun.

We do not have a conclusive empirical reason to prefer the approach we have taken here, but we do have a theoretical reason. We expect that modeling accommodation as pure comparison-class change will require multiplying comparison classes in an *ad-hoc* manner, far beyond the needs of the semantics of adjective-noun combinations. For now, then, we have chosen to hide comparison classes from view, to see how far we can get without them. We shall return briefly to this question in Sect. 7, with an example suggesting that they are needed anyway.

We turn now to the interpretation of $\mathcal{L}$. Imagine a pig that is on the threshold of becoming fat. Imagine also that you are well informed about the size of the pig – say, because you are looking straight at it. Now someone says that the pig is fat and someone else disagrees. In a case like this you may find yourself unable to agree with either of them. One possible explanation for this inability is that you are insufficiently informed: either the pig in question is fat or it is not, but you just do not know which. Another explanation for this inability, which coheres well with the approach we take, is that there are some pigs that are neither definitely fat, nor definitely not fat, and that this is one of them.

This second explanation suggests a *partial* interpretation for vague predicates. A partial interpretation assigns to each predicate both a positive and a negative extension, which need not exhaust the entire domain of quantification. A *borderline* individual is one that is neither in the positive nor in the negative extension of the predicate in question; for example, the pig described above is a borderline fat pig.

The notion that vagueness is semantic partiality is one of the main ideas underlying supervaluational treatments of vagueness. The other is the idea that vagueness can be reduced by resolving borderline cases one way or the other, while leaving determinate cases be. The different ways of making vague expressions more precise are *precisifications*. Precisifications correspond to partial interpretations.

Precisifications will enable us to make precise the suggestion, in Sect. 1, that accommodation involves 'stretching' the extensions of vague expressions. We shall treat accommodation as the adoption, for conversational purposes, of new senses of such expressions. These senses incorporate formerly borderline individuals either into the positive extensions of the expressions in question, or into their negative extensions. As such, they correspond to precisifications.

The intuitively understood meanings of expressions constrain precisifications. Some of these constraints, following Fine (1975), we shall call *penumbral connections*. For instance, the intuitive meanings of *"fat pig"* and *"skinny pig"* require that on any precisification, if a pig is at least as fat as a fat pig, then it too is a fat pig; if a skinny pig is at least as fat as another pig, then the other pig too is a skinny pig; and no skinny pig is a fat pig. Precisifications must also satisfy the constraints placed on them by the meanings of non-vague expressions. For instance, the intuitive meaning of *"at least as fat as"* requires that on any precisification, given any two pigs, one is at least as fat as the other. The intuitive meanings of *"at least as fat as"* and *"fatter than"* together require that on any precisification one pig is fatter than another just in case it is at least as fat as the other, but not the other way around.

We evaluate a sentence at a precisification that is *appropriate* insofar as it retains a degree of indeterminacy that reflects the intuitively understood meanings of vague expressions. But the truth value of a sentence at this appropriate precisification depends on the truth values it will obtain on the different ways of making it completely precise. A sentence is counted true on the appropriate precisification if it is true on each of its *complete* precisifications, and it is counted false if it is false on each of these. A sentence that is true on some and false on others has no truth value on the appropriate precisification.

We shall now make these ideas precise. A *model* $\mathcal{M}$ for $\mathcal{L}$ is a quadruple $\langle\ \mathcal{U},\ \mathcal{P},\ \leq,\ \mathcal{I}\ \rangle$. Here $\mathcal{U}$ is a non-empty set, the domain of quantification; $\mathcal{P}$ is a set of evaluation points; $\leq$ is a partial ordering on $\mathcal{P}$; and $\mathcal{I}$ is an interpretation function. We require that $\leq$ orders $\mathcal{P}$ as a tree, with a unique minimal element @, the *appropriate point*, at the base. $\mathcal{I}$ assigns to each n-place predicate or relation symbol R and evaluation point p two disjoint sets of n-tuples of elements of $\mathcal{U}$: $\mathcal{I}^+(R, p)$, the *positive extension* of R at p; and $\mathcal{I}^-(R, p)$, the *negative extension* of R at p. $\mathcal{I}$ must respect $\leq$: for each n-place relation R and all points $p, q \in \mathcal{P}$, if $p \leq q$ then $\mathcal{I}^+(R, p) \subseteq \mathcal{I}^+(R, q)$ and $\mathcal{I}^-(R, p) \subseteq \mathcal{I}^-(R, q)$. A *complete point* is a point $p \in \mathcal{P}$ such that for each n-place relation R, $\mathcal{I}^+(R, p) \cup \mathcal{I}^-(R, p)$ is the set of all n-tuples of elements of $\mathcal{U}$. The appropriate precisification is that which is induced by $\mathcal{I}$ at the appropriate point, and complete precisifications are those induced by $\mathcal{I}$ at complete points. Finally, $\mathcal{I}$ assigns to each individual constant of $\mathcal{L}$ some element of $\mathcal{U}$.

Valuation at a complete point p is classical. For any assignment a of the individual variables of $\mathcal{L}$ into the domain of $\mathcal{M}$, and for any individual term t, let $[t]_{\mathcal{M},a}$ be $\mathcal{I}(t)$ if t is a constant, and $a(t)$ if t is a variable. If ϕ is an atomic formula $Rt_1, \ldots, t_n$, then $[\phi]_{\mathcal{M},p,a} = true$ if and only if $\langle[t_1]_{\mathcal{M},a}, \ldots, [t_n]_{\mathcal{M},a}\rangle \in \mathcal{I}_{\mathcal{M}}^+(R, p)$. Otherwise, $[\phi]_{\mathcal{M},p,a} = false$. Formulas composed with the classical connectives and quantifiers obtain truth values in accordance with the usual recursive clauses involving the classical truth functions.

At any point p that is not complete, the satisfaction value of a formula is supervaluational: $[\phi]_{M,p,a} = true\ [false]$ if and only if for all complete points $q \in \mathcal{P}$ such that $p \leq q$, $[\phi]_{M,q,a} = true\ [false]$. We say a sentence ϕ is *true in M at p*, relative to a, just in case $[\phi]_{M,p,a} = true$; ϕ is *false in M at p* just in case $[\phi]_{M,p,a} = false$; otherwise, ϕ is *undefined*. Finally, truth in a model goes by the appropriate precisification: a sentence ϕ is *true* [*false/undefined*] in $\mathcal{M}$ just in case ϕ is *true* [*false/undefined*] in $\mathcal{M}$ at @.

To complete the truth definitions we must still consider expressions of the form $I(\phi)$. The truth value of such an expression at a complete point is not a function of the value of ϕ at that point. To see why not, consider the informal meaning of this expression. Informally speaking, it is indeterminate whether ϕ if there is no fact of the matter that ϕ expresses, i.e., if on some ways of making ϕ precise this sentence is true, on others, it is false. Thus, "*It is indeterminate whether ϕ*" expresses a fact about the semantic incompleteness of the interpretation of ϕ. Accordingly, we let the value of $I(\phi)$ at any point p depend on the value of ϕ at the appropriate point: $[I(\phi)]_{M,p,a} = true$ if and only if $[\phi]_{M,@,a}$ is undefined; otherwise, $[I(\phi)]_{M,p,a} = false$.[4] Since truth is supertruth, $[I(\phi)]_{M,p,a} = true$ if and only if there are complete points q and r such that $[\phi]_{M,q,a} = true$ and $[\phi]_{M,r,a} = false$.

We will be interested only in *acceptable* models. A model M is acceptable if for all points p and q: (1) for each non-vague predicate or relation symbol R, $\mathcal{I}(R,p) = \mathcal{I}(R,q)$; and (2) $\mathcal{I}$ induces an admissible precisification at p. The first constraint ensures that the interpretation of non-vague language does not vary from point to point within a model. From the second follows the logical validity, the truth in every model, of the following *lexical truths*:

(i) $\forall x, y(\textit{at-least-as-fat-as}(x, y) \rightarrow (\textit{fat-pig}(y) \rightarrow \textit{fat-pig}(x)))$,
(ii) $\forall x, y(\textit{at-least-as-fat-as}(x, y) \rightarrow (\textit{skinny-pig}(x) \rightarrow \textit{skinny-pig}(y)))$,
(iii) $\forall x, y(\textit{at-least-as-fat-as}(x, y) \& \neg \textit{at-least-as-fat-as}(y, x) \leftrightarrow \textit{fatter}(x, y))$,
(iv) $\forall x, y(\textit{at-least-as-fat-as}(x, y) \vee \textit{at-least-as-fat-as}(y, x))$,
(v) $\forall x(\textit{skinny-pig}(x) \rightarrow \neg \textit{fat-pig}(x))$,
(vi) $\forall x(\textit{fat-pig}(x) \rightarrow \textit{pig}(x))$,
(vii) $\forall x(\textit{skinny-pig}(x) \rightarrow \textit{pig}(x))$.

Our models give rise to the notion of entailment in the standard way. A set of sentences Γ entails a sentence ϕ, written $\Gamma \models \phi$, if and only if ϕ is true in every acceptable model in which each member of Γ is true.

We can now extend the notion of vagueness from the simple expressions of $\mathcal{L}$ to sentences. A sentence ϕ is *vague* if and only if there are acceptable models M and N and points p in $\mathcal{P}_M$ and q in $\mathcal{P}_N$ such that (1) all non-vague symbols of $\mathcal{L}$ (including individual constants) have the same extensions in M at p as they do in N at q; and (2) it is not the case that $[\phi]_{M,p} = [\phi]_{N,q}$. Not all sentences with vague symbols are vague; no penumbral truth is, for instance. It can easily be shown, however, that containing vague symbols is a necessary condition for vagueness.

---

[4] For a more detailed discussion of the interpretation of "*It is indeterminate whether*" see (Fine, 1975), pp. 287-289 and (Williamson, 1994), pp. 149–153.

2. Conveyed Meanings

A speaker often conveys more than he has literally said. We use *conveyed meanings* as a general term for the conventional meanings, conversational implicatures, and presuppositions of an utterance.

Consider definite descriptions. When someone says a sentence with a definite description he will in many cases convey that something fits the description. That is why, if he is not sure whether there is a pig but is sure there is none in the pen, it is misleading for him to say "*The pig is not in the pen.*" Instead he ought to say "*The pig is not in the pen, if there is a pig.*" By saying the former sentence, but not by saying the latter, he conveys something he does not believe to be true. He conveys that there is a pig.

Our treatment of accommodation presupposes a theory of conveyed meanings, but we shall not assume any particular theory. Instead, allowing others to fill in the details, we will write '$Cnv(s, c)$' to indicate the set of conveyed meanings of an utterance of the English sentence s in a context c; here, c and $Cnv(s, c)$ are understood to be sets of sentences of $\mathcal{L}$. When we come to worked examples in Sect. 6 we shall introduce assumptions about the function Cnv, making claims that hold for all accounts of conveyed meanings satisfying these assumptions.[5]

The above example illustrates one of these assumptions, namely, that the conversational implicatures of utterances override the potential presuppositions triggered by definite descriptions. Saying "*The pig is not in the pen*" is in many contexts enough to convey that there is a pig, which is the presupposition triggered by the definite description "*the pig*". For many contexts c, then, we can assume:

$$\exists x\, pig(x) \in Cnv(\text{"}The\ pig\ is\ not\ in\ the\ pen\text{"}, c).$$

An analogous assumption is made in examples 1 and 2 of Sect. 6. But things are different if you say instead "*The pig is not in the pen, if there is a pig*". One conversational implicature of this utterance is that you are unsure whether there is a pig, and this implicature seems to override the potential presupposition that there is one; among others Gazdar(1979b) and Karttunen(1973) address this matter. An acceptable account of conveyed meanings, then, will require for many contexts c:

---

[5] Modulo representation language, partial accounts that fill the bill can be found in (Gazdar, 1979b) and in Kamp's Discourse Representation Theory (Kamp & Reyle, 1995), once the latter has been suitably elaborated to take presupposition into account.

$\exists x\, pig(x) \notin Cnv(\text{``}The\ pig\ is\ not\ in\ the\ pen,\ if\ there\ is\ a\ pig\text{''}, c)$.

An assumption of this kind is made in Ex. 3 of Sect. 6.

3. CONVEYED MEANINGS AND CONTEXT GROWTH

What is conveyed by an utterance will often become a part of the assumed common beliefs and suppositions. Unless there is reason to think the speaker is mistaken or lying, the conveyed meanings of his utterance can often simply be added to the context. For instance, when the speaker says, "*The pig is not in the pen*," the context might grow to include the conventional meaning of this sentence as well as other conveyed meanings, such as the presupposition that there is a pig. Let '$c + s$' denote the context brought about by uttering sentence s in c. Then, for some contexts and sentences, the following holds:

$$c + s = c \cup Cnv(s, c).$$

As we suggested earlier, the context does not, in general, grow in this simple way. Before discussing the details of our proposed account of $+$, we shall argue this point in more detail. Consider again the case of the veterinarian who is about to give a farmer's not-quite-fat pig a shot. The farmer assumes that prior to the veterinarian's utterance of "*We will begin with the fat pig*," the two share the belief that the rounder pig is borderline fat. Let this pig be called Arnold. This piece of assumed common knowledge is represented by the sentence $I(fat\text{-}pig(Arnold))$. Suppose, in addition, that the context includes sentences expressing that Arnold and Babe are the only two pigs, that Arnold is the fatter of the two, and that Babe is a skinny pig. Thus, c is comprised of the following sentences:

$$I\,(fat\text{-}pig(Arnold)),$$

$$\forall x(pig(x) \rightarrow x = Arnold \vee x = Babe),$$

$$fatter(Arnold, Babe),$$

$$skinny\text{-}pig(Babe).$$

In any satisfactory account of conveyed meanings, the veterinarian's utterance of "*We will begin with the fat pig*" will convey that there is a fat pig, rendered $\exists x\, fat\text{-}pig(x)$. Now, the simple view of context change would have it that $c + $ "*We will begin with the fat pig*" $= c \cup$

$Cnv("We\ will\ begin\ with\ the\ fat\ pig", c)$. But c and the conveyed meaning $\exists x\, fat\text{-}pig(x)$ together entail:

$$(fat\text{-}pig(Arnold) \vee fat\text{-}pig(Babe)),$$

$$skinny\text{-}pig(Babe),$$

$$I\,(fat\text{-}pig(Arnold)).$$

In light of the penumbral connection ensuring that skinny pigs are not fat pigs, these sentences are not jointly satisfiable. So the simple view does not do justice to the context change brought about by the veterinarian's utterance, which the farmer will not find contradictory.

It appears that the view that context change is simple context growth must make way for a view compatible with the fact that a vague predicate can change its sense from context to context. In the example above, the context following the veterinarian's utterance should reflect a new sense of *"fat pig"*, wherein the fatter animal is truthfully characterized as a fat pig. In the next section we propose an account of the context shifts required to accommodate new senses of vague expressions.

4. Conveyed Meanings and Context Shifts

We have seen in the previous section that we cannot always retain the context prior to an utterance in its entirety. We seem to retain as much of it as possible, though. Thus, to elaborate our example somewhat, accommodating the speaker by agreeing to call Arnold a fat pig will not lead the farmer to call into question unrelated common knowledge, such as that Babe's tail is curly. The change involved seems to be *minimal* change. These considerations lead us to the following recipe for accommodation:

Take what is conveyed by an utterance. Then add as much of the original context as you can without introducing an inconsistency.

Notice that the accommodation which concerns us here does not require changes in contexts because the world represented therein has changed. Just *calling* a pig fat does not make it any fatter. Changes are not required because a participant in the discourse was mistaken, either. Rather, changes are required because vague language has come to be used differently. This suggests that accommodation ought not to lead us to reject any sentence that describes the world in purely non-vague terms. When we make minimal changes to regain consistency, only vague sentences ought to be sacrificed.

We will give the notion of minimal change a *syntactic* explication: a minimal change to a set of sentences will be one in which no vague sentences are unnecessarily deleted from it. The above recipe then comes to this:

Take what is conveyed by an utterance. Add all of the non-vague sentences from the former context. Finally, add as many of the remaining vague sentences as you can without introducing an inconsistency.

To put this recipe precisely, the following definition is useful:

For any two sets A and S of sentences, $A \perp S$ is the set $\{T : S \subseteq T \subseteq A \cup S, T \nvdash \perp$, and for all U, if $T \subseteq U \subseteq A \cup S$ and $U \nvdash \perp$, then $U = T\}$.[6]

Let c_{vague} be the subset of c that includes just the vague sentences, so that $c \setminus c_{vague}$ is the subset of those sentences of c that are not vague. And consider any set $c*$ in $c_{vague} \perp (Cnv(s, c) \cup c \setminus c_{vague})$. We take $c*$ to have the following significance: it is one possible result of making minimal changes to c so as to accommodate the speaker's utterance of s. It can of course happen that there is more than one such $c*$. For this reason we introduce a selection function Sel, which selects one set from among a number of them. Sel will assume the task of choosing from among a number of alternatives the best way of updating the utterance context. Finally, then, our proposal for context change is this:

$$c + s = Sel(c_{vague} \perp (Cnv(s, c) \cup c \setminus c_{vague})).$$

About Sel we have very little to say. The factors that make one way of updating c better than another are not a topic that we can go into here (though in Sect. 7 we will suggest one factor that ought to be reflected in Sel). In the simple examples we will use to illustrate the proposal, $c_{vague} \perp (Cnv(s, c) \cup c \setminus c_{vague})$ will contain just a single element. This leaves Sel with no choice, and it leaves us able to proceed without saying anything more about this function.[7]

---

[6] Thi s notion is borrowed from work in belief revision. See (Alchourrón et al., 1985). Its application to context-updating is natural, given the similarity of the project: we describe what is accepted as common knowledge following the addition of conveyed meanings to what was previously accepted common knowledge.

[7] We define + in terms of conveyed meanings, as registered in the function Cnv. Our discussion might be thought incompatible with a 'dynamic' account

5. Examples

To illustrate the proposed model of contextual change, we will now analyze several variants of the example with which we began. In the first two, the speaker uses a vague definite description to refer to a salient object, even though none satisfies the description. This anomalous situation triggers a shift to a context in which something does satisfy it. In the new context, this object is denoted by the definite description.

Example 1: Suppose there are just two pigs: a borderline fat pig and a skinny pig with a curly tail. The context c contains just the following sentences:

1. $I(fat\text{-}pig(Arnold))$
2. $skinny\text{-}pig(Babe)$
3. $\exists x(tail(Babe,x)\&curly\text{-}tail(x))$
4. $\forall x(pig(x) \rightarrow x = Arnold \lor x = Babe)$
5. $fatter(Arnold,Babe)$

Now the veterinarian says s: "*We will begin with the fat pig.*"

    This utterance ought to give rise to a new context in which "fat pig" has been precisified to the point that just one of the pigs – it will be Arnold – satisfies this description. The definite description will then denote that pig. We show that the following sentences are entailed by $c + s$:

$fat\text{-}pig(Arnold)$, $\neg fat\text{-}pig(Babe)$.

Demonstration: It can easily be seen, using the definition of a vague sentence given in section 2, that $c \setminus c_{vague} = \{4, 5\}$. Assuming a reasonable account of conveyed meaning, $Cnv(s, c) \models \exists x\ fat\text{-}pig(x)$. In virtue of lexical truths (i), (iii), and (vi), $\{\exists x\ fat\text{-}pig(x) \cup c \setminus c_{vague} \models fat\text{-}$

---

of meaning, which presupposes a notion of context change. Such an account can, for example, be found in the earlier mentioned work on DRT. It might be thought that to define context change in terms of conveyed meanings, and these in terms of context change, is circular. As far as we know, however, our discussion is quite compatible with dynamic accounts of conveyed meaning. The update function + models just the context change required to accommodate the existential presuppositions of vague definite descriptions. There is no reason to think that a dynamic account of Cnv, such as that which can be given in terms of DRT, must presuppose this particular kind of context change.

pig(Arnold). But in any model in which Sent. 1 is true, *fat-pig(Arnold)* is undefined. Therefore, $Cnv(s,c) \cup c \setminus c_{vague} \cup \{1\}$ is not satisfiable. Assuming, as is again reasonable, that $Cnv(s,c) \cup c \setminus c_{vague} \cup \{2,3\}$ is satisfiable, it follows that there is a single maximal subset of c_{vague} that is consistent with $Cnv(s,c) \cup c \setminus c_{vague}$, namely $\{2,3\}$. Therefore, $c_{vague} \perp (Cnv(s,c) \cup c \setminus c_{vague})$ has just a single element: $Cnv(s,c) \cup \{2,3,4,5\}$. This is then the set selected by *Sel* as the new context $c + s$. Clearly, by the earlier observation, $c + s \models$ *fat-pig(Arnold)*. And, since *skinny-pig(Babe)* $\cdot \in c + s$, by lexical truth (v) we have $c + s \models \neg fat\text{-}pig(Babe)$.

This example illustrates two things in passing. First, uttering a vague definite description can lead to contextual shifting: it is clear that $c+s$ is not a superset of c. Second, the contextual shifting involves only minimal change. The updated context includes vague sentences that are a part of the original context and are unaffected by the accommodation, such as $\exists x\,(tail(Babe,x)\,\&\,curly\text{-}tail(x))$.[8] In the following variant of Ex. 1, Babe is borderline fat, like Arnold, but less fat than he is:

Example 2: The context c contains just the following sentences:

1. $I\,(fat\text{-}pig(Arnold))$
2. $I\,(fat\text{-}pig(Babe))$
3. $\forall x\,(pig(x) \to x = Arnold \ \lor x = Babe)$
4. $fatter(Arnold, Babe)$

Now the veterinarian says s: "*We will begin with the fat pig.*" The following sentences are entailed by $c+s$: *fat-pig(Arnold)*, $I\,(fat\text{-}pig(Babe))$.

Again, $c_{vague} \perp (Cnv(s,c) \cup c \setminus c_{vague}$ contains just a single element, which contains Sent. 2 but not Sent. 1. In overview, the reason for this is that consistency with the conveyed meanings cannot be obtained by sacrificing Sent. 2 while retaining Sent. 1 because of lexical truth (i). Calling Babe fat requires calling Arnold fat too.

---

[8] The intuitively correct outcome depends on the inclusion of Sent. 5 in the context c, even though this sentence is entailed by the rest of c. Consider a variant of Ex. 1 in which c contains only Sents. 1-4. On reasonable assumptions about what is conveyed when s is uttered, one possible update following the utterance of s is a context $c*$ that includes Sents. 1,3,4. Consistency is maintained by sacrificing Sent. 2. It can easily be shown that $c* \models fat\text{-}pig(Babe)$ and $c* \models I(fatpig(Arnold))$. This is result is intuitively incorrect.

The final example of this section illustrates again the role the theory of conveyed meaning plays in our model of context change. Here, as in the previous examples, the veterinarian utters a sentence with a vague definite description that is not satisfied by any salient object. This time, however, the utterance does not create an anomolous situation, since the conveyed meanings of the utterance are compatible with the utterance context. The result is simple contextual growth.

Example 3: Earlier in the week, the farmer had said that he would buy a second pig: a fat pig, if possible, but at any rate, one fatter than the one he already has. Suppose the veterinarian knows that Arnold, the pig he already owns, is borderline fat, and of the new pig, Babe, he knows only what the farmer had earlier implied, that she is fatter than Arnold. The context c contains just the following sentences:

1. $I\,(fat\text{-}pig(Arnold))$
2. $\forall x\,(pig(x) \rightarrow x = Arnold\ \lor x = Babe)$
3. $fatter(Babe, Arnold)$

Now, while the veterinarian is gathering materials to give the pigs shots, he says s: "*We will begin with the fat pig, if there is one.*" We show that $c + s \not\models \exists x\ fat\text{-}pig(x)$.

Demonstration: Clearly $c \setminus c_{vague} = \{2, 3\}$. Assuming an acceptable account of conveyed meanings, $Cnv(s, c) \cup c \setminus c_{vague} \cup \{1\}$ is satisfiable. This is so even though s contains a definite description, the presence of which in other sentences triggers the presupposition that there is a fat pig. This is because s also contains the qualification "*if there is one*", which, in any acceptable account of conveyed meanings, cancels that presupposition. Therefore, there is a single maximal subset of c_{vague} that is consistent with $Cnv(s, c) \cup c \setminus c_{vague}$, namely, c_{vague} itself. The set $c_{vague} \perp (Cnv(s, c) \cup c \setminus c_{vague})$ again has just a single element, $Cnv(s, c) \cup \{1, 2, 3\}$, which is the set selected by Sel as the new context $c + s$.

6. ELABORATIONS

In this section, we shall describe ways in which our account might be elaborated. We shall also consider an example that suggests that our model is *too* accommodating, allowing senses of vague expressions to change too much. We shall conclude with an informal proposal for a less accommodating model.

Earlier we defined the context change function + relative to a selection function, reflecting the fact that in many cases, of the different possible ways of accommodating a speaker, one is preferred. Further elaboration of our account is required to characterize this selection function. So far the examples have skirted this issue, since in each case there was just a single way to accommodate. The following example concerns a case where there are at least two ways. The discussion suggests a factor that can make one alternative preferable to another.

Example 4: The farmer and the veterinarian are standing some distance from a feeder. Arnold is directly between them and the feeder. Babe is also between them and the feeder but much closer to the feeder and a little off to one side. The veterinarian says, "*We will begin with the pig in front of the feeder*". Arnold understands that he is referring to Babe.

Let *in-front-of-the-feeder* be the representation in $\mathcal{L}$ of the embedded predicate "*in front of the feeder*". We assume that the positive extension of *in-front-of-the-feeder* includes everything within a cone extending from the feeder for some distance in the direction of the speakers, and that in the context prior to the utterance, no pigs are located in this region. The veterinarian's utterance requires a change in the positive extension of *in-front-of-the-feeder*: it must stretch to include a single pig. But it could stretch in two different dimensions. It could come to include the pig at a greater distance from the feeder, or the one at a wider angle. Correspondingly, there will be two candidates for the selection function *Sel* to choose between. The updated context could represent Arnold as being in front of the feeder, or Babe.

Now it seems that following the veterinarian's utterance, the context changes so that Babe, and not Arnold, is represented as being in front of the feeder. (If you wish, alter the relative positions of the pigs so that "*the pig in front of the feeder*" seems to denote Babe.) The positive extension of *in-front-of-the-feeder* comes to include the pig at a wider angle rather than the one at a further distance. Somehow the former involves a lesser stretch. The selection function must somehow be made sensitive to the fact that some stretches are greater than others.

We will now consider an example that suggests that our account is too permissive.

Example 5: Suppose that there are just two pigs, both simply obese.

Though this is scarcely possible, one is even more so than the other. The context c contains just the following sentences:

1. *fat-pig(Arnold)*
2. *fat-pig(Babe)*
3. $\forall x\,(pig(x) \rightarrow x = Arnold \;\vee\; x = Babe)$
4. *fatter(Arnold,Babe)*

Now, the veterinarian says s: "*We will begin with the skinny pig.*"

The treatment of this example is analogous to that of Exs. 1 and 2. Here $c + s$ entails *skinny-pig(Babe)* and *fat-pig(Arnold)*. Intuitively, this case seems quite different, though. The farmer will not take the veterinarian to be talking about one or the other of these pigs. He will be unable to accommodate since pigs *this* fat just cannot be called skinny.

This example suggests that our model needs to be modified so that it does more justice to the idea that accommodation involves making vague expressions more precise and, therefore, that it preserves determinacy. The modified model would require the senses of vague expressions in revised contexts to be at least as precise as they were in the unrevised contexts. A context that supports, say, *fat-pig(Babe)* would be revisable only in ways that preserved the support for this sentence.[9] This modification of the model would allow for accommodation in many of the same cases that the original model does. In Exs. 1 and 2, for instance, a borderline fat pig comes to be called a fat pig – the speakers precisify. In Ex. 5, however, where accommodation is difficult, the modified model would not permit accommodation.

We think that making vague expressions more precise is the preferred mode of accommodation, and that the model should be modified to reflect this. Nonetheless, there are context shifts that seem not to involve precisifying. The final example illustrates one such case.

Example 6: Suppose the farmer's barn is filled with pigs. They are all very fat, but only Arnold is obese. The veterinarian arrives to give the pigs shots. He says, "*We will begin with the fat pig.*"

In this case, the farmer may be able to accommodate by moving to a context in which the only pig in the barn that is called fat is Arnold.

---

[9] See Manfred Pinkal (1983) for an account of context updating along these lines.

This context shift does not reflect a precisification. Except for Arnold, none of the pigs called fat pigs in the earlier context are so called in the updated context. One explanation for the shift is that the utterance causes *"fat pig"* to become minimally *less* precise, thereby making true the conveyed meaning that there is only one salient fat pig. On this view, the proposed modification is unsatisfactory since it would not permit such a shift.

We think it is more plausible, however, that examples like this one require a different treatment. In addition to the fine adjustments that can be made to a context by precisifying, it may be necessary to make more radical adjustments to the senses of vague expressions, by changing to different comparison classes in the manner alluded to in Sect. 1. Similarly, our home handyman can in many cases get by with his one crescent wrench, but a really big nut or a really small one may require a wrench of a different size.

7. CONCLUSIONS

We have argued that discourse participants can stretch the senses of vague expressions to suit their referential needs. We have described the changes to participants' common knowledge that accompany such stretching. And we have illustrated our account by considering several simple examples.

Other examples that we have looked at point toward elaborations of our proposal. Most significantly, they point the way toward a less permissive model which requires that the senses of vague expressions in updated contexts are at least as precise as in prior contexts. We believe that with this adjustment our proposal will account for more of the context shifts that take place following vague utterances. The final example suggests, however, that ultimately it must be combined with a model of comparison-class change.

REFERENCES

Alchourrón, C., Gärdenfors, P., and Makinson, P. (1985) On the theory of logic change: partial meet functions for contraction and revision. *Journal of Symbolic Logic* 50, 510-30.

Beaver, D. (1997) Presupposition. In J. Van Benthem and A. ter Meulen (1997) *Handbook of Logic and Language* Amsterdam: Elsevier.

Fine K. (1975) Vagueness, truth, and logic. *Synthese* 30, 265–300.

Gärdenfors, P. (1988) *Knowledge in Flux.* Cambridge, MA: MIT Press.

Gazdar, G. (1979a) *Pragmatics: Implicature, Presupposition and Logical Form.* New York: Academic Press.

Gazdar, G. (1979b) A solution to the projection problem. In: C.-K. Oh and D. A. Dinneen(1979) *Syntax and Semantics II: Presupposition* New York: Academic Press, 57–89.

Grice, H. P. (1975) Logic and conversation. In: P. Cole and J. Morgan (1975) *Syntax and Semantics,* 41–58, New York: Academic Press.

Heim, I. (1983) On the projection problem for presuppositions. *Proceedings of the West Coast Conference on Formal Linguistics,* Volume 2, 114–126.

Kamp, J. A. W. (1975) Two theories about adjectives. In: E. Keenan (1975) *Formal Semantics of Natural Languages* Cambridge: Cambridge University Press.

Kamp, H. and Reyle, U. (1995) *From Discourse to Logic.* Dordrecht: Kluwer Academic Publishers.

Kamp, H. and Partee, B. (1995) Prototype theory and compositionality *Cognition* 57(2), 129 –191.

Karttunen, L. (1973) Presuppositions of compound sentences. *Linguistic Inquiry* 4, 169–93.

Karttunen, L. and Peters, S. (1979) Conventional implicature. *Syntax and Semantics* 11, 1 – 56.

Karttunen, L. and Peters, S., Requiem for presupposition. In: *Proceedings of the Third Annual Meeting of the Berkeley Linguistic Society,* 360–371.

Levinson, S. C. (1983) *Pragmatics.* Cambridge: Cambridge University Press.

Lewis, D. (1979) Scorekeeping in a language game. *The Journal of Philosophical Logic* (8) 339–359. Reprinted in D. Lewis (1983) *Philosophical Papers*: Volume I. New York: Oxford University Press.

Marr, D. (1982) *Vision: a Computational Investigation into the Human Representation and Processing of Visual Information.* San Francisco: W. H. Freeman.

Pinkal,M. (1983) On the limits of lexical meaning. In: R. Bauerle, C. Schwarze, and A. von Stechow *Meaning, Use and Interpretation* Berlin: de Gruyter.

Pinkal, M. (1995) *Logic and Lexicon.* Dordrecht: Kluwer Academic Publishers.

Sorenson, R. (1988) *Blindspots.* Oxford: Clarendon Press.

Williamson, T. (1994) *Vagueness.* London: Routledge.

ROBIN COOPER

USING SITUATIONS TO REASON ABOUT THE INTERPRETATION OF SPEECH EVENTS

1. INTRODUCTION

Situation semantics in its first incarnation in Barwise and Perry (1983) emphasized the importance of reasoning about the subtle interactions between speech events, various informational resources which may contribute contextual information and the content of an utterance. The idea is that the notion of situation in situation theory can be used not only to illuminate semantic notions of content but also grammatical and pragmatic aspects of speech events and context. In the implemented grammar based on situation theory that Massimo Poesio and I have been developing in connection with the FraCaS project,[1] we have attempted to blend this philosophy with the kind of compositionality mechanisms which are associated with Montague's semantics and which have become standard in many approaches to computational semantics. This chapter discusses some of the issues involved in achieving this interaction between compositionality and reasoning about speech events, contextual information resources and the content of utterances. We will discuss first the way in which the grammar we are developing handles the interaction using a fairly rich variety of situation theoretic objects. We will then sketch an alternative view that would off-load some of the richness of the situation-theoretic universe by exploiting a type-theoretic approach to records.

In order to introduce the basic techniques of the grammar, we will go through some of the details involved in the compositional semantics

---

[1] The implementation is called EKNTOOL because it implements a grammar using the version of situation theory proposed in connection with Extended Kamp Notation (EKN) proposed by Barwise and Cooper(1991, 1993). It was developed from an implementation of situation theoretic DRT (STDRT) developed for the DYANA project by Phil Kime and Julian Day (Day, 1993). A smaller version of the EKNTOOL grammar was incorporated in CLEARS (Cooper et al., 1996).

H. Bunt and R. Muskens (eds.), Computing Meaning, Volume 1, 167–184.

for the simple sentence *"Smith hired Jones"*. We will start with the lexical meanings associated with the words.

We will talk of meanings as having roles for objects that need to be filled in by context. These roles will be expressed in terms of λ-abstraction as we will see below. The meaning of a proper name in our grammar has three context roles: one for the discourse situation, one for the described object or referent of the proper name utterance and one for a resource situation associated with that particular utterance of the proper name. Of these three the referent role needs least explanation, although we will see that the referent is dependent on a linking between the utterance of the proper name and its context in a way that is not the case in, for example, classical Montague semantics. All meanings according to our grammar will have a role for a discourse situation and all the subconstituents of a given discourse will share the same role for a single discourse situation, that is, the discourse situation associated with all the subutterances of a discourse will be the same one. The discourse situation will among other things support facts relating utterance events to aspects of the semantic content. In the case of an utterance of the name *"Smith"* (and *mutatis mutandis "Jones"*) the meaning requires that the discourse situation supports information about what the referent of the utterance is and which resource situation it exploits, thus relating the three context roles. The resource situation of the proper name utterance of *"Smith"* must support the fact that the referent is named Smith in order for the proper name utterance to have content. It is possible for the same discourse (even the same sentence) to contain different utterances of the same proper name which have different referents. The resource situations which provide the naming information for these referents may be different as well. That is, each separate utterance of a proper name in a discourse is provided with a unique role for a resource situation. For example, one use of *"Smith"* may refer to 'Smith at the bank' (i.e. with a resource situation relating to the bank) and another use may refer to 'Smith at the office'. Of course, the fact that the different utterances are provided with unique roles does not rule out the possibility that the same resource situation may be assigned to two or more of the roles as will often be the case in practice.

One may think that having a certain name is such a general relation that we should not relativize it to situations. That is, one might claim that a use of *"Smith"* is appropriate for a given referent just in case the referent is named Smith *tout court*, rather than that the referent is named Smith in a given resource. The reason that we have chosen the resource situation option is that we want the semantics to be straightforwardly embeddable in systems that reason about communication. For example, it may be important for participants in a dialogue to share resource situations associated with given utterances (or at least to have sufficiently similar resource situations for the communication to be successful). It is not sufficient for successful communication that the referent of a proper name use simply be appropriately named. Both dialogue participants must in addition have access to the information in their limited information resources. By including a role for a resource situation in the meaning of proper name utterances, our grammar provides a hook onto which such reasoning can be hung.

How can we have this kind of detailed reasoning about the relationship between utterances, contents and various information resources provided by context and still maintain something like the standard compositional regime that was proposed by Montague? A key tool that we have used in our grammar is a more enriched version of λ-abstraction than was available in traditional Montague semantics. For a given utterance u of "*Smith*", the meaning according to our grammar is represented arammar is represented as in (1).

$$(1)\ \lambda[\ \text{ds} \to D,\ < \text{do},u > \to Y,\ < \text{exploits},u > \to R_1]$$
$$(\lambda[P]((P.[Y])\!\restriction \genfrac{}{}{0pt}{}{(D\models\text{ref}(u,Y)\wedge(D\models\text{exploits}(u,R_1))\,)}{\wedge\ (R_1\models\text{named}(Y,\ \text{``Smith''})\,)}\ )\ )) $$

We use a form of simultaneous abstraction. The basic idea is that we abstract simultaneously over a number of free parameters which we want to be filled in by context. Along with the simultaneous abstraction comes a method of indexing the parameters that are abstracted over. This means that substitution of arguments for the abstracted parameters is governed not by the order in which the arguments are presented but by the role indices with which they are associated. This kind of indexing associated with λ-expressions is familiar from programming languages like lisp but not so common in the logical or linguistic literature. Barwise and Cooper (1991, 1993) base their work on the notion of simultaneous abstraction developed by Aczel and Lunnon (Aczel and Lunnon, 1991; Lunnon, forthcoming) and present it in the context of situation theory. However, there are now other versions of simultaneous abstraction, notably that developed by Peter Ruhrberg (1996). We will not go into further technical detail about it here but just explain enough to follow our notation.

Parameters are represented by upper case letters such as D, Y, P, R_1 etc. The indexing or labelling of parameters which are abstracted over is indicated by an arrow going from the index to the parameter. Thus ds $\rightarrow$ D in an abstract indicates that the argument that is to be supplied for D will play the role 'ds' ('discourse situation'). We will say more about why we chose certain role indices to be complex (e.g. < do, u >) below. When no role indices are indicated in an abstract (e.g. $\lambda[P]((P.[Y])))$ it is assumed that the role indices default to the natural numbers beginning with 1.

The basic format for a meaning is given in (2).

(2) $\lambda[context\ roles](content)$

This follows the Montague-Kaplan view that a meaning is applied to a context (modelled as an assignment to the roles of an abstract in our system) to obtain a content (corresponding to what Montague would call an intension). The use of simultaneous abstraction allows meanings for different phrases to have different numbers of context roles and indeed for the same phrase to be ambiguous with respect to the number of roles which depend on context, without this involving a difference in the number of levels of abstraction. That is, it enables us to gather all the context roles together 'in one bag' while still using different levels of abstraction within the same object for the 'compositional abstracts in the style of Montague. Thus the parametric object corresponding to the content in example (2) is itself an abstract in the style of Montague's treatment of proper names, shown in (3).

(3) $\lambda[P]((P.[Y])) \upharpoonright \begin{array}{l} (D \models \text{ref}(u, Y)\ ) \wedge (D \models \text{exploits}(u, R_1)\ ) \\ \wedge\ (R_1 \models \text{named}(Y,\ \text{``Smith''})\ ) \end{array}$)

Within this one can recognize a variant of the familiar Montague generalized quantifier treatment of proper names, i.e. (4).

(4) $\lambda[P](P.[Y])$

The additional material has to do with the fact that the situation semantic treatment of proper names is an indexical one, that is Y represents an individual parameter rather than a particular individual and the remaining material in (3) presents restrictions on what kind of individual can be assigned to Y.

We are exploiting simultaneous abstraction here to distinguish the context roles from the content roles. As is well-known, the Montague-style content may involve more than one level of abstraction as in the treatment of transitive verbs where there is first abstraction over the object and then over the subject.[2] It is both formally and computationally convenient to have all the context roles collected together in the topmost level of abstraction so that they are clearly distinguished from the content roles represented by abstractions embedded beneath them. Also the use of simultaneous abstraction means that there is no presumption about the order in which context role arguments should be provided.

Why do we want to use abstraction rather than leave the context parameters free and use abstraction just for the representation of the compositional content? One reason is that for the purposes of defining compositional semantics it is useful to gather the context roles together in one place and give them labels which identify them, e.g. 'resource situation of utterance u. Sometimes context roles can optionally be bound by existential quantification at the topmost level of an utterance or even within the content of a subconstituent of an utterance, for example within the scope of negation or a verb of propositional attitude. λ-abstraction gives us a convenient tool for giving general statements of these subtleties whereas arbitrary free parameters are difficult to identify in general rules. In implementation terms, it is hard to imagine an efficient implementation using free parameters for context which did not keep a list of the free parameters around as part of the general bookkeeping. Using abstraction means that the theory does the necessary bookkeeping and therefore specifies the implementation more precisely. (The nature of the bookkeeping is not left up to the implementor.) This argument might be seen as similar to an argument for using λ-abstraction for compositional semantics as opposed to passing around free prolog variables as in the classical programs using DCGs to construct predicate calculus representations of content.

Now let us look at the details of the context roles. The index on the discourse situation role is simply ds rather than an ordered pair such as $<ds,u>$. Making it simple is a technical device that will ensure that all constituents of the sentence will share the same discourse situation role, that is there will be only one discourse situation which is associated with all the subutterances of the utterances. The other two context roles, indexed by $< do,u >$ 'described object of utterance u and $< exploits,u >$, 'resource situation exploited by utterance u are on the other hand relativized to the particular utterance u of *"Smith"*.

---

[2] Actually, in free word order languages this layering can be a disadvantage and one could exploit simultaneous abstraction with role indexing so that there is no prescription of the order in which arguments should be supplied.

This ensures that the roles are not merged with similar roles for other constituents.

We wish to express restrictions to the effect that utterances only receive content when certain conditions are met. For example, an utterance of the sentence *"Smith hired Jones"* only makes sense in a context where the utterance of *"Smith"* refers to somebody named Smith and the utterance of *"Jones"* refers to somebody named Jones.[3] If these conditions are not met, the sentence is not simply perceived as false. Rather some failure in communication is perceived which is in need of repair. Thus these restrictions behave like a species of what has been called presupposition in the linguistic literature. The version of restrictions that we use is that proposed by Barwise and Cooper (1991, 1993). Any object may be restricted by a proposition. If the proposition is true then the restricted object is identical with the unrestricted object. If the proposition is false, the restricted object is undefined (that is, the restriction operation is only defined when the proposition is true). If the restricting proposition is parametric then the result of restricting an object with it is a new object which restricts the parameters in the restricting proposition, i.e. the only anchors which will yield a defined object from the restricted objects are those that satisfy the restricting proposition. Thus we have the restricted parametric object (1a) rather than simply (1b), repeating examples (3) and (4), respectively. Under an assignment to the parameters this becomes the content of an utterance of *"Smith"*.

(5) a. $\lambda[P]((P.[Y])\upharpoonright \begin{array}{l}(D\models\text{ref}(u,Y)\,)\wedge(D\models\text{exploits}(u,R_1)\,)\\ \wedge\,(R_1\models\text{named}(Y,\ \text{"Smith"})\,)\end{array})$

   b. $\lambda[P](P.[Y])$

This indicates that the content will only be defined if the discourse situation D supports the fact that Y is the referent of u and that R_1 is the resource situation exploited by u and furthermore that the resource situation R_1 supports the fact that Y is named Smith. (The reader may notice that the information expressed about the discourse situation appears to duplicate that expressed by the role indices on the abstract for the complete meaning in (1). We will return to this below.)

The meaning for *"hired"* also has three context roles in our grammar. As usual there is a role for the discourse situation with the index *ds*.

---

[3] Or to be more precise, dialogue participants have access to a shared resource situation in which they are appropriately named.

In addition there are two roles for times: one for the utterance time of the verb and one for event time, that is, the time at which the relation corresponding to the verb is asserted to hold of its arguments. The utterance time is taken to be the interval during which the verb is uttered. Normally, semantic theories take utterance time to be the time of the utterance of the sentence (or even discourse) thus idealizing away from the fact that utterances are events that happen in real time. For the most part such an idealization is harmless. However, I believe there to be examples in real speech where the fact that time progresses during the utterance becomes relevant to the interpretation of a single sentence as in (6).

(6) He kicks the ball and he kicked it straight into the goal

Relating the event time to the utterance time of the verb rather than the sentence of discourse would allow us to treat such examples.

Since the verb *"hired"* is in the past tense, we require that the event time is earlier than the utterance time. The 'earlier-than' relation on times is treated as a situation-theoretic type, that is something that holds between two times (intervals) *tout court* and does not need to be situated. The content of a transitive verb is treated in our grammar as a relation between individuals, curried in the standard Montague fashion. If u is an utterance of *"hired"*, then its meaning is given in (7).

$$(7) \quad \lambda[\, ds \to D, \; < \text{utt-time},u > \; \to T_{utt}, \; < \text{ev-time},u > \; \to T_{ev}]$$
$$(D \models \text{utt-time}(u, T_{utt})\,)$$
$$(\, \lambda[Y](\lambda[X](\text{hire}(X,Y,T_{ev})\restriction \wedge (D \models \text{ev-time}(u,T_{ev})\,)\;)))$$
$$\wedge \; T_{ev} < T_{utt}$$

The general strategy for composing meanings compositionally to find the meanings of larger constituents in our grammar can be described intuitively as follows. Suppose that we have two meanings represented schematically as in (8).

(8) a. $\lambda[\, \rho_1 \to X_1, \; \rho_2 \to X_2](c_1(X_1, X_2))$

   b. $\lambda[\, \rho_1 \to Y_1, \; \rho_3 \to Y_2](c_2(Y_1, Y_2))$

That is, we have two meanings which share a role index (ρ_1) and each have a role index which is not shared by the other (ρ_2 and ρ_3). The respective representations of the contents associated with the two meanings (c_1 and c_2) contain the parameters that have been abstracted over in the respective meanings (X_1, X_2 and Y_1, Y_2, respectively). Suppose that the relevant operation for combining the two contents is g. That is, we would represent the combined content as $g(c_1, c_2)$. In many cases, as in Montague's semantics, g would be application, which in our notation would be represented as $c_1.[c_2]$. However, as in Montague's semantics, it will not always be straightforward application. The intuition is that we want whatever semantic operation is used to combine the contents to be applied inside the abstraction over the context roles and the context roles to be gathered together as the topmost abstraction in the resulting meaning. Where a role is shared by the two constituents, like ρ_1 in this example, this should result in one role in the combined meaning. (The fact that ρ_1 is associated with different parameters in the representation of the two meanings should not hinder this falling together. The variant of λ-abstraction we use, like standard λ-abstraction, has α-equivalence, i.e. relettering of bound parameters does not result in a different object, given the standard restrictions avoiding the accidental capture of other parameters.) Thus the combined meaning resulting from (8a) and (8b) should have three context roles and be as shown in (9).

(9) $\lambda[\ \rho_1 \to X_1,\ \ \rho_2 \to X_2,\ \ \rho_3 \to X_3]$
$\quad (g(c_1(X_1, X_2), c_2(X_1, X_3)))$

We achieve this by a straightforward manipulation in the kind of λ-calculus we are using. Since we are using simultaneous λ-abstraction with indexing of roles, we do not supply single arguments to an abstract, but rather an assignment of arguments to the roles of the abstract. Thus application looks like the example in (10a) which by β-conversion is equivalent to (10b) in more or less the standard way.

(10) a. $\lambda[\ \rho_1 \to X_1,\ \ \rho_2 \to X_2](c(X_1, X_2))$
$\quad\quad\quad .[\ \rho_1 \to a,\ \ \rho_2 \to b]$

   b. $c(a, b)$

In our version of application we allow application when assignments are overdefined, that is (11a) is also equivalent to (11b).

(11) a. $\lambda[\ \rho_1 \to X_1,\ \ \rho_2 \to X_2](c(X_1, X_2))$
$\quad\quad\quad .[\ \rho_1 \to a,\ \ \rho_2 \to b,\ \ \rho_3 \to d]$

   b. $c(a, b)$

This means that if we have two abstracts with different or partially overlapping sets of roles we can find assignments that are appropriate to both abstracts. For example, the assignment (12c) is a appropriate to both (12a) and (12b).

(12) a. $\lambda[\, \rho_1 \to X_1, \ \rho_2 \to X_2](c_1(X_1, X_2))$

b. $\lambda[\, \rho_1 \to Y_1, \ \rho_3 \to Y_2](c_2(Y_1, Y_2))$

c. $[\, \rho_1 \to a, \ \rho_2 \to b, \ \rho_3 \to d]$

(12c) is a *minimal assignment* which is appropriate for both (12a) and (12b), that is, it is defined on precisely the union of the sets of roles for the two abstracts. If a minimal assignment for a set of abstracts provides a unique parameter for each role which does not occur in any of the abstracts we call it a *minimal index assignment* for those abstracts. The way, then, to achieve the combination of meanings where context roles percolate to the top is by applying each of the meanings to an appropriate minimal index assignment first, then do whatever content combination is required and finally use the minimal index assignment to form a new abstract. The result of this for our example is shown in (13a) which is equivalent by β-conversion to (13b).

(13) a. $\lambda[\, \rho_1 \to Z_1, \ \rho_2 \to Z_2, \ \rho_3 \to Z_3]$
$(g(\lambda[\, \rho_1 \to X_1, \ \rho_2 \to X_2](c_1(X_1, X_2))$
$\cdot[\, \rho_1 \to Z_1, \ \rho_2 \to Z_2, \ \rho_3 \to Z_3],$
$\lambda[\, \rho_1 \to Y_1, \ \rho_3 \to Y_2](c_2(Y_1, Y_2))$
$\cdot[\, \rho_1 \to Z_1, \ \rho_2 \to Z_2, \ \rho_3 \to Z_3]))$

b. $\lambda[\, \rho_1 \to Z_1, \ \rho_2 \to Z_2, \ \rho_3 \to Z_3]$
$(g(c_1(Z_1, Z_2), c_2(Z_1, Z_3)))$

By using this technique and standard combinations from Montague semantics adapted to take care of restrictions we obtain (13) for the maning of the sentence *"Smith hired Jones"*.

The adaptation to take care of restrictions involves setting up the situation theory in such a way that it will be ensured that retrictions will percolate up from their origin to the highest possible level. That is, as constituents are combined, restrictions associated with the constituents will become restrictions associated with the larger constitent to the extent that this does not involve passing beyond a λ-abstract. λ is the only operation that binds parameters. This percolation is achieved within the situation theory by having the restriction operation distribute over all operations which combine situation-theoretic objects except λ. This treatment is, however, not unproblematic as we will see below.

(14) $\lambda[\text{ds} \rightarrow D,$
$\qquad <\text{do},u_1 > \rightarrow X_1,$
$\qquad < \text{utt-time},u_2 > \rightarrow T_{utt},$
$\qquad < \text{ev-time},u_2 > \rightarrow T_{ev},$
$\qquad <\text{do},u_3 > \rightarrow X_3,$
$\qquad <\text{exploits},u_1 > \rightarrow R_1,$
$\qquad <\text{exploits},u_3 > \rightarrow R_3]$

$$\begin{aligned}
& (D\models\text{ref}(u_1, X_1)) \\
& \wedge\ (D\models\text{exploits}(u_1, R_1)) \\
& \wedge\ (D\models\text{utt-time}(u_2, T_{utt})) \\
& \wedge\ (D\models\text{ev-time}(u_2, T_{ev})) \\
(\text{hire}(X_1, X_2, T_{ev})\restriction\ & \wedge\ (D\models\text{ref}(u_3, X_3)) \qquad\qquad) \\
& \wedge\ (D\models\text{exploits}(u_3, R_3)) \\
& \wedge\ (R_1\models\text{named}(X_1, \text{``}Smith\text{''})) \\
& \wedge\ (R_3\models\text{named}(X_3, \text{``}Jones\text{''})) \\
& \wedge\ T_{ev} < T_{utt}
\end{aligned}$$

2. Two Problems

Getting the details of the treatment of restrictions to work is complicated. Barwise and Cooper (1991, 1993) go part way in spelling out what needs to be done. To date, nobody has been successful in defining a complete model which covers both the structured nature of the objects, the notions of parameters and anchors and the notion of restricted object which is intertwined of the notion of truth for propositions. Ruhrberg (1996) has a model of part of the system in terms of property theory and domain theory, although he allows only propositions to be restricted. At the same time, nobody to date has shown that it is not possible to construct a model for the system as it has been defined. Here we will concentrate on two specific problems that arose in the development of our grammar.

2.1. *The Division of Labour between Role Labels and Restrictions*

We noted briefly above that there seems to be a duplication of information in the role-indices of the grammar and the restrictions. The role indices are important for book-keeping so that we know what context roles are being reasoned about, e.g. resource situation of utterance u or described object of utterance v. However, the role indices are essentially arbitrary symbols. They do not, of themselves, require the truth of any particular proposition, e.g. a proposition that requires that some situation r actually is the resource situation of utterance u. We need the restrictions in order to be able to express this. This leaves an uneasy feeling that there should be some way of expressing the information just once and have it serve both the purposes of reasoning and book-keeping.

2.2. *Computing β-reduction when Restrictions are Present*

The only operation over which restriction does not distribute is the binding operation of abstraction since parameters in restrictions are bound by this operation. By rights we should have an axiom which allows distribution of restrictions in this case as well, when the restrictions do not contain parameters that are bound in the abstraction. This is expressed in (15).

(15) If γ contains no free parameters in the range of β,
   then $\lambda\beta(\alpha \restriction \gamma) \equiv \lambda\beta(\alpha) \restriction \gamma$

However, this axiom is currently ignored in our implemented systems because it makes reductions to canonical representations by β-reduction and distribution of restrictions difficult to handle. The problems arise when you have a restriction within an abstract of the form $p(X) \wedge q(Y)$ where, say, X is bound within the abstract but not Y. Intuitively, $q(Y)$ should percolate up and become a restriction external to the abstract whereas $p(X)$ with X bound within the abstract should remain internal to the abstract. However, following (15) the presence of the bound X would mean that no distribution would occur.

3. AN ALTERNATIVE APPROACH USING RECORDS AND DEPENDENT RECORD TYPES

The ideas sketched in this section take as their starting point the work of Betarte and Tasistro (forthcoming) which develops within Martin-Löf type theory a notion of record and dependent record type which provides mathematical objects corresponding to contexts in the sense of Martin-Löf type theory. Records are sequences of fields, i.e. pairs of labels and values. Values can themselves be records. In (16) are two examples of records in the notation that we shall use.

(16) a. $\begin{bmatrix} \text{phon} & = & \text{"Smith"} \\ \text{cat} & = & \text{np} \end{bmatrix}$

b. $\begin{bmatrix} \text{rel} & = & \text{hire} \\ \text{args} & = & \begin{bmatrix} \text{hirer} & = & a \\ \text{hired} & = & b \\ \text{ev-time} & = & t \end{bmatrix} \\ \text{pol} & = & 1 \end{bmatrix}$

These, of course, look very similar to the kind of feature structures that are used in HPSG, for example. One important difference is that these records are ordered, i.e. they are a sequence of fields (read from top to bottom in our representation). Record types in the formulation of Betarte and Tasistro (1998) are sequences of pairs of labels and the types to which the value belongs. Assuming some rather obvious names of types for the sake of illustration here the records in (16) could be said to be of the types in (17).

(17) a. $\begin{bmatrix} \text{phon} & : & \text{Word} \\ \text{cat} & : & \text{LexCat} \end{bmatrix}$

b. $\begin{bmatrix} \text{rel} & : & \text{Rel} \\ \text{args} & : & \begin{bmatrix} \text{hirer} & : & \text{Ind} \\ \text{hired} & : & \text{Ind} \\ \text{ev-time} & : & \text{Time} \end{bmatrix} \\ \text{pol} & : & \text{Bool} \end{bmatrix}$

Of course, these types also look like the kind of typed feature-structures which are found in HPSG. One important aspect of the Martin-Löf approach is that the formalism allows you to talk about both types and objects belonging to types. An important aspect of the treatment of record types by Betarte and Tasistro (1998) is that a record with additional fields not mentioned in the type will still be of that type. Thus, for example, (18) is also a record of type (17).

$$(18) \quad \begin{bmatrix} \text{rel} & = & \text{hire} \\ \text{args} & = & \begin{bmatrix} \text{hirer} & = & a \\ \text{hired} & = & b \\ \text{salary} & = & 100\text{Kecu} \\ \text{ev-time} & = & t \end{bmatrix} \\ \text{pol} & = & 1 \end{bmatrix}$$

To this I want to introduce the idea that records can classify other objects. This is not something that is present in Betarte and Tasistro (1998), although it can be seen perhaps as a distant relation of the view of propositions as types in Martin-Löf type theory and also the idea of classification introduced by Seligman (1990) and Barwise and Seligman (1997) where objects can be used to classify other objects. The idea is based on the intuitive notion that records give us a way of classifying objects. For example, (17a) is a record which might be regarded as classifying any situation which is an event of uttering the word *"Smith"*. Similarly, the record (17b) can be regarded as classifying situations in which a hires b at time t. I will use this classification relation in the construction of record types. Thus records as well as record types may appear to the right of the colon in record types. To save space and improve readability I will use the traditional situation theoretic notation for infons to abbreviate records corresponding to infons,[4] as in (19).

$$(19) \quad \text{a.} \quad \begin{bmatrix} \text{rel} & = & \text{hire} \\ \text{args} & = & \begin{bmatrix} \text{hirer} & = & a \\ \text{hired} & = & b \\ \text{ev-time} & = & t \end{bmatrix} \\ \text{pol} & = & 1 \end{bmatrix}$$

b. $\langle\!\langle \text{hire}, a, b, t \rangle\!\rangle$

An example of a record type which exploits the classify relation would be (20).

(20) $[\ \text{desc-sit} \quad : \quad \langle\!\langle \text{hire}, a, b, t \rangle\!\rangle\ ]$

The record (21) would be of this type just in case $\langle\!\langle \text{hire}, a, b, t \rangle\!\rangle$ classifies s.

---

[4] My idea is that all the structured objects found in situation theoretic domains should now be regarded as records, so the record actually is the infon.

(21) $[\ \text{desc-sit}\ =\ s\ ]$

Record types with such classifiers can be dependent. That is the representation of the classifying record can contain labels which occur previously in the record type or even references to other records. If r is a record and l is a label in r then we will use $r.l$ to represent the value in the field headed by l in r. An example of such a dependent record type is in (22), where the labels *ref* and *res* can be read as 'referent' and 'resource situation' respectively.

(22) $\left[\begin{array}{lll} \text{ref} & : & \text{Ind} \\ \text{res} & : & \langle\!\langle \text{named,ref, } \textit{``Smith''}\rangle\!\rangle \end{array}\right]$

(23) would be of this type just in case a is of type *Ind*, i.e. an individual, and s is classified by $\langle\!\langle\text{named},a,\ \textit{``Smith''}\rangle\!\rangle$, i.e. a situation which supports this infon.

(23) $\left[\begin{array}{lll} \text{ref} & = & a \\ \text{res} & = & s \end{array}\right]$

Here we see a record serving as an assignment to context roles and the dependent record type as providing a dynamic way of characterizing such contexts.

We will use functions from records to records to characterize meanings and contents, actually considering such functions as a kind of record. A simple example of such a function would be (1a) which is of the type (1b).

(24) a. $\lambda r{:}\left[\begin{array}{lll} \text{ref} & : & \text{Ind} \\ \text{res} & : & \langle\!\langle\text{named,ref, } \textit{``Smith''}\rangle\!\rangle \end{array}\right]$ $\left(\left[\begin{array}{lll} \text{phon} & = & \textit{``Smith''} \\ \text{cat} & = & \text{np} \\ \text{cont} & = & r.\text{ref} \end{array}\right]\right)$

b. $\left(\left[\begin{array}{lll} \text{ref} & : & \text{Ind} \\ \text{res} & : & \langle\!\langle\text{named,ref, } \textit{``Smith''}\rangle\!\rangle \end{array}\right]\right)$ $\left[\begin{array}{lll} \text{phon} & : & \text{Word} \\ \text{cat} & : & \text{LexCat} \\ \text{cont} & : & \text{Ind} \end{array}\right]$

Here now is a proposal for using this machinery to represent the meaning of *"Smith"* corresponding to example (1). If u is an utterance event classified by $[\ \text{phon}\ =\ \textit{``Smith''}\ ]$ then $[\![\ u\ ]\!]$, the meaning of u, is (1).

$$(25) \ \lambda r: \begin{bmatrix} u & : & \begin{bmatrix} \text{ref} & : & \text{Ind} \\ \text{res} & : & \langle\!\langle \text{named,ref, ``Smith''} \rangle\!\rangle \end{bmatrix} \end{bmatrix}$$

$$\left(\begin{bmatrix} u & = & \begin{bmatrix} \text{phon} & = & \text{``Smith''} \\ \text{cat} & = & \text{np} \\ \text{cont} & = & \lambda r_1 : [\ 1 \ : \ \text{Property}\ ] \\ & & (r_1.1([\ 1 \ = \ r.u.\text{ref}\ ])) \end{bmatrix} \end{bmatrix} \right)$$

Here we take *Property* to represent the type in (26)

$$(26)\ ([\ 1 \ = \ \text{Ind}\ ])\text{Infon}$$

i.e. the type of functions from records with a label '1' (for 'first argument') associated with an individual as value to infons.[5]

If u is an utterance of the word *"hired"*, i.e. u is a situation classified by $[\ \text{phon} \ = \ \text{``hired''}\ ]$ then $[\![\ u\ ]\!]$ is (1).

$$(27) \ \lambda r: \begin{bmatrix} u & : & \begin{bmatrix} \text{utt-time} & : & \text{Time} \\ \text{ev-time} & : & \text{Time} \\ \text{restr} & : & \text{ev-time} < \text{utt-time} \end{bmatrix} \end{bmatrix}$$

$$\left(\begin{bmatrix} u & = & \begin{bmatrix} \text{phon} & = & \text{``hired''} \\ \text{cat} & = & \text{tv} \\ \text{cont} & = & \lambda r_1 : [\ 1 \ : \ \text{Ind}\ ] \\ & & (\lambda r_2 : [\ 1 \ : \ \text{Ind}\ ] \\ & & (\langle\!\langle \text{hire}, r_2.1, r_1.1, r.u.\text{ev-time} \rangle\!\rangle)) \end{bmatrix} \end{bmatrix} \right)$$

The field $[\ \text{restr} \ : \ \text{ev-time} < \text{utt-time}\ ]$ needs some explanation. We take *ev-time < utt-time* to be an abbreviation for a record which, under appropriate substitution for 'ev-time' and 'utt-time', is a situation theoretic proposition using the situation theoretic type '$<$'. We will let propositions classify an element 'true' if they are true. Otherwise, they do not classify anything. The label *restr* corresponds to 'restriction'. Thus a record in the domain of the function in (27) would be one of the form (28a) where its being of the type (28b) guarantees that t_2 is earlier than t_1.

$$(28)\ \text{a.} \ \begin{bmatrix} u & = & \begin{bmatrix} \text{utt-time} & = & t_1 \\ \text{ev-time} & = & t_2 \\ \text{restr} & = & \text{true} \end{bmatrix} \end{bmatrix}$$

---

[5] We have given examples of infons but have not characterized the type precisely as that involves some complications not relevant to the present chapter.

$$\text{b.} \begin{bmatrix} u & : & \begin{bmatrix} \text{utt-time} & : & \text{Time} \\ \text{ev-time} & : & \text{Time} \\ \text{restr} & : & \text{ev-time} < \text{utt-time} \end{bmatrix} \end{bmatrix}$$

We now take a brief look at how compositional semantics might go on such an approach. Suppose that 'NP' and 'VP'are the types of any record containing the field $[\ \text{cat}\ =\ \text{np}\ ]$ and $[\ \text{cat}\ =\ \text{vp}\ ]$ respectively. Suppose further that we have a way of characterizing what it means for two utterance events, u_1 followed by u_2, to be assembled into a single larger utterance event, u_3, represented by $u_3 = u_1{}^{\sqcap}u_2$. In order to do compositional semantics we need a way of dependently conjoining two record types ρ_1 and ρ_2. We will represent the dependent conjunction as $\rho_1 \oplus \rho_2$. This conjunction is introduced as follows, using the notation $\rho[r]$ to represent the result of substituting, for any label l in r, the value $r.l$ for any occurrence of l in ρ.

(29) If ρ_1 is a record type
     and $\rho_2[r]$ is a record type for any $r : \rho_1$,
     then $\rho_1 \oplus \rho_2$ is a record type.

If $r : \rho_1$ and $r : \rho_2[r]$, then $r : \rho_1 \oplus \rho_2$.

This dependent conjunction is, of course, a relative of dynamic conjunction in dynamic semantics.

In (1) we give a simple inference rule for concluding that appropriately related NP and VP utterances constitute a sentence utterance.[6]

(30)
$$\frac{\begin{array}{l} [\![\, u_1 \,]\!] : (\rho_1) \begin{bmatrix} u_1 & : & \text{NP} \\ \end{bmatrix} \\ [\![\, u_2 \,]\!] : (\rho_2) \begin{bmatrix} u_2 & : & \text{VP} \end{bmatrix} \\ u_3 = u_1{}^{\sqcap}u_2 \end{array}}{[\![\, u_3 \,]\!] = m}$$

where m is $\lambda r : \rho_1 \oplus \rho_2$

$$\left(\begin{bmatrix} u_3 = \begin{bmatrix} \text{phon} & = & [\![\, u_1 \,]\!](r).u_1.\text{phon}{}^{\frown}[\![\, u_2 \,]\!](r).u_2.\text{phon} \\ \text{cat} & = & \text{s} \\ \text{cont} & = & [\![\, u_1 \,]\!](r).u_1.\text{cont} \\ & ([\,1 & = & [\![\, u_2 \,]\!](r).u_2.\text{cont}\,]) \end{bmatrix} \end{bmatrix} \right)$$

---

[6] The symbol '$\frown$' is used to represent the 'concatenation' of the two phonologies.

4. Conclusions

It seems to me that there are a number of potential advantages for using records and dependent record types in the situation theoretic approach to grammar:

— It relieves the situation theory of restricted objects which have always been regarded with some suspicion if not outright confusion.

— It replaces simultaneous abstraction with unary abstraction over records which is perhaps easier to understand.

— It seems possible to claim that all the structured semantic objects we need can be regarded as some kind of record. Thus records would provide a uniform way of structuring semantic objects which bears a family resemblence to the use of feature structures for other aspects of linguistic structure.

— Dependent record types are inherently dynamic and records can play a role similar to variable assignments. This potentially points to a pleasing relationship with dynamic semantics.

— The use of types, the separation between types and objects and the original proof-theoretic conception of dependent record types suggests the possibility of linking to various type-theoretical and type-logical approaches to grammar.

ACKNOWLEDGEMENTS

I am grateful to Massimo Poesio for the joint work on the FraCaS situation theoretic grammar which is reported on in this chapter. I am grateful to Bengt Nordström, Gustavo Betarte and other members of the type theory group at Gothenburg for discussion of dependent record types, although they are in no way responsible for what I have done (or failed to do) with them. Work on this chapter has been supported in part by FraCaS (EC project LRE 62-051) and S-DIME (NUTEK/HSFR Language Technology project F305/97).

REFERENCES

Aczel, P., D. Israel, Y. Katagiri and S. Peters (eds.) (1993) *Situation Theory and its Applications, Volume 3*, CSLI, Stanford.

Aczel, P. and R. Lunnon (1991) Universes and Parameters, in Barwise et al., eds, (1991).

Barwise, J. and R. Cooper (1991) Simple Situation Theory and its Graphical Representation, Indiana University Logic Group Preprint No. IULG-91-8 and in Seligman (1991)

Barwise, J. and R. Cooper (1993) Extended Kamp Notation: a Graphical Notation for Situation Theory, in Aczel, Israel, Katagiri and Peters (1993), 29–54.

Barwise, J., M. Gawron, G. Plotkin and S. Tutiya, eds, (1991) *Situation Theory and its Applications, Vol. 2* , CSLI Publications.

Barwise, J. and J. Perry (1983) *Situations and Attitudes*, MIT Press.

Barwise, J. and J. Seligman (1997) *Information Flow: the Logic of Distributed Systems*, Cambridge Tracts in Theoretical Computer Science, 44, Cambridge University Press.

Betarte, G. and A. Tasistro (1998) Extension of Martin-Löf's type theory with record types and subtyping. *Proceedings of the conference '25 Years of Constructive Type Theory'*, Oxford University Press.

Cooper, R., ed. (1993) *Integrating Semantic Theories*, DYANA-2 report R2.1.A, ILLC/Department of Philosophy, University of Amsterdam, http://www.fwi.uva.nl/research/illc/dyana/Home.html.

Cooper, R., R. Crouch, J. van Eijck, C. Fox, J. van Genabith, J. Jaspars, H. Kamp, D. Milward, M. Pinkal, M. Poesio, and S. Pulman (1996) *Building the Framework, Using the Framework*, FraCaS deliverables D15 and D16, Centre for Cognitive Science, University of Edinburgh, http://www.cogsci.ed.ac.uk/~fracas.

Day, J. (1993) The STDRT Implementation. In Cooper(1993)

Lunnon, R. (forthcoming) An Anti-Founded Model of a Theory of Sets and Functions, *Journal of Symbolic Logic*.

Ruhrberg, P. (1996) *Simultaneous Abstraction and Semantic Theories*, PhD thesis, Centre for Cognitive Science, University of Edinburgh.

Seligman, J. (1990) *Perspectives: a relativistic approach to the theory of information*, Ph.D. thesis, Centre for Cognitive Science, University of Edinburgh

Seligman, J., ed. (1991) *Partial and Dynamic Semantics III*, DYANA Deliverable R2.1.C, Centre for Cognitive Science, University of Edinburgh.

AARON N. KAPLAN AND LENHART K. SCHUBERT

SIMULATIVE INFERENCE IN A COMPUTATIONAL MODEL OF BELIEF

1. INTRODUCTION

If I see a glass begin to fall from a shelf, I can infer that the glass will probably break, by applying world knowledge such as:

1. When things fall, they collide with whatever is below them.
2. Glasses are fragile; floors are hard.
3. When a fragile thing and a hard thing collide, the fragile thing often breaks.

If I notice John looking at the glass as it begins to fall, I can infer that *John* believes the glass will break, under the assumption that he has similar world knowledge and similar reasoning abilities to mine. The reasoning process goes something like this:

- John believes the glass is falling (because people believe what they see).
- John believes facts 1-3 above (because everyone does).
- If I believed that the glass was falling, as well as facts 1-3, then I would conclude that the glass would break.
- Therefore, John believes that the glass will break.

This kind of reasoning is called *simulative inference*, since it involves using one's own reasoning faculties to simulate those of another agent.

Classical models of belief based on possible-worlds semantics are subject to the notorious 'logical omniscience' problem. In these models, if an agent has any beliefs, then it also believes all of the logical consequences of those beliefs, no matter how difficult those consequences may be to discover. A number of alternative semantics for belief that relax the logical omniscience requirement have been proposed. Many, such as the situation semantics approaches (e.g. Barwise and Perry, 1983), go to the opposite extreme: instead of requiring that agents discover all consequences of their beliefs, these models treat belief in one proposition as entirely independent of belief in other propositions.

H. Bunt and R. Muskens (eds.), Computing Meaning, Volume 1, 185–202.

If we want a semantics that licenses simulative inference, then we need something in between – a semantics in which belief in a set of sentences Φ entails belief in the easy-to-discover consequences of Φ, but not in the consequences that are too hard to find.

'Easy-to-discover' is not an intrinsic property of sentences themselves. Rather, it is relative to the inference mechanism doing the discovery. Therefore, our model of belief includes a model of an inference mechanism. The model is based on the following intuition: how an agent's inference mechanism is implemented, whether as a network of organic cells, as a computer program that applies deductive inference rules to logical axioms, or anything else, is irrelevant for the purposes of simulative inference. Only the mechanism's input/output characteristics are important. In our model, each agent has a *belief machine* to which it can make assertions and pose queries. An agent believes a sentence φ if its belief machine is in such a state that when it is queried about φ, it answers *yes*. The state of the machine can be changed by asserting new information.

In Sect. 2, we describe a logic whose semantics is built on the computational model of belief. We present a rule of simulative inference, and prove that it is sound. We also mention some completeness results that are proved elsewhere. In Sect. 3, we compare our model to other models of belief.

2. The Computational Model

In our model of belief, each agent has a *belief machine*, which is a computational inference mechanism along with some memory for maintaining state. The belief machine is characterized by two functions, ASK and $TELL$. If S is a possible state of the belief machine, and φ is a sentence (a formula with no free variables), then the value of $ASK(S, \varphi)$ is either *yes* or *no*. The intended significance of ASK is that the belief machine will answer *yes* if it is able to derive φ quickly from what it has already stored (in state S), and *no* otherwise. $TELL(S, \varphi)$ identifies the new state the belief machine would enter if, while in state S, it was informed that φ was true.

Our semantics will be used to interpret formulas of a first-order language L, defined like standard first-order logic, with the addition of the modal belief operator B. A sentence of the form $B(\alpha, \varphi)$ is true if and only if $ASK(S, \varphi) = yes$, where S is the state of the belief machine of the agent denoted by term α. We use the phrase *belief context* to mean the sentential argument of an occurrence of the belief operator; in $B(a, P(b))$, b occurs in a belief context, but a does not.

The only allowable belief machines are those that are guaranteed to halt; in other words, ASK and $TELL$ are computable functions. Note that a *no* answer does not necessarily mean that φ is disbelieved – it may be that an agent believes neither φ nor $\neg\varphi$, in which case its belief machine would answer *no* to both of them.

Quantifying-in (the binding from outside a belief context of a variable occurring within that context) is given a substitutional semantics: if agent a is in belief state S, then the sentence $\exists x B(a, P(x))$ is true if there is some term τ for which $ASK(S, P(\tau)) = yes$. For example, $\exists x B(john, Spy(x))$ (i.e. "there is some particular person whom John believes to be a spy") is true if there is some term τ for which John's belief machine assents to $Spy(\tau)$. The conditions for the truth of this sentence differ from those of $B(john, \exists x Spy(x))$ ("John believes that someone, though he might not know who, is a spy"), because John's belief machine might well assent to $\exists x Spy(x)$ without there being any name τ for which the machine assents to $Spy(\tau)$. The traditional, denotational interpretation of quantification is maintained wherever a variable is not quantified-in. For example, $\exists x P(x)$ is true if the extension of P is non-empty, even if there is no term τ for which $P(\tau)$ is true.

This model of belief is flexible enough to model a wide range of believers, but that range can be restricted by placing constraints on ASK and $TELL$. These constraints can be seen as analogous to the AGM postulates for belief revision (Alchourrón, Gärdenfors, and Makinson, 1985), in that they limit consideration to belief change functions with certain characteristics. For example, the axiom schema

$$B(\alpha, \varphi \wedge \psi) \rightarrow B(\alpha, \varphi)$$

is not valid in general, but its validity can be guaranteed by stipulating the following constraint on the belief machine: for any machine state S and sentences φ and ψ, if

$$ASK(S, \varphi \wedge \psi) = yes$$

then

$$ASK(S, \varphi) = yes \text{ and } ASK(S, \psi) = yes.$$

In general, each agent could be considered to have its own belief machine. However, our current reason for introducing this model of belief is to give a treatment of simulative inference, which is based on the approximation that all agents have functionally the same reasoning mechanism. Therefore, for the remainder of this chapter we will assume that the belief machines of all agents have the same input/output characteristics. Under this assumption, if two agents have different beliefs, it can be attributed only to their having acquired different information in the past.

2.1. *Definitions*

Formally, a *belief machine* is a structure $\langle \Gamma, S_0, TELL, ASK \rangle$, where

- Γ is a set of belief states, i.e. states of the machine.
- $S_0 \in \Gamma$ is the initial belief state. Each agent begins with this belief state, before it has *TELL*ed anything to its belief machine.
- $TELL : \Gamma \times L_c \to \Gamma$, where L_c is the set of closed formulas (sentences) of L, is a recursive function that describes how the machine changes state when fed a new assertion.
- $ASK : \Gamma \times L_c \to \{yes, no\}$ is a recursive function that describes how the belief machine responds to a query about the truth of a given sentence, when in a given belief state.

A model for interpreting the language L is a structure like a model for ordinary FOL, but augmented with a belief state for each agent. We will be interested in the truth values of formulas given a particular belief machine, so the machine is a parameter of the model structure rather than a constituent thereof. In other words, when we ask if $B(a, \varphi)$ logically entails $B(a, \psi)$, we are not asking if there is *any* belief machine that would conclude ψ from φ. Rather, we are asking about the belief machine we have already chosen. Where m is a belief machine, an m-model $M = \langle D, I, \gamma \rangle$ for L is composed of:

- D: the domain.
- I: an interpretation. I maps variables and individual, predicate, and function constants in Σ to set-theoretic extensions. Details are given below.
- $\gamma : D \to \Gamma$: a function mapping each individual to its belief state.

As a simplification, we do not distinguish between individuals that are believers and those that aren't – every individual in the domain is assigned a belief state (perhaps an empty one, though depending on the choice of belief machine there might be no state of the machine in which it answers *no* to everything). If the consequences of this simplification seem too undesirable, one could instead use a many-sorted logic, with *agent* being a distinguished sort, in the manner of Grove (1995).

A formula of L has a truth value with respect to a model $M = \langle D, I, \gamma \rangle$. We will write $|\alpha|^M$ to mean the denotation of term α with respect to model M. That denotation is defined as follows:

$$|\alpha|^M = \begin{cases} I(\alpha) & \text{if } \alpha \text{ is an individual constant} \\ & \text{or a variable} \\ I(f)(|\beta_1|^M, \ldots, |\beta_n|^M) & \text{if } \alpha \text{ is a functional term} \\ & f(\beta_1, \ldots, \beta_n). \end{cases}$$

The truth value of an ordinary (non-belief) atom with respect to a model is found as usual: where π is a predicate constant and α is a term, $M \models \pi(\alpha)$ iff $|\alpha|^M \in |\pi|^M$. The truth values of belief atoms are defined below.

The connectives and quantifiers of FOL are defined as usual. In particular, $\langle D, I, \gamma \rangle \models \exists \nu \varphi$ iff there is some other interpretation I' that differs from I by no more than its assignment to the variable ν, such that $\langle D, I', \gamma \rangle \models \varphi$. Similarly, $\langle D, I, \gamma \rangle \models \forall \nu \varphi$ iff for all interpretations I' that differ from I at most by their assignment to the variable ν, $\langle D, I', \gamma \rangle \models \varphi$.

Let σ be a *variable substitution*, which is a mapping from variables to ground terms. For formula φ, we define φ^σ as the sentence that results from replacing each *free* variable occurrence in φ with the term to which σ maps that variable. Note that bound variables in φ remain as variables in φ^σ. An *extension-preserving* variable substitution under model M is one that maps each variable to a term having the same extension as that variable under M.

Belief atoms are interpreted as follows, where $m = \langle \Gamma, S_0, TELL, ASK \rangle$, and M is an m-model: $M \models B(\alpha, \varphi)$ iff there is some variable substitution σ that is extension-preserving under M such that

$$ASK(\gamma(|\alpha|^M), \varphi^\sigma) = yes.$$

This gives a substitutional semantics to quantified-in beliefs. For example, $\exists x B(a, P(x))$ is true if there is some ground term τ for which $B(a, P(\tau))$ is true.

Note that a model assigns truth values to open formulas as well as sentences. In extensional contexts, free variables are interpreted in exactly the same way as constants. However, there is a difference between a free variable and a constant in belief contexts: $B(a, P(c))$ means that a believes the sentence $P(c)$, while $B(a, P(x))$ means only that there is *some* constant κ, which denotes the same thing as x, such that a believes the sentence $P(\kappa)$. The open formula $B(a, P(x))$ does not specify what constant occurs in the actual belief.

While all formulas, including open ones, are given truth values, note that the functions ASK and $TELL$ are only defined for sentential arguments. Wherever a meta-variable for a formula appears as an argument of ASK or $TELL$, it should be clear that it stands for a sentence, not an open formula.

We will use $TELL(S, \varphi_1, \ldots, \varphi_n)$ as an abbreviation for

$$TELL(\ldots TELL(TELL(S, \varphi_1), \varphi_2), \ldots, \varphi_n).$$

The notation $\mathcal{B} \cdot S$ means the belief set of belief state S, i.e.

$$\mathcal{B} \cdot S = \{\varphi | ASK(S, \varphi) = yes\}.$$

$\mathcal{M} \cdot S$ is the set of *monotonically acceptable* formulas for S, defined as

$$\mathcal{M} \cdot S = \{\varphi | \{\varphi\} \cup (\mathcal{B} \cdot S) \subseteq \mathcal{B} \cdot TELL(S, \varphi)\}$$

A sentence φ is monotonically acceptable for belief state S if entering (i.e. $TELL$ing) φ to a machine in state S will cause it to believe φ, and will not cause it to retract any of its prior beliefs.

2.2. *Simulative Inference*

In (Kaplan and Schubert, 1997, henceforth KS97), we present several inference rules for our logic. The most important rule, the one the logic was designed to license, is the rule of simulative inference:

$$\frac{B(\alpha, \varphi_1), \ldots, B(\alpha, \varphi_n)}{B(\alpha, \psi)} \text{ if } ASK(TELL(S_0, \varphi_1, \ldots, \varphi_n), \psi) = yes .$$

This rule relies on the assumption that we (the observers using the inference rule) have $ASK/TELL$ access to an implementation of the same belief machine used by agent α. The rule may or may not be sound, depending on the choice of belief machine. As Theorem 1, we will show that it is sound when the belief machine satisfies the constraints listed below. Though the inference rule only requires that $ASK(TELL(S_0, \varphi_1, \ldots, \varphi_n), \psi) = yes$ for one ordering of the φ_i, these constraints entail that if the φ_i can all be believed simultaneously, then the order in which they are $TELL$ed is not significant.

The simulative inference rule is sound when the belief machine satisfies the following constraints:

C1 (closure) *For any belief state S and sentence φ,*

$$\text{if } ASK(S, \varphi) = yes \text{ then } \mathcal{B} \cdot TELL(S, \varphi) = \mathcal{B} \cdot S.$$

C1 says that *TELL*ing the machine something it already believed does not change its belief set.

C2 (finite basis) *For any belief state S, there exist sentences $\varphi_1, \ldots,$ φ_n such that for $1 \leq i \leq n$, $\varphi_i \in \mathcal{M} \cdot TELL(S_0, \varphi_1, \ldots, \varphi_{i-1})$ and $\mathcal{B} \cdot TELL(S_0, \varphi_1, \ldots, \varphi_n) = \mathcal{B} \cdot S$.*

C2 says that for each belief state, an equivalent state (in terms of the beliefs in that state) can be reached from the initial state by a finite succession of *TELL*s, each of which supplies a monotonically acceptable sentence. It requires that even if a machine reached its current state via a sequence of sentences that were not all monotonically acceptable, there is some monotonically acceptable sequence that would have put it in an equivalent state. In other words, when belief revision occurs, the resulting beliefs are ones that can also be induced monotonically from S_0.

C3 (commutativity) *For any belief state S and sentences φ and ψ, if*

$$\varphi \in \mathcal{M} \cdot S \text{ and } \psi \in \mathcal{M} \cdot TELL(S, \varphi)$$

then

$$\psi \in \mathcal{M} \cdot S \text{ and } \varphi \in \mathcal{M} \cdot TELL(S, \psi)$$

and

$$\mathcal{B} \cdot TELL(S, \varphi, \psi) = \mathcal{B} \cdot TELL(S, \psi, \varphi).$$

C3 says that if two inputs are successively monotonically acceptable for a given belief state, then they are monotonically acceptable in either order, and the resulting belief set is the same regardless of the order. In other words, the belief machine may be sensitive to the order of a sequence of two *TELL*s only if it revises its beliefs at some point in that sequence.

This constraint, in combination with C4, entails commutativity for arbitrarily long sequences of sentences, not just pairs of sentences. This is shown below, as Lemma 1. Henceforth, when the phrase "monotonically acceptable for belief state S" is used to describe a sequence of formulas, it should be taken to mean that the elements of the sequence are successively monotonically acceptable, starting from S. The commutativity lemma says that if a sequence of formulas is monotonically acceptable, then any permutation of the sequence is also monotonically acceptable.

C4 (robustness) *For any belief states S and S' and sentence φ,*

$$\text{if } \mathcal{B} \cdot S = \mathcal{B} \cdot S' \text{ then } \mathcal{B} \cdot TELL(S, \varphi) = \mathcal{B} \cdot TELL(S', \varphi).$$

C4 says that if two belief states store the same beliefs, then the two are behaviorally indistinguishable. It means that for the purposes of predicting how a machine will react to future $TELL$s and ASKs, knowing its current belief set is as good as knowing its internal state.

From constraints C3 and C4, we can prove that a stronger form of commutativity follows:

LEMMA 1 (COMMUTATIVITY) For belief state S and sentences $\varphi_1, \ldots,$ φ_n such that $\varphi_i \in \mathcal{M} \cdot TELL(S, \varphi_1, \ldots, \varphi_{i-1})$ for $1 \leq i \leq n$, and for any permutation ρ of the integers $1 \ldots n$,

$$\varphi_{\rho(i)} \in \mathcal{M} \cdot TELL(S, \varphi_{\rho(1)}, \ldots, \varphi_{\rho(i-1)}), 1 \leq i \leq n \quad \text{and}$$

$$\mathcal{B} \cdot TELL(S, \varphi_1, \ldots, \varphi_n) = \mathcal{B} \cdot TELL(S, \varphi_{\rho(1)}, \ldots, \varphi_{\rho(n)}) \ .$$

That is, any sequence of successively monotonically acceptable $TELL$ed formulas can be permuted freely – the formulas remain successively monotonically acceptable, and the resulting belief state has the same belief set.

Proof. See Appendix.

We are now ready to prove the soundness of the simulative inference rule under the above constraints.

THEOREM 1 (SOUNDNESS OF SIMULATIVE INFERENCE) For belief machine $m = \langle \Gamma, S_0, TELL, ASK \rangle$ satisfying constraints C1–C4, m-model $M = \langle D, I, \gamma \rangle$, and sentences $\varphi_1, \ldots, \varphi_n$ and ψ, if $M \models B(\alpha, \varphi_i)$ for each of the φ_i, and $ASK(TELL(S_0, \varphi_1, \ldots, \varphi_n), \psi) = yes$ then $M \models B(\alpha, \psi)$.

Proof. See Appendix. The proof can be summarized as follows: by the finite basis axiom, agent α's current belief state (call it S) can be reached by $TELL$ing the belief machine some sequence of sentences $\chi_1, \ldots, \chi_m$ which are monotonically acceptable for S_0. By the closure axiom, $\varphi_1, \ldots, \varphi_n$ are monotonically acceptable for S. This means that the whole sequence $\chi_1, \ldots, \chi_m, \varphi_1, \ldots, \varphi_n$ is monotonically acceptable for S_0. By the definition of 'monotonically acceptable' and the commutativity lemma,

$$\mathcal{B} \cdot TELL(S_0, \varphi_1, \ldots, \varphi_n) \subseteq$$
$$\mathcal{B} \cdot TELL(S_0, \chi_1, \ldots, \chi_m, \varphi_1, \ldots, \varphi_n).$$

From the premises, we know that ψ is in the former belief set, so it must be in the latter as well. By the closure axiom, the latter is the same as $\mathcal{B} \cdot S$, so α believes ψ.

2.3. Completeness

In (KS97), we introduce a number of other inference rules, and prove each of them sound. In addition to the rule of simulative inference, we use a rule of negative simulative inference, a modified form of Skolemization, and the ordinary rules of $\wedge$-introduction, $\wedge$-elimination, double negation, substitution of equals (with the restriction that the substitution may not occur within a belief context), and universal instantiation (restricted to apply only if no occurrence of the variable is in a belief context).

Depending on the choice of belief machine, these inference rules may or may not be complete. In (KS97) we prove that for some interesting belief machines, no complete proof system can exist. However, we also show that for all belief machines, the above rules are refutation-complete for a restricted subset of the language. Loosely stated, the restriction is that universal quantification into a positively embedded belief context is not allowed.

To make the definition of a positive embedding precise, we treat $\exists \nu \psi$ as an abbreviation for $\neg \forall \nu \neg \psi$, and $\psi \to \chi$ as an abbreviation for $\neg \psi \vee \chi$. Another complication is that universal quantification can be "disguised" as existential quantification by nesting an existential formula inside the scope of a universal quantifier: $\forall x \exists y [x = y \wedge B(a, P(y))]$ is logically equivalent to $\forall x B(a, P(x))$. For the completeness theorem, we define L_1 to be a language constructed like L, but with the restriction that when all existential quantifiers are rewritten as universal quantifiers with negation, no free variable of the belief argument of a positively embedded belief atom is bound by a positively embedded (universal) quantifier, nor by a negatively embedded (universal) quantifier that is inside the scope of a positively embedded one.

THEOREM 2 (RESTRICTED REFUTATION COMPLETENESS) If sentence $\varphi \in L_1$ is unsatisfiable, then $\varphi \vdash \bot$.

Proof. The proof is an extension of the completeness proof for standard FOPC. The details can be found in (KS97). There are two main steps: first, it is shown that any consistent sentence $\varphi \in L_1$ can be extended to a Hintikka set Δ^+. The restriction against universal quantifying-in allows us to show that this can be done so that Δ^+, though it may be infinite, contains only finitely many belief atoms for each believer. Second, we show that every such Hintikka set has a model. This is the contrapositive of the refutation completeness theorem, so the theorem itself follows.

2.4. Competence

Our model of belief is a syntactic one, where the belief relationship is between agents and sentences. Since $P(a) \wedge P(b)$ is a different sentence from $P(b) \wedge P(a)$, it is possible for an agent to believe one but not the other. This goes against intuitions about what belief and conjunction are. We can codify these intuitions in *competence constraints*, which are lower bounds on the reasoning abilities of agents in the model. The following are examples of some natural competence constraints:

1. if $ASK(S, \varphi) = yes$ then $ASK(S, \neg\varphi) = no$
2. $ASK(S, \varphi \wedge \psi) = ASK(S, \psi \wedge \varphi)$
3. $ASK(S, \varphi \wedge \psi) = yes$ if and only if
   $ASK(S, \varphi) = ASK(S, \psi) = yes$

As with any kind of constraint, we need to be careful not to choose competence constraints so strong that no belief machine can satisfy them. It is possible, for example, to specify a set of constraints that require the machine to be complete for first-order logic; but since provability for first-order logic is undecidable, no belief machine could satisfy all of those constraints.

3. RELATED WORK

3.1. The Deduction Model of Belief

Our model of belief is similar in some respects to the deduction model of Konolige (1986). In that model, a believer is represented by a *deduction structure*, which is composed of a set of sentences (the base beliefs) and a set of inference rules. An agent's belief set is the set of all sentences that can be derived from the base beliefs by exhaustive application of the inference rules. Belief sets are not necessarily closed under logical consequence, because the set of inference rules is not required to be complete. The deduction model is an interesting step towards describing simulative inference, but we believe it is both more restrictive and more idealized than it needs to be. Our computational model addresses the following shortcomings of the deduction model:

- In the deduction model, agents always apply their inference rules exhaustively. Depending on the inference rules used, this may result in an agent having an uncomputable belief set. In the computational model, agents' belief sets must be computable.

- If one has implemented a complex reasoning mechanism, and one wants to know if simulative inference using that mechanism will yield correct results, the deduction model is only helpful if one can construct a deduction structure that is functionally equivalent to the mechanism. While this is possible for *some* computational mechanisms, Konolige does not provide criteria for deciding whether this is the case for a given one. In contrast, our constraints C1–C4 are simple conditions on the input/output behavior of a machine in a general model of computation, so they should be relatively easy to apply in practice.

- In the straightforward extension of the deduction model to a temporal logic, a monotonic increase of information is the only kind of belief change that could be represented straightforwardly. In contrast, our model provides a framework for describing how an agent's beliefs change when it learns new information, even if that information contradicts what was previously believed.

- Agents in the deduction model can make only sound, deductive inferences. The computational model itself does not impose this restriction, though our constraints C1–C4 do rule out belief machines that perform interesting kinds of non-deductive inference. In a future publication, we will introduce a modified form of simulative inference that is sound under a weaker set of constraints, which will permit belief machines that perform some kinds of non-deductive inference.

See (KS97) for a more detailed comparison of the computational model with the deduction model.

3.2. *Other Related Work*

Haas (1986) describes another kind of simulative inference, within the framework of a temporal logic. His inference rule is this: if we know that an agent believes the sentences in set Φ, and that the agent began attempting to prove a conclusion ψ by time t, and we observe that our own theorem prover can prove ψ from Φ in time δ, then the rule of simulative inference licenses the conclusion that the agent believes ψ by time $t + \delta$. Because it keeps track of the time at which each consequence is discovered, Haas' technique is applicable to a larger class of reasoning mechanisms than the technique we described in this paper. Specifically, it does not have a closure requirement – the fact that belief in ψ can eventually follow from belief in Φ does not entail that the beliefs generated from $\Phi \cup \{\psi\}$ in a certain amount of time are the same as those generated from Φ alone in the same amount of time. The tradeoff is that in order to apply this form of simulative inference, one needs an extra bit of information, namely the fact that the agent posed a query to its belief machine by a certain time. Since the two simulative techniques are applicable in different circumstances, a complete system could make use of both.

Moore (1977) suggested that the rule of simulative inference might be taken as a default rule, rather than a sound, deductive rule. Then belief could be taken to be a simple relation between agents and sentences, with no entailments between belief in one sentence and belief in another. If simulation ever led to a conclusion that was contrary to other information, then that conclusion could simply be discarded. Chalupsky and Shapiro (1996) have described such a system. In this system, if an agent believes the elements of set Φ, and we are able to prove ψ from Φ, then the rule of simulative inference allows us to conclude that the agent believes ψ, barring evidence to the contrary. This holds regardless of how much time and effort it takes us to discover the proof of ψ from Φ.

Simulative inference is based on the assumption that the agent about whom we're reasoning thinks just like we do. In most cases this is only an approximation, so simulation will sometimes give incorrect results. Making simulative inference a defeasible rule is an appropriate way of dealing with this possibility. However, we have shown that even in cases where the approximation is correct, simulative inference may *still* give incorrect results, depending on the reasoning mechanism being used. In such cases, to make the simulative inference rule defeasible is simply to sweep the problem under the rug. Our contribution has been to demonstrate conditions under which simulative inference is guaranteed to give correct results, given that the reasoner being simulated has the same reasoning mechanism as the one doing the simulation.

Halpern, Moses, and Vardi (1994) describe a very general model in which each agent has a local state l and an algorithm A. The algorithm takes a local state and a sentence as input, and answers "yes," "no," or "?." An agent's explicit beliefs are those sentences φ for which $A(\varphi, l) =$ "yes." The local state is analogous to our belief state, and the algorithm A is analogous to our ASK, but there is nothing in their model analogous to our $TELL$; that is, the model does not specify what causes agents to move from one local state to another. There is no discussion in (Halpern, Moses, and Vardi, 1994) of conditions under which simulative inference is sound.

Ballim and Wilks (1991) contend that there can be no satisfactory semantics for a formal logic of belief. Logical semantics, they claim, is a "heap view" of belief, meaning that all beliefs are lumped together in an unstructured heap of sentences. Since real agents have complex mechanisms for storing and manipulating their beliefs, the results of the heap view are bound to differ from the real thing. Though we are presenting a formal semantics for belief, our central claim is really not very different from theirs. Like them, we think an accurate model of belief must take the agent's reasoning mechanism into account explicitly. The difference is that the believer's reasoning mechanism is a *parameter* of our model, while their model incorporates a *particular* reasoning mechanism.

In (KS97), we examine the axioms of the classical modal logics T, S4, and S5 (see Hughes and Cresswell, 1968), and discuss the restrictions that can be placed on the belief machine to ensure that those axioms are valid. We show that some of the axioms are valid only for trivial belief machines, while others are valid for some more interesting machines.

4. CONCLUSIONS

AI system designers have long realized that the theoretical problem of logical omniscience can sometimes be finessed in practice: when reasoning about another agent's beliefs, an AI system has only finite resources itself, so it will only discover some of the many conclusions the other agent supposedly believes according to the possible-worlds model. This is simulative inference, and it has been in use at least since the early 1970s (Moore, 1973).

Unfortunately, if a system is based on possible-worlds semantics, but uses simulative inference to control the logical omniscience problem, it might as well have no formal semantics at all. The advantage of having a formal semantics for a knowledge representation is that one can give precise arguments for the appropriateness of the inference methods the system uses. If the semantics doesn't properly specify which consequences of its beliefs an agent will discover and which it won't, then there is no way to make such arguments.

The reason agents discover only some of the consequences of their beliefs is that there are resource limitations on the computation they perform. Therefore, in order to model belief accurately, a semantics for belief should incorporate a model of bounded computation. Konolige's deduction model includes a very idealized model of computation, namely the exhaustive application of deductive inference rules. That model allows some unrealistic agents and prohibits some realistic ones, so we have adopted a different model. In our model, the computational mechanism that generates new beliefs from old ones can be any arbitrary algorithm, as long as it is guaranteed to return a yes/no answer within a finite amount of time.

We have described a logic based on the computational model of belief. In general, simulative inference is not sound in the logic. To make it sound, we adopted constraints C1 (closure), C2 (finite basis), C3 (commutativity), and C4 (robustness). In a separate paper (Kaplan and Schubert, 1997), we introduce some additional inference rules and show that this set of rules is complete for a subset of the logic.

The basic computational model allows many kinds of reasoners that can't be described in the deduction model, but in order to make simulative inference sound, we had to introduce the above constraints, some of which are implicit in the deduction model. Even with these constraints, the computational model allows some interesting agents that can't be described in the deduction model. A belief machine describes not only an agent's beliefs at a fixed time, but how its beliefs change when the agent learns new information, even if the new information contradicts what the agent previously believed.

APPENDIX 1. Proofs

4.1. *Proof of Lemma 1*

For belief state S and sentences $\varphi_1, \ldots, \varphi_n$ such that $\varphi_i \in \mathcal{M} \cdot TELL(S, \varphi_1, \ldots, \varphi_{i-1})$ for $1 \leq i \leq n$, and for any permutation ρ of the integers $1 \ldots n$,

$\varphi_{\rho(i)} \in \mathcal{M}\text{·}TELL(S, \varphi_{\rho(1)}, \ldots, \varphi_{\rho(i-1)}), 1 \leq i \leq n$, and $\mathcal{B}\text{·}TELL(S, \varphi_1, \ldots, \varphi_n)$
$= \mathcal{B} \cdot TELL(S, \varphi_{\rho(1)}, \ldots, \varphi_{\rho(n)})$.

Proof. We will first show that if the order of any two consecutive formulas in the sequence is reversed, the elements of the sequence are still successively monotonically acceptable, and the resulting belief set is not changed. Let $S_1 = TELL(S, \varphi_1, \ldots, \varphi_{i-1})$. It was a premise of the lemma that

$$\varphi_i \in \mathcal{M} \cdot S_1$$

and that

$$\varphi_{i+1} \in \mathcal{M} \cdot TELL(S_1, \varphi_i).$$

By the commutativity constraint (C3), it is also true that

$$\varphi_{i+1} \in \mathcal{M} \cdot S_1$$

and that

$$\varphi_i \in \mathcal{M} \cdot TELL(S_1, \varphi_{i+1})$$

and that

$$\mathcal{B} \cdot TELL(S_1, \varphi_i, \varphi_{i+1}) = \mathcal{B} \cdot TELL(S_1, \varphi_{i+1}, \varphi_i).$$

Hence, applying the robustness constraint (C4) $n - i - 1$ times,

$$\varphi_j \in \mathcal{M} \cdot TELL(S_1, \varphi_{i+1}, \varphi_i, \varphi_{i+2}, \ldots, \varphi_{j-1}), i + 2 \leq j \leq n$$

(i.e. $\varphi_{i+1}, \varphi_i, \varphi_{i+2}, \ldots, \varphi_n$ are successively monotonically acceptable starting from S_1), and

$$\mathcal{B} \cdot TELL(S_1, \varphi_i, \varphi_{i+1}, \varphi_{i+2}, \ldots, \varphi_n) =$$
$$\mathcal{B} \cdot TELL(S_1, \varphi_{i+1}, \varphi_i, \varphi_{i+2}, \ldots, \varphi_n).$$

By the way we chose S_1, it follows that the elements of the sequence

$$\varphi_1, \ldots, \varphi_{i-1}, \varphi_{i+1}, \varphi_i, \varphi_{i+2}, \ldots, \varphi_n$$

are successively monotonically acceptable starting from S_0, and that

$$\mathcal{B} \cdot TELL(S, \varphi_1, \ldots, \varphi_n) =$$
$$(10.1) \qquad \mathcal{B} \cdot TELL(S, \varphi_1, \ldots, \varphi_{i-1}, \varphi_{i+1}, \varphi_i, \varphi_{i+2}, \ldots, \varphi_n).$$

Now we prove the commutativity lemma by induction on n, the number of $TELL$s in the sequence. The basis is $n = 1$. Assume that the lemma holds for $n = m$. Any permutation of the $m + 1$ sentences $\varphi_1, \ldots, \varphi_{m+1}$ is of the form

$$\varphi_{\rho(1)}, \ldots, \varphi_{\rho(i)}, \varphi_{m+1}, \varphi_{\rho(i+1)}, \ldots, \varphi_{\rho(m)}, 0 \leq i \leq m$$

for some permutation ρ of the integers $1 \ldots m$ (for $i = 0$, φ_{m+1} comes first, immediately before $\varphi_{\rho(1)}$; for $i = m$, φ_{m+1} is last, immediately after $\varphi_{\rho(m)}$).

$$\mathcal{B} \cdot TELL(S, \varphi_{\rho(1)}, \ldots, \varphi_{\rho(i)}, \varphi_{m+1}, \varphi_{\rho(i+1)}, \ldots, \varphi_{\rho(m)})$$
$$= \mathcal{B} \cdot TELL(S, \varphi_{\rho(1)}, \ldots, \varphi_{\rho(m)}, \varphi_{m+1})$$

by $m - i$ applications of (10.1)

$$= \mathcal{B} \cdot TELL(S, \varphi_1, \ldots, \varphi_m, \varphi_{m+1})$$

by the induction hypothesis

Similarly, the elements of the sequence $\varphi_{\rho(1)}, \ldots, \varphi_{\rho(m)}, \varphi_{m+1}$ are successively monotonically acceptable starting from S_0 by $m - i$ applications of (10.1), and therefore

$$\varphi_i \in \mathcal{M} \cdot TELL(S, \varphi_1, \ldots, \varphi_{i-1}), 1 \leq i \leq m + 1$$

by the induction hypothesis.

4.2. Proof of Theorem 1

For belief machine $m = \langle \Gamma, S_0, TELL, ASK \rangle$ *satisfying constraints C1–C4,* m-*model* $M = \langle D, I, \gamma \rangle$, *and sentences* $\varphi_1, \ldots, \varphi_n$ *and* ψ, *if* $M \models B(\alpha, \varphi_i)$ *for each of the* φ_i, *and* $ASK(TELL(S_0, \varphi_1, \ldots, \varphi_n), \psi) = yes$, *then*

$$M \models B(\alpha, \psi).$$

Proof. Assume that

$$(10.2) \quad M \models B(\alpha, \varphi_i)$$

for all $1 \leq i \leq n$, and assume that

$$(10.3) \quad ASK(TELL(S_0, \varphi_1, \ldots, \varphi_n), \psi) = yes.$$

Let $S = \gamma(|\alpha|^M)$, i.e. the belief state of the agent denoted by α. From (10.2) and the semantics of the operator B, it follows that for each φ_i, there is an extension-preserving variable substitution σ_i such that

$$(10.4) \quad ASK(S, \varphi_i^{\sigma_i}) = yes.$$

Furthermore, since the rule only applies when the φ_i have no free variables, φ_i^σ is the same as φ_i for any σ. Therefore, (10.4) is equivalent to

$$(10.5) \quad ASK(S, \varphi_i) = yes, 1 \leq i \leq n$$

According to the finite basis constraint (C2), there is some sequence of sentences $\chi_1, \ldots, \chi_m$ such that the sequence $\chi_1, \ldots, \chi_m$ is monotonically acceptable for S_0 and

(10.6) $\mathcal{B} \cdot TELL(S_0, \chi_1, \ldots, \chi_m) = \mathcal{B} \cdot S$

From (10.5) and the closure constraint (C1), it follows that the sequence $\varphi_1, \ldots, \varphi_n$ is monotonically acceptable for S, so by (10.6) and the robustness constraint (C4) $\varphi_1, \ldots, \varphi_n$ is monotonically acceptable for $TELL(S_0, \chi_1, \ldots, \chi_m)$. From this we can conclude that the whole sequence $\chi_1, \ldots, \chi_m, \varphi_1, \ldots, \varphi_n$ is monotonically acceptable for S_0. By the commutativity lemma, the sequence $\varphi_1, \ldots, \varphi_n, \chi_1, \ldots, \chi_m$ is also monotonically acceptable for S_0, and

(10.7) $\mathcal{B} \cdot TELL(S_0, \varphi_1, \ldots, \varphi_n, \chi_1, \ldots, \chi_m) = \mathcal{B} \cdot S$

Since the sequence $\varphi_1, \ldots, \varphi_n, \chi_1, \ldots, \chi_m$ is monotonically acceptable for S_0, the sequence $\chi_1, \ldots, \chi_m$ is also monotonically acceptable for $TELL(S_0, \varphi_1, \ldots, \varphi_n)$, by the definition of monotonically acceptable, and hence

(10.8) $\mathcal{B} \cdot TELL(S_0, \varphi_1, \ldots, \varphi_n)$
$\subseteq \mathcal{B} \cdot TELL(S_0, \varphi_1, \ldots, \varphi_n, \chi_1, \ldots, \chi_m)$

Equation (10.3) says that

(10.9) $\psi \in \mathcal{B} \cdot TELL(S_0, \varphi_1, \ldots, \varphi_n)$

From (10.9) and (10.8), it follows that

(10.10) $\psi \in \mathcal{B} \cdot TELL(S_0, \varphi_1, \ldots, \varphi_n, \chi_1, \ldots, \chi_m)$

which, according to (10.7), is the same as

(10.11) $\psi \in \mathcal{B} \cdot S$

or, equivalently,

(10.12) $ASK(S, \psi) = yes$

Since ψ was assumed to have no free variables, ψ^σ is the same as ψ for any variable substitution σ. By the semantics of B and our choice of $S = \gamma(|\alpha|^M)$, the desired conclusion follows:

(10.13) $M \models B(\alpha, \psi)$

ACKNOWLEDGEMENTS

This work was supported in part by ARPA grant F30602-95-1-0025 and NSF grant IRI-9503312. Rajesh Rao contributed several useful ideas in a 1992 term paper and subsequent discussions with LKS.

REFERENCES

Alchourrón, C. E., Gärdenfors, P., and Makinson, D. (1985) On the logic of theory change: partial meet functions for contraction and revision. *Journal of Symbolic Logic* 50, 510 – 530.

Ballim, A. and Wilks, Y. (1991) *Artificial Believers: The Ascription of Belief.* Hillsdale, NJ: Lawrence Erlbaum Associates.

Barwise, J. and Perry, J. (1983) *Situations and Attitudes.* Cambridge: MIT Press.

Chalupsky, H. and Shapiro, S. C. (1996) Reasoning about incomplete agents. *Proceedings of the Fifth International Conference on User Modeling.*

Grove, A. J. (1995) Naming and identity in epistemic logic part II: a first-order logic for naming. *Artificial Intelligence* 74, 311 – 350.

Haas, A. R. (1986) A syntactic theory of belief and action. *Artificial Intelligence* 28, 245 – 292.

Halpern, J. Y., Moses, Y., and Vardi, M. Y. (1994) Algorithmic knowledge. *Theoretical Aspects of Reasoning about Knowledge: Proc. Fifth Conference.* San Francisco: Morgan Kaufmann, 255 – 266.

Hughes, G. E. and Cresswell, M. J. (1968) *An Introduction to Modal Logic.* London: Methuen.

Kaplan, A. N. and Schubert, L. K. (1997) *Simulative Inference in a Computational Model of Belief.* Technical Report 636, University of Rochester Computer Science Department, Rochester, New York.

Konolige, K. (1986) *A Deduction Model of Belief.* Los Altos, California: Morgan Kaufmann.

Moore, R. C. (1973) D-script: A computational theory of descriptions. *Third International Joint Conference on Artificial Intelligence*, 223 – 229.

Moore, R. C. (1977) Reasoning about knowledge and action. *Proceedings of the International Joint Conference on Artificial Intelligence*, 223 – 227.

INDEFINITES AS EPSILON TERMS: A LABELLED
DEDUCTION ACCOUNT

1. INTRODUCTION

It is a well known problem of on-line parsing that quantified NPs, in particular indefinites, may be interpreted as giving rise to logical forms in which they have a scope very different from that indicated by the surface sequence of expressions in which they occur – a problem which cannot be reduced to positing referential uses of indefinites; cf. (Farkas, 1981; Abusch, 1994). Various computational and formal systems have tackled this ambiguity problem, either, as is familiar, by positing processes of restructuring or storage (Montague, 1974; Cooper, 1983; May, 1985; Morrill, 1994; Pereira, 1990), or by building underspecified structures including unscoped or partially scoped representations of quantified NPs (Alshawi & Crouch, 1992; Reyle, 1993; Pereira & Pollack, 1991). In all of these cases, there is implicit recognition that the determination of scope choice is not incremental, but can only be defined once the total structure is complete. In this chapter we propose that the interpretation of indefinite NPs involves an anaphoric-like dependency, in which the indefinite is lexically projected as involving a dependent name for which the *anchor* of the dependency has to be chosen on-line. The dependency is represented by an indexing on the name, the index indicating the expression to which the dependent element is to be anchored. The anchor dictates the mode of combination of the parts and the construction of the resulting dependent term.

The account is set within a model of utterance interpretation as a structure-building operation assigning logical forms to a sentence through a mixed process of labelled type deduction and other operations. This model is part of a general programme developing a deductive framework for natural language understanding (cf. Gabbay & Kempson, 1992; Finger et al., forthc.; Kempson et al., forthc.). The formal tools we use are labelled deduction (*LDS*) to define type deduction and other mixed modes of inference (Gabbay, 1996), the epsilon calculus as the selected logical language (Meyer Viol, 1995), and the modal tree

H. Bunt and R. Muskens (eds.), Computing Meaning, Volume 1, 203–218.

as the selected logical language (Meyer Viol, 1995), and the modal tree logic LOFT for modelling the architecture within which the setting out of premises for type deduction takes place (Blackburn & Meyer Viol, 1994). Utterance processing is taken to be a goal-driven inferential task, in which the goal is to establish a logical formula of type t using information as incrementally provided on a left-right basis by a given input string. The system has been partly implemented in Sicstus Prolog as part of a longer-term project.

Within this system, all NPs project onto formulas labelled with type e, with *epsilon* and *tau* terms for quantified NPs of existential and universal force respectively. Context dependence is reconstructed as a syntactic choice defined over the configurations built up during the interpretation process allowing content to be initially underspecified. All determiners lexically define such partial specifications of content, projecting specialised metavariables which are resolved in various ways. Anaphora resolution, for example, is assumed to involve an initial metavariable which is associated with a very free choice mechanism, restricted only by a locality constraint precluding representations which are too local to the point in the structure in which the metavariable is itself projected. Indefinites, on the other hand, project a metavariable corresponding to an incomplete epsilon term; a choice mechanism selects as the anchoring index some other representation projected in the interpretation process; and the elimination rules then progressively compute the formula in which the effect of this choice of anchoring is made explicit.

2. THE ϵ-CALCULUS: OVERVIEW AND APPLICATIONS

The ϵ-calculus gives us a quantifier free language which has all the expressivity of a first-order language (plus some more). It gives us a way to represent all noun phrases as entities of type e. Instead of quantified formulas the ϵ-calculus uses quantified terms to achieve the same purpose. These terms are constructed with *variable binding term operators* (Costa, 1980), each such operator ν corresponding to a quantifier. The building principle of these terms is: whenever ϕ is a formula of the language, then $\nu x\phi$ is a *term* in which all occurrences of x free in ϕ are bound by the operator νx. In this chapter we will use only two such operators: epsilon ϵ, and tau τ. These give rise to ϵ-terms and τ-terms:

- The term $\epsilon x \phi$ denotes some arbitrary d in the domain which has the property ϕ, if there are any such objects, and an arbitrary d *tout court* if there are no such objects. Given this choice of d, it is evident that $\phi[\epsilon x \phi / x]$ is true precisely if $\exists x \phi$ is. So we have the equivalence $\exists x \phi \leftrightarrow \phi[\epsilon x \phi / x]$.
- We interpret the term $\tau x \phi$ as shorthand for $\epsilon x \neg \phi$, i.e. it denotes an arbitrary object d s.t. d does *not* have the property ϕ if there is such an object, otherwise an arbitrary d. The following equivalence holds: $\forall x \phi \leftrightarrow \phi[\tau x \phi / x]$.

Variable binding term operators can be introduced for all (generalized) quantifiers. For instance, in *"Most men walk"* the term $a = \text{most} x (\text{man}(x) \rightarrow \text{walk}(x))$ would denote a walking man if indeed most men walk and some arbitrary non-walker otherwise. So $\text{walk}(a)$ holds exactly iff most men walk.[1] And in *"No man walks"* the term $b = \tau x (\text{man}(x) \rightarrow \neg \text{walk}(x))$ would give the right denotation. That is, $\text{man}(b) \rightarrow \neg \text{walk} (b)$ holds iff no man walks. In the quantified formula $Q x \phi$, the binding structure of the variable x in the matrix ϕ is completely described by the triple $\langle q, x, \phi \rangle$, where q denotes the *mode* of quantification of x and ϕ denotes the *scope* of that quantification. In the calculus with variable binding term operators this description is substituted, as it were, for x thus eliminating the need for the quantifier.

In the ϵ-calculus quantifier scope interactions are exhibited as term dependencies. For example, the two readings of *"Every nurse visits a patient"* translate as follows into the quantifier free calculus.

Narrow Scope Object $Nu(b) \rightarrow (Vis(b, a_b) \wedge Pat(a_b))$ where

1. $a_y = \epsilon x (Vis(y, x) \wedge Pat(x))$
2. $b = \tau y (Nu(y) \rightarrow (Vis(y, a_y) \wedge Pat(a_y)))$
3. $a_b = \epsilon x (Vis(b, x) \wedge Pat(x))$

Here the patient is construed as a term depending on the subject of *"visits"* i.e. *"every nurse"*. This dependence is reflected in the fact that the τ-term for *"nurse"* (b) occurs inside the final representation of *"patient"* (a_b).

---

[1] As it stands the use of the implication sign might be confusing, though note that we do get the right interpretation. In general, but not in this chapter, we are considering to let operators like *"most"* bind variables in pairs of formulas. *"Most men"*, would start its life as $\langle \mu, x, Men(x) \rangle$ without a semantic interpretation and get its definitive shape $\mu x(Men(x), Walk(x))$ by some rule like the one for τ-terms presented in this chapter.

Wide Scope Object $(Nu(b) \rightarrow (Vis(b_a, a)) \wedge Pat(a))$ where

    1. $a = \epsilon x Pat(x)$
    2. $b_x = \tau y(Nu(y) \rightarrow Vis(y, x))$
    3. $b_a = \tau y(Nu(y) \rightarrow Vis(y, \epsilon x Pat(x)))$

In this case, the patient does not depend on anything. In fact, in this calculus $\epsilon x Pat(x)$ occurs inside the representation of the term for *"every nurse"*. In the narrow scope reading the term derived from *"a patient"*, $\epsilon x(Vis(y, x) \wedge Pat(x))$ has the variable y free, i.e. the value of the term $\epsilon x(Vis(y, x) \wedge Pat(x))$ covaries with or depends on the value of y according to the extension of the *visit* relation (seen as a set of ordered pairs). In the wide scope reading where the patient is the same for each nurse the term $a = \epsilon x Pat(x)$ is independent, i.e. contains no free variables[2].

2.1. *Construction of the Terms*

The parsing process is essentially a two stage affair (although in practice the stages may be interleaved, as in the current prototype implementation). In the first stage a 'parse tree' is constructed in which the leaves are decorated with functions and arguments to these functions. The second phase of the parse then consists in iteratively applying functions to arguments among sister nodes and depositing the result on the mother node. After the first phase of the parse, quantified noun phrases in the string have resulted in leaves on which the *quantificational mode* of the NP is specified (indefinite, universal, etc.), the *restrictor* and scope information, couched in terms of *dependence*. These pieces of information suffice for the second stage of the parsing process to *algorithmically* compute the definitive shape of the quantified terms.

    In the first stage of parsing *"Every nurse visits a patient"* the noun phrases *"a patient"* and *"every nurse"* end up as 'unscoped' proto ϵ-terms $\langle \epsilon, x, Pat(x) \rangle$ and $\langle \tau, x, Nu(x) \rangle$ respectively. *At this point the terms are not given a semantics as they stand*, but the parse tree contains enough information to algorithmically compute the eventual shape of the terms which do get an interpretation. The reason for this delay of interpretation is that restrictors of the terms may have to be extended in the course of the computation (*"a patient who smiles,..."*),

---

    [2] Note that the restrictor $\phi(x)$ of an epsilon term $\epsilon x \phi(x)$ may represent both the natural language *content*, of the quantified NP — the common noun *"patient"* in *"a patient"* — and the *scope* of that NP in the entire clause.

or that the restrictor of the term still has to 'recombine' with the nuclear scope: terms starting their life as, for instance, $\langle \tau, x, \phi(x)\rangle$, $\langle \text{'no'}, x, \phi(x)\rangle$ or $\langle \text{'most'}, x, \phi(x)\rangle$ have to be restructured so as to incorporate the nuclear scope. For instance, in processing the sentence *"Every nurse visits a patient"* the proto term $\langle \tau, x, Nu(x)\rangle$ is not interpreted as the term $\tau x Nu(x)$ but if the dependence information states a dependence of *"a patient"* on *"every nurse"* (i.e., narrow scope object), then the term giving *"a patient"* its definitive semantic shape is constructed by the following Narrow Scope rule.

DEFINITION 1 (NARROW SCOPE OBJECT) Suppose ϕ free of λ, and L some sequence, possibly empty, of *lambda v*'s.

1. $\lambda x L\phi[x/y] + \epsilon y\psi = L(\phi[\epsilon y(\phi \wedge \psi)/y] \wedge \psi[\epsilon y(\phi \wedge \psi)/y])$
2. $\lambda x L\phi[x/y] + \tau y\psi = L(\psi[(\tau y(\psi \rightarrow \phi))/y] \rightarrow \phi[\tau y(\psi \rightarrow \phi)/y])$

That is, we use function application 'with a twist': in applying we 'recombine' the restrictor and nuclear scope. Here we derive the object narrow scope reading of our example sentence

1. **Visit + a Patient**:
   $\lambda u \lambda y Vis(y, u) + \epsilon x Pat(x)) = \lambda y(Vis(y, a_y) \wedge Pat(a_y))$
2. **Visit a Patient + every Nurse**:
   $\lambda y(Vis(y, a_y) \wedge Pat(a_y)) + \tau y Nu(y) =$
   $Nu(b) \rightarrow (Vis(b, a_b) \wedge Pat(a_b))$
   where

   a) $a_y = \epsilon x(Vis(y, x) \wedge Pat(x))$
   b) $b = \tau y(Nu(y) \rightarrow (Vis(y, a_y) \wedge Pat(a_y)))$
   c) $a_b = \epsilon x(Vis(b, x) \wedge Pat(x))$

If parsing *"Every nurse visits a patient"* results in the proto term $\langle \epsilon, x Pat(x)\rangle$ with the information that there is no dependence (or, alternatively, a dependence on the time index/world of evaluation[3]) then the Wide Scope application rule is called for.

DEFINITION 2 (WIDE SCOPE OBJECT) Suppose ϕ free of λ, and L some sequence, possibly empty, of *lambda v*'s. Let $X(x, \chi)$ be the *smallest subformula* of χ containing all free occurrences in χ of the variable x.

---

[3] There is an unresolved issue here concerning whether the world should be represented in a (two-sorted) object language or whether the world *labels* the formula; cf Finger & Gabbay, 1993).

1. $\lambda x L\phi[x/y] + \epsilon y\psi = L(\phi[\epsilon y\psi/y] \wedge \psi[\epsilon y\psi/y])$
2. $\lambda x L\phi[x/y] + \tau y\psi = L\phi[\xi/X(y,\phi)])$
   where
   $\xi = \psi[(\tau y(\psi \to X(y,\phi))/y] \to X(y,\phi)[\tau y(\psi \to X(y,\phi))/y]$

1. **Visit + a Patient:**
   $\lambda u\lambda v Vis(v,u) + \epsilon x Pat(x) = \lambda y(Vis(y,a) \wedge Pat(a))$
2. **Visit a Patient + every Nurse:**
   $\lambda y(Vis(y,a) \wedge Pat(a)) + \tau y Nu(y) =$
   $(Nu(b) \to (Vis(b_a,a)) \wedge Pat(a)$
   where

   a) $a = \epsilon x Pat(x)$
   b) $X(y, \lambda y(Vis(y,a) \wedge Pat(a))) = Vis(y,a)$
   c) $b_x = \tau y(Nu(y) \to Vis(y,x))$

This semantic notion of dependency can be conceptually separated from the syntactic notion of scope (see e.g. Farkas, forthc.). We make use of the notion of dependency in the way scope relations are determined as a by-product of the sequential parsing process. As was mentioned above quantified NPs are interpreted initially as unscoped 'proto-terms' but there is the option to fix dependencies on variables so as to place constraints on the eventual scope relations. For instance in the above sentence processing *"every nurse"* results in the proto-term $\langle \tau, y, Nu(y) \rangle$. At the point where *"patient"* is encountered there are two options:

2. a) $\langle \epsilon, x, Pat(x) \rangle$
   b) $\langle \epsilon, x, dep(y), Pat(x) \rangle$

Option (2a) triggers the combination rule resulting in the wide scope reading for the indefinite in (1) and option (2b) triggers the rule which results in the narrow scope reading. If we express the dependency of the variable x in (2a) on the world/temporal index directly in the representation language, then indefinites can be given a unitary characterisation as $\langle \epsilon, x, dep(y), Pat(x) \rangle$ with y to be chosen much like an anaphoric choice. Like anaphoric resolution this choice is primarily on-line but to account for (marked) cases where scope does not correspond to left-right order we need to allow dependency on a metavariable which is instantiated later: In the first parsing stage of *"A nurse visits every patient"*, *"a nurse"* starts its life as the proto term $\langle \epsilon, x, dep(\mathbf{u}), Nu(x) \rangle$. At the end of that stage, the dependence has been resolved to $\langle \epsilon, x, dep(\mathbf{a}), Nu(x) \rangle$ where $\mathbf{a} = \langle \tau, x, Pat(x) \rangle$. The second stage of the parse then uses the dependence information to construct the semantic representation as below Definition 1.

In choosing the source of dependence in these terms there are several options. We may choose the constructed term (if already in its definitive shape), or we may choose the variable associated with it (if we are dealing with a quantified NP). An altogether different possibility is to make a proto term dependent on the location in the *tree* where the anchor is located, or even on the identifier of the *task* it is associated with. All these options are currently being explored.

3. CONSTRUCTION ALGORITHM AND IMPLEMENTATION

The interpretation process is formalised in a LDS framework in which type-logical formulas as labels guide the parser in the goal-directed process of constructing labelled formulas or *declarative units (DUs)*. The goal of the parser is the deductive task *show(t)* (derive a formula of type t); this is achieved by generating a succession of subtasks *show(e)*, *show(e→t)* etc. In this section we define declarative units and *task states* and describe the rules which license transitions between states, with some remarks concerning implementation considerations.

3.1. *Declarative Units*

The *formula* of a declarative unit is the side representing the content of the words supplied in the course of a parse. In the fragment used in this chapter a formula is either a term of type e or a lambda-expression. The *labels* annotate this content with linguistic features and control information. These include:

(i) the logical types expressed as type-logical formulas: e, cn, t are types and for any types a, b; $a \rightarrow b$ is a type.

(ii) Tree node identifiers: these identifiers and other properties of the nodes are described by LOFT (Logic of Finite Trees), a logic for a propositional modal language which allows nodes of a tree to be defined in terms of the relations that hold between them (Blackburn & Meyer Viol 1994). In the system described in this chapter we only employ the modality $\langle d \rangle$ or 'down': $\langle d \rangle P$ holds at tree-node i iff P holds at a daughter of i.

(iii) Features specifying other syntactic information such as *Case*,
$+Q$ for questionhood etc.

Declarative units are represented as finite sets of formulas

$$\{Lab_1(l_1), \ldots, Lab_n(l_n), Form(\phi)\} \ .$$

Each such set is called a *DU-formula*.

3.2. *Task States*

A *Task state* is a description of the state of a task. The four feature
dimensions of a task state are

Goal Values on this dimension are the semantic types in the label set
Ty.

Tree Node
This feature fixes the location of the task in question within a tree
structure.

Discrepancy (ToDo)
Values are (finite sequences of) *DU*-formulas. This dimension tells
us what has to be found/constructed before the goal object can be
constructed.

Result (Done)
Values are lists, sequences, of *DU*-formulas. These values will be
(partial) declarative units.

We will represent a task state either graphically by

show **G**
N
ToDo: α
Done: β

or as the string $\{Tn(N), \ Goal(G), \ ToDo(\alpha), \ Done(\beta)\}$.

In the rules given below, tasks are identifed by the tree node identifier Tn since there is a one-to-one correspondence between tasks and
nodes. In the prototype implementation of this system task states are
recorded in the Prolog database as unit clauses of the form `task(Tn,
show(Goal), ToDo, Done)` where `ToDo` and `Done` are lists. This not
only simplifies the programming task of accessing and updating task

states but according to the particular Prolog implementation may allow fast direct access to any task state via the mechanism of indexing clauses for a predicate by their first argument (see e.g. Shieber et al., 1995). We can distinguish three kinds of task states:

Task Declaration Nothing has yet been achieved with respect to a goal G:
$$\{Goal(G), Tn(N), ToDo(G), Done(\emptyset)\}$$

Tasks in Progress In the middle of a task:
$$\{Goal(G), Tn(N), ToDo(\beta), Done(\alpha)\}$$

If things are set up right, then $\alpha\beta \Rightarrow G$ by some rule of combination.

Satisfied Task $\{Goal(G), Tn(N), ToDo(\emptyset), Done(\alpha)\}$
Soundness of the deductive system amounts to the fact that the goal G can be computed, derived, from α in case $ToDo$ is empty.

3.3. *Parse States and Dynamics: The Basic Transition Rules*

A parse state consists of a pair: a bookkeeping device which gives a value for the parsing pointer identifying the current task and the string counter which represents the location of the current word in the input string; and a sequence S of task states (to avoid cluttering the definitions, we generally omit details of the bookkeeping device in what follows). In the following definitions the symbols $X, Y, Z, \ldots$ will range over individual DU-formulas, the symbols α, $\beta, \ldots$ will range over (possibly empty) sequences of such formulas, D, $D', \ldots$ will range over (possibly empty) sequences of tasks, and w_i, $w_{i+1}, \ldots$ will range over words.

The dynamics of the parse process consists of reaching a final parse state or *Goal State* starting from a begin state, the *Axiom State*:

(1) **Axiom**: $\{Goal(t), Tn(1), ToDo(Ty(t)), Done(\emptyset)\}$

(2) **Goal**: $(\{Goal(t), Tn(1), ToDo(\emptyset), Done(Ty(t), \ldots)\}.D)$
    where elements of D are task states with fully specified DU-formulas.

As was stated in Sect. 2, the parsing process consists of two conceptually separate phases, namely constructing a function-argument tree (in the process recognising a grammatical sentence) and iteratively applying functions to arguments to derive a logical form. In our system

the 'structure-building' rules which construct the initial parse tree are
Introduction, **Subordination** and **Scanning**, while the 'interpretive' rules are **Completion** and **Elimination**. These rules are defined
below.

(3) **Scanning**: For some string position s and tree node i:

if $\mathrm{LEX}(w_{s+1}) = Y$, $U \epsilon Y$; set $s := s + 1$ then

$$(D.\{Tn(i), \ Goal(X), \ ToDo(U, \beta), \ Done(\alpha)\}.D')$$

$$(D.\{Tn(i), \ Goal(X), \ ToDo(\beta), \ Done(\alpha, Y)\}.D')$$

The side condition specifies that Y is the lexical entry retrieved for the
current word in the string, with type-specification U. This rule licenses
the introduction of material from the lexicon as long as it satisfies the
conditions specified in *ToDo*. These conditions are established by the
rule of **Introduction**.

(4) **Introduction**

$$(D.\{Tn(i), \ Goal(X), \ ToDo(Z, \beta), \ Done(\alpha)\}.D')$$

$$(D.\{Tn(i), \ Goal(X), \ ToDo(\langle d \rangle Y_0, \ldots, \langle d \rangle Y_n, \beta), \ Done(\alpha)\}.D')$$

where $Y_0, \ldots Y_n \Rightarrow Z$

The relation $\Rightarrow$ stands for some mode of combination; in the current
system we employ Modus Ponens over the type system, restricted to
combinations of the types which occur in the grammar of the language
being parsed (namely t plus the types of lexical items).

This rule licenses the introduction of a set of new subgoals as long as
there is some mode of combination reducing the subgoals to the original
one. **Introduction** itself sets up the need for a rule transferring the
requirement on the daughter to a *ToDo* at which the requirement has
to be met:

(5) **Subordination**

$$(D.\{Tn(i), \ Goal(X), \ ToDo(((\langle d \rangle Ty(x)), \beta), \ Done(\alpha)\}.D')$$

$$(D.\{Tn(i), \ Goal(X), \ ToDo(((\langle d \rangle Ty(x)), \beta), \ Done(\alpha)\}.D'. \\ \{Tn(k), \ Goal(x), \ ToDo(Ty(x))), \ Done(\emptyset)\})$$

where k stands in the daughter relation to i

Subordination is one of a pair of rules which license the transition from a task to be carried out on a daughter to the creation of a task corresponding to that daughter. Like **Introduction**, it relies on a converse rule, **Completion**, which defines the transition back to the mother:

(6) **Completion**

$$\frac{(D.\{Tn(i),\ Goal(X),\ ToDo((\langle d\rangle Y,\beta),\ Done(\alpha)\}.D'.}{\{Tn(k),\ Goal(Y),\ ToDo(\emptyset),\ Done(U_0,\ldots,U_n)\}.D'')}$$

$$(D.\{Tn(i),\ Goal(X),\ ToDo((\beta),\ Done(\alpha,\langle d\rangle(U_0,\ldots,U_n))\}.D'.$$
$$\{Tn(k),\ Goal(Y),\ ToDo(\emptyset),\ Done(U_0,\ldots,U_n\}.D'')$$

where k stands in the daughter relation to i

Completion then feeds **Elimination**, the rule twinned with **Introduction**:

(7) **Elimination**

$$\frac{(D.\{Tn(i),\ Goal(X),\ ToDo(\beta),\ Done(\alpha,\ \langle d\rangle Y_0,\ldots,\langle d\rangle Y_n)\}.D')}{(D.\{Tn(i),\ Goal(X),\ ToDo(\beta),\ Done(\alpha,Z)\}.D')}$$

where $Y_0,\ldots,Y_n \Rightarrow Z$

This rule effects the converse of **Introduction**, so that type specifications of subtasks are progressively derived. The rule schema $Y_0,\ldots,Y_n \Rightarrow Z$ is realised by a generalised Modus Ponens, where type-deduction is combined with the variant of function application described in Sect. 2:

(8) **Generalised MP**

$$\frac{\langle d\rangle(Ty(a) \wedge Form(\phi)) \wedge \langle d\rangle(Ty(a \to b) \wedge Form(\psi))}{Ty(b) \wedge Form(\psi(\phi))}$$

The above rules between them define the state space of the parser, and various options are available for traversing that space. In the prototype program we have chosen to interleave the structure-building and interpretive rules, with a simple recursive definition shown in Fig. 1, whereby the rules are invoked in turn until the `goalstate` predicate succeeds. (This predicate attempts to call the `task` predicate with the goal `show(t)`, empty ToDo and with `ty(t)` as an element of Done). The order in which rules are applied is dictated in part by efficiency considerations. For instance, the **Scanning** rule is always called to check whether the type of the current word in the string matches the current task specification before invoking **Introduction** and **Subordination** to generate new tasks; this minimizes unwanted backtracking.

```
parse:-goalstate.
parse:-eliminate,parse.
parse:-complete,parse.
parse:-scan,parse.
parse:-subord,parse.
parse:-intro,parse.
parse:-backtrack,parse.
```
Main Parse Loop

This inference regime results in a top-down parsing strategy, with backtracking over the **Introduction** rule until a task specification is generated which results in successful application of **Scanning**. An alternative approach would be to combine top-down and bottom-up techniques by making **Introduction** sensitive to the type(s) defined for the current word in the lexicon.

3.4. *Example*

As an illustration we exhibit a sequence of snapshots of the parsing of *"Every nurse visits a patient"*.

Parse state 1: Axiom state `task(1, show(t), [ty(t)], [ ])`.

Parse state i: All words in the input string have been consumed. As a result of the interleaved inference regime **Elimination** and **Completion** have applied to the type e tasks. The state of task 5, representing the indefinite *"a patient"*, assumes a non-deterministic choice of the variable x associated with task 2 as the 'anchor of dependency'.

```
┌─────────────────────────────┐
│ show t                      │
├─────────────────────────────┤
│ 1                           │
│   ToDo:                     │
│   ⟨d⟩Ty(e → t)              │
│   Done:                     │
│   ⟨d⟩(Ty(e), Form(⟨τ, x, Nu⟩)) │
└─────────────────────────────┘
```

```
┌──────────────────────────────┐
│ show e                       │
├──────────────────────────────┤
│ 2                            │
│   ToDo: ∅                    │
│   Done:                      │
│   Ty(e), Form(⟨τ, x, Nu⟩)    │
└──────────────────────────────┘
```

```
┌──────────────────────────────────────────────┐
│ show e → t                                   │
├──────────────────────────────────────────────┤
│ 3                                            │
│   ToDo: Ty(e → t)                            │
│   Done:                                      │
│   ⟨d⟩(Form(λuλvVis(v,u)), Ty(e → (e → t)))   │
│   ⟨d⟩(Ty(e), Form(⟨ε, y, dep(x), Pat⟩))      │
└──────────────────────────────────────────────┘
```

```
┌──────────────────────────────┐
│ show e → (e → t)             │
├──────────────────────────────┤
│ 4                            │
│   ToDo: ∅                    │
│   Done:                      │
│   Ty(e → (e → t)),           │
│   Form(λuλvVis(v,u))         │
└──────────────────────────────┘
```

```
┌──────────────────────────────┐
│ show e                       │
├──────────────────────────────┤
│ 5                            │
│   ToDo: ∅                    │
│   Done:                      │
│   Ty(e),                     │
│   Form(⟨ε, y, dep(x), Pat⟩)  │
└──────────────────────────────┘
```

Parse state j: The rules of Elimination and Completion apply to tasks 1 and 3, applying the specialised λ-reduction rule given in Sect. 2. The indicated dependency triggers the Narrow Scope clause of the rule (see Definition 1), where the constructed term $a_x = \epsilon y(Vis(x,y) \wedge Pat(y))$ has the variable x free.

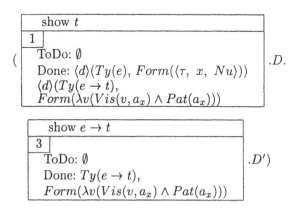

Parse state k: The final step in deriving a formula of type t is application of Elimination to the top-level task $Tn(1)$, again invoking the λ-reduction rule:

$$\left(\begin{array}{|l|} \hline \text{show } t \\ \hline \boxed{1} \\ \text{ToDo: } \emptyset \\ \text{Done: } Ty(t), \text{Form}(\ Nu(b) \to (Vis(b, a_b) \wedge Pa(a_b))) \\ \hline \end{array} \right. \quad . \ D')$$

where:

(i) $b = \tau x (Nu(x) \to (Vis(x, a_x) \wedge Pa(a_x)))$
(ii) $a_b = \epsilon y (Vis(b, y) \wedge Pat(y))$

4. Conclusion

This LDS$_{NL}$ model relates to categorial analyses manipulating labelled type deduction (e.g. Morrill, 1994; Oehrle, 1995; Joshi & Kulick, 1995), though it is unlike these in addressing issues of underspecification, and in its explicitly procedural perspective. It is close to semantic accounts of underspecification (Alshawi & Crouch, 1992; Reyle, 1993, Farkas, forthc.), though unlike these formalisms, the process of resolving dependencies is assumed to be an on-line choice which is simultaneously context-dependent and nevertheless syntactic. So a semantics is defined only for the output of this process, not for the underspecified lexical input. The model is similar to the Candide system of (Pereira & Pollack, 1991) where the interpretation process divides into structure-building *conditional interpretation* rules and interpretive *discharge* rules, except that in the Candide system it is the tree-building operation which is deterministic, with decisions on quantifier scope and modifier attachment postponed to the semantic-pragmatic discharge phase.

The novelty of the present system lies in (a) the application of the epsilon calculus, and (b) its analysis of wide scope effects as a phenomenon falling together with anaphora. Its conceptual advantage over its competitors is that the indefinite is no longer seen as a determiner which is exceptional in virtue of having term-like properties; and its idiosyncratic freedom of scope choice follows directly from the anaphoric nature of the process resolving its lexical underspecification. Aspects of the research that are currently being developed are the precise nature of the relation between the concept of dependency implicit in the indexing and that defined within the epsilon calculus, the expansion of the system to incorporate dependencies on and between expressions denoting time, and the application to a broader range of quantifiers.

ACKNOWLEDGEMENTS

This research was supported by the UK Engineering and Physical Sciences Research Council under grant reference GR/K67397, "A Labelled Deductive System for Natural Language Understanding" The LaTeX macros used in the box diagrams in this chapter were originally developed by John Barwise and Robin Cooper.

REFERENCES

Abusch, D. (1994) The scope of indefinites. *Natural Language Semantics* 2 (2), 83 – 135.

Alshawi, H. & Crouch, R. (1992) Monotonic semantic interpretation. in *Proceedings 30th Annual Meeting of the Association of Computational Linguistics*, 32 – 38.

Blackburn, S. & Meyer Viol, W. (1994) Linguistics, logic and finite trees. *Bulletin of Interest Group in Pure and Applied Logics* 2 (1), 3 – 29.

Cooper, R. (1983) *Quantification and Syntactic Theory*. Dordrecht: Reidel.

da Costa, N. C. (1980) A model–theoretic approach to variable binding term operators. In: A. I. Aruda, R. Chuaqui, N. C. da Costa (1980) *Mathematical Logic in Latin America*. Amsterdam: North Holland Publishing Company.

Farkas, D. (1981) Quantifier scope and syntactic islands. *Chicago Linguistic Society 17th Meeting*, 59 – 66.

Farkas, D. (1997) Indexical scope. In: A. Sczabolsci (1997) *Ways of Scope-Taking*. Dordrecht: Reidel, 183 – 216.

Finger, M. & Gabbay, D. (1993) Adding a temporal dimension to a logical system. *Journal of Logic, Language and Information* 1, 203 – 33.

Finger, M., Kibble, R., Kempson, R. & Gabbay, D. (forthc.) Parsing natural language using LDS: a prototype. *Bulletin of Interest Group in Pure and Applied Logics*.

Gabbay, D. (1996) *Labelled Deductive Systems*. Oxford: Oxford University Press.

Gabbay, D. & Kempson, R. (1992) Natural language content: a proof–theoretic perspective. *Proceedings of 8th Amsterdam Semantics Colloquium*. Amsterdam, 173 – 96.

Joshi, A. & Kulick, S. (forthc.) Partial proof trees as building blocks for a categorial grammar. *Linguistics and Philosophy*.

Kempson. R., Meyer Viol, W. & Gabbay, D. (forthc.) Syntactic computation as labelled deduction. In: R. Borsley, & I. Roberts, *Syntactic Categories*. New York: Academic Press.

May, R. (1985) *Logical Form*. Cambridge: MIT Press.

Meyer Viol, W. (1995) Instantial Logic. Utrecht: PhD dissertation.

Milward, D. (1993) Dynamics, dependency grammar and incremental interpretation. *COLING* 14, 1095 – 9.

Montague, R. (1974) *Formal Philosophy.* Yale: Yale University Press.

Morrill, G. (1994) *Type–logical Grammar.* Dordrecht: Kluwer.

Oehrle, R. (1995) Term–labelled categorial type systems. *Linguistics & Philosophy* 17.6, 633 – 78.

Pereira, F. (1990) Categorial semantics and scoping. *Computational Linguistics* 16, 1 – 10.

Pereira, F. & Pollack, M. (1991) Incremental interpretation. *Artificial Intelligence* 50, 37 – 82.

Reyle, U. (1993) Dealing with ambiguities by underspecification. *Journal of Semantics* 10, 123 – 79.

Shieber, S., Schabes, Y. & Pereira, F. (1995) Principles and implementation of deductive parsing. *Journal of Logic Programming* 24 (1–2), 3 – 36.

LENHART SCHUBERT

DYNAMIC SKOLEMIZATION

1. INTRODUCTION

The phenomenon of 'donkey anaphora' has been much discussed in the linguistic semantics literature (e.g., see Carlson & Pelletier, 1995; Chierchia, 1995), and has given rise to new theories of logical form based on various kinds of 'dynamic semantics'.[1] Although these theories appear to account for donkey anaphora in a natural way, they have not had much impact so far on knowledge representation in AI. This is surprising since – as I will argue – much of the 'common-sense' knowledge needed for ordinary reasoning and language understanding characteristically involves donkey anaphora, when this knowledge is expressed in words. The reason may be that the development of knowledge representations has been influenced more by the need for efficient inference than the need for capturing linguistically conveyed information.

This chapter explores the extent to which the phenomena addressed by dynamic semantics theories can be systematically addressed within a more standard representational framework. The main proposal is a mechanism called *dynamic skolemization* for conversion of logical forms containing anaphoric terms to ones containing constants and functional terms with a standard, non-dynamic semantics. The resultant formulas seem to be equivalent (in a sense) to corresponding formulas in logics using dynamic semantics, in cases where the latter are able to represent the anaphoric relations involved (esp. donkey anaphora). A fortuitous advantage of dynamic skolemization is that it can be recast as automatic creation of script-like or frame-like structures (as understood in AI), and enables referring into these structures in ways beyond the capabilities of dynamic semantics. This is not to say that dynamic skolemization rivals dynamic semantics accounts of donkey anaphora on a theoretical level, but it does appear to have practical potential, and to be connected in interesting ways to the latter.

---

[1] I would prefer to use Chierchia's term 'dynamic binding', but do not wish to imply particular theoretical commitments here.

H. Bunt and R. Muskens (eds.), Computing Meaning, Volume 1, 219–253.

The following sentences illustrate the problems encountered when we attempt to represent sentences involving donkey anaphora in standard first-order logic.

(1) If *a farmer* buys *a donkey*, *he* pays for *it* in cash.

(2) If John bought *a donkey* at the fair, he paid for *it* in cash.

Note that (1) has a generic flavor, in that it quantifies over cases where a farmer buys a donkey. Sentence (2) admits both a generic and a specific reading. On the generic reading, it quantifies over past instances of John buying a donkey (perhaps with different instantiations of *"the fair"*, or perhaps with a single instantiation of a very long fair). On the specific reading, (2) seems to refer to just a single visit by John to the fair, and a possible donkey-purchase during that visit.

Both sentences and both readings of (2) illustrate the problem at issue, but the specific reading of (2) does so most simply and starkly. If we interpret indefinites in terms of existential quantification (as has been customary in philosophical logic and much of AI), then the logical form of the specific reading of (2) appears to be

$$[(\exists x)D(x) \wedge B(J, x)] \;\rightarrow\; P(it, M),$$

ignoring implicit events. But how are we to disambiguate the anaphoric pronoun? We cannot set it to x, since this would lead to a free occurrence of x outside the scope of its quantifier, where this free occurrence is semantically disconnected from the prior bound occurrence. We also cannot appeal to a 'wide-scope reading' of the indefinite, giving the existential quantifier wider scope than the conditional and thus bringing the pronoun within its scope. This would give a reading to the effect that something x is such that if it is a donkey and John bought it at the fair, then he paid for it in cash. But such a statement is true virtually independently of John's donkey purchases and manner of payment, as long as there is *something* that is not a donkey, or *something* that John didn't buy, thus rendering the antecedent (protasis) of the conditional false and the conditional as a whole true.

Finally, we cannot appeal to some principle of quantifier scope widening analogous to conversion to prenex form, since this would convert the negatively embedded existential quantifier to a wide-scope universal. If it happens that John bought several donkeys at the fair, truth of (2) would then require John to have paid for *all* of them in cash. But this is wrong (though it is sometimes an implicature), as can be seen by augmenting (2) as follows:

(3) John took enough money to the fair to buy a donkey. So, if he bought a donkey at the fair, he paid for it in cash.

Clearly we do not want to infer that if John was so impressed with the livestock offerings that he went on a donkey-buying spree, he paid for *all* his donkeys in cash. Yet (2) remains true in this context. The point is even clearer for the following variant of (2):

(4) If John bought a donkey at yesterday's fair, he rode it home.

This seems perfectly true even in a case where John bought two donkeys, but rode only one home while leading the other. Another argument against the scope-widening solution is that it plainly leads to incoherence for variants of (1) involving explicit generic quantification, such as

(5) If a farmer buys a donkey, he {*usually/ sometimes/ rarely*} pays for it in cash.

Why, then, should the KR community care about this problem? I claim that much of the knowledge needed for common-sense reasoning is of this form. For instance, the following are some general facts that everyone presumably knows:

(6) If a hungry predator encounters a smaller creature, it may well try to attack and eat it.

(7) If a conspicuous action occurs within plain sight of a person (in a normal state of alertness), the person will notice it.

(8) If an adult attacks a child, that is an extremely wicked action.

(9) If someone does something extremely wicked, and others find out about it, they will want to punish him severely.

(10) If one (physically) enters something, one will then be inside it (and will have been outside it immediately before).

(11) If you eat at a restaurant, you enter (it), get a table to sit at, select a meal from a menu, place your order with a waiter, etc.

The first five items are taken loosely from the encodings in (Schubert & Hwang, 1989, Hwang & Schubert 1993a) of the knowledge needed to understand some small fragments of a fairy tale (Little Red Riding Hood). We found that dozens of axioms of this sort, encoded in EL (Episodic Logic, an NL-like representation) were typically required to enable the EPILOG system to make sense of a sentence in a story (also represented in EL), i.e., to infer the 'obvious' causal, temporal, part-of, and other coherence relations. Of course, the claim that story understanding is a knowledge-intensive activity is a truism in AI nowadays (thanks to the work of Roger Schank and his co-workers, and many others in the 70's and 80's), but the present point concerns the particular form of the required facts when stated in ordinary language. Evidently, all five sentences involve at least one instance of donkey anaphora. (In the third sentence, the deictic *that* is in effect a reference to an action whose existence is implicit in the antecedent if-clause.)

The last sentence is intended to echo the kind of knowledge often encoded in script-like representations. Setting aside the role of *you*, the consequent clauses clearly involve tacit or explicit references to the restaurant in question, and these references are again of the 'donkey' variety.

The need to convey huge numbers of mundane generalities to machines remains a frustrating bottleneck in the effort to endow machines with ordinary understanding and common sense. There are several possible ways of attacking the problem, the most direct being the systematic hand-coding of the requisite facts (Lenat, 1995). However, this approach is very labor-intensive, and the task would be greatly lightened if the bulk of the necessary knowledge could be conveyed directly through language.

The problem of donkey anaphora presents a formidable obstacle in this endeavor. The next section includes a brief review of some proposed solutions based on dynamic semantics. These solutions deal very plausibly with examples like (1-4), but have some drawbacks from an AI perspective. One is that their implementation in a reasoning system would require a significant reworking of the usual inference mechanisms so as to allow for the context dependence of the meanings of dynamically interpreted formulas. In addition, I will show that the dynamic semantics approach has difficulty representing reference to dependent entities (e.g., ones that play a role in a certain type of event), where the dependency was established by prior discourse or hinges on general world knowledge. Such dependent entities would be frequently encountered in attempting to 'tell machines about the world'.

In Sect. 3, I will then develop the proposal I call *dynamic skolemization*, showing how it deals both with standard donkey anaphora and the more challenging cases described in Sect. 2. Dynamic skolemization can be augmented so as to introduce new concepts (predicates) that 'summarize' the content of the formulas comprising the scope of the skolemized variables. When this is done, the representations becomes quite concise, and strongly reminiscent of scripts and frames in AI.

In Sect. 4 I discuss some further issues in the application of dynamic skolemization, including limitations of the approach when it is used to represent reference relations across clauses whose connective lies in a negative polarity environment; as well, I will briefly discuss 'generic passages' in the sense of (Carlson & Spejewski, 1997), the issue of 'strong readings', and the 'proportion problem'. In the final section I reiterate my conclusions about the status and scope of dynamic skolemization, and its potential utility in knowledge encoding.

2. DYNAMIC SEMANTICS

The difficulties posed by donkey anaphora have spurred new developments in the logical analysis and representation of ordinary language. Sentence (1), repeated here as (12), will serve to illustrate two well-known approaches very briefly:

(12) a. If a farmer buys a donkey, he pays for it in cash

b.

$$
\boxed{\;\boxed{\begin{array}{l} x \quad y \\ \hline F(x) \\ D(y) \\ B(x,y) \end{array}} \;\Rightarrow\; \boxed{\begin{array}{l} z \quad w \\ \hline P(z,w) \\ z = x \\ w = y \end{array}}\;}
$$

c. $(x, y : F(x), D(y), B(x,y)) \Rightarrow (z, w : P(z, w), z = x, w = y)$

(13) $[(\exists x, y) F(x) \wedge D(y) \wedge B(x, y)] \rightarrow P(x, y)$

Perhaps the best-known framework for dealing with anaphora is Discourse Representation Theory (DRT) (Kamp, 1981; Heim, 1982). The representation of (1), repeated here as (12a), would be a Discourse Representation Structure (DRS) as shown in (12b). This DRS contains a conditional whose antecedent (protasis) and consequent (apodosis) are again DRSs. The indefinites "*a farmer*" and "*a donkey*" are represented as variables called *discourse referents*, comprising the syntactically separate *universe* of the antecedent DRS. Corresponding *conditions* $F(x)$ and $D(y)$ appropriately constrain them in the antecedent DRS. The treatment of the definites in the consequent DRS is analogous, and the anaphoric references are resolved by the equations in the consequent DRS. An alternative, non-pictorial syntax could be as illustrated in (ref12c).

What is crucial here is the semantics, in particular the dynamic way in which discourse referents are added to the domain of a partial assignment function in the course of semantically evaluating a DRS. Roughly speaking, a conditional DRS like (12b) is taken to be true relative to a model and a partial assignment if every way of making the antecedent true by adding its discourse referents (here, x and y) to the domain of the assignment can be extended to a way of making the consequent true by adding its discourse referents (here, z and w) to the domain of the assignment.

Clearly, then, the way DRT treats the anaphoric pronouns in the consequent of a conditional is both syntactically and semantically dependent on the presence of co-referring discourse referents in the antecedent. Syntactically, the translations of the pronouns need to be equated to 'accessible' referents (such as those in the antecedent, or in the universe of an embedding DRS), and semantically the equations succeed in making the desired connection because of the way partial assignment functions get extended in the antecedent, and the way this extension is carried forward to the consequent.

A disadvantage of DRT as a meaning representation is that it requires a mapping from surface linguistic form to logical form that is hard to reconcile with a compositional semantics. Dynamic Predicate Logic (DPL) (Groenendijk & Stokhof, 1991) provides a compositional alternative. DPL would assign (12) the logical form shown in (13). Note that in DPL we can actually substitute the quantified variables x and y for the anaphoric pronouns, much as we were tempted to do – but couldn't make formal sense of – in the case of *it* in (2). The way DPL makes sense of (13) is by treating formulas much like computer programs, where variables are assigned values in earlier subformulas, and these values persist to later subformulas. In particular, an existential formula $(\exists x)\Phi$ is thought of as denoting a *nondeterministic assignment* to x, followed by a *test* Φ. Truth corresponds to 'executability' (for some initial values of the variables and some nondeterministic choices during execution). Technically, this is formalized in terms of state-change semantics, where a state is a (total) variable assignment; i.e., the semantic value of $(\exists x)\Phi$ relative to a model consists of the pairs of states such that the formula can (nondeterministically) transform one into the other. For a conditional $\Phi \rightarrow \Psi$, successful execution (truth) requires that for every way of executing Φ, the resultant state allows execution of Ψ.

Again, the dynamic change in the context of evaluation induced by the prior material is apparent, as is the need for 'accessible' prior referents. Another significant point to note is that both approaches lead to a universal ('strong') interpretation of indefinites in the antecedent of a conditional. In DRT, this is because of the iteration over *all* ways of making the antecedent true (in the present example, all ways of picking a farmer and a donkey such that the farmer buys the donkey). Similarly, in DPL this is because of the iteration over successful executions of the antecedent. So this semantics is somewhat appropriate for (12) but hardly for the specific reading of (2). However, one could define a 'specific conditional' within DRT or DPL that does justice to intuitions about (2) (see Chierchia, 1995). EL, mentioned above, would assign much the same logical form as DPL to (12) (neglecting events), but would employ a distinctive 'generic conditional' to obtain a quasi-universal reading. For the material conditional, EL's particular brand of DRT-like dynamic semantics would give the desired specific reading for (2).

The reliance of these theories on the presence of accessible referents for interpreting anaphora can be a serious handicap. This is apparent for passages where 'dependent entities' are introduced in one sentence, and then referenced in another, as in

(14) There were several instances at the fair where a farmer bought a donkey. In each instance, *the farmer* paid for *the donkey* in cash.

The dynamic semantics approaches provide no easy way to logically represent the referential definites in the second sentence so that they refer to the appropriate farmer and donkey in each of the instances under discussion. This is apparent if we write down a DPL-like or EL-like logical form for these sentences (enriching the basic syntax slightly so as to allow restricted quantifiers and some set-theoretic constructs):

(15) a. $(\exists S : set\text{-}of\text{-}instances(S))$
$\qquad (\forall e : e \in S)$
$\qquad\quad (\exists x : F(x))(\exists y : D(y))B(x, y, e).$

b. $(\forall e : e \in S)(\exists e' : e' \sqsubseteq e)$
$(The\ z\ :\ F(z))(The\ w\ :\ D(w))P(z,w,e').$

This interprets the 'instances' in (14) as donkey-purchases by farmers, and accordingly introduces a Davidson-like event variable into B ("*buys*") and likewise into P ("*pays in cash for*"). While I do not regard this approach to event representation adequate (see Hwang & Schubert, 1993b) it will do for present purposes.

Note, first of all, that the referential connection between the bound occurrence of S at the beginning and the free occurrence later on will be made successfully by the dynamic semantics approaches mentioned. However, the same is not true of the definites $(The\ z\ :\ F(z))$ and $(The\ w\ :\ D(w))$. Substituting the farmer-variable x from the first sentence for z, and the donkey-variable y for w, simply does not lead to a coherent result in any of the theories, since $(\exists x\ :\ F(x))$ and $(\exists y\ :\ D(y))$ lie within the scope of a universal quantifier. Intuitively, the first sentence posits various values of x and y depending on the choice of $e \in S$, and in the second sentence z and w should refer to these values as a function of e, but no such function is available.

In other words, when the desired referents are dependent entities embedded within a prior quantified context, they cannot do the required context-setting for interpreting the anaphoric descriptions. In fact, the only way we appear to have of solving the reference problem in (14) is to reformulate the second sentence so that it *repeats* the content of the first sentence antecedently, making the required referents directly accessible:

(16) a. In each instance, if *a farmer* bought *a donkey*, *the farmer* paid for *the donkey* in cash.

b. $(\forall e : e \in S)\ [(\exists x : F(x))(\exists y : D(y))B(x,y,e)] \rightarrow$
$(\exists e' : e' \sqsubseteq e)P(x,y,e')$

However, besides being cumbersome and *ad hoc*, this importation of material ought to be redundant. After all, the discourse prior to (16a) already characterized the instances in question as instances in which a farmer buys a donkey, so why should we have re-specify this property?

This is not the worst case. There are familiar kinds of reference where the required antecedent material is not merely submerged in the prior discourse, but hidden in the tacit knowledge of the speaker and hearer. The following is an example:

(17) a. John *dined at Mario's.* He left a big tip for *the waiter.*

  b. $(\exists e)D(J, M, e).\ (\exists x : T(x))(\exists e' : e' \sqsubseteq e)$
     $(The\ y : W(y))L(J, x, y, e')$

Any of the dynamic semantics approaches would now require retrieving and instantiating a 'dining out' scenario, at least in part, and incorporating this antecedently into the representation of the second sentence. Only then would we be able to resolve the definite description $(The\ y : W(y))$ to the appropriate referent, i.e., the waiter who served John. This approach would be laborious and hard to systematize, keeping in mind that stored scenarios could be quite complex, and that multiple scenarios could be relevant to a single sentence (e.g., *"At the business dinner at Mario's, the waiter spilled coffee on the CEO just when he was about to put up some pie-charts"*). These are just the sorts of problems that hampered full exploitation of 'scripts' in story-understanding research in the 70's and 80's.

  My goal in the following is to provide a straightforward and concise method of interpreting sentences involving anaphora as in (14) and (17), as well as the more innocuous cases of donkey anaphora. The idea is to make available *Skolem functions* (constants, in the simplest cases) for establishing referential connections. For instance, in the case of (17) we want to make available a 'waiter function' that picks out the waiter of any dining-out event, as a function of that event. In the following I develop such an approach, beginning with simple cases of (non-donkey) anaphora.

3. DYNAMIC SKOLEMIZATION

3.1. Skolem constants

Let's begin with a very simple example of cross-sentential anaphora, the sort that invites the use of Skolem constants – and has been dealt with in that way in countless natural-language systems:

(18) a. John bought a donkey. He paid for it in cash.

  b. $(\exists x : D(x))(\exists e)B(J, x, e).\ (\exists e')P(J, it, e').$

  c. $D(A) \wedge B(J, A, E).\ P(J, A, E').$

(18b) shows the preliminary logical form of (18a) (again with Davidsonian event arguments). In (18c), the variable x for the newly introduced donkey has been skolemized to A and the variable e for the newly introduced buying event has been skolemized to E. The anaphoric pronoun has also been replaced by A, unproblematically making the cross-sentential connection. Note that (as in some previous examples) there is also an implicit relation between the paying event and the buying event, i.e, the paying is understood to be part of the buying. Various theories have been proposed for deriving this sort of connection systematically (e.g., Webber, 1988; Hwang & Schubert, 1992; Lascarides *et al.*, 1992). By whatever means the connection is derived, the skolemization of event variables facilitates its representation, e.g., as $E \sqsubseteq E'$.

We should note in passing that skolemization is not a logically sound transformation. Rather, it amounts to a logical strengthening, since predicating constraints on a constant will filter out some possible models. But the strengthening is trivial in the sense that it is guaranteed to preserve satisfiability, and that no new sentences are entailed, other than some that involve the Skolem constant. (See the 'conservative extension' proposition below. This is why skolemization is legitimate in refutation proofs, such as resolution proofs.)

If one now considers a conditional sentence like (2) (repeated here as (19a)), one feels intuitively that the anaphoric connection is made just as in (18a), the non-conditional case.

(19) a. If John bought a donkey at the fair, he paid for it in cash.

   b. $[(\exists x)D(x) \wedge B(J, x)] \rightarrow P(J, it)$

   c. $[D(A) \wedge B(J, A)] \rightarrow P(J, A)$.

One conceptualizes the situation of John buying a donkey, and in doing so, establishes some conceptual token for the donkey. This token is then available for reference, whether the context-setting sentence supplies a fact or a proviso.

Of course, the discourse referents of DRT and the existential variables of DPL provide just such tokens, but we are seeking a solution admitting a standard semantics, and one extendable to functionally dependent entities. At first sight, Skolem constants and functions seem to fail us here. If we assign to (19a) the preliminary logical form (19b) (neglecting events for simplicity) and then attempt to skolemize and resolve the referent as we did in (18c), the result (19c) is patently defective. This is apparent from the fact that (19c) is the skolemized form of $(\exists x)[D(x) \wedge B(J, x) \rightarrow P(J, x)]$, i.e., "There is a thing x such that if it is a donkey and John bought it, then he paid for it in cash"; but this is trivially true if we can find any x that is not a donkey or was not bought by John, rendering the antecedent false.

However, it is interesting to note that (19c) fails as a representation of (19a) by being too weak, rather than too strong. Given (19a) and given that John bought a donkey, it should follow that there is a donkey that John bought, and paid for in cash. But if we replace (19a) as a premise in this argument by (19c), the conclusion no longer follows. This is because the existence of a donkey that John bought fails to entail $D(A) \wedge B(J, A)$, the antecedent of (19c).

This suggests a simple remedy: we supplement the skolemization in (19c) with the following stipulation:

(20) $(\exists x : D(x))B(J, x) \rightarrow D(A) \wedge B(J, A)$.

I will use the term *dynamic skolemization* for the two steps of (i) skolemizing an existential variable, and (ii) stipulating a supplementary condition like (20) above, relating the unskolemized existential formula to its skolemized form. (This is stated more formally, and generalized, below.) I will also refer to the supplementary condition itself as a 'Skolem conditional'.

Given (20), falsity of $D(A) \wedge B(J, A)$ implies that John didn't buy a donkey. So $D(A) \wedge B(J, A)$ can no longer be trivially false, and (19c) trivially true, as a result of A not being a donkey or John not having bought it. Some additional points are worth noting. First, the Skolem conditional can be turned into a biconditional, by existential generalization. This makes it natural to think of (20) as a partial *definition* of the newly introduced constant A. As such it provides a *conservative extension* of any theory framed in a vocabulary exclusive of A, as shown later.

Second, when we resolve the pronoun in (19a,b) to the constant A, introduced through dynamic skolemization, the resultant reading is *non-universal* ('weak'). To obtain a past-habitual reading of (19a), a generic or habitual quantifier (arguably, over events) would have to be introduced into the logical form (19b). Examples of this sort will be seen later.

A third, related point concerns the logical consequences of readings based on dynamic skolemization. Suppose we are told after (19a) that John *did* buy a donkey (within the relevant time frame), namely Archie (A'):

$D(A') \land B(J, A')$.

It does *not* follow that John paid for Archie in cash. This is because it does not follow that $A' = A$. Yet it seems intuitively natural to draw that conclusion. I will assume that this intuition arises from a scalar implicature of existential sentences that there is at most one verifying instance of that sentence.[2] For (19b) the implicature could be written as

$$[(\exists x : D(x))B(J, x)] \ \rightarrow \ (\exists! x : D(x))B(J, x),$$

or, using the Skolem constant in (19c), as

$$(\forall x : (D(x) \land B(J, x)))(x = A).$$

This clearly leads to the desired conclusion concerning Archie. But note that the uniqueness assumption is cancellable, for instance in a context like "*I don't know how many donkeys John bought, if any. But if he did buy a donkey, he rode it home*". Here it may well be that John bought a donkey that he rode home, and another that he didn't ride home. I leave further discussion of the uniqueness assumption to Sect. 5.3.

Abstracting from the above example, we can define dynamic skolemization as follows, for an existential sentence that occurs outside the scope of all other quantifiers:

(21)

> Given an occurrence of a (closed) sentence of form $(\exists x : \Phi)\Psi$ in the provisional logical form of an English sentence being interpreted,
>
> a. assert the Skolem conditional
> $$(\exists x : \Phi)\Psi \ \rightarrow \ \Phi_{C/x} \land \Psi_{C/x},$$
> where C is a new constant;
> b. replace the original occurrence of $(\exists x : \Phi)\Psi$ by the consequent of the above implication.

---

[2] E.g., (Kadmon, 1990). Such a uniqueness implicature is present in many contexts, and appears to be the result of the hearer's assumption that if the speaker thought there might have been multiple instances of the indefinite, and such instances are relevant to the purposes of the exchange, then he would have made this possibility explicit. This is similar to Gricean scalar implicatures in sentences such as "*Some / Most* students passed the exam", or "If *some / most* students passed the exam, John will be pleased", where the speaker seems to assume that not all students passed the exam.

The notation $\Phi_{C/x}$ stands for the result of substituting C for all free occurrences of x in Φ.[3] The 'provisional logical form' of a sentence refers to the logical form we would obtain *before* finalizing the representation of pronouns and referential definites, but *after* analyzing phrase structure, applying rules of logical-form composition corresponding to phrase structure rules (grounding these in a lexicon that supplies logical translations of lexical items), and scoping quantifiers.

What do the representations of pronouns and referential definites look like before they are finalized? I would like to leave this somewhat open. One possible assumption is that they are represented as unscoped restricted quantifiers, as in the quasi-logical forms of Schubert & Pelletier (1982),[4] *coindexed* with their referents (simple or functional terms) within the logical forms of the prior discourse or knowledge base. They are not assumed to be interpretable as parts of their embedding expressions, but only as transient forms still reflecting surface syntax and 'waiting' to be replaced by interpretable terms. In assuming coindexing of anaphoric terms, I am setting aside the problem of determining their referents, which is separate from that of appropriately representing them in the final logical form. Another possible provisional representation of anaphoric terms would be as DPL-variables, suitably chosen to refer to the desired referents. This would have the advantage of being fully interpretable – but only under a dynamic semantics, and only as long as we are dealing with the sorts of local reference that DPL can handle (as opposed to reference into quantificational contexts).

One implicit assumption in the above rule is that the embedded existential sentence $(\exists x : \Phi)\Psi$ is itself a final logical form, free of provisional (or dynamic) representations of anaphoric terms; otherwise the meaning of the Skolem conditional would not be well-defined. Thus dynamic skolemization of an existential sentence must be preceded by full anaphora processing within its scope.

Let us note some properties of dynamic skolemization, beginning with the following simple

Proposition. *The Skolem conditional (21a) provides a conservative extension of any theory framed in a vocabulary exclusive of the new Skolem constant C.*

---

[3] I use the particular variable x and constant C here for readability, but these are of course arbitrary.

[4] Or as generalized quantifiers.

What this means is that no new sentences follow from the theory together with the definition, other than ones involving the defined term C. The proposition is easily proved by considering any formula Φ not involving C that is entailed by a given theory $\mathcal{T}$ (not involving C) together with the Skolem conditional. For any model $\mathcal{M}$ of theory $\mathcal{T}$, let $\mathcal{M}' = \mathcal{M}$ if the antecedent of the Skolem conditional is false in $\mathcal{M}$; otherwise let $\mathcal{M}'$ differ from $\mathcal{M}$ only in assigning a value to C that makes the consequent of the Skolem conditional true. Then $\mathcal{M}'$ is a model of $\mathcal{T}$ together with the Skolem conditional, and so by assumption is a model of Φ. But $\mathcal{M}$ and $\mathcal{M}'$ agree on Φ, hence $\mathcal{M}$ is a model of Φ. Thus $\mathcal{T}$ entails Φ. I leave the generalization of the proposition (and proof) for the case of Skolem *functions* (below) to the reader.

Another property that (21) ought to satisfy is that it should give the expected result in simple declarative contexts – keeping in mind that it was motivated by existential sentences within conditional antecedents. It is easy to see that it does. For instance, consider (once again) (18a). First, note that the skolemization specified by (21b) yields the sentence $D(A) \wedge B(J, A)$ (*modulo* the choice of arbitrary new constant) as previously specified in (18c). But since this sentence occurs at the top level of the text being interpreted, it is *asserted*. As such it entails the Skolem conditional (previously given as (20), since it coincides with the consequent. Hence the Skolem conditional is redundant. In other words, in the case of simple declaratives (21) just describes ordinary skolemization of top-level existentials.

Finally, before proceeding to the more general case, we should note that the above rules of dynamic skolemization will need some modification in certain negative polarity environments. Examples are *"John didn't buy a donkey and pay for it in cash"*; and *"If John bought a donkey and paid for it in cash, then he rode it home"*. In both cases, *"a donkey"* occurs within a negative polarity environment, and is referred to anaphorically within the same environment. For the time being we ignore such cases, but take them up again in Sect. 5.2.

3.2. *Skolem functions, concept definitions*

The generalization of dynamic skolemization (21) to existential formulas containing free variables (i.e., embedded within the scope of other quantifiers) is straightforward:

(22) | Given an occurrence of a formula $(\exists y : \Phi)\Psi$, containing free variables $x_1, ..., x_m$, in the provisional logical form of an English sentence being interpreted,

   a. assert the Skolem conditional

$$(\forall x_1)...(\forall x_m)[(\exists y : \Phi)\Psi \rightarrow$$
$$\Phi_{f(x_1,...,x_m)/y} \wedge \Psi_{f(x_1,...,x_m)/y}],$$

   where f is a new m-place function symbol;

   b. replace the original occurrence of $(\exists y : \Phi)\Psi$ by the consequent of the above implication.

As before, we assume that the embedded formula $(\exists y : \Phi)\Psi$ is free of unresolved referring expressions. A simple illustration is provided by the following type of quantified donkey sentence, often used as central example in the literature; (we neglect events):

(23) a. Every farmer who bought a donkey paid for it in cash.

    b. $(\forall x : F(x) \wedge (\exists y : D(y))B(x,y))\, P(x,it)$

    c. Assert:
      $(\forall x)[(\exists y : D(y))B(x,y) \rightarrow D(f(x)) \wedge B(x, f(x))]$
      Subst.: $(\forall x : F(x) \wedge D(f(x)) \wedge B(x, f(x)))\, P(x, f(x))$

Note the resolution of the anaphoric pronoun in (23c). The reading this encodes is *non-universal* for donkeys, i.e., any one farmer purchasing multiple donkeys need only have paid for one in cash. I believe this is correct, based on examples analogous to (3) and (4), although we often generalize to a universal interpretation (see Sect. 5.3). For example, an analog of (4) is

(24) Every farmer who bought a donkey rode it home,

which seems true even if the farmers involved rode only one donkey each.

    It is clear that repeated application of (22) to a formula with multiple existential quantifiers, $(\exists y_1 : \Phi_1)...(\exists y_n : \Phi_n)\Psi$ will be equivalent to simultaneous skolemization of the y_i to $f_1, ..., f_n$. I will henceforth freely apply it in this way. The following is an interesting variant of (1), illustrating the case $n = 2$; (25b) is the Skolem conditional, and (25c) the logical form of (25a) after substitution:

(25) a. Whenever a farmer bought a donkey, he paid for it in cash.

    b. $(\forall e)[(\exists x : F(x))(\exists y : D(y))B(x,y,e) \rightarrow$
        $F(f(e)) \wedge D(g(e)) \wedge B(f(e),g(e),e)]$

    c. $(\forall e)[F(f(e)) \wedge D(g(e)) \wedge B(f(e),g(e),e) \rightarrow$
        $(\exists e')\, P(f(e),g(e),e')]$

The *whenever*-clause calls for universal event quantification, and this leads to the introduction of a farmer-function f and donkey-function g on events. In this case, we obtain a reading that effectively quantifies universally over farmers and donkeys, assuming that in distinct action predications such as $B(x,y,e)$, $B(x',y',e')$, e and e' cannot be the same buying-event unless x and y are the same as x' and y' respectively. This seems intuitively correct.

There remains a certain inelegance in these examples of dynamic skolemization from a practical computational perspective, in that we are repeating variants of the original existential formula, $(\exists y_1 : \Phi_1)...$ $(\exists y_n : \Phi_n)\Psi$, three times: twice in the Skolem conditional (in the antecedent and consequent) and once in the logical form of the given text. I will therefore introduce a space-saving notation, called *concept definition* that avoids redundancy.

Before defining the notation formally, the idea is just this: when we encounter a wff $(\exists y_1)...(\exists y_n)\Phi$ that is to be skolemized, we first define a new predicate that is simultaneously equivalent to (i) this wff, for all values of the free variables (those not bound by the $(\exists y_i)$), and (ii) the skolemized version of the wff. We then substitute the newly defined predicate into the source text. Formally, the concept definition schema is this:

(26) | For Π a new m-place predicate constant, $f_1, \ldots, f_n$ new m-place function constants, and Φ a formula possibly containing free occurrences of variables $x_1, \ldots, x_m$ and $y_1, \ldots, y_n$ (and no others),
    (Def $\Pi(x_1, \ldots, x_m)$ $(f_1, \ldots, f_n)$ $\Phi_{\underline{f}/\underline{y}})$
abbreviates (with underlining indicating vectors)
    $(\forall x_1) \ldots (\forall x_m)[\Pi(x_1, \ldots, x_m)$
    $\leftrightarrow (\exists y_1) \ldots (\exists y_n)\Phi \leftrightarrow \Phi_{\underline{f}(x_1,\ldots,x_m)/\underline{y}}]$

$x_1, ..., x_m$ are the *variables* of the Def-schema, $f_1, ..., f_n$ are the *roles* (role functions, Skolem functions), and $\Phi_{\underline{f}/\underline{y}}$ is the *body* of the definition. Note that in this body we are using function symbols (without arguments) in place of variables, so that the result will not be a well-formed formula. This avoids having to repeat the variables $x_1, ..., x_m$ on which each role depends.

Applying the Def-schema to (25) as described above, we get a more concise and transparent representation of the dynamic skolemization (now formulated as a concept definition, (27a)) and the resultant logical form, (27b); *FBD* is the newly defined concept (mnemonic for "farmer buys donkey"):

(27) a. (**Def** *FBD* (e) (f, g) $F(f) \wedge D(g) \wedge B(f, g, e))$

  b. $(\forall e)$ *FBD* $(e) \rightarrow (\exists e') P(f(e), g(e), e')$

We are now well-equipped to return to the farmers at the fair, and Mario's restaurant. Looking back at (15a), note that we will first skolemize S, the set of instances mentioned, to some new constant (but I will retain S here). The next existential sentence encountered is $(\exists x : F(x))(\exists y : D(y))B(x, y, e)$. Hence we get the definition

  (**Def** *FBD*(e) (f, g) $F(f) \wedge D(g) \wedge B(f, g, e))$.

Substituting the defined concept in the provisional logical form (15a), we obtain (28a); we can now easily resolve the references in (15b) to $f(e)$ and $g(e)$, as shown in (28b):

(28) a. $(\forall e : e \in S)$ *FBD*(e).

  b. $(\forall e : e \in S)(\exists e' : e' \sqsubseteq e)P(f(e), g(e), e')$.

To deal with the example of Mario's restaurant, (17), we naturally need to presuppose some prior knowledge of 'what happens when' a person dines out. While people are unlikely to first acquire this information in the form of a tidy verbal package, it would help with knowledge bootstrapping if this were possible for computers. So suppose we tell our NLP system something like the following:

Generally, when a person dines at a restaurant, s/he enters the restaurant, gets seated at a table, selects a meal from a menu, tells the order to a waiter, etc.

I will assume that *generally* quantifies over dining-at-restaurant episodes here, binding an episodic variable:

$(Gen\ e :(\exists x : P(x))(\exists y : R(y))D(x,y,e))$
$\qquad (\exists e_1 : e_1 \sqsubseteq e \wedge starts(e_1,e))\ Enter(\hat{x},\hat{y},e_1)\ \wedge$
$\qquad (\exists e_2 : e_2 \sqsubseteq e \wedge \hat{e} \prec e_2)\ Get\text{-}seated(\hat{x},e_2)\ \wedge$
$\qquad (\exists e_3 : e_3 \sqsubseteq e \wedge \hat{e}_2 \prec e_3)\ Select(\hat{x},e_3)\ \wedge$
$\qquad (\exists w : W(w))(\exists e_4 : e_4 \sqsubseteq e \wedge \hat{e}_3 \prec e_4)$
$\qquad\qquad\qquad Tell\text{-}order(\hat{x},w,e_4)\ \wedge$
$\qquad\qquad \ldots \qquad\qquad)$

Note that the first line of this expression comprises the *restrictor* of the *Gen* quantifier. The symbols with carets are an *ad hoc* abbreviation for anaphoric terms, used for readability. For instance, $Enter(\hat{x},\hat{y},e_1)$ abbreviates

$(The\ z : R(z))Enter(s/he,z,e_1),$

i.e., s/he enters the restaurant; the particular symbols used, such as $\hat{x}$ and $\hat{y}$, are intended to suggest to the reader the expected referents of these terms.

The first existential sentence encountered is the restrictor of the *Gen* quantifier. Thus we apply dynamic skolemization and concept definition to it:

$\qquad (\textbf{Def}\ \ PDR\ \ (e)\ (f,g)\ P(f) \wedge R(g) \wedge D(f,g,e)).$

Having substituted the defined predicate in the restrictor, and knowing that x is now $f(e)$ and y is $g(e)$, we can also resolve $\hat{x}$ and $\hat{y}$ to $f(e)$ and $g(e)$ respectively in the matrix of the *Gen* construct. Next we apply dynamic skolemization and concept definition to the matrix. Here I allow myself a slight liberty, skolemizing all of the conjoined existential sentences at once (processing them in succession would yield multiple definitions rather than a single one, but would otherwise be equivalent):

$\quad (\textbf{Def}\ \ PDRsteps\ \ (e)\ (f_1,f_2,f_3,h,f_4,\ldots)$
$\qquad f_1 \sqsubseteq e \wedge starts(f_1,e) \wedge Enter(f,g,f_1) \wedge$
$\qquad\qquad \ldots$
$\qquad W(h) \wedge f_4 \sqsubseteq e \wedge f_3 \prec f_4 \wedge Tell\text{-}order(f,h,f_4) \wedge$
$\qquad\qquad \ldots \qquad\qquad)$

Substituting in the matrix of *Gen*, we then obtain

$\qquad (Gen\ e :PDR(e))PDRsteps(e).$

Having accommodated the background knowledge in this way, we are now ready to interpret the definite description *the waiter* in (17), repeated here as (29a). The result is (29b), and after further skolemization, (29c):

(29) a. John dined at Mario's. He left a big tip for *the waiter*.

b. $D(J, M, E)$.
$(\exists x : T(x))(\exists e : e \sqsubseteq E)L(J, x, h(E), e)$.

c. $D(J, M, E)$. $T(C) \wedge E' \sqsubseteq E \wedge L(J, C, h(E), E')$.

There is still a hidden ambiguity, however. As far as the stored background knowledge is concerned, the agent of E is $f(E)$ and the restaurant is $g(E)$. To link these to *John* and *Mario's* respectively, we again need to invoke a 'uniqueness of roles' assumption concerning dining-out events:

$$(\forall e)(\forall x, y, x', y')D(x, y, e) \wedge D(x', y', e) \rightarrow x{=}x' \wedge y = y'.$$

Again, this is an intuitively reasonable assumption.

4. SCRIPTS, FRAMES AND KNOWLEDGE BOOTSTRAPPING

As previously hinted, there is a close resemblance between the above encodings of the farmers-at-the-fair and dining-at-Mario's examples on the one hand, and scripts and frames as understood in AI (e.g., Schank & Abelson, 1977; Minsky, 1975) on the other. For instance, Minsky suggests that a person entering an office retrieves and instantiates an office frame featuring *slots* for the expected parts and furnishings (floor, ceiling, walls, door, desk, chair, etc.). These slots quickly become bound to perceived parts and furnishings, and the knowledge associated with them helps to guide further perception and action. Now this is just the sort of structured representation we would obtain by skolemizing a description of the form, "*An office generally has a floor, a ceiling, four walls, a door, a desk, etc., with such-and-such properties and related in such-and-such ways...*". Assuming a provisional logical form like

$(Gen\ x : Office(x))\ [(\exists y_1 : Floor(y_1)\ ...\ ],$

we would define of a concept such as *Office-interior*(x) corresponding to the body of the *Gen*-formula, with roles (Skolem functions) that pick out the parts and furnishings of the office. It would then be straightforward to interpret the definites in general and particular sentences like

(30) An office belonging to a professor often has piles of books and papers on *the desk*.

(31) Mary went into her office and sat down at *the desk*.

Note that the *Gen*-formula for an office does not involve any existential quantifiers in the restrictor, and so does not give rise to a concept definition for the restrictor (in contrast with the examples of the farmers at the fair and Mario's restaurant). Thus the formula supplies information about the pre-existing concept of an office, rather than about newly introduced episodic notion such as that of dining at a restaurant. This is typically how frames have been employed in knowledge-based systems, i.e., they are used to supply information about familiar, usually non-episodic concepts such as that of an office, a wage earner, a particular product, etc., expressible with a lexical or compound noun.

In the case of general episodic knowledge, the tie-in with scripts is by now clear. The dining-out example was of course intended as a parallel to Schank and Abelson's (1977) restaurant script. While their script is not formally interpreted, the name of the script can be viewed as a defined concept similar to *PDR* above; further, it involves roles for the participating entities that are clearly analogous to some of the skolemized roles in the definitions of *PDR* and *PDRsteps*, and it involves steps that are analogous to the skolemized subepisodes in *PDRsteps*. An interesting difference is that it is not possible to access the roles in a script 'from the outside', as seems to be required for representing general or particular sentences such as

(32) When a person dines at a *fancy* restaurant, s/he pays *the waiter* directly, not at a cash register.

(33) When Mary dined at Mario's, *the waiter* turned out to be an an ex-classmate of hers.

For (32), a traditional script-based approach would have to create a variant script for fancy dining, as a context in which to place the new fact (assuming that the pre-existing restaurant script is noncommittal about how the bill is paid). This could be done in some *ad hoc* way by modifying a copy of the regular script, or directly inserting an alternative track into that script. In the approach based on dynamic skolemization, we would automatically create a separate concept of dining at a fancy restaurant, and, recognizing that dining at a fancy restaurant entails dining at a restaurant, make use of the role functions in the *PDR* and *PDRsteps* definitions to pick out the waiter (and the implicitly referenced bill). For (33), the traditional approach would expand out an instance of the restaurant script, thus gaining access to the waiter in that script instance. In the approach based on dynamic skolemization, it is sufficient to recognize Mary's dining at Mario's as an instance of a person dining at a restaurant (hence instantiating PDR); this immediately makes available the role functions in $PDRsteps$ (as was illustrated for (29a).

It has been known for a long time that frame slots involve Skolem-like functions, logically speaking (Hayes, 1979). Furthermore, role functions have been proposed in the planning literature for picking out steps in goal-oriented courses of action (e.g., Kautz 1991). However, the representational devices employed in scripts, frames and plans were conceived on purely computational and introspective grounds, with no formal links to the syntax/semantics interface. So it seems auspicious that considerations arising from problems in linguistic anaphora lead directly to script/frame-like representations, and in doing so also provide solutions to some traditionally difficult reference problems.

Schank and his collaborators were very interested in the problem of *learning* scripts by generalization from particular narratives containing repetitive patterns of events (Schank, 1982). While this type of generalization learning is undoubtedly of crucial importance for AI, the present work clears some obstacles from a more direct path to the acquisition of such knowledge, namely explicit description of the general patterns in ordinary language. Lenat (1995), as mentioned earlier, has already mounted a large-scale effort to encode general knowledge directly in a frame-like representation. But this has depended so far on familiarizing the contributors to this effort with the internal representation, and entrusting to their intuitions the correct formulation of common-sense facts in this representation. Such an effort would surely benefit from an effective linguistic input channel. Language is the shared medium for the exchange of common-sense human knowledge, and as such would provide a much faster, much more natural means for knowledge boot-strapping; as well, if the mapping from the internally stored information to language were straightforward and systematic, browsing and verifying the stored knowledge, and any inferences drawn from it, would become much easier.

5. FURTHER ISSUES

A variety of issues remain concerning the scope and details of dynamic skolemization. Most require further research, but I want to at least provide a preliminary discussion.

5.1. *Generic passages*

In the discussion of the restaurant scenario so far, I have oversimpli-
fied matters. In particular, I assumed just one tacit all-encompassing
generic quantifier and restrictor (roughly, *"For most situations e in
which there is a person x and a restaurant y such that x dines at y,
..."*). More realistic examples are considered in (Carlson & Spejewski,
1997) under the heading of *generic passages*. These may (tacitly or
explicitly) involve a succession of different quantifiers and restrictors.
For instance, the restaurant scenario might contain a subpassage such
as

If the restaurant is informal, the menus are *often* already on the table. If it
is formal the waiter *usually* brings the menus. When the waiter arrives at the
table, he *usually* begins by requesting orders for drinks. He *always* asks the
ladies first...

It can be seen that successive sentences can add their own restrictions
to one implied by the preceding context, and can supply their own
generic quantifier. (Arguably the quantifier is always there, explicitly
or tacitly.) The quantification implicitly refers to the overall event type
(i.e., dining-out) and may in addition be restricted by the subordinate situation types specified in previous sentences. For instance, the
last sentence above (about asking the ladies first) quantifies implicitly
over events of requesting orders for drinks (introduced in the *previous*
sentence) that are part of a dining-out event.

   Thus the logical form of a generic passage will be something like

$$(Ge : \phi(e))$$
$$(G_1e_1 : \phi_1(e_1))\psi_1(e_1) \wedge ... \wedge (G_ne_n : \phi_n(e_n))\psi_n(e_n),$$

where $G, G_1, ..., G_n$ are various generic event quantifiers (such as *"generally", "usually", "sometimes",* etc.). The ϕ_i and ψ_i can of course
contain arbitrary additional quantifiers, and in particular the ψ_i will
typically introduce new existentially quantified events/situations (e.g.,
the waiter's arriving at the table, the waiter's requesting orders for
drinks, etc.) Now there is a difficulty here very similar to the one
encountered in the 'farmers at the fair' example. We have a series of
quantificationally closed sentences, yet we need to relate events introduced in the ψ_i to each other temporally (and in other ways); and in
addition, as noted the restrictors (i.e., the ϕ_i) need to refer to event-

types introduced in previous sentences, as well as to the overall event type.

In a DRT-based approach such as is developed in (Carlson & Spejewski, 1997) these phenomena require a great deal of forward propagation of material from both restrictor clauses and main clauses, in order to restrict each successive quantifier appropriately, and make temporal and other connections. (This is similar to techniques used in the DRT literature for modal subordination.) Something quite analogous would have to be done in a DPL representation.

The promise of dynamic concept definition lies in the fact that it would automatically supply both Skolem functions for the events introduced in the ψ_i, and new event predicates corresponding to ϕ (the main event-type being described) and those of the ϕ_i and ψ_i that involve existential quantification. These are precisely what we need to relate the events in the generic passage in time (etc.), and to succinctly express the restrictions ϕ_i, *without* carrying forward any of the prior material. Thus it appears the earlier remarks about the advantages of adding dynamic concept definition to the process of logical-form calculation gain further support when we move from simplified scenarios to genuine generic passages. The technique should enable us to obtain direct, succinct representations of such passages, in a form that admits a non-dynamic semantics and allows the application of familiar inference techniques.

5.2. *Anaphora within negative environments*

In all of the examples of anaphora seen so far, the indefinite E_i and the coindexed pronoun or definite D_i were 'positively linked' in the following sense: they occurred within a sentential complex of the form

$$\Phi(E_i) \ op \ \Psi(D_i),$$

where the connecting operator *op* lies in a positive polarity (upward entailing) environment. For instance, this is true for anaphoric links across the two components of a (top-level) conjunction or a (top-level) if-then sentence. This bias in our examples (and elsewhere in the literature) in favor of positive environments is a consequence of the fact that extended negative environments are rare in natural language.

Nonetheless, it is of interest how dynamic skolemization fares in negative environments. My tentative conclusion is that dynamic skolemization needs to be modified in such environments. In particular, the Skolem conditionals need to take account of all of the material within such environments – i.e., in terms of the above schema, both the Φ-material and the Ψ-material.

The following are some relevant examples, with corresponding provisional logical forms shown in (b) (using free variables, as in DPL or EL, to provisionally represent any anaphoric pronouns). The (c)-items show the corresponding dynamically skolemized representations that would be obtained if we applied the same rewriting rules to negatively linked indefinite-definite pairs as to positively linked pairs. In each case the unmodified Skolem conditional would be $(\exists x : D(x))B(J,x) \rightarrow D(A) \wedge B(J,A)$.

(34) a. John did not buy a donkey

　　 b. $\neg(\exists x : D(x))B(J,x))$

　　 c. $\neg(D(A) \wedge B(J,A))$

(35) a. John didn't buy a donkey and pay for it in cash.

　　 b. $\neg[((\exists x : D(x))B(J,x)) \wedge P(J,x)]$

　　 c. $\neg(D(A) \wedge B(J,A) \wedge P(J,A))$

(36) a. If John bought a donkey and paid for it in cash, then he rode it home.

　　 b. $[((\exists x : D(x))B(J,x)) \wedge P(J,x)] \rightarrow R(J,x)$

　　 c. $(D(A) \wedge B(J,A) \wedge P(J,A)) \rightarrow R(J,A)$

(37) a. It's not the case that if John bought a donkey, he paid for it in cash.

　　 b. $\neg[(\exists x : D(x))B(J,x) \rightarrow P(J,x)]$

　　 c. $\neg[(D(A) \wedge B(J,A)) \rightarrow P(J,A)]$

The first example, (34), involves an explicitly negative context for skolemization, but no anaphora. Despite the flagrant violation of the conditions under which ordinary skolemization would be licensed, the skolemized representation, (34c), evidently has the desired truth conditions, taken together with the Skolem conditional.

(35) is our first example of a negative linkage between an indefinite and an anaphoric pronoun. Does (35c) (along with the Skolem conditional) capture the intuitive meaning of (35a) (which corresponds to the DPL meaning of (35b))? Well, it does as long as we let a uniqueness assumption stand. For, if John bought just one donkey, then by the Skolem conditional, $D(A) \wedge B(J, A)$ holds, and hence from $\neg(D(A) \wedge B(J, A) \wedge P(J, A))$, $\neg P(J, A)$ holds, i.e., John did not pay in cash for the one donkey he bought. However, we can preempt the uniqueness implicature by prefacing (35a) with the disclaimer, "*I don't know how many donkeys, if any, John bought, but...*". Even in this context (35a) says that John did not pay in cash for *any* donkey he bought, no matter how many he bought; whereas (35c) incorrectly allows for the possibility that John bought two donkeys and paid for one (but not the other) in cash.

As already indicated, I believe that the correct Skolem conditional for (35) would take account of all of the material in the negatively embedded conjunction; i.e., we need to define A as any donkey that John bought *and paid for in cash*, if there is such a donkey. It is as if we tacitly widened the scope of the existential quantifier in (35b) so that its scope is the entire conjunction, allowing it to bind the pronoun (non-dynamically). Here it is worth citing an analogous example involving a universal quantifier, apparently requiring expansion of the quantifier binding scope:[5]

(38) John didn't go to each donkey and give it a sugar cube.

Example (36) further illustrates anaphoric binding within a negatively embedded conjunction, since the conjunction comprises the antecedent of a (positively occurring) conditional. Again (c) fails to provide correct truth conditions for (a) if John bought more than one donkey. For if A picks out any donkey John bought, and he happened to pay for that donkey by credit card, then (36c) will be true (in virtue of the falsity of the conjunctive antecedent) – even if John bought a second donkey, paid for it in cash, and didn't ride any donkey home. Once again the correct Skolem conditional would be one that amalgamates the content of both clauses of the conjunction.

Example (37) is a little harder to get an intuitive hold on, but I think it illustrates the same point. In this case the anaphoric linkage

---

[5] However, I am not suggesting quantifier scope widening as the actual mechanism to be be employed in such cases, but rather a direct expansion of the Skolem conditional to incorporate the extra material.

bridges the clauses of a negatively embedded conditional, rather than a negatively embedded conjunction. Sentence (37a) implies that it's not the case that John either didn't buy a donkey, or bought a donkey that he paid for in cash. Hence John did buy a donkey, but didn't buy a donkey that he paid for in cash. But again (37c) merely entails that John bought a donkey A and didn't pay for A in cash – incorrectly leaving open the possibility that he bought another donkey A' and paid for it in cash. The correct Skolem conditional should again express that A is a donkey that John paid for in cash, if there is such a donkey, i.e., it should amalgamate the material from the antecedent and consequent of the negatively embedded conditional.[6] Then (37c) would entail (*via* the Skolem conditional) that there is no donkey that John bought and paid for in cash, while also entailing $D(A)$ and $B(A)$ (he did buy a donkey).

The details of the above modification of dynamic skolemization for negative anaphoric linkages, when the coindexed terms lie within arbitrarily complex sentences, are a matter for further research. The need to change the rules of dynamic skolemization for negative anaphoric linkages would diminish its appeal as an *alternative* to dynamic semantics, if it were offered as such. However, that is not the intention; the very fact that dynamic skolemization involves the stipulation of new definitions disqualifies it as a *semantic* theory (especially if we are partial to compositional semantics). Its promise lies elsewhere, namely in the way it links up dynamic semantic representations with 'standard' knowledge representations, and in the way it implements functional anaphoric connections.

Finally, let me mention a very tangentially related point concerning apparent cases of external reference into negated contexts, as in

(39) John didn't buy a DONKEY. It was a mule.

The result of dynamically skolemizing the indefinite in the negated context would again be unsatisfactory. In particular, it would fail to capture the entailment that John bought a mule. But this is to be expected, since the interpretation of (39) depends upon a presupposition, mediated by the indicated stress on A DONKEY, that John did

---

[6] If we wish to view this amalgamation in terms of scope widening, we would first have to rewrite the conditional $\Phi \to \Psi$ as $\neg\Phi \lor (\Phi \land \Psi)$, confining the scope-widening to the conjunction. But this would have the undesirable consequence of generating two Skolem conditionals, one for each disjunct.

buy SOMEthing. It appears, then, that the correct referent for the pronoun comes from that presupposition, rather than from the negative sentence.

5.3. *Uniqueness and strong readings*

I invoked uniqueness implicatures in connection with arguments like the following.

If John bought a donkey, he paid for it in cash. John bought a donkey named Archie. Therefore, John paid for Archie in cash.

Now while the existence of uniqueness implicatures is widely acknowledged, their role in donkey anaphora remains controversial. One point that is frequently made is that uniqueness implicatures cannot be used to justify a 'lazy definite' account of anaphoric pronouns (such as suggested by Geach, 1962; Partee, 1975; Evans, 1980). On such an account, we could reformulate "*If John bought a donkey, he paid for it in cash*" as "*If John bought a donkey, he paid for the donkey he bought in cash*". Here successful reference by the phrase "*the donkey he bought*" depends on the uniqueness of that donkey, if John bought one at all. But since uniqueness is merely implicated, the implicature may be cancelled, as in the following sentence due to Kratzer (1995:158) (a variant of Heim's 'sageplant' sentences):

(40) When a house has a barn, it often has a second one right next to it (the first barn).

Clearly the final "*it*" cannot be rephrased as "*the house's barn*". However, this is not a problem for the Skolem-function approach. Even when the uniqueness implicature is cancelled, the Skolem function still refers uniquely. In other words, the Skolem-function approach is more akin to a 'lazy indefinite' account of anaphoric pronouns in this respect.

However, there is a general objection to any sort of pronoun-of-laziness account, which would also carry over to dynamic skolemization: we are left with no account of strong readings of donkey sentences, which appear to quantify universally over all verifying instances of an existential sentence. For instance, "*If John bought a donkey, he paid for it in cash*" is claimed to have a strong reading, even on a nongeneric construal. According to this reading, John paid for *every* donkey he bought in cash. Note that this would provide an alternative justification for the above argument concerning Archie the donkey.

LENHART SCHUBERT

246

Kamp (1981) and Heim (1982) and most researchers after them took it as their central task to account for strong readings, and formulated their dynamic semantics accordingly. Schubert and Pelletier (1989) pointed out the importance of weak (nonuniversal) readings, taking these as basic while suggesting that strong readings arise from generic construals. Chierchia (1995) considers these matters in detail and concludes that weak readings are basic, in the sense that dynamic binding yields weak rather than strong readings. Nonetheless, he maintains (with Kanazawa, 1994) that many donkey sentences, even nongeneric ones, have strong readings, and offers a novel account of these. An example he attributes to Heim is

(41) Every man who owned a slave owned his offspring

(Chierchia, 1995:64). Certainly one feels that this sentence tends to rule out cases where a slave owner owns the offspring of some, but not all, of his slaves. Chierchia suggests that in addition to a dynamically bound reading, donkey pronouns can also have an E-type reading (Evans, 1980), specifically one which uses a contextually determined function whose value may be a plural entity. On this account, there is a reading of "*his offspring*" in (40) tantamount to "the offspring of *the slaves owned by* the given slave-owner"; evidently this yields the strong reading. So we are invoking a plural-valued (or at least number-neutral) function "*the slaves owned by*", somehow supplied by the linguistic context (where the subject noun phrase presumably plays the key role).

From the present perspective such a suggestion is rather attractive insofar as we already have in hand a simple mechanism for extracting functions from context; we could implement Chierchia's suggestion by allowing for definition of set- or collection-valued Skolem functions.[7] However, my own intuitions about examples like (41) are uncertain. It seems possible to me that this sentence has no direct entailments concerning a slave owner's 'extra slaves', if any. Rather, it may make a definite claim only about one slave per slave owner – but may invite inference of a stronger statement to cover the cases left open by the uniqueness implicature.[8] Such inferences may derive from our dispo-

---

[7] In the case where $(\exists x : \Phi)\Psi$ contains no free variables, we would stipulate $\forall x.(x \in C) \leftrightarrow (\Phi \wedge \Psi)$. When there are free variables $x_1, ..., x_m$ in the existential formula, we would use Skolem function $f(x_1, ..., x_m)$ in place of C and add external $\forall$-quantifiers for $x_1, ..., x_m$.

[8] Some unconditional sentences where a uniqueness presupposition is likely to be undermined by general knowledge also appear to have a 'strong reading':

sition to make sense of what we are told in terms of more general principles and trends, and to reconcile the phrasing and content of the claims made with our knowledge of the world and of conversational maxims. In the case of (40), we might make sense of the weak reading (which has no entailments for a slave owner's 'extra slaves') in terms of some presumed law of ownership likely to be in effect during times of slavery, and conclude that there is no reason why this law would not extend to the 'extra slaves', thus arriving at the strong 'reading'.

I would point out that such strengthened interpretations seem to arise even in the absence of explicit indefinites, for instance in

(42) Everyone who burped said "excuse me",

where we tend to conclude that repeat-burpers made repeated apologies. It would be a stretch to invoke a function from people to sets of burps here, as a way of capturing this inference. Rather (as in the case of the slave-ownership sentence), we seem to generalize over the event type at issue (burping) in a way that goes beyond the explicit quantification over people who burped at least once (cf. the appeal to implicit quantification over times in Evans, 1980). Another example where it is hard to see how context could supply a suitable function for a strong reading is the following:

(43) If there is an extraterrestrial civilization, it hasn't contacted humanity.

This appears to rule out contact with all extraterrestrial civilizations, however many there might be. We would need something like a function from sectors of the universe to the set of civilizations in that sector (where the contextually relevant sector is the universe exclusive of Earth), to implement Chierchia's suggestion here. My inclination is again to regard the strong interpretation as an explanatory inference: why would anyone make a claim like (43), if not as a comment on the lack of evidence for an extraterrestrial civilization? And if there is no evidence for one, there is no evidence for any.

More familiar sentences of this form, such as (44), appear susceptible to the same kind of account:

(44) a. If John bought a donkey he didn't pay for it in cash.

"*I have no money in my pocket*"; "*John has a strong arm and a sharp eye*"; "*John is scarcely aware of his next-door neighbor*"; etc.

b. $[((\exists x : D(x))B(J,x)] \rightarrow \neg P(J,x)]$

c. $\neg(D(A) \wedge B(J,A) \wedge P(J,A))$

Again a strong reading appears to be dominant,[9] and I would again surmise that this derives from a generalization from the weak reading. John's not paying in cash for one donkey suggests he was unable or unwilling to come up with the cash, and this makes it very unlikely that he would pay cash for any *additional* donkeys. For comparison note the following variant of a sentence due to Kanazawa (1994), where the weak reading does prevail:

(45) If John has an umbrella, he surely didn't leave it at home today.

5.4. *The proportion problem*

A further question of interest is how dynamically skolemized donkey sentences fare with respect to the 'proportion problem' (e.g., Kadmon, 1987). For example, consider the following sentence:

(46) In most instances, if a bee stings a man, he survives.

The problem is that if we count every 'stinging event' e of the sort $Stings(x,y,e)$ as distinct, a single instance where a man died after being stung by a thousand bees will outweigh hundreds of nonfatal stingings by isolated bees, and lead to the incorrect prediction that the sentence is false.

One option here is to treat *"in most instances"* as a quantifier that selectively binds times and men, but not stinging events and bees. This corresponds to a paraphrase of (46) as *"For most pairs (t,y) of times and men such that there is a bee x and a stinging event e at time t where x stings y in e, y survives"*. A disadvantage of this approach is its *ad hoc* introduction of a time variable and its nonuniform treatment of indefinites as sometimes bound by adverbial quantifiers and sometimes

---

[9] If we try to express the strong reading of (44) unambiguously, we have to be careful about phrasing. Since that reading is supposed to express iteration over all verifying instances of the indefinite, we might try to express it as *"If John bought a donkey, he didn't pay for every donkey he bought in cash"*. However, this is essentially the weak reading, since the negation in the matrix clause tends to outscope the quantifier, making the matrix clause equivalent to *"for some donkey John bought, he didn't pay for that donkey in cash."*

existentially quantified (with a dynamic semantics). Be that as it may, such an approach would be compatible with dynamic skolemization. We would obtain the following Skolem conditional and skolemized sentence:

$$(\forall y)(\forall t)[[(\exists x : B(x))(\exists e : At-time(e, t))(M(y) \wedge Stings(x, y, e))]$$
$$\leftrightarrow [B(f(y, t)) \wedge At-time(g(y, t), t) \wedge$$
$$M(y) \wedge Stings(f(y, t), y, g(y, t))]$$
$$(Most\, y,\, t : B(f(y, t)) \wedge M(y) \wedge At-time(g(y, t), t) \wedge$$
$$Stings(f(y, t), y, g(y, t))) \; Survives(y),$$

ignoring the event variable of *Survives*, which should be related in some way to the time t. Though the Skolem functions pick out a particular bee and stinging by that bee for any given man and time, there is no presumption that the selected bee is acting alone.

To me a more attractive option is to treat the adverbial as quantifying only over events (more generally, situations / eventualities / episodes), but not Davidsonian ones. We regard events as being determined not just by atomic predications, but also by more complex formulas such as $(\exists x : B(x))Stings(x, y)$, as in Situation Semantics (Barwise & Perry, 1983) or Episodic Logic (Hwang & Schubert, 1993b). Then we can quantify over 'coarse-grained' stinging events that may involve multiple bees. Without going into details (which would require a digression into SS or EL), such an approach would treat both indefinites in (46) as existentially quantified. If we narrow-scope the bee-quantifier and wide-scope the man-quantifier with respect to the operator that connects event variables with sentences describing the events ("$\models$" in SS and "**" in EL), the preferred reading emerges. Dynamic skolemization can be applied to existential quantifiers outside the scope of this operator, and in the case of (46) this leads to an event-dependent function supplying the victim of a bee-stinging (where any number of bees may be involved).

6. CONCLUDING REMARKS

I have shown how one can dynamically skolemize indefinites encountered in natural language input, so that the resultant constants and functions are available for subsequent reference. This provides a new way of dealing with donkey anaphora and other cases of anaphora standardly handled through some version of dynamic semantics. The advantages are that the resulting representations are context-independent and admit a standard semantics, and that referential connections can be made for instances of functional anaphora that are problematic for dynamic semantics.

The kinds of anaphora at which dynamic skolemization is aimed pervade ordinary language, particularly the sort of language used to express commonsense generalizations about the world. So the possibility of dealing straightforwardly with heretofore refractory cases should prove very helpful in the effort to impart commonsense knowledge to machines through language.

Moreover, I showed that the representations of general facts obtained through dynamic skolemization, aided by concept definitions, are strikingly similar to the frame-like and script-like representations that are the stock-in-trade in knowledge representation and reasoning. This convergence between certain kinds of linguistically and nonlinguistically motivated representations provides some reason for optimism about the possibility of a unified approach to representation and inference.

I have also tried to explore some areas of potential difficulty for dynamic skolemization, including anaphora within negative polarity environments, the proportion problem, and strong readings. This indicated the need for some refinement of the technique for certain kinds of embeddings of coindexed terms, but as far as I can tell there are no insurmountable obstacles to its broad application in natural language processing.

There appear to be some interesting links between my proposal and an approach to anaphora proposed by Meyer Viol (1995). (See also Meyer Viol *et al.*, this volume.) The latter is based on *instantial logic*, a development of Hilbert's ϵ-calculus. As noted by Meyer Viol, there is a close connection between skolemization and *epsilon*-terms. In fact, the indefinite in a sentence such as *"John owns a donkey"* would be represented by an ϵ-term $\epsilon x(D(x) \wedge O(J,x))$, which can be thought of a picking out an arbitrary donkey owned by John, if there is such a donkey. However, Meyer Viol's goal is not to provide 'standard' logical translations of NL sentences, but rather to develop a logic containing ϵ-terms, and to employ that logic to represent quantification and reference (among other things) in NL. His account of anaphoric pronouns is, in fact, a lazy-indefinite account. The reconstructed content of a pronoun often depends not only on the material in the sentence that introduces the indefinite antecedent of the pronoun, but potentially also on subsequently added material. In particular, successive occurrences of a pronoun that we might naively take as having the same implicit content are taken to have different content; e.g., this is the case for the two occurrences of *"he"* in *"A man walked in. He was wearing a hat. He smiled.*" where the first is interpreted as having the content "*a man who walked in*", while the second has the content "*a man who walked in and was wearing a hat*". By contrast, dynamic skolemization would resolve both pronouns to the same Skolem constant. Meyer Viol offers a novel account of strong readings of donkey sentences, based on incorporating the entire content of such sentences into the reconstructed pronoun. For example, the pronoun in "*Every farmer who owns a donkey beats it*", on a strong reading, is rendered as (roughly) "*some donkey owned by the farmer which he doesn't beat*". Evidently this entails that each farmer beats all of his donkeys, for if he had any donkeys he doesn't beat, such a donkey would be picked out by the ε-term, rendering the matrix clause false (indeed logically false). It would be possible in principle to incorporate this idea into dynamic skolemization, but I would hesitate to complicate the the dynamic skolemization rule to that extent.

As a final comment, I would also mention the possibility of transmuting dynamic skolemization into a truly semantic theory. The idea would be incorporate the creation of functions, corresponding to indefinites in quantified contexts, into dynamic predicate logic. This may be possible by generalizing variable assignments so that variables can be dynamically bound to functions, as well as to individuals, and requiring all occurrences of existential quantifiers to bind distinct variables (which could then be used freely outside their binding context). The attraction of such a move would be that it would dispense with separately asserted Skolem conditionals, preserve a DPL-like compositional semantics for donkey sentences, and extend this semantics to functional anaphora. Script- and frame-like structures would be created even more directly than in the scheme proposed herein, since it would no longer be necessary to substitute Skolem terms for indefinites – the names of the corresponding existential variables would already denote the requisite individuals or functions.

ACKNOWLEDGEMENTS

This work was supported in part by NSF grant IRI-9503312 and by grant F30602-95-1-0025 from ARPA/SSTO. I am grateful to Greg Carlson for useful pointers to the literature (including the draft of his paper with Beverly Spejewski on generic passages), and to Wilfried Meyer Viol and Ruth Kempson for alerting me to the cited work on instantial logic, and providing helpful comments on its application to anaphora.

REFERENCES

Allen, J. F. and L. K. Schubert (1991) The TRAINS project. Tech. Rep. 382, Dept. of Computer Science, Univ. of Rochester, Rochester, NY. Also slightly revised as "Language and discourse in the TRAINS project", in A. Ortony, J. Slack, and O. Stock (eds.), *Communication from an Artificial Intelligence Perspective*. Heidelberg: Theoretical Springer-Verlag, 91-120, 1993.

Barwise, J. and J. Perry (1983) *Situations and Attitudes*. Cambridge, MA: Bradford Books, MIT Press.

Carlson, G. N. and F. J. Pelletier (1995) *The Generic Book*. Chicago: Univ. of Chicago Press.

Carlson, G. N. and B. Spejewski (1997) Generic passages. *Natural Language Semantics 5*, 1-65 (to appear).

Chierchia, G. (1995) *Dynamics of Meaning*. Chicago: Univ. of Chicago Press.

Evans, G. (1980) Pronouns, quantifiers and relative clauses (I). In M. Platts (ed.), *Reference, Truth and Reality*, New York: Routeledge, Kegan Paul.

Geach, P. (1962) *Reference and Generality*. Ithaca, N.Y.: Cornell University Press..

Groenendijk, J. and M. Stokhof (1991) Dynamic predicate logic. *Linguistics and Philosophy 14*, 39-100.

Hayes, P. J. (1979) The logic of frames. In D. Metzing (ed.), *Frame Conceptions and Text Understanding*, New York: de Gruyter.

Heim, I. (1982) *The Semantics of Definite and Indefinite Noun Phrases*. Ph.D. Dissertation, U. Mass.

Hwang, C. H. and L. K. Schubert (1993a) Episodic Logic: a comprehensive, natural representation for language understanding. *Minds and Machines 3*(4): Special Issue on KR for NLP, 381-419.

Hwang, C. H. and L. K. Schubert (1993b) Episodic Logic: a situational logic for natural language processing. In P. Aczel, D. Israel, Y. Katagiri and S. Peters (eds.), *Situation Theory and its Applications, v.3 (STA-3)*, CSLI, Stanford, CA, 303-338.

Hwang, C. H. and L. K. Schubert (1992) Tense trees as the 'fine structure' of discourse. *Proc. of the 30th Ann. Meet. of the Assoc. for Computational Linguistics (ACL-92)*, U. Delaware, Newark, DE, June 28 - July 2, 232-240.

Kadmon, N. (1987) *On Unique and Non-Unique Reference and Asymmetric Quantification*. Ph.D. Dissertation, U. Mass., Amherst, MA.

Kadmon, N. (1990) Uniqueness. *Linguistics and Philosophy 13*, 273-324.

Kamp, H. (1981) A theory of truth and semantic representation. In J. Groenendijk, T. Janssen, and M. Stokhof (eds.), *Formal Methods in the Study of Language*, Mathematical Centre-tracts, U. Amsterdam, Amsterdam, Netherlands.

Kanazawa, M. (1994) Weak vs, strong readings of donkey sentences and monotonicity inferences in a dynamic setting. *Linguistics and Philosophy 17*(2), 109-158.

Kautz, H. A. (1991) A formal theory of plan recognition and its implementation. In J.F. Allen, H.A. Kautz, R.N. Pelavin, and J.D. Tenenberg, *Reasoning about Plans*, San Mateo, CA: Morgan Kaufmann, 69-125.

Kratzer, A. (1995) Stage-level and individual-level predicates. In (Carlson and Pelletier, 1995), 125-175.

Lascarides, A., N. Asher, and J. Oberlander (1992) Inferring discourse relations in context. In *Proc. of the 30th Ann. Meet. of the Assoc. for Computational Linguistics (ACL-92)*, U. Delaware, Newark, DE, June 28 - July 2, 1-8.

Lenat, D. (1995) CYC: A large-scale investment in knowledge infrastructure. *Comm. of the ACM 38*(11), 33-38.

Meyer Viol, W. P. M. (1995) *Instantial Logic.* IILC Dissertation Series 1995-11, Inst. for Logic, Language and Computation, Univ. of Amsterdam.

Minsky, M. (1975) A framework for representing knowledge. In P.H. Winston (ed.), *The Psychology of Computer Vision*, New York: McGraw-Hill, 211-277.

Partee, B. (1975) Bound variables and other anaphors. In D. L.,Waltz (ed.) *Theoretical Issues in Natural Language Processing-2 (TINLAP-2)*, July 25-27, Univ. of Illinois at Urbana-Champaign, 79-85.

Schank, R. C. (1982) *Dynamic Memory: A Theory of Reminding and Learning in Computers and People.* New York: Cambridge Univ. Press.

Schank, R. C. and R. P. Abelson (1977) *Scripts, Plans, Goals and Understanding.* Hillsdale, NJ: Lawrence Erlbaum Assoc.

Schubert, L. K. and C. H. Hwang (1989) An episodic knowledge representation for narrative texts. *Proc. of the 1st Int. Conf. on Principles of Knowledge Representation and Reasoning (KR-89)*, May 15-18, Toronto, Canada, 444-458.

Schubert, L. K. and F. J. Pelletier (1989) Generically speaking, or, using discourse representation theory to interpret generics. in G. Chierchia, B. Partee, and R. Turner (eds.), *Properties, Types, and Meanings II*, Dortrecht: Reidel, 193-268.

Schubert, L. K. and F. J. Pelletier (1982) From English to logic: Context-free computation of 'conventional' logical translations. *Am. J. of Computational Linguistics 8*, 27-44, 1982. Reprinted in B. J. Grosz, K. Sparck Jones, and B. L. Webber (eds.), *Readings in Natural Language Processing.* Los Altos, CA: Morgan Kaufmann, 293-311, 1986.

Webber, B. L. (1988) Tense as discourse anaphor. *Computational Linguistics 14*(2), 61-73.

JONATHAN GINZBURG

SEMANTICALLY-BASED ELLIPSIS RESOLUTION WITH SYNTACTIC PRESUPPOSITIONS

1. INTRODUCTION

A central issue since the late 1960's has been the issue of whether ellipsis resolution processes are syntactic or semantic in nature.[1] Recently, works that take a more generalized discourse view (Prüst et al, 1993; Asher, 1993; Kehler, 1994) have suggested the need for an approach which eschews a purely syntactic or semantic approach, but rather is conditioned by discourse structure. Kehler, for instance, has modified the approach of Hankamer and Sag (1976, 1984) so that whether the resolution arises from syntactic copying or is semantic i.e. derives from material already integrated in the discourse model, is determined by whether the coherence relation between clauses is parallel or not. Thus, on the Sag/Hankamer/Kehler view, syntactic parallelism is not expected indeed not possible in resolution where the source has been integrated in the discourse model. In this chapter, I show that *short answers* as they occur in extended dialogue involve a resolution process that is perplexing for current models of ellipsis, both purely syntactic or semantic, and mixed ones such as Kehler's. In particular, I demonstrate that elliptical options are possible

- at essentially unbounded distance from the original source,
- long after integration of material must have taken place in the discourse model,
  and yet,
- (partial) syntactic parallelism obtains.

However, I defend the semantic nature of the resolution procedure itself. Nonetheless, I suggest that the syntax/semantics interface as far as interrogative meaning, and ultimately quite generally, needs to

---

[1] This chapter summarizes work presented in much greater detail in chapters 4 and 5 of a soon to be completed book, tentatively titled *Moving on the Dialogue Gameboard: a Semantics for Interaction in Dialogue*. The aforementioned chapters are available from ftp.cogsci.ed.ac.uk:pub/ginzburg

H. Bunt and R. Muskens (eds.), Computing Meaning, Volume 1, 255–279.

be modified, arguing that the data motivates reconstructing the idea of *syntactically-based* presuppositions first broached in Lakoff (1971). I will argue that, at least as far as this type of ellipsis goes, syntax does have a material role to play, not in *constructing* interpretations but in *constraining* interpretations. More specifically: in ensuring that the contents of phrasal utterances get associated with the right *semantic* argument-roles. This will provide a natural account for *why* (a very limited amount of) syntax needs to be preserved across utterances and in what cases it does not, for instance the short-answers used to respond to y/n questions.

My own account is based on combining the dialogue dynamics developed in Ginzburg (1994, 1995a, 1995b, forthcoming) with information structure. The latter will serve as motivation for introducing the notion of a *a syntactic presupposition on a semantic argument-role*. I will show how such presuppositions can be captured within a slightly modified version of a sign-based grammar like HPSG. The essential idea will be to construct λ-abstracts over *utterances* in such a way that the argument-roles also carry syntactic appropriateness restrictions. This involves using a number of tools from situation semantics, including the reification of utterances and parameters bearing restrictions. The idea of using restrictions to capture such syntactic presuppositions follows up on ideas first put forward in Cooper (1993). Finally, I will suggest that, with certain independently motivated modifications, such abstracts have similar semantic expressiveness to abstracts that lack such appropriateness restrictions.

2. DIALOGUE DYNAMICS

I review here the basics of the semantic framework I presuppose, based on Ginzburg (1994, 1995a, 1995b, forthcoming).

2.1. *Individuals in Dialogue*

How to talk about a dialogue participant (DP)? Ginzburg (1994) proposes the following schematic partition. On the one hand, we need a way of talking about some *quasi*-shared object, each DP's version of the common ground, relative to which the conventionalized interaction of the dialogue, both locutionary (uttering) and illocutionary (asserting, querying) takes place. I will call this component the *dialogue gameboard* (DGB) (cf. Hamblin's notion of *individual commitment slate*). Separate from this will be the *non-publicized* aspects of each participant's individual mental state. I will call this the DP's *unpublicized mental situation* (UNPUB-MS(DP)), where typically, such things as goals and general inferential capabilities are represented. In the current chapter attention will be focussed exclusively on the dialogue gameboard: a gameboard is a situation which represents a DP's view of certain attributes of the dialogue situation. These attributes need to include at least the following:

- FACTS: set of commonly agreed upon facts;
- QUD ('questions under discussion'): partially ordered set that specifies the currently discussable questions. If q is topmost in QUD, it is permissible to provide any information specific to q.
- LATEST-MOVE: content of *latest move* made: it is permissible to make whatever moves are available as reactions to the latest move.

With this view of context, *discussion* can be modelled as the consequence of a particular question q being maximal in QUD. This structures the context to accept either any information σ that is *about q* or questions q_1 on which q *depends*. Here *about* and *depend* are semantic notions, relations respectively between informational items and questions, and between two questions described and formalized in Ginzburg (1995a). Whereas the standard view of assertion *that p* due to Stalnaker only accommodates acceptance or rejection of p as followups, the current view allows us to explicate why an assertion commonly gives rise to a discussion of *whether p*. An assertion is modelled as a sequence of actions that starts out with the question *whether p* as maximal in QUD. The context is then structured either to accept *that p* as information that resolves the question or to lead to a discussion sequence of *whether p*.

2.2. *Semantic Ontology*

The semantic framework utilized here is situation theory (e.g. Barwise and Cooper, 1991). The view of questions utilized here is the framework described in Ginzburg (1995a, 1995b). A proposition is notated $p = (s!\tau)$, where s is a situation and τ is a **soa**. This is the kind of entity that can be believed or disbelieved and is the descriptive content of an assertion.

(1) $p = (s!\tau)$ is TRUE iff τ is a *fact* of s: denoted as: $s \models \tau$

Thus, the proposition $(s!\langle WALK, j; + \rangle)$ is TRUE iff $s \models \langle WALK, j; + \rangle$. That is, intuitively, if j's walking is a fact of s.

A question will be an entity $(s?\mu)$, constructed from a situation s and an n-ary abstract $\mu = \lambda X_1, \ldots, X_n \sigma(X_1, \ldots, X_n)(n \geq 0)$. For instance:

(2) a. a use of *"Did Bill leave"* has as its content: $(s?\langle LEFT, b; +\rangle)$,

   b. a use of *"who left"* has as its content $(s?\lambda x \langle LEFT, x \rangle)$

Questions are related to soa's via two principal relations, *about* ('partial answerhood') and *resolves* ('contextually relativised exhaustiveness'). Both relations are formally characterized in Ginzburg (1995a) using the notion of informational subsumption within a soa-algebra.

3. SHORT ANSWERS

I turn now to one prominent semantic application of the semantic framework for dialogue briefly sketched above. One of the most obvious ways in which a query use of an interrogative changes the context is to enable elliptical followups, *short answers*, phrasal utterances used to respond to queries. Let us start by considering short answers to unary wh-questions. An initial formulation of a rule for interpreting such utterances is (3):[2]

(3) S $\rightarrow$ XP

   Content(S)[DGB_0] = (SIT(DGB_0 | Max-QUD) ! λ-Abstr(DGB_0 | Max-QUD)[Content(XP)])

The rule says that in a DGB configuration DGB_0, any XP can be expanded as an S whose content is calculated as follows: it is a proposition of the form $(s!\sigma)$. Here s is the situation component of the question maximal in QUD; σ arises by predicating of the XP the abstract component of the question maximal in QUD.[3]

This is exemplified in (4), where many significant details such as tense have been simplified away:

---

[2] For expository simplicity, I use here a phrase structure, rule-to-rule description; as will become clear in chapter 5, my approach crucially presupposes a sign-based approach, where syntax and semantics can interact and influence each other in significant ways.

[3] The rule assumes that such fragments are sentential by nature and, hence, potentially embeddable as complements. This potential is fulfilled, *contra* Steedman (1990), as originally pointed out by Morgan (1973):

(4) a. [In a train depot, the driver needs to be decided]
A: Who will drive the train?
B: Bill.

b. The question expressed: $(s_{train-journey}?\lambda x \langle WILL-DRIVE-THE-TRAIN, x \rangle)$

c. Content of answer phrase: (reference to the individual) **b**.

d. Content of the short answer: $(s_{train-journey}!\langle WILL-DRIVE-THE-TRAIN, b \rangle)$

The rule in (3) is, putting aside framework-related differences, similar to rules for interpreting short-answers prevalent in the so-called categorial approach to interrogatives, approaches that interpret interrogatives as denoting n-ary relations (see e.g. Hull, 1975; Hausser and Zaefferer 1979). The main innovation here pertains to the reference to QUD, which connects up to context in an explicit way, in particular enabling an account of short-answers used an arbitrary distance away from the question to which they pertain, as illustrated in section 5.1.

3.1. Generalizing the Short-Answer Rule

The rule in (3) needs to be generalized. As it stands it does not account for quantified short answers, as in (5a) for sentential adverbials used to respond to y/n–questions, as in (5b), nor to answers to multiple wh–questions, as in (5c,d):

(5) a. A: Who attended the meeting? B: No students./ A friend of Jill's.

b. A: Did Bill attend the meeting? B: Yes./ Maybe.

c. A: Who was interacting with whom at the party? B: Bill with Mary./ Some of my friends with each of her friends./ One thing's for sure: None of my friends with none of my sister's friends

---

(i) A: What is the default font-size? B: I'd been assuming that 12 point.

(ii) A: What does Nixon want for breakfast? B: Kissinger says eggs. (Morgan (1973))

(iii) A: Why is she leaving town? B: It seems that because Max is no longer here.

d. A: Who arrived when? B: Bill at 5, Mustafa a couple of hours later./ Several of us in the morning, everyone else at noon.

There is a familiar strategy one could employ to deal with unary quantified answers and adverbial answers to y/n–questions, namely to view the *short–answer phrase* as the operator, rather than the abstract associated with the question. Such a strategy has been advocated in somewhat distinct forms by Groenendijk and Stokhof (1984), and by Ginzburg (1995b). I do not adopt this strategy here primarily because it does NOT generalize to cover short answers to multiple wh–questions.[4] How to interpret such answers? The most pressing question perhaps is the relative scope of the answer phrases: which one composes first with the abstract provided by the question? One could imagine a number of possible strategies that might emerge, perhaps based on word order or grammatical hierarchy. However, what the data seems to suggest is perhaps most consonant with a non-elliptical syntax presupposed here, namely *neither answer takes scope over the other*: this means that what emerges can be analyzed either as a *branching* reading (see e.g. Barwise, 1979; Westerståhl, 1985; Sher, 1991) or in terms of cumulative quantification over groups (see e.g. Landman, 1995). Thus, whereas a dependent reading in which the subject NP takes scope over the object PP for (6a) would be equivalent to a $\forall\exists$ reading, the actual reading exhibited is one whose truth conditions entail that the set of my friends kept apart from the set of my sister's friends Similarly, in (6b), a dependent reading means that *a lot* of inter-sexual arguing was taking place, whereas the branching reading, the one that seems to occur, involves relatively little such discord:

(6)   A: Who was interacting with whom at the party?

a. B: One thing's for sure: None of my friends with none of my sister's friends.

b. B: Some liberals with most conservatives but few men with few women.

These data constitute, to the best of my knowledge, one of the few cases where branching quantification contents arise as the *sole* interpretational possibility, arguably as a consequence of a particular constructional meaning.

---

[4] For further discussion of this alternative strategy see chapter 4 of Ginzburg (forthcoming).

Given this, I propose to generalize our original schema (3) in the following way:

(7) $S \rightarrow (Adv),(XP_1),\ldots,(XP_n)$

Content(S)(context) = (SIT(MAX-QUD) ! Content(Adv)
(Branch-closure(Quant-Content(XP_1),...,Quant-Content(XP_n),
⟨Rel:μ, r_1: Content(XP_1),...,r_n: Content(XP_n) ⟩)))

Context: $\mu = \lambda$-Abstr(Max-QUD)

The 0-ary case corresponds to y/n questions, where the phrasal utterance is a sentential modifier (*"yes"*, *"probably"*, *"no"*, *"maybe next week"*, etc.), which takes as its argument the 0-ary λ-abstract associated with the question currently under discussion, i.e. maximal in QUD, which is simply a **soa**. When n $\geq$ 1, the content arises by predicating the λ-abstract associated with the question maximal in QUD, of the contents associated with the phrasal utterances; in case these latter are quantified, the content that arises is the branching-quantificational closure of these quantifiers, with nuclear scope the λ-abstract.[5] When we restrict attention to the most common case, n = 1, branching closure reduces to ordinary quantificational closure.

(7) seems to leave open a crucial issue that concerns the syntax–semantics interface: how to ensure the correct association between semantic roles and phrasal utterances? Thus, consider (8):

---

[5] For concreteness, I will adopt the following schema due to Barwise (1979), restricted for simplicity to two quantifier phrases. (See Westerståhl, 1987 and Sher, 1990 for background and a more general and uniform condition.):

(i) Branch-closure($Q_1x_1A, Q_2x_2B, \mu(x_1,x_2)$) $\leftrightarrow \exists X \subset A, \exists Y \subset B$ [$Q_1AX \land Q_2BY \land (X \times Y \subset Extension(\mu) \cap A \times B)$] ($Q_1, Q_2$

(ii) Branch-closure($Q_1x_1A, Q_2x_2B, \mu(x_1,x_2)$) $\leftrightarrow \exists X \subset A, \exists Y \subset B[Q_1AX \land Q_2BY \land (Extension(\mu) \cap A \times B \subset X \times Y)]$ (Q_1, Q_2 monotone decreasing quantifiers)

Thus, given these schemas B's response in (iii) will involve the truth–conditions in (iv) and (v):

(iii) A: Who was arguing with whom? B: Some liberals with most conservatives but few men with few women.

(iv) There exist sets X, Y; X consists of liberals, Y is such that most conservatives are in Y and for each x $\in$ X and y $\in$ Y, x argued with y.

(v) There exist sets X, Y; X is either empty or consists of few men, Y is either empty or consists of few women and those men/women pairs who engaged in arguing are included in $X \times Y$.

(8) A: Who depends on whom? B: John on Mary./ Most students on most teachers.

Both short answers here are quite unambiguous: in (8a) *"John"* is the depender and *"Mary"* dependent, in (8b) *"most students"* is the depender and *"most teachers"* dependent. In any account which involves reconstruction/deletion at some level of analysis, this is not difficult to enforce. But what about the present account, which eschews such mechanisms? (7) itself does not offer a way out. A solution to this problem will emerge in section 7, *without in any way altering* (7); the alteration will be in the nature of the abstract associated with the question, which will encode certain syntactically-based presuppositions on its argument-roles.

4. SURFACE SEMANTICS V. RECONSTRUCTION

The discussion concerning (8) suggests we should consider an alternative to the surface semantics approach outlined in the previous section, namely a *syntactic* approach to short answer resolution, based on some form of reconstruction or deletion, say. My concern in this section is to argue against the desirability of such an approach, which has in fact been widely assumed to be necessary since Morgan (1973). Specifically, I will offer some arguments towards refuting the following claim:

(9) Well-formedness of short answers involves checking whether their reconstruction correlates are well-formed. (Morgan, 1973)

My claim will be that in general the short answer diverges from plausible surface correlates of the reconstructed form both syntactically and semantically.

4.1. *Syntactic Divergences*

I start by considering syntactic divergences between the short answer and those surface forms that are plausible correlates of a reconstruction analysis. For reasons of space I restrict attention to one class of cases, a much wider discussion is to be found in the extended version of the chapter.

One of the biggest challenges for the surface semantics approach is Morgan's claim that well-formedness of fragments involves checking whether reconstructed forms satisfy binding theory (BT). If this were indeed the case, the implication would be that syntactic information of the *entire* source is relevant. However, I will argue that Morgan's BT data is actually preferably explained otherwise. Morgan's idea is that, for instance, condition B of BT would be invoked to explain why examples such as (10) are infelicitous:

(10) a. A: Who does Bill$_i$ like? B: himself$_i$/# him$_i$ (felicitous if stressed)

    b. Bill likes himself$_i$ /# him$_i$

However, as the following examples illustrate, the ill-formedness of the reconstructed form is not, as a general rule, a good predictor of short-answer felicity[6]:

(11) a. A: Who will punish Bill$_i$ if he fails? B: he himself/himself/#he/ #him (both felicitous if stressed)

    b. # He himself$_i$/* himself$_i$ will punish Bill$_i$ if he fails.

(12) a. A: What caused the computer to break down? B: Power surge? A: perhaps, but the most intriguing answer is: [the computer itself]$_i$ /itself$_i$ /#it

    b. #The computer itself$_i$/*Itself$_i$ caused the computer$_i$ to break down.

(13) a. A: Who were the cause of John and Mary's worst problems? B: Each other.

    b. *Each other were the cause of John and Mary's worst problems.

---

[6] In the discussion here I assume that the surface correlate ('spellout') of reconstruction is simply the form obtained by, roughly speaking, inserting the short answer in the *in situ* position of the interrogated wh-phrase, as commonly assumed (see e.g. Morgan, 1973; Von Stechow, 1991; Rooth, 1992). In the extended version of the chapter, I offer both syntactic and semantic arguments that an alternative assumption according to which the deletion source/reconstruction output is either a pseudo-cleft or a cleft does not strengthen the reconstructionist's case.

(14) a. A: Whose complaints annoyed Bill and Jill most intensely?
         B: Each other's.

      b. # Each other$_i$'s complaints annoyed [Bill and Jill]$_i$ most intensely.

Thus, BT + reconstruction undergenerates: many fragments are felicitous despite the fact that their reconstructed surface correlate violates BT. A better explanation of such cases is provided by the two independently motivated assumptions that a short answer is focal and hence must be accented, and that accented pronouns in English must be contrastive. This has the consequence of ruling out coreference in examples such as (15):[7,8]

(15) A: Who does Bill$_i$ like? / B: HIM$_i$

Support for the focus-based explanation comes from (16). Here what reconstruction + BT predicts should be licit (the unstressed pronominal) is infelicitous, whereas a resolution that is *outlawed* by reconstruction is acceptable:

(16) a. A: Who does Jill think Bill desires? B: Herself/Her.

      b. Jill thinks Bill desires herself.

      c. Jill thinks Bill desires her.

4.2. *Semantic Divergences*

Let us consider now semantic divergences between short answers and their reconstructed correlates. The first set of data I discuss is based on some interesting observations by Corblin (1995); his data is based on French, I will discuss similar examples from Hebrew (if anything the Hebrew data makes the point somewhat more strongly.) The observations are these:

----

[7] I wish to thank Joe Taglicht for helpful discussion of this point that helped sharpen my previous proposal.

[8] Cremers (1983) proposes a related explanation for 'the absence of clitics or relative pronouns from being a proper part of a well-formed ellipse.' (Cremers, 1983, p. 148.) Cremers is concerned with gapping and sluicing, which he argues to be instances of a general ellipsis schema. He proposes an essentially phrase-structure account and advocates separating away issues of well-formedness from issues of interpretability of ellipsis.

- the short answer (17a) has only a ∀∃ reading [for (17a) this amounts to a reading where everyone met at least one visitor.]
- the reconstructed version only has the reading in which no meetings/no inspections took place (in French this is the *preferred* reading; ∀∃ also available)

(17) a. A: mi lo pagash af exad mihamevakrim? B2: af exad.

A: who not met no one of the visitors? B2: no one.

"Who met none of the visitors?" "No one"

b. af exad lo pagash af exad mihamevakrim.

"No one met any of the visitors"

The surface semantics approach explains the short-answer part of Corblin's observation. The reading provided for (17a) is the following:

(18) a. $\lambda P \neg \exists x[\text{person}(x) \wedge P(x)](\lambda z \neg \exists y(\text{visitor}(y) \wedge \text{met}(z,y))) =$

$= \neg \exists x[\text{person}(x) \wedge \neg \exists y(\text{visitor}(y) \wedge \text{met}(x,y))]$

$= \forall x[\text{person}(x) \rightarrow \exists y(\text{visitor}(y) \wedge \text{met}(x,y))]$

An analogous argument can be constructed with responses to multiple wh-questions. Here, as we saw in section 3, short-answers are to be analyzed as involving scope-less quantification, either branching quantification or cumulative quantification *not* scope-ful quantification. However, it is the latter that is, at the very least, the preferred interpretation of the reconstruction correlates. One such example is provided in (19): for (19a) the reading exhibited is one whose truth conditions entail that the set of men keeps apart from the set of women, whereas (19b) is preferably understood as indicating the lecherous nature of men; this reading is accentuated if *"few"* in the object NP *"few women"* receives a pitch accent. Similar phonology does *not* have a similar effect in (19a):

(19) a. A: who interacts with whom here these days? B: As far as I can tell few men with few women. (Unambiguously branching/cumulative reading, regardless of stress.)

b. Few men interact with few women. (Preference for scoped reading, especially with accent on second *"few"*)

5. CATEGORY CONCORD IN (LONG-DISTANCE) DIALOGUE ELLIPSIS

5.1. Data

The data considered in the previous two sections underlines the fact that short answers diverge markedly from their reconstructed correlates both on the syntactic and the semantic front. In particular, this suggests the following conclusion: *the syntax of short answers does not require reference to the syntactic properties of the* **entire source**. It does *not* follow from this, however, that: *no* syntactic properties of *any* constituent of the source are relevant. In fact, I will now attempt to establish the following two claims:[9]

- Reference must be made to the syntactic properties of the argument-role associated with the interrogated wh-phrase.[10]
- This constraint holds across (in principle) unbounded stretches of dialogue.

I consider here solely nominal complements, though analogous data exists with verbal complements. A language like English, where case is irregularly marked, is not an ideal stalking ground; the phenomenon is more straightforward to demonstrate in languages where case is more pervasive. In (20), I offer an example from Hebrew whose analogues in a variety of inflected languages (e.g. German, Greek, Russian) demonstrate a similar point: the Hebrew verb "siyea" (*"help"*) takes PP's headed by "lo" (*"to"*), whereas the verb "tamax" (*"support"/"vote"*) takes PP's headed by "be" (*"in"*). The short-answers must be headed by the requisite preposition.

Does this data reflect idiosyncratic subcategorisation requirements or is it to be explained in terms of (something like distinctness in thematic roles? While one can never fully rule out an explanation of the latter type, this seems rather unlikely: the fineness of grain needed to distinguish the thematic roles of, say, "siyea" (*"help"*) and "tamax" (*"support"*), cuts across any default thematic-role–to–syntax mappings that might plausibly be proposed: PP[+le] is associated with *goal* argument-roles, whereas PP[+be] is associated with *location* argument-roles. By

---

[9] Data from Korean supporting the first claim are also provided in Morgan (1989).

[10] For the y/n case (with no focussing), the claim amounts to: *no* syntactic dependence, see the extended version for exemplification.

most tests, the PP-object of either verb is in fact a *goal*, so by default we should expect both PP's to be realized as PP[+le].

(20)

a.	A: be/*le mi tamaxta babxirot?	A: *be/le mi siya'ta babxirot?
b.	B: ba/*la xazit haislamit	B: *ba/la xazit haislamit
c.	A: haxevre shel Darawsha	A: haxevre shel Darawsha
d.	B: shel Dahamshe	B: shel Dahamshe
e.	A: ah ken.	A: ah ken.
f.	B: vekamuvan gam be/*leAhmad	B: vekamuvan gam *be/leAhmad
g.	A: yafe	A: yafe.
h.	B: leca'ari gam ba/*la tembel hahu.	
		B: leca'ari gam *ba/latembel hahu

(Gloss: *A: Who did you help/support in the elections? B: (to)//(in) the Islamic front; A: (to)//(in) Darawshe's guys?; B: Dahamshe's! A: Right; B: And (to/in) Ahmad;A:Nice; B: And also unfortunately (to/in) that idiot.*)

5.2. *The Moral*

In considering how to capture syntactic dependencies such as those exemplified in this section, it is important to bear in mind the fact that the dependence is maintained across unbounded stretches of dialogue. This means that capturing the dependence using *reconstruction* of the source is problematic, not only for the syntactic and semantic reasons mentioned above, but also for two processing-related reasons: first, there is psycholinguistic data that shows syntactic information as a whole decays rapidly,[11] which is why one would not wish to posit a syntactic structure over unbounded stretches of dialogue. Second, for a short answer such as (20f) or (20h) above, occuring as it does while the question is in the midst of being discussed, it seems quite clear that the question expressed in (20a) *has been incorporated in the discourse model* as a semantic entity (it has been understood and is under discussion). Hence, given that the relevant semantic object (the abstract representing the queried property) is available anyway, it would be an otiose processing strategy to keep on performing syntactic reconstruction each time an XP appropriate to serve as an answer is

---

[11] The classic experiment usually taken to show this is reported in Sachs (1967). For recent overviews of results in this area, which suggest a more mixed picture, see Baddeley (1997) and Cohen (1997). I argue in Ginzburg (forthcoming) that consideration of the update process effected by an utterance suggests that, in principle, a significant amount of information concerning *how meanings are put together* does get maintained long-term in the context.

encountered. The unbounded nature of the syntactic dependency and the concomitant likelihood that the question must get integrated sooner or later in the discourse model also weakens the applicability of the Sag-Hankamer-Kehler approach to discourse ellipsis—one where syntactic dependencies arise solely when resolution makes recourse to material *not yet integrated in the discourse model.*

6. QUD AND FOCUS

I shall follow a strategy according to which context can influence the *form* of an utterance, at least that part of the utterance often dubbed the *focus.* In order to spell out this hypothesis, we need to fix concretely the notions of *focus/ground* (henceforth: f/g). I will keep things rather simple here, basing them on the following assumptions:

– [Partition] Every utterance-type can be partitioned into two components (not necessarily syntactic constituents) one of which constitutes the ground, the other the focus. Every utterance-type contains a focus, though some utterances might contain only a focus (cf. Engdahl and Vallduví, 1996).

– [QUD and Focus] An utterance with a given f/g partition requires for its felicity the maximality in QUD of a certain question, one whose defining property is identical with the scope generated by the focus constituent(s) (cf. the 'question test' for diagnosing the focus of an utterance, and the theories of focus semantics of Von Stechow, 1991 and Rooth, 1992).

My formulation of 'QUD and Focus' follows Rooth in viewing the effect of focus as being presuppositional in nature—requiring the maximality in QUD of a particular question:

(21) a. [JILL]$_{FOCUS}$ [likes Bill]$_{GROUND}$ presupposes QUD-maximality of the question (denoted by) *who likes Bill* i.e.
(s ? $\lambda x \langle$LIKE, liker:x,likee:b $\rangle$))

b. [Jill likes]$_{GROUND}$ [BILL]$_{FOCUS}$ presupposes QUD-maximality of the question (denoted by) *who does Jill like* i.e.
(s ? $\lambda x \langle$LIKE, liker:j,likee:x $\rangle$))

7. Specifying the Structure of Foci: The Emergence of Syntactic Presuppositions

7.1. *The Intuition*

In the previous section I proposed that the fact that a given question q is maximal in QUD has the consequence of making utterances with a particular f/g structure felicitous in that context – those utterances whose focus has as its scope the individuating property of q. I now want to concentrate on one subcase: the one that pertains to utterances which contain nothing but focus. The basic idea is simply that an interrogative utterance creates a context where it is permissible to provide an utterance in which *only* the focus is realized, on condition that the form *and* content of such an utterance matches the specification provided by QUD. Hitherto, I assumed that QUD consisted merely of questions, which in turn are partially specified in terms of n-ary λ-abstracts. Henceforth, we enrich the notion of *question*: these will now also implicitly carry a specification for the structure of possible foci. This specification originates from the utterance of a *focus-establishing-constituent* (f-e-c), which in the current chapter will exclusively be a wh-phrase.

The proposal I put forward is based on the idea that the abstract created by scoping wh-phrases in a question possesses argument-roles that carry appropriateness restrictions on the category of utterance which can associate with them. The current proposal is indebted to and builds on a number of ideas first put forward in Cooper (1993).[12] This view of the syntax/semantics interface suffices to overcome the problems pointed out above for other accounts of ellipsis. I will suggest

---

[12] Cooper's paper offers a number of arguments from attitude reports, linguistic communication and ellipsis for the position that 'linguistic interpretation involves objects of information that integrate information from various different sources. In particular... that what is traditionally considered syntactic information in linguistic theory needs to be integrated into the kind of informational objects we would normally consider to be the semantic content of linguistic utterances.' (Cooper, 1993, p. 1). One proposal Cooper explores is that meanings, which he takes to be abstracts where the variables abstracted over represent the contextual parameters, should carry restrictions that pertain to the structure of the utterance-types of their constituents. In that paper, following on some earlier work on sluicing by the current author, Cooper suggests that such abstracts could be used to capture the inter-utterance case-dependencies also exhibited in sluicing, an idea further developed in the extended version of this chapter.

that this proposal is ontologically conservative in the sense that the
notion of abstract appealed to, viz. an abstract that has argument-
roles that carry syntactic appropriateness restrictions, is already in
essence presupposed in sign-based grammars like HPSG. Before this
and before considering how to implement the idea, let me sketch the
underlying intuition. Assume that with the interrogative sign *"who
relies on whom"* we now associate the following abstract:

(22) $\lambda X, Y \langle$RELY,reli-er:X,reli-ee:Y;$+\rangle$
RESTRICTIONS: utterance associated with X is of syntactic category NP[+nom], utterance associated with Y is of syntactic category PP[+on].

If the question expressed by *"who relies on whom"* is introduced into
QUD, then in particular the abstract used in resolution of a short-
answer is the one in (22). Now consider what happens when we encounter an utterance such as:

(23) John on Mary

Interpretation can proceed directly using the schema from section 3,
repeated here:

(24) S $\rightarrow$ (Adv),(XP$_1$),...,(XP$_n$)

Content(S)(context) = (SIT(MAX-QUD) ! Content(Adv)
(Branch-closure(Quant-Content(XP$_1$),...,Quant-Content(XP$_n$),
$\langle$Rel:μ, r$_1$: Content(XP$_1$),...,r$_n$: Content(XP$_n$))))))

Context: $\mu = \lambda$-Abstr(Max-QUD)

The referent of the utterance *John* can *only* be fed to the role covered by
the X parameter, given the restriction it carries ('utterance associated
with X is of syntactic category NP[+nom]'), whereas the referent of the
utterance of *"on Mary"* can *only* be fed to the role covered by the Y
parameter, given the restriction it carries ('utterance associated with Y
is of syntactic category PP[+on]'). So, for a start, there is no potential
for ambiguity as to which phrase associates with which argument-role,
as a purely semantic approach would necessarily involve – the apparent
problem raised by the schema (7), discussed in section 3 is defused.
Second, the syntactic dependency has been captured simply by having
it stated *once*, as part of the compositional creation of the content of the

interrogative. The sign description of the short-answer itself requires absolutely no stipulation of *syntactic* presuppositions. Third, we do not appeal to any essentially hybrid entities, as for instance a pair of a question and utterance, as would be required in any reconstruction-based approach. Rather, the value that QUD takes is simply a question, one that is individuated in terms of a situation and an abstract. Fourth, and perhaps most importantly, we have something like an explanation for, a raison d'être, for the emergence of *syntactic* presupposition(s). This explanation is completely compatible with the fact that the *content* of the question is already available in the context, which as mentioned previously renders performing syntactic reconstruction each time an XP appropriate to serve as an answer is encountered an otiose processing strategy: In the 0-ary question case, that is, y/n-questions, phrasal utterances involve only sentential modifiers. There is no potential ambiguity, no associations to establish; no syntactic presuppositions carry over from the interrogative utterance. With unary wh-questions there is one association to be made, between the phrasal utterance and the role it fills or quantifies over. In the case of binary wh-questions, the syntactic presuppositions ensure that when a phrasal utterance occurs, each sub-utterance phrase associates with the right role.

The final virtue to mention about this type of account is that the syntax of the source does not play any role in *constructing* the interpretation of the short answer.[13] That is, it is not *reused* in computing the content of the short answer. It is, therefore, entirely compatible both with long-term memory degradation of syntactic information and with cases, discussed in the extended version of the chapter, where no overt utterance antecedent exists. Insofar as one can remember content and forget its structure the prediction is that one can produce an interpretable albeit not entirely syntactically felicitous ellipsis.

7.2. *Abstracts with Restrictions*

The notion of an abstract whose argument-roles carry restrictions is prevalent in situation semantics (see e.g. Gawron and Peters, 1990; Barwise and Cooper, 1991; Cooper, 1993). For instance:

(25) a. $\lambda X \langle \text{STAND,stand-er:X;+} \rangle$
    $\sqrt{}$ $(s_0 \ ! \ \langle \text{NAMED,'JOHN',X} \rangle)$

---

[13] Of course, the syntax of the source played an important role in computing the content of the original question and this content is used in resolving the content of the short-answer.

b. $\lambda X \langle SEE, see\text{-}er\text{:}j,\ see\text{-}ee\text{:}X;+\rangle$
   $\sqrt{}\ (s_0\ !\ \langle BOOK,X\rangle)$

Here the material to the right of $\sqrt{}$ is the proposition specifying the restrictions: thus, (25a) specifies a role for an entity that stands, carrying the restriction that it be named 'John', whereas (25b) specifies a role for an entity seen by j, carrying the restriction that it be a book. There are two basic components of the idea: *restricted objects* and *application of a restricted object to an assignment*.

(26) **Definition. Restricted objects:** given any object X and proposition p,

   $X\ \sqrt{}\ p = X$, if p is true

   $= $ undefined, if p is false

In the case where p contains free parameters, p does not have a truth-value. In such a case, the restriction becomes a precondition on possible anchors for $X\ \sqrt{}\ p$: only anchors f such that p[f] is true need to be considered. By the same token, when a parameter contained in a restricted object undergoes abstraction, the restriction becomes an appropriateness condition on that argument-role. This means that when this abstract is applied to an assignment, the application will be successful if and only if the entities in the assignment satisfy the restrictions.

(27) **Definition. Application for restricted objects:** given an abstract with restrictions, $\mu\ \sqrt{}\ p$, and an assignment f,

   $\mu\ \sqrt{}\ p\ o\ [f] = \mu[f]$, if p[f] is true

   $= $ undefined, if p[f] is false

As an example take (25a): let f be the assignment $[X \mapsto j]$: then

(28) $\lambda X \langle STAND, stand\text{-}er\text{:}X;+\rangle\ \sqrt{}\ (s_0\ !\ \langle NAMED,`JOHN',X\rangle)\ o\ [X \mapsto j]$
   $= \langle STAND, stand\text{-}er\text{:}\ j;+\rangle$ if $s_0 \models \langle NAMED,`JOHN',\ j\rangle$
   $= $ undefined   otherwise

Thus, the abstract from (25a) can only apply to assignments for which the assigned object satisfies the condition: $s_0 \models \langle NAMED,`JOHN',j\rangle$. (28) shows that it is quite straightforward to impose appropriateness restrictions that involve *naming* because the name an entity bears is a property of that entity which transcends a given context. The problem is: how to relate the *entities* to which this abstract applies to *utterances* whose content they potentially constitute? A given entity **e** might in some context be the content of a nominative NP, but in others the content of an accusative NP or some other category. As a prelude to the solution, let us consider how signs are specified and selected in a sign-based grammar like HPSG.

7.3.   *Specifying Signs with Abstraction and Restrictions*

In a sign-based grammar like HPSG (Pollard and Sag, 1994), grammar rules are taken to specify *signs*, types of utterances. A sign is specified in terms of three attributes, a PHON(OLOGY) attribute, a SYNSEM attribute and in the case of signs that have constituents, that is *phrases*, a DTRS attribute, which specifies its (immediate) constituents.[14] It is *Synsem* objects that a head selects for: these encapsulate part-of-speech-hood, valency, case, agreement, and semantic content and context. Using abstraction and restrictions we can formulate this quite simply. As a starting point, I take the Situation Theoretic Grammar (STG) formulation of Cooper (1990), computationally implemented in Black (1992), where utterances are taken to be situation/event-like entities which in addition to such familiar attributes as SPEAKER, ADDRESSEE, LOCATION are also defined for attributes such as CONTENT and CATEGORY. An 'NP utterance', say u_1, will involve facts such as the following:[15]

---

[14] I am ignoring unbounded dependencies (UDC's) in the current discussion. PHON values will also not be referred to apart from my assumption that no utterances have a null PHON value.

[15] One point to note about (29) is that, following Cooper, all soa's which involve an attribute of the utterance should be construed as shorthand for soa's in which the utterance fills the role of predicatee:

(i) $u_1 \models \langle$ CAT,u_1, NP[nom] $\rangle \wedge \langle$ AGR,u_1, 3rd-person-singular-masculine $\rangle \wedge \langle$ CONTENT,u_1, X$\rangle$

Here the self-reference is exploited to avoid the need to postulate situations whose identity and motivation is unclear. Consider that, alternatively, we decided to assume that some other situation, u_3 say, was the situation that supported the soa's in (i) Such an assumption raises the questions: what is u_3? What other information does it carry? By contrast, once we reify utterances as real-world events/situations, the existence of u_1 is not at issue and the conditions in (i) can be taken as the information which characterizes it. For more detailed discusion of this point see the works by Cooper and Black.

(29) $u_1 \models \langle \text{CAT,NP[nom]} \rangle \land \langle$ AGR, 3rd-person-singular-masculine $\rangle$
$\land \langle$ CONTENT,$X \rangle \land \langle \text{NAMED,'JOHN'},X \rangle$

What of a functor utterance? The idea I propose is to use *restrictions* as a means for encoding the specifications the complements need to satisfy: in the prototypical case a complement projects two parameters, one is fed to an argument-role of the functor; the other represents the *utterance* of that complement, it is not a constituent of the *body* of the abstract, but figures solely in the restrictions. Thus, a vanilla transitive verb will involve utterances of the type exemplified here by u_3:

(30) a. $u_3 \models \langle \text{CAT, V[+fin]} \rangle$

    b. $u_3 \models \langle \text{CONTENT, } \lambda u_1,X,u_2,Y \langle \textbf{INVITE,arg-1:Y,arg-2:X;} \rangle$
      $\sqrt{} \ (u_1 \ ! \ \langle \text{CAT,NP[+acc]} \rangle \land \langle \text{CONTENT,}X \rangle)$
      $\land \ (u_2 \ ! \ \langle \text{CAT, NP[+nom]} \rangle \land \langle \text{CONTENT,}Y \rangle \land \langle \text{AGR,3sing} \rangle)$

Here, u_1 and u_2 serve to as it were mediate between argument-role fillers and the structural conditions they might need to satisfy. Since u_1 and u_2 are not constituents of the *body* of the abstract in (30) (that which is in bold-face), the set of application-instances of the abstract is a (not necessarily proper) subset of the set of application-instances of the abstract in (31); the application instances that get thrown out involve fillers that do not satisfy the restrictions.

(31) $\lambda X,Y \langle \text{INVITE,arg-1:Y,arg-2:X} \rangle$

How does a phrase get formed? As far as category specification, we might use the standard HPSG inheritance principle. The content arises by functional application: this will be successful, given the definition of application for restricted objects in (27) if and only if the utterance(s) fed into the abstract together with the argument-role filler(s) satisfy the restrictions. It might seem a little bit strange that the utterance of the complement serves also as an argument of the content, its function there is (merely) as a 'test', to ensure that the semantic entity fed in is indeed the content of an utterance with the right structure. This 'redundancy' can be eliminated in favour of a notation that uses merely utterance-parameters: the argument-role fillers can be bypassed by treating CONTENT as a function-symbol, just like in the following number theoretic lambda-term:

(32) $\lambda n.[\text{Succ}(n) \geq 5]$ ('the property of being a number whose successor is greater than 5')

(30) would then become:

(33) $u_3 \models \langle \text{CONTENT}, \lambda u_1, u_2 \langle \text{INVITE}, \text{arg-1}: \text{CONTENT}(u_1),$
          $\text{arg-2}:\text{CONTENT}(u_2)\rangle; \rangle$
          $\sqrt{} \ (u_1 \ ! \ \langle \text{CAT}, \text{NP}[+\text{acc}]\rangle)$
          $\wedge \ (u_2 \ ! \ \langle \text{CAT}, \text{NP}[+\text{nom}]\rangle \ \wedge \langle \text{AGR}, 3\text{sing}\rangle)$

The 'redundant' format used in (30) makes it perhaps a little easier to see the relation between 'normal' and 'utterance-based' abstracts; (33) is to be regarded as the official formulation for which (30) serves as a more familiar substitute. Phrases, then, are specified as follows:

(34) $u_0 \models \langle \text{ CAT}, \text{CAT}(u_1) \rangle$
     $\wedge \ \langle \text{CONTENT}, \text{CONTENT}(u_1) \text{ o } \text{CONTENT}(u_2)\rangle$
     $\wedge \ \langle \text{HEAD-DTR}, u_1 \rangle \wedge \langle \text{COMP-DTR}, u_2 \rangle$

7.4. *Questions and Utterance Abstracts*

In the previous section I considered the essence of how signs get specified and selected in a theory like HPSG. I provided an alternative formulation of this specification using the tools of abstraction and restrictions and this lead one to posit abstracts some of whose roles are roles for utterances. The full version of the chapter contains a revised specification for interrogative signs, which shows in particular how such contents can be put together. I also show there that, with certain modifications, such abstracts can both carry out the duties envisaged for 'abstracts with argument-roles that carry syntactic appropriateness restrictions' in section 7.1, as well as function as the abstracts with which questions are individuated. Let me here merely explain the potential conflict: in 7.1 I proposed to associate with the interrogative sign *"who relies on whom"* an abstract informally specified as in (22) repeated here as (35):

(35) $\lambda X, Y \langle \text{RELY}, \text{reli-er}:X, \text{reli-ee}:Y;+\rangle$
     RESTRICTIONS: utterance associated with X is of syntactic category NP[+nom], utterance associated with Y is of syntactic category PP[+on].

Given the discussion in the previous section, we can now see that (35) spells out as:

(36) $\lambda u_1, X, u_2, Y \langle \text{RELY,reli-er:X,reli-ee:Y;+} \rangle$
$\sqrt{}$ (u_1 ! $\langle \text{CONTENT, X} \rangle \wedge \langle \text{CAT,NP[+nom]} \rangle$) $\wedge$ (u_2 ! $\langle \text{CONTENT, Y} \rangle$
$\wedge \langle \text{CAT,PP[+on]} \rangle$)

It should be fairly clear that (36) is up to the job of both providing the right content for a short-answer and enforcing the syntactic presupposition—after all it is (one possible construal of the content of) an HPSG functor sign. It is less obvious that such an abstract can be used to individuate a question: I dub the standard, syntactic-restriction-*less* abstracts encountered in section 2 *pure abstracts*; those posited in the previous section *utterance-argument abstracts*. The most concrete criterion of adequacy for abstracts as individuators of questions involves checking whether the answerhood relations specified by the utterance-argument abstract differ intrinsically from those specified by the pure abstract. The potential problem is that an entity **e** that is in the extension of the pure abstract will fail to be in the extension of the utterance-argument abstract since **e** does not constitute *the content* of any utterance. The way out, discussed and motivated in the extended version, is to modify the construal of an utterance-argument abstract μ by allowing other kinds of information-acquiring events in addition to linguistic utterances to constitute instantiators of the *'utterance argument'*. μ will now not merely relate entities to utterances of a certain structure which have **e** as their content, but will also relate any such **e** to other situations in which **e** is involved in some way. Of course once we make such a move, the attribute CONTENT also needs to be construed more generally as a multi-modal term covering e.g. linguistic reference, gesture, and visual or auditory perception, whereas for all but the linguistic mode the attribute CAT will not be applicable. This necessitates conditionalizing the appropriate structural presuppositions, a move independently motivated by the need to accommodate deictic, non-linguistic answers.

8. CONCLUSIONS

In this chapter I have considered the resolution process in short-answers. I have offered a variety of syntactic, semantic and processing reasons which suggest that this resolution process, despite exhibiting certain syntactic parallelism effects, cannot be adequately analyzed in terms of a syntactic reconstruction or deletion mechanism. The main contribution of the chapter was to offer an account for *why* partial syntactic parallelism is exhibited and how this parallelism can be captured without invoking syntactic ellipsis mechanisms. This involved developing the notion of a λ-abstract over *utterances* in such a way that the argument-roles also carry syntactic appropriateness restrictions. In Ginzburg (forthcoming), the account is generalized to account for other types of ellipsis and anaphora. These include phrasal utterances used in grounding/clarification of an utterance (A: *"Jill left."* B: *"Jill?/left?"*), as well as cases similar to short answers, where the existence of syntactic parallelism has been taken as an indication of a syntactically-based resolution process, including sluicing and gapping.

ACKNOWLEDGEMENTS

Thanks to Mary Dalrymple, Caroline Heycock, Rob Koeling, Dimitra Kolliakou, and Yael Ziv for comments about the extended version of this chapter. For discussion thanks also to Nicholas Asher, Robin Cooper, Edit Doron, Graham Katz, Andy Kehler, John Nerbonne, Ivan Sag, Josef Taglicht, though none of them necessarily endorses my conclusions. Thanks also to audiences at IATL 12, Jerusalem; at IWCS 2, Tilburg; at Groningen, and at Tübingen, where earlier versions of this work were presented. The author was supported by an Alon Fellowship during the time this paper was written.

REFERENCES

Asher, N. (1993), *Reference to Abstract Objects in English: a Philosophical Semantics for Natural Language Metaphysics*. Dordrecht: Kluwer.

Baddeley, A. (1997) *Human Memory: Theory and Practice*. Hove: Psychology Press.

Barwise, J. and R. Cooper (1991) Simple Situation Theory and its graphical representation. In: J. Seligman (ed.) DYANA Report R2.1.C.

Black, A. (1992) *Computational Situation Theory*. PhD Dissertation, University of Edinburgh.

Cohen, G. (1997) *Memory in the Real World*. Hove: Psychology Press.

Cremers, C. (1983) One the form and interpretation of Ellipsis. In: A. ter Meulen (ed.)*Studies in Modeltheoretic Semantics*. Dordrecht: Foris.

Cooper, R. (1991) Three lectures on Situation Theoretic Grammar. In: M. Filgueiras et al. (eds.) *Natural Language Processing: Proceedings of EAIA 90*, Lecture Notes in Artificial Intelligence no. 476, Berlin: Springer Verlag, 101-140.

Cooper, R. (1993) Integrating different information sources in linguistic interpretation. In: Y.H. Lee (ed.) *Proceedings of Chosun University Linguistic Seminar.*

Corblin, F. (1994) Multiple Negation Processing. University of Edinburgh HCRC Research Paper, RP-62.

Gawron, M. and Peters, S. (1990) *Anaphora and Quantification in Situation Semantics.* CSLI publications, Stanford: CSLI.

Ginzburg, J. (1994) An Update Semantics for Dialogue. In: H. Bunt, R. Muskens, G. Rentier (eds.) *Proceedings of the International Workshop on Computational Semantics.* Tilburg: ITK.

Ginzburg J. (1995a) Resolving Questions, I. *Linguistics and Philosophy 18,* 5:359 – 423.

Ginzburg, J. (1995b) Interrogatives: questions, facts and dialogue. In: S. Lappin (ed.) *Handbook of Contemporary Semantic Theory.* Oxford: Blackwell.

Ginzburg, J. (forthcoming) *Moving on the Dialogue Gameboard: a Semantics for interaction in Dialogue.* Stanford: CSLI.

Hankamer, J and I. Sag (1976) Deep and Surface Anaphora. *Linguistic Inquiry, 7,* 391 – 426.

Hausser, R. and D. Zaefferer (1979) Questions and Answers in a Context Dependent Montague Grammar. In: Guenthner and Schmidt (eds.) *Formal Semantics and Pragmatics for Natural Languages.* Dordrecht: Reidel.

Hull R. (1975) A semantics for superficial and embedded questions in natural language. In: E. Keenan (ed.), *Formal Semantics of Natural Language.* Cambridge: Cambridge University Press.

Kehler, A. (1994) Common topics and coherent situations: interpreting ellipsis in the context of discourse inference. ACL 32.

Lakoff, G. (1971) Presupposition and relative well-formedness. In: D. Steinberg et al (eds.) *Semantics: An Interdisciplinary Reader.* Honolulu: University of Hawaii Press.

Morgan, J. (1973.) Sentence fragments and the notion 'sentence'. In: B. Kachru et al (eds.) *Issues in Linguistics: papers in honour of Henry and Rene Kahane.* Urbana: University of Indiana Press.

Morgan, J. (1989) Sentence Fragments Revisited. CLS 25.

Pollard, C. and I. Sag (1994) *Head-driven Phrase Structure Grammar.* Chicago: University of Chicago Press.

Prüst, H, R. Scha, and M. van den Berg (1994) Discourse grammar and Verb Phrase Ellipsis. *Linguistics and Philosophy 17.*

Rooth, M. (1992 A Theory of Focus Interpretation. *Natural Language Semantics 1,* 75 – 116.

Sag, I. and J. Hankamer (1984) Towards a Theory of Anaphoric Processing. *Linguistics and Philosophy 7.*

Sher, G. (1991) *The Bounds of Logic.* Cambridge, MA: MIT Press.

Steedman, M. (1990) Gapping as Constituent Coordination, *Linguistics and Philosophy 13.*

Vallduví, E and E. Engdahl (1996) Information Packaging in HPSG. In: C. Grover and E. Vallduví (eds.) *Edinburgh Working Papers in Cognitive Science: Studies in HPSG*. Centre of Cognitive Science, University of Edinburgh

Von Stechow, A. (1991) Focusing and Background Operators. In: W. Abraham (ed.) *Discourse Particles*. Amsterdam: John Benjamins.

Westerståhl, D. (1993) Branching Generalized Quantifiers and Natural Language. In: P. Gärdenfors (ed.) *Generalized Quantifiers*, Dordrecht: Reidel.

EMIEL KRAHMER AND PAUL PIWEK

PRESUPPOSITION PROJECTION AS PROOF CONSTRUCTION

1. INTRODUCTION

Van der Sandt's (1992) anaphoric account of presupposition is generally considered to be the theory which makes the best empirical predictions about presupposition projection (see e.g. Beaver 1997:983). The main insight is that there is an interesting correspondence between the behavior of anaphoric pronouns in discourse and the projection of presuppositions in complex sentences. Van der Sandt proposes to 'resolve' presuppositions just like anaphoric pronouns are resolved in *Discourse Representation Theory* (DRT, Kamp & Reyle, 1993). Van der Sandt contends that there is also an important *difference* between pronouns and presuppositions: when there is no antecedent for an anaphoric pronoun, the sentence containing the pronoun cannot be interpreted. However, when there is no antecedent for a presupposition – and the presupposition has sufficient descriptive content – then the presupposition can be accommodated and, as it were, create its own antecedent. This combination of resolution and accommodation constitutes the empirical strength of van der Sandt's approach.

A problem with van der Sandt's approach is that it does not take the influence of world knowledge into account (see e.g. Beaver, 1995: 64-66). Consider:

(1) a. If John is married, his wife probably walks the dog.

    b. If John buys a car, he checks the motor first.

    c. If Spaceman Spiff lands on planet X, he will be annoyed by the fact that his weight is higher than it would be on earth. (Beaver, 1995)

Example (1a) contains a definite description, *"his wife"*, which triggers the presupposition that John has a wife. For the correct treatment of this example, a rather trivial piece of world knowledge is needed: if

H. Bunt and R. Muskens (eds.), Computing Meaning, Volume 1, 281–300.

a man is married, he has a wife. But, if we do not take this piece of world knowledge into account, the theory of van der Sandt (1992) is not able to treat being *"married"* as an 'antecedent' for the presupposition triggered by *"his wife"*. Being married creates an (implied) antecedent for *"his wife"*. A more substantial usage of world knowledge is required for example (1b), which is an example of the notorious *bridging phenomenon* (Clark, 1975). The description *"the motor"* presupposes the existence of a motor. Since there is no proper antecedent for this definite description, the theory of van der Sandt (1992) predicts that the presupposition is accommodated. But this fails to do justice to the intuition that the mentioning of a car somehow licenses the use of *"the motor"* and that the motor is part of the car which John buys. Example (1c) also illustrates the need for world knowledge. The *"the fact that S"* construction presupposes S; thus the consequent of (1c) presupposes that Spaceman Spiff's weight is higher than it would be on earth. Since there is no obvious way to bind this presupposition, van der Sandt's account incorrectly predicts that it is accommodated.

The claim that world knowledge has an influence on presupposition projection is hardly revolutionary. For instance, van der Sandt seems to assume that world knowledge somehow influences presupposition projection (van der Sandt, 1992:375, fn. 20), but he gives no clues on how world knowledge interacts with his theory of presupposition. The central question addressed in this chapter is *how* to account for the influence of world knowledge on presupposition projection. We argue that employing a class of mathematical formalisms known as *Constructive Type Theories* (CTT, see e.g. Martin-Löf, 1984, Barendregt, 1992) allows us to answer this question. To do so, we reformulate van der Sandt's theory in terms of CTT. CTT differs from other proof systems in that for each proposition which is proven, CTT also delivers a proof-object which shows *how* the proposition was proven.[1] As we shall see, the presence of these proof-objects is useful from the presuppositional point of view. Additionally, CTT contexts contain *more* information than is conveyed by the ongoing discourse, and there is a formal interaction between this 'background knowledge' and the representation of the current discourse. This means that the reformulation of van der Sandt's theory in terms of CTT is not just a nice technical exercise, but actually creates interesting new possibilities where the interaction

---

[1] For us, the *constructive* aspect resides in the explicit construction of proof-objects; we are not committed to an underlying intuitionistic logic.

between presupposition resolution and world knowledge is concerned.[2]

2. PRESUPPOSITIONS AS ANAPHORS

Van der Sandt (1992) proposes to *resolve* presuppositions, just like anaphoric pronouns are resolved in DRT. For this purpose he develops a meta-level resolution algorithm. The input of this algorithm is an underspecified *Discourse Representation Structure* (DRS), which contains one or more unresolved presuppositions. When all these presuppositions have been resolved, a proper DRS remains, which can be interpreted in the standard way.[3] Consider (2), and its van der Sandtian representation:

(2) If a Chihuahua enters the room, the dog snarls.

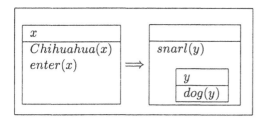

The definite description "*the dog*" presupposes the existence of a dog. Van der Sandt models this by adding an embedded, presuppositional DRS to the representation of the consequent (expressing that there is a dog). To resolve the presuppositional DRS, we do what we would do to resolve a pronoun: look for a suitable, accessible antecedent.

---

[2] In spirit, our work is related to Ahn (1994), Beun & Kievit (1995) and Krause (1995). Krause presents a type-theoretical approach to presuppositions. His system not only allows binding of presuppositions, but also has the possibility to globally accommodate them using an abductive inferencing mechanism. One important difference with our approach is that we take the entire theory of van der Sandt (including intermediate and local accommodation) and rephrase it in terms of CTT. Ahn and Beun & Kievit use CTT for dealing with the resolution of definite expressions. The latter focus on selecting the right referent (which may be found in the linguistic context, but also in the physical context) using concepts such as prominence and agreement.

[3] In Krahmer (1995, 1998), van der Sandt's theory is combined with a version of DRT with a *partial* interpretation. In this way, DRSs which contain unresolved presuppositions can also be interpreted, which is shown to have several advantages.

In this case, we find one: the discourse referent x introduced in the antecedent *is* accessible, and suitable since a Chihuahua is a dog. As said above, it is unclear *how* this information can be employed in van der Sandt's theory, but for now let us simply assume that we can *bind* the presupposition. The presuppositional DRS is removed, and the y in the condition $snarl(y)$ is replaced with the newly found antecedent: x.

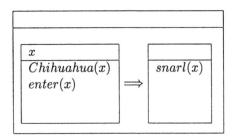

Anaphoric pronouns need to be bound. For presuppositions this is different: they can also be accommodated, provided the presupposition contains sufficient descriptive content. Reconsider example (2): on van der Sandt's approach (globally) *accommodating* the presupposition associated with "*the dog*" amounts to removing the presuppositional DRS from the consequent DRS and placing it in the main DRS, with the following DRS as result.

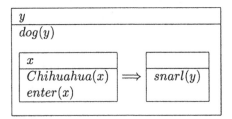

This DRS represents the 'presuppositional' reading of (2), which may be paraphrased as "*there is a dog and if a Chihuahua enters, the aforementioned dog snarls*".[4] Now we have *two* ways of dealing with the presupposition in example (2), so the question may arise which of these two is the 'best' one. To answer that question, van der Sandt (1992:357) gives some general rules for preferences, which may be put

---

[4] This DRS (as the previous ones) are presented in the usual 'pictorial' fashion. Below we also use a linear notation which we trust to be self-explanatory. For example, in this linear notation the current DRS looks as follows: $[y|\ dog(y),\ [x\ |\ Chihuahua(x), enter(x)] \Longrightarrow [\ |snarl(y)]]$.

informally as follows: *1.* Binding is preferred over accommodation, *2.* Accommodation is preferred as high as possible, *3.* Binding is preferred as low as possible. Thus: according to van der Sandt the second DRS discussed above (the 'binding' reading) is preferred over the third one (the 'accommodation' reading).[5] The second preference rule suggests that there is more than one way to accommodate a presupposition, and indeed there is. Consider:

(3) It is not true that I feed John's Chihuahua, since he doesn't have one!

Here global accommodation of the presupposition triggered by *"John's Chihuahua"* yields an inconsistent DRS. This is prohibited by one of van der Sandt (1992:367)'s conditions on accommodation. Therefore the presupposition is accommodated *locally*, i.e., within the scope of the negation.

In the next section, we discuss CTT and show how van der Sandt's approach can be rephrased in terms of it. In the section thereafter, we will see how the examples in (1), which are problematic for van der Sandt's approach as it stands, can be dealt with. We believe that the CTT approach leads to better results than adding a proof-system to DRT, as done in e.g. Saurer (1993). The main advantage of CTT is that it is a standard proof system developed in mathematics with well-understood meta-theoretical properties (see Ahn & Kolb (1990) for discussion on the advantages of reformulating DRT in CTT). Moreover, the presence of explicit proof-objects turns out to have some additional advantages for our present purposes.

3. The Deductive Perspective

We introduce CTT by comparing it with DRT; this comparison is based on Ahn & Kolb (1990), who present a formal translation of DRSs into CTT expressions. In CTT, a context is modelled as an ordered sequence of introductions. Introductions are of the form $V : T$, where V is a variable and T is the type of the variable. Consider example (4a) and its DRT representation (4b) (in the linear notation, cf. footnote 4).

---

[5] It has been argued that examples like (2), in which there is a *partial match* between anaphor and antecedent are ambiguous between a binding and an accommodation reading. See e.g. Krahmer & van Deemter (1997) for an analysis of partial match ambiguities. Here we will ignore this issue.

(4) (a) A dog snarls.

(b) $[x \mid dog(x), snarl(x)]$

A discourse referent can be modelled in CTT as a variable. A referent is added to the context by means of an introduction which not only adds the variable but also fixes its type. We choose *entity* as the type of discourse referents. Thus, we add $x : entity$ to the context. *entity* itself also requires introduction. Since *entity* is a type, we write: *entity* : *type*.

In general, a type T can only be used after the type of T itself (or the parts of which T has been composed) has been specified in the context with an introduction (e.g. $T : T'$). However, the introduction of the aforementioned type *type* is not carried out in the context; it is taken care of by an axiom which says that $type : \Box$ (where $\Box$ is to be understood as the 'mother' of all types) can be derived in the empty context ($\epsilon \vdash type : \Box$).

DRT's conditions correspond to introductions $V : T$, where T is of the type *prop* (short for proposition, which comes with the following axiom: $\epsilon \vdash prop : \Box$). For instance, the introduction $y : (dog \cdot x)$ corresponds to the condition $dog(x)$. The type $dog \cdot x$ (of type *prop*) is obtained by applying the type dog to the object x. Therefore, it depends on the introductions of x and dog. Since $dog \cdot x$ should be of the type *prop*, dog must be a (function) type from the set of entities into propositions, i.e., $dog : entity \to prop$.

The introduction $y : dog \cdot x$ involves the variable y (of the type $dog \cdot x$). The variable y is said to be an inhabitant of $dog \cdot x$. Curry and Feys (1958) came up with the idea that propositions can be seen as classifying proofs (this is known as the *propositions as types – proofs as objects* interpretation). This means that the aforementioned introduction states that there is a proof y for the proposition $dog \cdot x$. The second condition of (4b), $snarl(x)$, can be dealt with along the same lines (this yields $z : snarl \cdot x$). Thus, the CTT counterpart to the DRS (4b) contains the following three introductions: $x : entity, y : dog \cdot x, z : snarl \cdot x$.

Dependent Function Types   In DRT, the proposition *Everything sucks* is translated into a DRS containing an implicative condition of the form $[x \mid thing(x)] \implies [\mid suck(x)]$. In CTT, this proposition corresponds to the type $(\Pi x : entity.suck \cdot x)$, which is a dependent function type. It describes functions from the type *entity* into the type $suck \cdot x$. The range of such a function $(suck \cdot x)$ depends on the object x to which it is applied. Suppose that we have an inhabitant f of this function type, i.e., $f : (\Pi x : entity.suck \cdot x)$. Then we have a function which, when it is applied to an arbitrary object y, yields an inhabitant of the proposition $suck \cdot y$. Thus, f is a constructive proof for the proposition that *Everything sucks*.

Of course, function types can be nested. Consider the predicate *"snarl"*. We suggested to introduce it as a function from entities to propositions. One could, however, argue that *"snarl"* is a predicate which only applies to dogs. In that case, it would have to be introduced as a function from entities to another function, i.e., the function from a proof that the entity is a dog to a proposition, that is $snarl : (\Pi x : entity.(\Pi p : dog x.prop))$. We will abbreviate this as $snarl : ([x : entity, p : dog \cdot x] \Rightarrow prop)$.

Inference The core of CTT consists of a set of derivation rules with which one can determine the type of an object in a given context. These rules are also suited for searching for an object belonging to a particular type. There is, for instance, a rule which is similar to modus ponens in propositional logic (in the rule below, $T[x := a]$ stands for a T such that all free occurrences of x in T have been substituted by a. Furthermore, $\Gamma \vdash E : T$ means that in context Γ, the statement $E : T$ holds):

$$\frac{\Gamma \vdash F : (\Pi x : A.B) \quad \Gamma \vdash a : A}{\Gamma \vdash F \cdot a : B[x := a]}$$

For instance, if a context Γ contains the introductions $b : entity$ and $g : (\Pi y : entity.suck \cdot y)$ (Everything sucks), then we can use this rule to find an inhabitant of the type $suck \cdot b$. In other words, our goal is to find a substitution S such that $\Gamma \vdash P : suck \cdot b[S]$. The substitution S should assign a value to P. P is a so-called *gap*. A CTT expression with a gap is an underspecified representation of a proper CTT expression: if the gap is filled, then a proper CTT expression is obtained. The deduction rule tells us that $(g \cdot b)$ can be substituted for P, if $\Gamma \vdash g : (\Pi y : entity.suck \cdot y)$ and $\Gamma \vdash b : entity$. Both so-called judgements are valid, because we assumed that $g : (\Pi y : entity.suck \cdot y)$ and $b : entity$ are members of Γ. Thus, we can conclude that $\Gamma \vdash (g \cdot b) : suck \cdot b$.

Presuppositions as Gaps A DRS is the end product of the interpretation of a sentence with respect to a main DRS. Ahn & Kolb (1990) show that this end product can be translated into a corresponding CTT context. Van der Sandt's presuppositional DRSs can be seen as a kind of proto DRSs of which the presuppositional representations have not yet been resolved. Only after binding and/or accommodation of the presuppositional representations a proper DRS is produced. Analogously, in CTT terms, a construction algorithm could translate a sentence into a proto type before a proper type (of the type *prop*) is returned.[6] This proper type (i.e., proposition) can then be added to the main context by introducing a fresh proof for it. For example, this is the appropriate proto type for example (2):[7]

(5) $[x : entity, y : chihuahua \cdot x, z : enters \cdot x] \Rightarrow$
    $(snarl \cdot Y)_{[Y : entity, P : dog \cdot Y]}$

Thus, if x is an entity, y is a proof that x is a Chihuahua and z is a proof that x enters, then there exists a proof that Y snarls, where Y is a gap to be filled by an entity for which we can prove that it is a dog.[8] The presuppositional annotation consists of a sequence of introductions with gaps.

To be complete, let us give the *syntactic* definition of proto types. For that we need the definition of a proper type:

$$T \quad ::== \quad V \mid type \mid prop \mid \square \mid (\Pi V : T.T) \mid (\lambda V : T.T) \mid (T \cdot T).$$

A proto type T' can be obtained by substituting gaps (G) for one or more of the types of some proper type T. The result is a Type with Gaps (TG). An annotation has to be attached to T (with gaps) for specifying the types of the gaps. A TG with one or more annotations (A) is a Proto Type (PT).

$$
\begin{aligned}
TG \quad &::== \quad G \mid V \mid type \mid prop \mid \square \mid (\Pi V : TG.TG) \mid \\
&\qquad (\lambda V : TG.TG) \mid (TG \cdot TG) \\
A \quad &::== \quad TG : TG \mid A \otimes A
\end{aligned}
$$

---

[6] We assume that one sentence translates into one type. The attentive reader may wonder how this agrees with our earlier translation of (4a). In fact, it corresponds to the following single introduction: $g : (\Sigma x : entity.(\Sigma y : dog \cdot x.snarl \cdot x))$, given some appropriate, standard derivation rules (e.g. Martin-Löf, 1984; Ranta, 1994).

[7] Recall that this abbreviates $\Pi x : entity.(\Pi y : chihuahua \cdot x.(\Pi z : enters \cdot x.(snarl \cdot Y_{[Y : entity, P : dog \cdot Y]})))$.

[8] The notion of gaps can also be applied to the analysis of questions in CTT (Piwek, 1997, 1998). A question introduces gaps, which can be filled by extending the context of interpretation with the answer provided by the dialogue participant. A question is answered, when the associated gaps can be filled.

$$PT \quad ::== \quad TG \mid PT_A \mid (\Pi V : PT.PT) \mid (\lambda V : PT.PT) \mid$$
$$(PT \cdot PT)$$

$P \otimes Q$ represents the concatenation of sequences P and Q (often written as P, Q). Notice that the definition permits annotation of expressions which are already annotated. This is required for representing embedded presuppositions.

Filling the Gaps Before we can evaluate the CTT representation (5) given some context Γ, we first have to resolve the presupposition by filling the gaps. For this purpose, we have developed an algorithm (sketched in the appendix) which can be seen as a re-implementation of van der Sandt's resolution algorithm, but now operating on CTT expressions. The first thing we do after starting the resolution process, is try to fill the gap by 'binding' it. The question whether we can bind the presupposition triggered by *"the dog"* in example (2) can be phrased in CTT as follows: is there a substitution S such that the following can be proven?[9],[10]

(6) $\Gamma, x : entity, y : chihuahua \cdot x, z : enter \cdot x \vdash_\Delta$
$(Y : entity, P : dog \cdot Y)[S]$

In words: is it possible to prove the existence of a dog from the global context Γ extended with the local context (the antecedent of the conditional)? The answer is: that depends on Γ. Suppose for the sake of argument that Γ itself does not introduce any dogs, but that it does contain the information that a Chihuahua is a dog. Technically, this means that (7) is a member of Γ:

(7) $f : ([a : entity, b : chihuahua \cdot a] \Rightarrow (dog \cdot a))$

Given this function, we find a substitution S for (6), mapping Y to x and P to $(f \cdot x \cdot y)$ (which is the result of applying the aforementioned function f to x and y).[11] So we fill the gaps using the substitution S, remove the annotations (which have done their job) and continue with the result:

---

[9] In general: $\Gamma \vdash_\Delta C_1, \ldots, C_n$ abbreviates $\Gamma \vdash C_1, \ldots, \Gamma \vdash C_n$.

[10] Interestingly, Zeevat (1992) compares the van der Sandtian resolution of a presupposition with answering a 'query' in PROLOG, requiring the instantiation of a variable.

[11] The "·" (representing function application) is left-associative, thus $f \cdot x \cdot y$ should be read as $(f \cdot x) \cdot y$.

(8) $[x : entity, y : chihuahua \cdot x, z : enter \cdot x] \Rightarrow (snarl \cdot x)$

Thus, intuitively, if an interpreter knows that a Chihuahua is a dog, she will be able to bind the presupposition triggered by the definite "the dog" in (2). Now suppose the interpreter does not know that a Chihuahua is a dog or is of the opinion that Chihuahuas simply are not 'proper' dogs. That is, Γ does not contain a function mapping Chihuahuas to dogs. Then, still under the assumption that Γ does not introduce any dogs, the interpreter will not be able to prove the existence of a dog. She can then try to accommodate the existence of a dog by replacing the gaps Y and P with fresh variables, say y' and p', and extending the context Γ with $y' : entity, p' : dog \cdot y'$. Of course, it has to be checked whether this move is *adequate*, whether the result of accommodation is consistent and informative.[12] For more details on the resolution algorithm (also of intermediate[13] and – our alternative for – local accommodation) the reader is referred to the appendix.

4. USING WORLD KNOWLEDGE

Bridging   From our perspective, bridging amounts to using world knowledge to fill gaps. Consider example (1b) again, with its CTT representation given in (9).

(9) $[x : entity, y : car \cdot x, z : buy \cdot x \cdot j] \Rightarrow$
    $(check \cdot Y \cdot j)_{[Y : entity, P : motor \cdot Y]}$

Before we can add this expression to some context Γ, we have to resolve the presuppositional expression. We first search for a substitution S such that (10) can be proven:

(10) $\Gamma, x : entity, y : car \cdot x, z : buy \cdot x \cdot j \vdash_{\Delta}$
     $(Y : entity, P : motor \cdot Y)[S]$

When can "the motor" be understood as a bridging anaphor licensed by the introduction of a car? If the interpreter knows that a car has a motor. Modelling this knowledge could go as follows: Γ contains two

---

[12] For more information on the background and formalization of these constraints see van der Sandt (1992:367-369).

[13] Intermediate accommodation is not entirely uncontroversial. For instance, it has been argued that the 'intermediate readings' are achieved in a different way, e.g. by quantificational restriction (see e.g. Beaver, 1995).

functions: one function which maps each car to an entity, $f : ([a : entity, b : car \cdot a] \Rightarrow entity)$, and one function which states that this entity is the car's motor $g : ([a : entity, b : car \cdot a] \Rightarrow (motor \cdot (f \cdot a \cdot b)))$. Using these two functions, we find a substitution S in (10), mapping Y to $f \cdot x \cdot y$ and P to $g \cdot x \cdot y$. We can look at the resulting proof-objects as the 'bridge' which has been constructed by the interpreter; it makes the link with the introduction of a car explicit (by using x and y) and indicates which inference steps the user had to make to establish the connection with the motor (by using the functions f and g). So, we can fill the gaps, assuming that the proofs satisfy certain conditions. Of course, they have to satisfy the usual van der Sandt conditions. Additionally, the bridge itself has to be 'plausible'. What plausibility exactly is, is beyond the scope of this chapter (but see Section 5). We would like to point out, however, that the presence in CTT of explicit proof-objects indicating precisely which pieces of knowledge have been used, facilitates plausibility-checking. For example, we contend that the complexity of the proof-object is inversely proportional to the plausibility of the bridge.[14]

Let us now consider a somewhat more complex example.

(11) John walked into the room. The chandelier shone brightly. (after Clark, 1975)

Assume that the first sentence of (11) has already been processed, which means that the context Γ at least contains the following introductions: $x : entity, y : room \cdot x, z : walk\_in \cdot x \cdot j$. Now, we encounter the CTT representation of the second sentence:

(12) $q : shine \cdot Y_{[Y:entity, P:chandelier \cdot Y]}$

We want to resolve the presupposition triggered by *"the chandelier"* in the context Γ (assuming that Γ does not introduce any chandeliers). When would an interpreter be able to link *the chandelier* to the room John entered? Of course, it would be easy if she had some piece of knowledge to the effect that every room has a chandelier (if her Γ would contain functions which for each room produce a chandelier). However, such knowledge is hardly realistic; many rooms do not have a chandelier.

---

[14] For a given proof-object we can determine which atomic proof-objects from the context have been used and how many times. Thus, in the aforementioned $f \cdot x \cdot y$ three atomic proofs are used, namely f, x and y.

In a more realistic scenario, the following might happen. The interpreter tries to prove the existence òf a chandelier, but fails to do so. However, she knows that a chandelier is a kind of lamp and the existence of a lamp *can* be proven using the room just mentioned and the background knowledge that rooms have lamps. Formally, and analogous to the *motor*-example, Γ contains one function which produces an entity for each room; $f : ([a : entity, b : room \cdot a] \Rightarrow entity)$, and one which states that this entity is a lamp; $g : ([a : entity, b : room \cdot a] \Rightarrow (lamp \cdot (f \cdot a \cdot b)))$. Since the speaker has uttered (11) the interpreter will *assume* that (one of) the lamp(s) in the room is a chandelier.[15] In terms of the CTT approach: the interpreter *infers* that the room which John entered contains an entity which is a lamp (applying the aforementioned piece of knowledge; the functions f and g), and then binds *part* of the presupposition by filling the Y gap with $f \cdot x \cdot y$ (the inferred lamp). The remaining part of the presupposition (that the lamp is in fact a chandelier) is now *accommodated* in the usual way by filling the P gap with a fresh variable.[16,17]

Summarizing: if the 'bridge' between would-be anaphor and would-be antecedent is fully derivable using world knowledge, the presupposition can be bound. Thus, binding plays a more substantial rôle than in van der Sandt's original theory, as presuppositions can be bound to both inferred and non-inferred antecedents. On the other hand, if the 'bridge' between anaphor and antecedent is not fully derivable,

---

[15] Notice that according to this picture both the anaphor *and* the antecedent play a role in constructing the bridge (see, for instance, Milward, 1996).

[16] Where does bridging fit in with van der Sandt's preference hierarchy? We hypothesize that rule *1*, mentioned in Section 2, should be restated as, *1a* Binding to a non-inferred antecedent is preferred to accommodation, and *1b* Binding to a non-inferred antecedent is preferred to binding to an inferred antecedent. Whether binding to an implied antecedent is preferred over accommodation or vice versa cannot be stated in a general way: this again depends on the 'plausibility'.

[17] It has been observed that binding a pronominal anaphor to an implied antecedent is generally impossible. This follows from our present approach: the descriptive content of a pronoun is *so* small, that there will in general be many inferred objects meeting what little descriptive content there is, thus resulting in an 'unresolvable ambiguity'. Notice that this approach does not preclude that sometimes a pronoun *can* refer back to a inferred antecedent. Consider: *"Did you hear that John finally is going to get married? She must be very rich"*. In such cases, one implied antecedent ('John's future wife') seems to be more prominent than all others.

the 'missing link' will be accommodated. So, accommodation is still a repair-strategy, as in van der Sandt's original approach, but now there is generally less to repair. In most cases, accommodation will amount to 'assuming' a more specific description of a deduced object (in this case, that the lamp whose existence has been proven is actually a chandelier).[18] Notice, finally, that our approach to bridging is deliberately *not* lexical.[19]

(13) Yesterday somebody parked a car in front of my door, and the dog howled awfully.

This example can be understood in a bridging-manner given the 'right' background knowledge. Suppose, it is well known between the speaker and the interpreter that the former lives opposite a dog hotel somewhere in the countryside, and all the cars which stop in front of this hotel (and hence in front of the speaker's door) either drop a dog or pick one up. In this context, the hearer will have no trouble constructing the required bridge (since she has a mental function which produces a dog for each car stopping in front of the speaker's door). For more examples, we refer to Piwek & Krahmer (1999).

Conditionals and Presuppositions One attractive feature of the CTT view on discourse is that we get 'discourse markers' for propositions for free. This is useful, for instance, in the case of propositional presuppositions, of which *the fact that S* construction is an example (cf. (1c)). According to Stalnaker (1974), a proposition which is presupposed should be part of the context (common background). In terms of CTT, this means that a proof for the proposition should be derivable in the context. The latter interpretation agrees nicely with the dictum

---

[18] In this respect our approach to bridging is comparable to the one advocated in Hobbs (1987) and, in particular, in Hobbs *et al.* (1993). One important difference between our approach and theirs is that we take the *presuppositionhood* of the bridging anaphor as one of the central characteristics. This separation of presupposed and asserted material enables us to resolve bridging anaphors even in cases where the asserted material is inconsistent with the context. A similar point is made in Asher & Lascarides (1998), who argue that rhetorical relations are an important factor for processing bridging NPs.

[19] As opposed to e.g. Bos, Buitelaar & Mineur (1995), where bridging is analyzed by the addition of *qualia-structures* to van der Sandt's presupposition theory. As Bos, Buitelaar & Mineur put it, a qualia-structure can be seen as a set of lexical entailments. Our main objection to this approach is that not all implied antecedents are *lexical* entailments, as example (13) illustrates.

of presuppositions as anaphors: the proof of the proposition acts as the required antecedent (cf. Ranta, 1994).

In order to make this idea more precise, let us give the proto type for example (1c). For the sake of simplicity we treat *"annoyed by the fact that"* as a (complex) predicate: *annoyed* is a function which applied to a person, a proposition and a proof for the proposition yields a new proposition, $annoyed : [x : entity, q : prop, r : q] \Rightarrow prop$:

(14) $[p : land \cdot sp \cdot plx] \Rightarrow$

$\quad (annoyed \cdot sp \cdot (weigth\_higher \cdot sp) \cdot P)_{[P : weight\_higher \cdot sp]}$

The basic structure of this proto type is $\Phi \Rightarrow \Psi_\pi$.[20] The algorithm sketched in the appendix proceeds as follows. It first tries to bind the presupposition, in the context of Γ extended with Φ (the conditional's antecedent). In this case, Φ seems to provide no proper antecedent for the presupposition. World knowledge can, however, change the picture dramatically. Suppose that the interpreter knows that: *"if something lands on planet X, then its weight will be higher than it would be on earth"*, formally $f : ([x : entity, q : land \cdot x \cdot plx] \Rightarrow weight\_higher \cdot x)$. In that case, the presupposition can be bound. The appropriate substitution for the presupposition P, namely $f \cdot sp \cdot p$, is obtained by using world knowledge and the information given in the conditional's antecedent.

Now, suppose there is not sufficient information in the context to find a binder for the presupposition. Then some piece of information will have to be accommodated. First, the algorithm attempts to globally accommodate the presupposition. This results in a rather awkward reading, paraphrasable as *"Spaceman Spiff's weight is higher than it would be on earth, and if he lands on planet X, it will bother him (that his weight is higher than it would be on earth)"*. Beaver explains this awkwardness by pointing out that the sentence will typically be uttered in a situation where Spiff is hanging somewhere in space. Most of us know that in space one is weightless. So for the average interpreter, global accommodation of *"Spiff's weight is higher than it would be on earth"* can be blocked: adding this proposition to a context containing the information that Spiff is weightless will enable the interpreter

---

[20] The proto type (14) contains some simplifications: the meaning of some parts of the sentence has not been analysed to the fullest detail: we stipulate that *"Spiff's weight is higher than it would be on earth"* corresponds to $weight\_higher \cdot sp$. Additionally, some presuppositions are already resolved: *"Spiff"* to the variable sp and *"planet X"* to plx.

to derive an inconsistency (given some other fairly common pieces of information, e.g., 'on earth one is not weightless'). If global accommodation is ruled out, there are two possibilities left: intermediate and local accommodation. Here, let us consider the reading involving local accommodation (cf. footnote 13). We model van der Sandt's local accommodation as follows: given a CTT expression of the form $\Phi \Rightarrow \Psi_\pi$ (as (14)), the algorithm adds $\Phi \Rightarrow \pi$ to the *global* context, i.e.: we model local accommodation as global accommodation of a *conditional* presupposition.[21]

5. CONCLUSIONS

We rephrased van der Sandt's *presuppositions as anaphors* theory in terms of CTT, and showed that this facilitates the formal interaction between world knowledge and presupposition projection. To illustrate this interaction, we applied the CTT version of the presuppositions as anaphors approach to Clark's bridging cases and Beaver's conditional presuppositions. These phenomena, which are beyond the scope of the theory presented in van der Sandt (1992), could be dealt with in a straightforward fashion. An important factor in our analyses is the presence of explicit proof objects, which is one of the characteristic properties of CTT.

There are, however, still a lot of open questions. When is bridge a illformed? Why do listeners prefer one bridge over another? And, why should a listener construct a bridge in the first place? In fact, Clark (1975) already provided part of the answers to these questions. For example, he noted that bridging is a *determinate* process, which has to satisfy certain criteria. Among other things, Clark proposes a general *stopping rule* which essentially says that listeners build the

---

[21] The advantage of this alternative can be illustrated using another example from Beaver (1995): *"It is unlikely that if Spaceman Spiff lands on planet X, he will be annoyed by the fact that his weight is higher than it would be on earth."*. Van der Sandt's local accommodation produces the following interpretation for this sentence: *"It is unlikely that if Spaceman Spiff lands on planet X, his weight will be higher than it would be on earth and he will be annoyed by this fact"*. Beaver (1995) remarks that van der Sandt's reading does not entail that *"if Spaceman Spiff lands on planet X, his weight will be higher than it would be on earth"* (it even suggest the opposite), whereas it intuitively should. According to our re-definition of local accommodation the latter sentence does follow from the (adjusted) global context.

shortest possible bridge that is consistent with the context. In Piwek & Krahmer (1999) it is argued that the CTT perspective can account for this constraint, as well as 'softer' constraints having to do with *relevance* and *plausibility*, in an elegant manner as conditions on proof-objects.

APPENDIX: THE RESOLUTION ALGORITHM

Let Φ be the CTT representation of the current utterance, and Γ the current global context. The following algorithm, written in *Pseudo PROLOG*, tells us how to resolve the presuppositions of Φ (if any) in the context of Γ. C is a variable representing the relevant context, consisting of the Γ extended with temporary assumptions (e.g. antecedents of conditionals). Initially, C is set equal to Γ (i.e. $C := \Gamma$). The *basic* clause goes as follows:

$$\texttt{resolve}(\Phi, C, \Phi) \text{ :- } \texttt{atomic}(\Phi).$$

If Φ is atomic, i.e. not of the form $\Pi V : \Phi.\Psi$ (also abbreviated as $[V : \Phi] \Rightarrow \Psi$) and does not contain presuppositional annotations, then the resolution of Φ in the context of C is Φ. Here is the recursive clause, which deals with Π-expressions ($\otimes$ stands for concatenation).

$$\texttt{resolve}(\Pi V : \Phi.\Psi, C, \Pi V : \Phi'.\Psi') \text{ :- } \quad \texttt{resolve}(\Phi, C, \Phi'),$$
$$C' := C \otimes (\Gamma - C),$$
$$\texttt{resolve}(\Psi, C' \otimes V : \Phi', \Psi').$$

In words: when the resolution algorithm encounters an expression of the form $\Pi V : \Phi.\Psi$ in context C then it first resolves all the presuppositions in Φ, and when Φ is totally devoid of presuppositional annotations the algorithm resolves the presuppositions of Ψ with respect to the modified context (the original C possibly extended with the accommodation of presuppositions which arose in Φ[22]) and $V : \Phi'$.[23] The first clause to deal with resolution proper is the one for *binding*.[24]

$$\texttt{resolve}(\Phi_\chi, C, \Phi') \text{ :- } \texttt{binder}(\chi, C, S),$$
$$\texttt{resolve}(\Phi[S], C, \Phi').$$

----

[22] $\Gamma - C$ gives those introductions which are present in Γ but not in C, i.e. have been added to the global context Γ since the beginning of resolution.

[23] $V : \Phi'$ is temporarily added ('assumed') to the context in order to resolve any presuppositions in Ψ.

[24] We have decided to code the preferences (binding over accommodation, etc.) into the algorithm itself. This choice is not forced upon us, it is just more efficient than calculating all possible resolutions, and order them afterwards.

where binder is defined as follows:

$$\text{binder}(\chi, C, S) :- S \in \{S^* | C \vdash \chi[S^*]\},$$
$$\text{preferred}(S).$$

When there is more than one possible binding, it is determined which is the most preferred one (where preference is defined in terms of the number of intervening introductions, the complexity of proof-objects, etc.). If there are two equally preferred bindings, an unresolvable ambiguity results. If there is no 'binder' for a presupposition, we try to *globally accommodate* it.

$$\text{resolve}(\Phi_\chi, C, \Phi') :- \text{adequate}(\chi[S'], C),$$
$$\text{add}(\chi[S'], \Gamma),$$
$$\text{resolve}(\Phi[S'], C \otimes \chi[S'], \Phi').$$

Here and elsewhere S' is the assignment which maps any gaps in Φ to Γ-fresh variables of the right type. Thus: if it is possible to accommodate the presupposition, then we may add it to the context Γ, and go on resolving any remaining presuppositions in Φ with respect to the new, extended context. adequate checks whether the result of accommodation in a given context meets the van der Sandtian conditions, i.e. is consistent and informative.[25] If binding *and* global accommodation are not possible, we try *intermediate accommodation*:

$$\text{resolve}(\Phi_\chi, C, \Phi') :- \text{not empty}(C - \Gamma),$$
$$\text{adequate}((\chi \Rightarrow \Phi)[S'], C),$$
$$\text{resolve}((\chi \Rightarrow \Phi)[S'], C, \Phi').$$

Thus: if we are in an embedded configuration (that is: there is a difference between Γ – the global context – and C – the extension of the global context with a local context –), and the result of intermediate accommodation is adequate, then we use intermediate accommodation. Finally, here is our version for *local accommodation*.[26]

---

[25] $V : T$ is *consistent* in the context of Γ if it is not the case that there is an E such that $\Gamma, V : T \vdash E : \bot$ (that is, adding $V : T$ to Γ makes $\bot$ provable). $V : T$ is *informative* in the context of Γ if it is not the case that there is an E such that $\Gamma \vdash E : T$ (i.e. T does not follow from Γ already). A *sequence* of introductions is informative if it contains an informative introduction. Notice that adequacy is tested w.r.t. to C while the presupposition is added to Γ. This is done to capture the 'sub-DRSs clause' of van der Sandt (1992: 367 (iii)). Notice moreover, that van der Sandt's *trapping-condition* (which states that no variable may end up being free after resolution) is encoded in the CTT framework itself: a variable cannot occur in a context where its type is not declared.

[26] Since χ may consist of a number of introductions $a_1 : b_1, \ldots, a_n : b_n$ we use an abbreviation here. For instance: $g : ([x : entity, p : car \cdot x] \Rightarrow [a_1 : entity, a_2 :$

resolve($\Phi_\chi, C, \chi' \otimes \Phi'$) :- empty($C - \Gamma$),
$\quad \chi' := \chi[S']$
$\quad$ resolve($\Phi[S'], C \otimes \chi', \Phi'$).

resolve(Φ_χ, C, Φ') :-   not empty($C - \Gamma$),
$\quad \Delta := C - \Gamma$,
$\quad$ adequate($f : (\Delta \Rightarrow \chi)[S'], \Gamma$),
$\quad$ add($f : (\Delta \Rightarrow \chi)[S'], \Gamma$),
$\quad$ resolve($\Phi[S'], C \otimes f : (\Delta \Rightarrow \chi)[S'], \Phi'$).

We distinguish two cases: $\Phi_\chi \Rightarrow \Psi$ and $\Phi \Rightarrow \Psi_\chi$. Notice that van der Sandt's local accommodation of χ in $\Phi \Rightarrow \Psi_\chi$ is modelled as global (!) accommodation of a function $f : \Phi \Rightarrow \chi$ (where f is Γ-fresh).

ACKNOWLEDGEMENTS

Thanks are due to René Ahn and Kees van Deemter for their comments on earlier versions of this paper, and to the audience of IWCS-II (1997), in particular Jerry Hobbs and Nicholas Asher, for comments and questions. The research by Paul Piwek has been performed as part of the DENK project (see Bunt et al., 1998), sponsored by the Brabant Universities Cooperation Agency (SOBU), grant SOBU DK9. The authors are mentioned in alphabetical order.

REFERENCES

Ahn, R. (1994) Communicating Contexts: a Pragmatic Approach to Information Exchange. In: *Proceedings of the BRA workshop: Types of Proofs and Programs*. Sweden:Baastad.

Ahn, R. & H-P. Kolb (1990) Discourse Representation meets Constructive Mathematics. In: L. Kálmán & L. Pólos (1990) *Papers from the 2nd Symposium on Logic and Language*. Budapest.

Asher, N. & A. Lascarides (1998) Bridging. *Journal of Semantics* 15:83–113.

Barendregt, H.P. (1992) Lambda Calculi with Types. In: Abramsky, S., D. Gabbay and T. Maibaum (eds.), *Handbook of Logic in Computer Science*. Oxford: Oxford University Press.

Beaver, D. (1995) *Presupposition and Assertion in Dynamic Semantics*. Ph.D. thesis, Edinburgh.

$motor \cdot a1$]) is an abbreviation of $g_1 : ([x : entity, p : car \cdot x] \Rightarrow entity)$ and $g_2 : ([x : entity, p : car \cdot x] \Rightarrow (motor \cdot g_1 \cdot x \cdot p))$.

Beaver, D. (1997) Presupposition. In: J. van Benthem and A. ter Meulen (eds.), *Handbook of Logic and Language*. Amsterdam: Elsevier, 939–1008.

Beun, R.J. & L. Kievit (1995) *Resolving Definite Descriptions in dialogue*. DENK-report 16, Tilburg.

Bos, J., P. Buitelaar & M. Mineur (1995) Bridging as Coercive Accommodation. In: E. Klein, S. Manandhar, W. Nutt and J. Siekmann (eds.), *Edinburgh Conference on Computational Logic & Natural Language Processing*. Edinburgh: HCRC.

Bunt, H.C., Ahn, R., Beun, R.J., Borghuis, T. & Overveld, K. van (1998) Multimodal Cooperation with the DENK System. In: H.C. Bunt, R.J. Beun & T. Borghuis (eds.) *Multimodal Human-Computer Communication*. Berlin: Springer.

Clark, H. (1975) Bridging, In: R. Schank and B. Nash-Webber (eds.) *Theoretical Issues in Natural Language Processing*. MIT.

Curry, H.B. & R. Feys (1958) *Combinatory Logic*. Vol. 1, Amsterdam: North-Holland.

Hobbs, J.R. (1987) *Implicature and Definite Reference*. Stanford: Report No. CSLI-87-99.

Hobbs, J.R., M. Stickel, D. Appelt & P. Martin (1993) Interpretation as Abduction. In: *Artificial Intelligence*, 63:69–142.

Kamp, H. & U. Reyle (1993) *From Discourse to Logic*. Dordrecht: Kluwer Academic Publishers.

Krahmer, E. (1995) *Discourse and presupposition*. PhD. thesis, Tilburg University.

Krahmer, E. (1998) *Presupposition and Anaphora*. CSLI Lecture Notes, Number 89. Stanford: CSLI Publications.

Krahmer, E. & K. van Deemter (1998) On the Interpretation of Anaphoric Noun Phrases: Towards a Full Understanding of Partial Matches. *Journal of Semantics* 15: 355–392.

Krause, P. (1995) Presupposition and Abduction in Type Theory. In: E. Klein, S. Manandhar, W. Nutt and J. Siekmann *Edinburgh Conference on Computational Logic and Natural Language Processing*. Edinburgh: HCRC.

Martin-Löf, P. (1984) *Intuitionistic Type Theory*. Napels: Bibliopolis.

Milward, D. (1996) Integrating Situations into a Theory of Discourse Anaphora. In: P. Dekker and M. Stokhof (eds.) *Proceedings of the Tenth Amsterdam Colloquium*, Amsterdam: ILLC. 538–519.

Piwek, P. (1997) The Construction of Answers. In: A. Benz and G. Jäger (eds.) *Proceedings of MunDial: the München Workshop on the Formal Semantics and Pragmatics of Dialogue*, CIS-Bericht 97-106, University of Münich: Department of Computational Linguistics.

Piwek, P. (1998) *Logic, information and conversation*. PhD. thesis, Eindhoven University of Technology.

Piwek, P. & E. Krahmer (1999) Presuppositions in Context: Constructing Bridges. In: P. Brézilon and M. Cavalcanti (eds.) *Formal and Linguistic Aspects of Context*, Dordrecht: Kluwer Academic Publishers.

Ranta, A. (1994) *Type-theoretical grammar*. Oxford: Clarendon Press.

Saurer, W. (1993) A Natural Deduction System for Discourse Representation Theory. *Journal of Philosophical Logic*, 22:249–302.

Stalnaker, R. (1974) Pragmatic Presuppositions. In: M.K. Munitz & P.K. Unger (eds.) *Semantics and Philosophy*. New York: New York University Press, 197–213.

van der Sandt, R. (1992) Presupposition Projection as Anaphora Resolution, *Journal of Semantics*, 9:333–377.

Zeevat, H. (1992) Presupposition and Accommodation in Update Semantics. *Journal of Semantics*, 9:379–412.

DYNAMIC DISCOURSE REFERENTS FOR TENSE AND MODALS

1. INTRODUCTION

Example (1) illustrates anaphora involving NP's, VP's (VP ellipsis), tense, and modals:

(1) a. **NP:** John gave *a presentation*. People enjoyed *it*.

   b. **VP:** John *gave a presentation*. Harry did not *VPE*.

   c. **Tns:** John *past* give a presentation, and he *past* leave.

   d. **Mod:** John *might* give a presentation. He *would* use slides.

In each case, the anaphorically related elements are italicized. In (1a), *"a presentation"* is the antecedent for the pronoun *"it"*, and in (1b), *"gave a presentation"* is the antecedent for the VPE. Similarly, in (1c), we view the *"past"* in the first clause as the antecedent for the *"past"* in the second clause. This links the time of leaving to the time of giving the presentation. In (1d), we regard *"John might give a presentation"* as describing a possibility and thereby providing the antecedent for the modal *"would"*. This is why the claim of John using slides is relativized to just those states of affairs in which he gives the presentation.

The analogy between tenses and pronouns is an old one (Reichenbach, 1947; Partee, 1973); data like (1d), first discussed in (Roberts, 1986; Roberts, 1989), has led a number of researchers recently to draw a similar analogy between modals and pronouns (Kibble, 1994; Portner, 1994; Geurts, 1995; Kibble, 1995; Frank and Kamp, 1997; Stone, 1997). While the interpretation of tenses and modals is clearly influenced by context, it is more controversial whether this influence can be described by a simple mechanism like anaphora. Tenses and modals have a wide range of interpretations, even in ordinary talk. Other researchers have argued that to account for these interpretations requires more complex and powerful theories involving general principles of relevance or

H. Bunt and R. Muskens (eds.), Computing Meaning, Volume 1, 301–319.

accommodation (Lascarides and Asher, 1991; Roberts, 1989). In this chapter, we propose to derive many such interpretations as instances of *sloppy* anaphora, as already observed with NP's and VP's. On our view, such sloppy interpretations actually confirm the parallels between tense and modals and pronouns, and illustrate the potential power and attractiveness of combining simple theories of anaphora with simple theories of attentional state in computational systems.

The following is a general characterization of sloppy identity:[1]

(2) C1 ... $[_{XP}$ ... $[_{YP}]$ ... $]$ ... C2 ... $[_{XP'}]$

(C1, C2: 'controllers' of sloppy variable **YP**)

We have an antecedent of category XP containing a sloppy variable YP. The interpretation of YP switches from controller C1 to C2. The following are familiar examples of sloppy identity, with the antecedent in italics:

(3) a. **[NP [NP]]** Smith spent *[[his] paycheck]*. Jones saved it.

  b. **[VP [NP]]** Susan *[loves [her] cat]*. Jane does too.

In (3a), the NP *"his paycheck"* is the antecedent for the pronoun *"it"*. The embedded NP *"his"* is sloppy, switching from *"Smith"* to *"Jones"*. In (3b), the VP *"loves her cat"* is the antecedent for the VPE. The embedded NP *"her"* is sloppy, switching from *"Susan"* to *"Jane"*. Now we give two examples of sloppy identity involving tense and modals:

(4) a. **[VP [Tns]]** You past *[think I [past] be crazy]*. You probably still pres do VPE.

  b. **[Mod [NP]]** John would use slides *[if [he] had to give the presentation]*. Bill would just use the chalkboard.

In (4a), the antecedent for VPE is *"think I past be crazy"*. Here, the embedded tense *"past"* is the sloppy variable. It is anaphorically linked to the matrix past tense; the time I was (thought to be) crazy is the same as the thinking time. At the ellipsis site, the tense associated with *"be crazy"* could be resolved in a *strict* or *sloppy* manner: on the strict reading, the tense is still associated with the past thinking time of the first sentence. On the sloppy reading, the tense switches to the present matrix tense of the second sentence.

---

[1] This framework has been applied to NP anaphora and VP ellipsis in (Hardt, 1993; Hardt, 1999).

In (4b), the antecedent for the modal *"would"* is the possibility evoked by *"if he had to give the presentation"*. Furthermore, *"he"* is linked to *"John"*. In the second sentence, the modal *"would"* is anaphorically linked to the same possibility: *"if he had to give the presentation"*. The most natural reading here is sloppy: *"he"* switches to *"Bill"*. On the other hand, a continuation like *"Bill would assist him"* shows that strict reference is also possible.

To account for these facts, we permit all anaphors, including tense and modals, to access *dynamic* discourse referents – discourse referents that record the *meaning* of an earlier constituent. Our general characterization of sloppy identity, in which any antecedent with an embedded anaphor can have a sloppy interpretation, emerges naturally in this framework. We show how the framework accounts for a broad pattern of sloppy identity involving tense and modals. This pattern encompasses the above facts and many others.

These facts have not, to our knowledge, been previously observed in the literature. While they receive a simple, natural account within our framework, they pose problems for many other accounts of anaphora, ellipsis, and modal interpretation.

2. FRAMEWORK

To begin, we briefly outline a semantic framework, adapting the compositional discourse representation theory (CDRT) of (Muskens, 1995).[2] Muskens's proposal encodes dynamic meanings as terms in typed λ-calculus, complementing the familiar types e (individuals), τ (times), ϵ (eventualities) and w (possible worlds) with a new type s that represent *environments* or states of the discourse model. Discourse markers are functions from environments to objects; these objects may have any type. In this chapter we will consider simple discourse referents with values of type e (introduced by NP's), τ (introduced by tense), ϵ (introduced by VP's), as well as (wt) (introduced by mood). Later, we

---

[2] (Muskens, 1995) is a more detailed presentation in the spirit of (Muskens, 1996), which includes an ontology of times, worlds and eventualities as well as ordinary individuals. The adaptations presented here to handle modal referents are motivated and described in more detail in (Stone, 1997). Other compositional presentations of DRT exist (including notably (Groenendijk and Stokhof, 1990; Dekker, 1993)) and could be adapted along similar lines to those presented here. We find Muskens's presentation particularly straightforward.

will also consider *dynamic* discourse referents for all of the same types, in order to handle sloppy identity.

Muskens introduces an axiomatic theory that describes a relationship of branching possibility among worlds and events. He has a single domain for all possible worlds, but an existence predicate, *e* **in** *w*, says that event or entity *e* exists in world *w*. (Times exist in all possible worlds.) Further axioms define a predicate **mk** true of discourse markers and use **mk** to ensure that markers and environments behave as we would expect for variables and assignments. Given this ontology, the meaning of a sentence φ is described by a relation that holds between environments *i* and *j* just in case *j* is an environment that might result from the interpretation of φ in environment *i*. The contents of the environment at any point determine the discourse markers that are *accessible* to pronouns or other anaphoric devices.

Muskens treats the usual syntax of DRT as syntactic sugar that abbreviates more elaborate terms of typed λ-calculus. We will adopt the same strategy here; thus, despite differences in some of the underlying forms, we will be able to provide familiar and succinct meaning-representations for discourse.

These differences arise because modality requires some changes in the types of objects and in the definition of accessibility. The anaphoric interpretation of modals leads us to regard the antecedents of conditionals as introducing possibilities, which not only the consequent, but also subsequent sentences, can go on to describe. Contexts must be rich enough to capture these possibilities, and accessibility of referents must be relativized to the possibility in which those referents are needed.

Modality requires a type-theoretic change because conditional sentences describe sets of circumstances. For example, (5) describes possible wolves that could come in:

(5) If a wolf comes in, it will eat you. Then it will eat me.

There are many possible worlds under consideration here; the identity of the wolf will vary from world to world. CDRT leaves the sets implicit by using a quantifier as part of the identity of the wolf will vary from world to world. CDRT leaves the sets implicit by using a quantifier as part of the meaning of "*if p q*": $\lambda i \lambda j.\ i = j \wedge \forall k(pik \supset \exists h.\ qkh)$. The different possible wolves are described by the different alternative values of the environment *k*. Now, however, the set of circumstances must remain available for future assertions and thus must be explicit.

Our resolution to this problem involves three steps. First, we have markers for sets of worlds. These will be the markers that modals introduce and refer to; because they are sets, they can faithfully represent the possibilities evoked by *"if"* clauses as in (5). To establish such sets of worlds, we borrow from (Lewis, 1973) a ternary relation **closer** on worlds, such that **closer**(w, w', w'') holds just in case w' is more like w than w'' is. To describe the possibility *"if p"*, we use this relation to obtain the set of worlds closest to the actual world where p is true.[3] Second, different values of a discourse marker may now be needed across possible worlds, so all discourse markers depend on the current world as well as the current environment. Thus, the expression δiw picks out the entity associated with marker δ in environment i and world w – in keeping with Muskens's representation of discourse markers as typed functions from context to value. Even world discourse markers have this dependence: which worlds they refer to depends on the current world where they start. We will therefore use expressions of the form $\forall ww'(w' \in \omega iw \supset Pw')$ to impose property P on all the worlds w' that a marker ω could describe in store i. (We let δ range over discourse markers – typically over events, entities and times – and ω range over world-set markers.) Finally, each atomic condition in a DRS is required to hold throughout a set of worlds; abbreviating such conditions is facilitated by the assumption that each primitive predicate and relation has a distinguished world argument.[4]

We recast Muskens's abbreviations to these assumptions, starting with formulas licensing changes in environments across worlds:

(6) $i[\omega : \delta_1...\delta_n]j$ $\forall \nu((\mathbf{mk}(\nu) \wedge \delta_1 \neq \nu \wedge ... \wedge \delta_n \neq \nu) \supset$
                   $\forall w(\nu iw = \nu jw)) \wedge \forall ww'(w' \in \omega jw \supset$
                   $(\delta_1 jw'$ **in** $w' \wedge ... \wedge \delta_n jw'$ **in** $w'))$

    $i[\omega : \omega_2]j$ $\forall \nu((\mathbf{mk}(\nu) \wedge \omega_2 \neq \nu) \supset \forall w(\nu iw = \nu jw)\wedge$
                   $\forall w(\neg \exists w'(w \in \omega jw') \supset \neg \exists w'(w' \in \omega_2 jw)))$

Like Muskens's original definitions, the conditions in (6) express that i and j differ at most in the values of $\delta_1, ..., \delta_n$ or ω_2. However, (6) also imposes constraints on the new values of these markers. An individual

---

[3] A better alternative may be to follow (Kratzer, 1989) in using an ontology of *situations* rather than worlds, which (at the cost of a less familiar setup) may allow for more and smaller cases to be considered, and for a more precise statement of the truth-conditions of counterfactuals and other conditionals.

[4] Again, a number of other options have been proposed in the literature (Kibble, 1994; Portner, 1994; Geurts, 1995; Kibble, 1995; Frank and Kamp, 1997); we adopt this one for simplicity and clarity. We find the others difficult to adapt to Muskens's framework; they all involve rather more complicated types and ontology.

marker's value at a world reachable by ω must exist there, while a set-marker's value at a world must be empty unless reachable by ω.

We abbreviate atomic conditions as in (7); at each world reachable from ω, we test the relation or equality using the markers' value there for the current environment:

(7) $R\{\omega, \delta_1, ..., \delta_n\}$ $\lambda i.\forall ww'(w' \in \omega iw \supset R(w', \delta_1 iw', ..., \delta_n iw'))$

δ_1 is$_\omega$ δ_2 $\lambda i.\forall ww'(w' \in \omega iw \supset \delta_1 iw' = \delta_2 iw')$

The definitions in (8) follow Muskens closely:

(8) $[\omega : u_1...u_n | \gamma_1...\gamma_m]$ $\lambda i \lambda j (i[\omega : u_1...u_n]j \wedge \gamma_1(j) \wedge ... \wedge \gamma_m(j))$

$K; K'$ $\lambda i \lambda j \exists k (Kik \wedge K'kj)$

The treatment of modal notions, however, requires some new notation. Statements of the form $\mathbf{if}(\omega_1, \omega_2, K)$ are dynamic transitions with the same type as boxes and the meaning given in (9):

(9) $\lambda i \lambda j.(\exists k(i[\omega_1 : \omega_2]k \wedge Kkj) \wedge \forall h(\exists k(i[\omega_1 : \omega_2]k \wedge Kkh) \supset$
$\forall ww'(w \in \omega_1 iw' \supset$
$\forall w_h w_j(w_h \in \omega_2 hw \wedge w_j \in \omega_2 jw \wedge$
$\mathbf{closer}(w, w_h, w_j) \supset \mathbf{closer}(w, w_j, w_h)) \wedge$
$\forall w_h(w_h \in \omega_2 hw \supset$
$\exists w_j(w_j \in \omega_2 jw \wedge \mathbf{closer}(w, w_j, w_h))))))$

Their effect is threefold. The marker ω_2 is introduced into the discourse model, and thereby made available for reference inside the box K. Then we update by K. Finally, we ensure that any comparable values for ω_2 (obtained similarly) involve either a smaller or a more distant set of worlds. This makes ω_2 the set of closest K-worlds to ω_1.[5]

The conditions given by **may** and **not** in (10), meanwhile, are predicates of environments – the type of conditions in boxes.

(10) $\mathbf{not}(\omega_1, \omega_2)$ $\lambda i.\forall ww_1(w_1 \in \omega_1 iw \supset \neg(w_1 \in \omega_2 iw_1))$

$\mathbf{may}(\omega_1, \omega_2)$ $\lambda i.\exists ww_1(w_1 \in \omega_1 iw \wedge w_1 \in \omega_2 iw_1)$

In contrast to ordinary dynamic theories, where such notions are captured by quantifying over environments, these definitions simply relate two sets of possible worlds. Given two markers, **may** says the second is possible from the first; **not** says the second is impossible from the

---

[5] As Kibble (1995) points out, the condition defining ω_2 as *the* set, rather than *a* set, illustrates a general tendency of plural anaphors to refer to maximal sets (a phenomenon underscored in an E-type analysis).

first. We shall use these in conjunction with $\mathbf{if}(\omega_1, \omega_2, K)$ statements in interpreting natural language negation, *"may"* and *"might"*. For example, *"not"* will transform one sentence parameterized by times and worlds into another, as in (11).

(11) $\mathbf{not}^{\omega_i}$ $\lambda K \lambda t \lambda \omega.$ $\mathbf{if}(\omega, \omega_i, K t \omega_i); [\ |\ \mathbf{not}(\omega, \omega_i)]$

Note that a counterfactual scenario is correctly made available for subsequent reference.

As presented in (Muskens, 1996), accessibility is now a weak notion, and does not even ensure the existence of the referent in the world where it is needed. We will therefore augment accessibility with an existence presupposition, which we formalize as follows. Existence of individual-marker δ throughout world-marker ω at a environment i is represented as $E u \omega i \equiv \forall w u' (w \in w i w' \supset u i w$ in $w)$. To test this as a presupposition, we must make sure that it would have held in the current environment no matter how, consistent with the prior discourse, that environment was obtained. We use the simple definition of (12), modeled after Muskens's definition of accessibility, to capture this condition. $\mathbf{pre}(u, \varphi, j, \alpha)$ is true iff variable-occurrence u in φ satisfies presupposition α starting from environment j. (We gloss over the intricacies pointed out in e.g., (Saeboe, 1996; van der Sandt, 1992; Geurts, 1995).)

(12) $\mathbf{pre}(u, \varphi, j, \alpha)$ $\qquad = \alpha(j)$, if φ is atomic
$\mathbf{pre}(u, \mathbf{if}(\omega, \omega_1, K), j, \alpha) = \mathbf{pre}(u, K, j, \alpha)$, if u occurs in K
$\mathbf{pre}(u, [...|\gamma_1...\gamma_m], j, \alpha) = \mathbf{pre}(u, \gamma_i, j, \alpha)$, if u occurs in γ_i
$\mathbf{pre}(u, K_1; K_2, j, \alpha) \qquad = \mathbf{pre}(u, K_1, j, \alpha)$ if u occurs in K_1
$\qquad\qquad\qquad\qquad\qquad = \forall h(K_1 j h \supset \mathbf{pre}(u, K_2, h, \alpha))$,
$\qquad\qquad\qquad\qquad\qquad$ if u occurs in K_2

Thus u is ω-accessible in DRS γ if and only if $u \in \mathbf{acc}(u, \gamma)$ and $\forall i.$ $\mathbf{pre}(u, \gamma, i, E u \omega)$.

Now we have a formal explanation of why discourses such as (13) are infelicitous, at least on the most natural interpretation:

(13) A wolf might come in. #It is hairy.

On that interpretation, we introduce a new world-marker with *"might"*, and introduce an individual marker relative to that world-marker to represent the possible wolf. The new world-marker need not include all the worlds compatible with reality (or what we know about it: remember how possibilities branch), so the new individual marker may have a nonexistent value in some of them. This is an unsuitable value for *"it"*, because the realistic verb *"is"* must refer to reality.

Let us consider in more detail the analysis of (5), repeated below as (14):

(14) If a wolf comes in, it will eat you. Then it will eat me.

We shall treat (5) as arising from the indexed syntactic representation shown in (15):

(15) $[\text{POS}_{\omega_0} [\text{FUT}_{t_0} [\text{if}^{\omega_1} [a^{u_1}_{\omega_1,t_0} \text{ wolf } [\text{ come in}^{e_1,t_1}]]$
$[\text{FUT}_{t_1} [\text{it}_{u_1} [\text{eat}^{e_2,t_2} \text{ you }]]]]]] ;$
$[\text{POS}_{\omega_1} [\text{FUT}_{t_2} [\text{it}_{u_1} [\text{eat}^{e_3,t_3} \text{ me }]]]]$

The abstract operators, coindexing, and application highlight a number of assumptions we make about how the anaphoric dependencies of sentences factor into the dependencies of their constituent words and phrases.

First, sentence meanings are constructed as abstracts which return context changes only when provided a time marker and a world marker. Since time markers are functions from environments and worlds to times, world markers are functions from environments and worlds to sets of worlds, and context changes are relations on environments, this gives sentence abstracts the intricate type $((\mathbf{sw}\tau)(\mathbf{swwt})\mathbf{sst})$. We will abbreviate this type as μ. Anaphoric values for these parameters are determined as the final stage of semantic composition, by the action of abstract tense and modal operators (here FUT for future and POS for possible). The actual contribution of these operators is a presupposition about their referent, but for our purposes quite simple meanings suffice:

(16) POS_{ω_i} (or any modal) $\lambda \mathcal{J}.\mathcal{J}\omega_i$
FUT_{t_i} (or any tense) $\lambda \mathcal{K}\lambda\omega.\mathcal{K}t_i\omega$

In (15), the referents for the first sentence are a free modal marker ω_0 representing reality and a free temporal marker t_0; the referents for the second sentence are the modal marker ω_1 representing the possibility that a wolf comes in and the time marker t_2 representing the duration of the results of the possible wolf eating you. We adopt this system because it streamlines the treatment of nested *"if"* and *"when"* clauses. In (15), because *"if"* takes sentence abstracts as arguments, we can easily ensure that both antecedent and consequent describe the same modal marker ω_1, and that the sentence as a whole depends on appropriate mood and time markers. The meaning of *"if"* that does this is:

(17) if^{ω_i} $\lambda\mathcal{K}\lambda\mathcal{J}\lambda t\lambda\omega$. $\text{if}(\omega,\omega_i,\mathcal{K}t\omega_i)$; $\mathcal{J}\omega_i$

As this discussion of parameters anticipates, we assume that the tense of a telic VP introduces not only an event marker e_i but also, following (Webber, 1988), a temporal marker for the duration of its result state, written $\mathbf{dr}(e_i)$. Reference to this marker allows time to move forward in the discourse. Thus, the meanings for *"come in"* and *"eat"*, when introducing duration t_j, are:

(18) $\lambda u\lambda t\lambda\omega.$ [$\omega : e_i, t_j$ | $come\text{-}in\{\omega, t, e_i, u\}$, t_j $\mathbf{is}_\omega$ $\mathbf{dr}(e_i)$]
      $\lambda\mathcal{Q}\lambda u.$ $\mathcal{Q}(\lambda v\lambda t\lambda\omega.$ [$\omega : e_i, t_j$ | $eat\{\omega, t, e_i, u, v\}$, t_j $\mathbf{is}_\omega$ $\mathbf{dr}(e_i)$])

While the temporal and modal interpretation of verbs and *"if"* and *"when"* clauses is governed by top-level referents for the entire sentence, NP meanings refer directly to a time marker and to a world marker. For example, (19) shows the meaning of *"a"*:

(19) $\text{a}^{u_i}_{\omega_j, t_k}$ $\lambda P\lambda Q\lambda t\lambda\omega.$ [$\omega_j : u_i$ |] ; $Pu_i t_k \omega_j$; $Qu_i t\omega$

As always, this is a function from an $\bar{\text{N}}$ meaning, P, and a VP meaning, Q, to a sentence meaning; it introduces an individual marker u_i and ensures that both P and Q hold of u_i. Both P and Q depend on a world and time argument: for Q, the VP, they are passed on to top level; for P, however, they are fixed by reference as ω_j and t_k. This referential mechanism is consistent with observations of (Enç, 1986; Reinhart, 1995) and others about the relatively unconstrained temporal and modal scope of noun phrases.

The remaining meanings involved in the composition of (15) are unsurprising:

(20) wolf $\lambda u\lambda t\lambda\omega.$ [| $wolf\{\omega, t, u\}$]
      it$_{u_i}$ $\lambda Q\lambda t\lambda\omega.$ $Qu_i t\omega$
      you $\lambda Q\lambda t\lambda\omega.$ $Q(you)t\omega$
      me $\lambda Q\lambda t\lambda\omega.$ $Q(me)t\omega$

The final translation of (5) in this system is given in (21):

(21) $\text{if}(\omega_0, \omega_1, [\omega_1 : u_1, e_1, t_1$ | $wolf\{\omega_1, t_0, u_1\}$,
          $come\text{-}in\{\omega_1, t_0, e_1, u_1\}$, t_1 $\mathbf{is}_{\omega_1}$ $\mathbf{dr}(e_1)]$);
      $[e_2, t_2 | eat\{\omega_1, t_1, e_2, u_1, you\}$, t_2 $\mathbf{is}_{\omega_1}$ $\mathbf{dr}(e_2)]$;
      $[e_3, t_3 | eat\{\omega_1, t_2, e_3, u_1, me\}]$]

The reader can check that the meaning given in (21) is derivable from the meaning in (15) using the definitions in (17)–(20), the identities of the λ-calculus and Muskens's axioms on environments; and that referents satisfy accessibility and existence conditions when necessary.

3. DYNAMIC DISCOURSE REFERENTS AND SLOPPY IDENTITY

Hardt (1999) proposes that sloppy identity involves references to *dynamic* discourse referents. Dynamic discourse referents can record the *meaning* of a constituent; when that meaning is recovered, its interpretation can be sloppy because of the intervening context change. Formally, whereas an ordinary discourse marker has type $\mathbf{sw}\alpha$, a dynamic discourse referent is typelifted over parameterized context changes; the dynamic marker has type $\mathbf{sw}(((\mathbf{sw}\alpha)\mu)\mu)$.[6]

We manipulate dynamic discourse referents by *assigning* meanings as their values, using a condition $\zeta \leftarrow f$, and by *applying* those values to arguments, using a parameterized box $\zeta \downarrow a$. These notions are defined thus:

(22) $\quad \zeta \leftarrow f \quad \lambda i. \forall w \, (\zeta i w = f)$
$\quad\quad\, \zeta \downarrow a \quad \lambda t \lambda w \lambda i \lambda j. \exists w (\zeta i w a t w i j)$

(We use variables x_i to represent dynamic individuals, z_i for dynamic times, P_i for dynamic properties, ξ_i for dynamic sets of worlds, and ζ_i to schematize over any of these types.) As befits meanings, (22) ensures that the values of dynamic referents exist, and are in fact the same, in all possible worlds. Since this is the case, to use a dynamic marker we can pick its value at any possible world arbitrarily, and apply that to its argument.

We formalize the changes in context between uses of dynamic markers using the notion of *center-shift*. For each type of marker α we assume

---

[6] Dynamic markers must take their values from a suitably restricted set of functions: dynamic markers cannot store arbitrary functions or even the denotations of arbitrary terms without introducing paradoxes of cardinality and self-reference – see (Muskens, 1995, pp. 179–180). The dynamic values we use, however, are clearly unobjectionable; they are the values of closed terms that do not themselves refer to dynamic markers. (More generally, we might restrict updates for a dynamic marker ζ to values that can be specified with a closed term referring only to dynamic markers that properly precede ζ in some ordering – for example, an ordering on dynamic markers with centers last and others ordered according to their introduction into the discourse.) We therefore regard specifying the right collection of functions for dynamic markers as an important but primarily technical issue for further research.

a distinguished marker $\delta_{\alpha 0}$ that represents the discourse center of that type. Expressions with a referent marked by * reassign the discourse center to point to that object. Reassignment is defined as in (23):

(23) $\delta_0 :=_\omega \delta_2 \ \lambda i \lambda j (i[\omega : \delta_0]j \wedge (\delta_0 \ \mathbf{is}_\omega \ \delta_2)j)$

Expressions marked by * pick out the value of the discourse center. In the case of individuals, center-shift draws on the centering theory of (Grosz et al., 1995); in the case of times, center-reassignment corresponds to standard methods of updating the reference time of tense later in time as discourse progresses (Hinrichs, 1986; Partee, 1984; Muskens, 1995).

4. TENSE AND SLOPPY IDENTITY

We now examine examples of sloppy identity and tense, using the semantic framework we have developed. Consider the following example:

(24) You thought I was crazy. You still do.

We assign (24) the indexed syntactic representation shown in (25):

(25) [REAL$_{\omega *}$ [PAST$_{t*}$ [you [^{P_1} think$^{e_2, \omega_2}$
          [PAST$_{t*}$ [I [be crazy^{e_3}]]]]]]];
     [REAL$_{\omega *}$ [PRES$^{t_4 *}$ [still [you [$_{P_1}$ do]]]]]

As before, the indexing of this example requires some additional explanation. The second sentence of (24) exhibits VP ellipsis, which we interpret using dynamic property markers. The definitions in (26) dictate that a fully realized VP adds a new property to the context and an occurrence of VP ellipsis accesses a property from the context.

(26) $[^{P_i} \ _{VP}] \ \lambda P \lambda u \lambda t \lambda w. \ [\ \omega : P_i \mid P_i \leftarrow P \ ] ; P_i \downarrow utw$
     $[_{P_i} \ _{VP}] \ \lambda u \lambda t \lambda w. \ P_i \downarrow utw$

These definitions account for the subscripted and superscripted brackets in (25).

As stative predicates, "think" and "be crazy" neither introduce new time markers nor move discourse time forward (Hinrichs, 1986). However, "think" does introduce a marker for the embedded context in which "I was crazy" is claimed to hold. Following (Portner, 1994), such markers account for free indirect discourse – main sentences taken as implicit descriptions of an individual's mental state.

Under these assumptions, the main VP of the first sentence means:

(27) $\lambda u \lambda t \lambda w.$ [$w : P_1 \mid P_1 \leftarrow \lambda u \lambda t \lambda w.$ [$w : w_2, e_2, e_3 \mid$
$\qquad\qquad think\{w, t, e_2, u, w_2\}, \; crazy\{w_2, t_0, e_3, I\}$]] ;
$\quad P_1 \downarrow utw$

Composition with subject, tense and modal operators imposes the dynamic property given by P_1 on *"you"* at t_0 and w_0. This step actually introduces the ordinary discourse referents described by the utterance.

The next sentence receives the following interpretation:

(28) [$w_0 : t_4 \mid$] ; $t_0 :=_{w_0} t_4$; [$\mid still\{w_0, t_4\}$] ; $P_1 \downarrow (you) t_4 w_0$

What does *this* occurrence of P_1 impose? Since time t_0 has shifted in value from its previous past value to the present time t_4, we get a sloppy tense reading for the elided VP. That is, the VP meaning P_1 represents the property *"think I be crazy at time t_0"* – i.e., *"think I am crazy"*.

Note that a strict tense reading is also possible, if we do not have the center shift of the tense. This is achieved by indexing the second sentence as follows:

(29) [$REAL_{w*}$ [$PRES^{t_4}$ [still [you [$_{P_1}$ do]]]]]

On this indexing, its interpretation is just:

(30) [$\dot{w}_0 : t_4 \mid$] ; [$\mid still\{w_0, t_4\}$] ; $P_1 \downarrow (you) t_4 w_0$

Because the center does not shift to t_4, the meaning of the elided VP, *"think I be crazy at time t_0"*, is equivalent to *"think I was crazy"*.

Where (24) shows sloppy temporal reference within VP ellipsis, (31) shows sloppy temporal reference in the interpretation of a pronoun.[7]

(31) A woman over thirty-five has a better chance to marry today than she did in the 1950s.

The explicit noun phrase *"a woman over thirty-five"* contains a temporal reference whose antecedent is *"today"*, but *"she"* is interpreted as *"a woman over thirty-five in the 1950s"*. We can capture that schematically by the following indexing:

(32) A^2 woman over thirty-five$_*$ has a better chance to marry today^{1*} than she$_2$ did in the 1950s^{3*}.

---

[7] This sentence is taken from Stephanie Coontz's book, *The Way We Never Were*.

Reference to a dynamic individual, together with temporal center-shift, from today to the 1950s, will explain the change in interpretation. As a naturally-occurring example, (31) inevitably contains features like genericity and comparison that make its complete explication beyond the scope of this presentation. Nevertheless, sloppy temporal reference, of the sort we predict, will have to be a part any such analysis.

5. Modals and Sloppy Identity

We now turn to sloppy modal discourse referents, as exemplified in (33):

(33) John will use slides if he gives the presentation. Bill will just use the chalkboard.

We assign an indexed structure to this example as follows:

(34) [John$_{\omega_1,t_0}^{u_1*}$ [POS$_{\omega_1}$ [FUT$_{t_0}$ [if$^{\xi_2}$ [he$_{u*}$ [presents]]
        [FUT$_{t_0}$ [ϵ_{u*} [use slides]]]]]]]]
[Bill$_{\omega_1,t_0}^{u_2*}$ [POS$_{\xi_2}$ [FUT$_{t_0}$ [ϵ_{u*} [just use chalkboard]]]]]

In these examples, we must assume *"John"* and *"Bill"* each raise to a position higher than the *"if"* clause in order to account for the ability to refer to them using a pronoun inside the *"if"* clause. With this assumption, the first sentence composes:

(35) [$\omega_1 : u_1$ | $john\{\omega_1, t_0, u_1\}$] ; $u_0 :=_{\omega_1} u_1$;
     [$\omega_1 : \xi_2$ | $\xi_2 \leftarrow \lambda \mathcal{J} \lambda t \lambda \omega.\mathbf{if}(\omega, \omega_2, [|presents\{\omega_2, t, u_0\}])$; $\mathcal{J}\omega$];
     $\xi_2 \downarrow \lambda \omega.[| use\text{-}slides\{\omega, t_0, u_0\}]$]

Evaluating the application of ξ_2 introduces the possibility that John gives the presentation, and asserts that John uses slides there. The second sentence composes thus:

(36) [$\omega_1 : u_2$ | $bill\{\omega_1, t_0, u_2\}$] ; $u_0 :=_{\omega_1} u_2$;
     $\xi_2 \downarrow \lambda \omega.[|use\text{-}chalkboard\{\omega, t_0, u_0\}]$

Because of the individual-level center-shift, application of ξ_2 introduces the possibility that *Bill* gives the presentation, and asserts that Bill uses the chalkboard there.[8]

---

[8] An anonymous reviewer draws our attention to the following variant of (33):

6. ALTERNATIVE APPROACHES

We have identified a large space of possible sloppy identity configurations, involving pairs of categories ranging over VP, NP, Tense, and Modal. We have described a uniform view of sloppy identity which accounts for the entire space of possibilities in terms of the general mechanisms for anaphora resolution. In this section, we examine alternative accounts of sloppy identity and modal interpretation, in the light of the data presented here. While no other theories would account for the entire space of sloppy identity possibilities, we will examine some accounts which might be expected to cover certain parts of the space.

Consider first the theory of Fiengo and May (1994), which accounts for VP ellipsis in terms of a syntactic identity condition between the antecedent and the reconstructed elided material. This identity condition is insensitive to certain differences in feature values; for example, a pronoun can differ in number and gender, as in the following examples:

(38) a. John fed his cat, and Susan did too. (fed *her* cat)

  b. John fed his cat, and the other boys did too. (fed *their* cats)

This difference in feature values under ellipsis is termed *vehicle change*. One might account for our *sloppy tense* examples as a reflection of vehicle change, where a verb differs in a tense feature. This account seems problematic, in that it does not treat tense as anaphoric, and thus the above effect is unrelated to the sloppy identity variation of pronouns under ellipsis. It appears, therefore, that this account would permit examples like (39):

(39) Harry thinks I am crazy, and Tom does, too. (think I *was* crazy)

But (39) cannot mean that. This follows from our account, since there is no *"past"* controller in the second sentence for the embedded verbal tense to switch to.

Another prominent account of sloppy identity in VP ellipsis is that of (Dalrymple et al., 1991). In this approach, higher-order matching

---

(37) If a professor gives the presentation he will use slides. Bill will use the chalkboard.

We feel the sloppy reading – *"Bill will use the chalkboard if Bill gives the presentation"* – is somewhat degraded, although still possible. One way to permit this reading in our approach would be to allow the NP *"a professor"* to refer to the center as a pronoun does, and not establish a new center. We leave this as an issue for further study.

is used to solve equations that represent ellipsis occurrences. Consider the following example:

(40) a. Harry thought I was crazy. Tom did too.

b. $P(Harry) = thought(Harry, crazy(I))$

The solution for P is $\lambda x.thought(x, crazy(I))$. This represents the semantic value of the elided VP. In setting up the equation, one must first determine the pairs of *parallel elements* in the antecedent and elliptical clause. In the above example, there is one such pair: ⟨Harry, Tom⟩. (Dalrymple et al., 1991) point out that *tense* can also be treated as a parallel element. This would permit an account of sloppy tense similar to that of our approach. Consider (4a), repeated as 41a:

(41) a. You thought I past be crazy. You probably still pres do.

b. P(you,past) = think(you, past, crazy(I, past))

In this case, we have two pairs of parallel elements: ⟨you,you⟩ and ⟨past,pres⟩. This would permit two solutions for P[9]:

(42) a. $P_1 = \lambda⟨x,Tns⟩.think(x,Tns,crazy(I, Past)))$

b. $P_2 = \lambda⟨x,Tns⟩.think(x,Tns,crazy(I, Tns))$

Applied to the parallel elements of the ellipsis clause, we would get these readings:

(43) a. P_1 ⟨you,pres⟩ = think(you,pres,crazy(I, past)))

b. P_2 ⟨you,pres⟩ = think(you,pres,crazy(I, pres))

This corresponds to the strict and sloppy tense readings, respectively. By λ-abstracting over tense as a parallel element in this way, we are in effect capturing the anaphoric connection involving tense. Thus, the equational framework permits an account similar to the one proposed in this chapter. Of course, it should be emphasized that our account achieves this effect without the mechanism of higher order matching. Furthermore, it is not at all clear how similar sloppy identity effects not involving ellipsis would be captured, such as those involving modals.

We now turn to the approach of (Roberts, 1989) to modal interpretation, as in (5), repeated here as (44):

---

[9] The 'primary occurrence constraint' discussed in (Dalrymple et al., 1991) rules out two other potential solutions for P.

(44) If a wolf comes in, it will eat you. Then it will eat me.

The first sentence is analyzed as the following DRS:

(45) $\Diamond$ [w | $wolf(w)$, $enter(w)$]

The second sentence is analyzed as a conditional involving a missing antecedent, which is recovered by copying the contents of the previous DRS, resulting in the following:

(46) [[w | $wolf(w)$, $enter(w)$] $\Rightarrow$ [x, z | $you(x)$, $eat(z, x)$, $z = w$]]

This approach differs from the current approach in that it uses a special copying mechanism to capture the relativized force of modals in discourse, while in the current approach we appeal simply to the general mechanism for the recovery of anaphoric expressions. Furthermore, Roberts' mechanism of copying DRS's would not permit sloppy identity, as in example 4b, repeated as (47):

(47) John would use slides if he had to give the presentation. Bill would just use the chalkboard.

To account for this in Roberts' approach, it would be necessary to introduce some mechanism for reassignment of discourse markers in DRS's, such as our center shift mechanism. This would make it possible to handle sloppy identity, but it would be distinct from the mechanisms for other types of sloppy identity.

7. CONCLUSION

We have argued that tense and modality are anaphoric, and we have presented new data showing that they participate in the following general pattern for sloppy identity:

(48) $C1 \dots [_{XP} \dots [_{YP}] \dots] \dots C2 \dots [_{XP'}]$

(C1, C2: 'controllers' of sloppy variable **YP**)

We have shown that simple extensions to a dynamic semantics framework make it possible to give a uniform account of sloppy identity involving tense and modals.

Since XP and YP can range over NP, VP, Tense and Modal, this pattern gives rise to the following space of 16 possible patterns for sloppy identity:

(49) [VP [NP]]   [NP [NP]]   [Tns [NP]]   [Mod [NP]]
      [VP [VP]]   [NP [VP]]   [Tns [VP]]   [Mod [VP]]
      [VP [Tns]]   [NP [Tns]]   [Tns [Tns]]   [Mod [Tns]]
      [VP [Mod]]   [NP [Mod]]   [Tns [Mod]]   [Mod [Mod]]

Examples of the four cases involving VP's and NP's are given in (Hardt, 1999). In this chapter, we have presented new data in the categories [VP [Tns]], [NP [Tns]], and [Mod [NP]]. The following examples illustrate additional patterns in this space:

(50) a. **[Mod [VP]]**   Harry's vices can make him compliant – or belligerent. When Harry gambles, *if I asked him not to VPE*, he would stop. When he drinks, he'd only continue with renewed vigor.

b. **[Mod [Tns]]**   On Tuesdays, we respond quickly to problems. *If Bill came then*, I could answer him in a week. However, on Wednesdays, we are very slow, and I wouldn't have the answer for almost two weeks.

We expect that the remaining patterns in this space are also possible, although perhaps with some awkwardness. Alternative approaches are only able to deal with limited sections of this space – ellipsis theories like (Fiengo and May, 1994) and (Dalrymple et al., 1991) would at most deal with the four cases with a VP containing another category, while modal theories like (Roberts, 1989) might deal with cases where a modal antecedent contains another category. However, none of these accounts could provide the basis of a uniform account for the entire space. This is the primary virtue of our account.

ACKNOWLEDGEMENTS

The first author is supported by an IRCS graduate fellowship; the second, by NSF grant IRI-9502257.

REFERENCES

Dalrymple, M., Shieber, S., and Pereira, F. (1991) Ellipsis and higher-order unification. *Linguistics and Philosophy*, 14(4).

Dekker, P. (1993) *Transsentential Meditations*. PhD thesis, University of Amsterdam.

Enç, M. (1986) Towards a referential analysis of temporal expressions. *Linguistics and Philosophy*, 9(3):405–426.

Fiengo, R. and May, R. (1994) *Indices and Identity*. MIT Press, Cambridge, MA.

Frank, A. and Kamp, H. (1997) On context dependence in modal constructions. In *SALT-97*, Stanford, CA. Stanford.

Geurts, B. (1995) *Presupposing*. PhD thesis, University of Stuttgart.

Groenendijk, J. and Stokhof, M. (1990) Dynamic Montague grammar. In Kálmán, L. and Pólos, L., editors, *Papers from the Second Symposium on Logic and Language*, pages 3–48, Budapest. Akadémiai Kiadó.

Grosz, B. J., Joshi, A. K., and Weinstein, S. (1995) Centering: A framework for modeling the local coherence of discourse. *Computational Linguistics*, 21(2):203–225.

Hardt, D. (1993) *VP Ellipsis: Form, Meaning, and Processing*. PhD thesis, University of Pennsylvania.

Hardt, D. (1999) Dynamic interpretation of verb phrase ellipsis. *Linguistics and Philosophy* 22(2): 187–221.

Hinrichs, E. (1986) Temporal anaphora in discourses of English. *Linguistics and Philosophy*, 9(1):63–82.

Kibble, R. (1994) Dynamics of epistemic modality and anaphora. In Bunt, H., Muskens, R., and Rentier, G., editors, *International Workshop on Computational Semantics*, Tilburg, NL. ITK.

Kibble, R. (1995) Modal subordination, focus and complement anaphora. In *Proceedings of the Tbilisi Symposium on Language, Logic and Computation*.

Kratzer, A. (1989) An investigation of the lumps of thought. *Linguistics and Philosophy*, 12:607–653.

Lascarides, A. and Asher, N. (1991) Discourse relations an defeasible knowledge. In *Proceedings of ACL 29*, pages 55–62.

Lewis, D. K. (1973) *Counterfactuals*. Harvard University Press, Cambridge, Massachusetts.

Muskens, R. (1995) Tense and the logic of change. In *Lexical Knowledge in the Organization of Language*, volume 114 of *Current Issues in Linguistic Theory*, pages 147–184. John Benjamins, Philadelphia.

Muskens, R. (1996) Combining Montague semantics and discourse representation. *Linguistics and Philosophy*, 19(2):143–186.

Partee, B. H. (1973) Some structural analogies between tenses and pronouns in English. *Journal of Philosophy*, 70:601–609.

Partee, B. H. (1984) Nominal and temporal anaphora. *Linguistics and Philosophy*, 7(3):243–286.

Portner, P. (1994) Modal discourse referents and the semantics-pragmatics boundary. Manuscript.

Reichenbach, H. (1947) *Elements of Symbolic Logic*. Macmillan, New York.

Reinhart, T. (1995) Interface strategies. Manuscript, Utrecht.

Roberts, C. (1986) *Modal Subordination, Anaphora and Distributivity.* PhD thesis, University of Massachusetts, Amherst.

Roberts, C. (1989) Modal subordination and pronominal anaphora in discourse. *Linguistics and Philosophy,* 12(6):683–721.

Saeboe, K. J. (1996) Anaphoric presuppositions and zero anaphora. *Linguistics and Philosophy,* 19(2):187–209.

Stone, M. (1997) The anaphoric parallel between modality and tense. Technical Report IRCS 97-6 and CIS 97-9, University of Pennsylvania. Submitted.

van der Sandt, R. (1992) Presupposition projection as anaphora resolution. *Journal of Semantics,* 9(2):333–377.

Webber, B. L. (1988) Tense as discourse anaphor. *Computational Linguistics,* 14(2):61–73.

LUCA DINI AND VITTORIO DI TOMASO

LINKING THEORY AND LEXICAL AMBIGUITY: THE CASE OF ITALIAN MOTION VERBS

1. INTRODUCTION

This chapter takes into account the interactions between motion verbs and spatial prepositions in Romance languages, considering Italian as a case study. We will show that, contrary to traditional approaches (Zingarelli, 1995; Serianni, 1988), there is no need to assume that spatial prepositions in Italian are almost systematically ambiguous between a *static* and a *dynamic* interpretation. Such an assumption, which is made in analogy with Germanic languages, hides the generalization that monosyllabic static and dynamic Italian locative prepositions are not distinct. This is shown below, where in the first use the preposition *"a"* heads a PP denoting the goal of the motion, while in the second one it heads a PP denoting the location where the event takes place:

(1) a. Leo è andato *a* Viareggio
Leo has gone to Viareggio

b. Leo ha dormito *a* casa
Leo has slept at home

The present approach has been developed with the purpose of providing an efficient way of parsing Italian locative expressions, while retaining a principle based organization of the grammar (HPSG). One of the major sources of inefficiency in traditional, declarative, NLP systems is indeed represented by lexical ambiguity. Nevertheless, lexicalist principle based theories such as HPSG (in its standard formulation, Pollard and Sag, 1994) rely on the multiplication of lexical entries (sometimes exploiting generative mechanisms such as lexical rules) to account for phenomena which would be otherwise analyzed through particular phrase structure rules. This makes it difficult to integrate such theories into practical NLP systems.

Here we suggest that a careful reconsideration of certain phenomena can overcome this conflict between efficiency and linguistic adequacy. A full implementation of our approach has been given using

H. Bunt and R. Muskens (eds.), Computing Meaning, Volume 1, 321–337.

the PAGE system from DFKI (Krieger and Schäfer, 1994a; 1994b; Neumann, 1993), adopting TDL as a type description language. In this treatment, Italian monosyllabic spatial prepositions, with the exception of *"per"* ('to/towards'), have *only* a static meaning: the PP denotes a state relating an individual and a region of space. The alleged goal interpretation of these prepositions is derived by letting them interact compositionally with verbal semantics, in such a way that the state they denote becomes the resulting state of the dynamic event. This composition triggers a shift of *aktionsart* from atelicity to telicity, as the classical test of *for/in*-adverbials modification proves:

(2) a. Leo corse per/*in due ore Leo ran for/in two hours

    b. Leo corse a Viareggio *per/in due ore
       Leo ran to Viareggio for/in two hours

Dynamic spatial prepositions which are distinct from the static counterpart behave differently. As Jackendoff (1996) shows for English, they interact with verbal *aktionsart* in a more complex way: depending on the type of path they refer to, they contribute to the determination of *aktionsart* at VP (or sentence) level. So, for example, *"verso"* identifies an unbounded path and determines atelicity, *"fino a"* identifies a bounded path and determines telicity.[1]

(3) a. Leo è andato verso Viareggio *in/per due ore Leo went towards Viareggio *in/for two hours

    b. Leo è andato fino a Viareggio in/*per due ore
       Leo went to Viareggio in/*for two hours

Section 3 of this chapter describes lexical entries for prepositions; Sect. 4 introduces the theory of events which has been adopted in this chapter; Sect. 5 addresses some issues concerning verbal semantics. We describe lexical entries for motion verbs and provide a compositional mechanism which relates the syntactic argument structure to the semantic representation (Linking Theory), based on the standard assumption that aspectually relevant constituents behave as arguments rather than adjuncts (Krifka, 1992; Tenny, 1994; Verkuyl, 1993). Finally, we show how Control Theory can be used to identify, through index binding, the participant which effectively undergoes a change of position in the motion event.

---

[1] We will not address this issue here, but see Di Tomaso (in preparation).

In the following we will rely on a *typed feature structure* language (Carpenter, 1992), where *sort resolvedness* is assumed. The organization of the grammar conforms standard HPSG (Pollard and Sag, 1994), except for revisions to the semantic part of the sign, which will be described shortly.

2. Related Work

The class of 'motion verbs' (and of 'motion complexes', i.e. verb plus preposition) has been considered a central case study in many linguistic theories: decompositional analysis (Jackendoff, 1983; 1990), formal semantics (Asher and Sablayrolles, 1995; Higginbotham, 1995; Verkuyl, 1993), typological description of regularities either within a single language (Sablayrolles, 1993; Boons, 1987; Laur, 1991), or across languages (Talmy, 1985), interface between semantic structure and argument structure (Levin and Rappaport Hovav, 1995), compositional analysis of aspectual properties (Tenny, 1995). Lack of space prevents us from reviewing in detail all these approaches; our analysis is close to Levin and Rappaport Hovav's view view that many of the properties of motion verbs are syntactically represented, but semantically determined (Levin and Rappaport Hovav, 1995).

The problem of representing knowledge about motion is also central for Artificial Intelligence, although the majority of AI works which take into account the linguistic level seem to concentrate more on static locative expressions than on dynamic ones (Herskovits, 1986; Lang, 1993; Olivier and Gapp, in press). Nevertheless, a detailed treatment of dynamic locative expressions is provided by Kalita and Lee (1996), where the goal of "developing a semantic representation which can be implemented in order to drive execution of physical tasks" leads the author to consider concepts close to physical world, such as force, motion and geometry, as integral part in the specification of lexical meanings; cf. also Hobbs et al. (1987); Marconi (1997); and work on the interaction between language and vision (Mc Kevitt, 1995).

3. Prepositional Relations

In this section we will describe the information to be encoded in the lexical entries of prepositions in order to avoid prepositional ambiguity and to build the proper semantic representation for locative expressions.

The role played by the information concerning geometrical features of objects (or, to be more precise, the spatial region they identify) is outside the scope of this chapter: we assume that alternative geometric conceptualizations (Talmy, 1983; Herkovits, 1986: Lang, 1993) are specified via coercion functions implemented along the lines of Dini and Busa (1994) and Dini and Di Tomaso (1995).

Spatial prepositional relations are encoded as types which introduce two attributes: LOCATUM and REF-OBJ. Each of them requires its filler to be of a certain type: the LOCATUM is either an individual or an event, while the REF-OBJ is a region of space identified by an object. For instance, the semantic content of a preposition expressing a *spatial relation* will look like the following, where the type *index* subsumes both *event-index* and *ref-index*:

(4)
$$\text{spatial-relation}\begin{bmatrix} \text{LOCATUM} & index \\ \text{REF-OBJ} & region \end{bmatrix}$$

We assume two types of locative prepositional relations: *static* and *dynamic*. Static locative expressions are classified into relations stating the presence of the LOCATUM inside (outside, next to, etc.) the region identified by REF-OBJ and relations (only one relation, to be precise) stating the absence of the LOCATUM from the spatial region identified by the REF-OBJ. In Italian, static relations are also used with motion verbs to express the destination of the moving object (the LOCATUM). The central claim of this chapter is that this coincidence is not by chance: lack of a clear explanation for the identity of these two classes of prepositions turns into the loss of an explanation of the well known generalization by Talmy (1985) concerning the different lexical conflation pattern of motion verbs across languages (see Sect. 5.1).

Italian path prepositions, like *"per"* ('to/towards'), *"verso"* ('towards'), *"lungo"* ('along')) are used only in dynamic cases and differ from the static prepositions in that (i) the LOCATUM has to be an event (type: *ev-ind*) whereas standard static prepositions, as we have seen, can range over both events (*"the cat ran on the floor"*) and individuals (*"the cat is on the ground"*); (ii) they never change the verbal *aktionsart*; (iii) they always behave as adjuncts rather than complements (for instance, they are never obligatory). We distinguish purely dynamic relations into *destination* (*"verso"*, *"per"*) and *path location*, the latter being specialized into path location *within* the reference object (*"per"*) and path location *through* the reference object (*"attraverso"*).

These distinctions, which are still coarse-grained, are reported in the hierarchy in Fig. 1.[2]

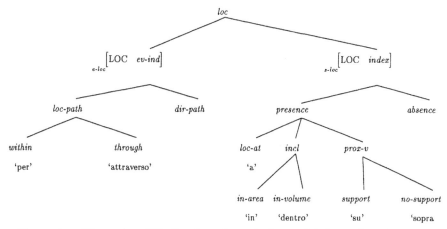

Figure 1.   Hierarchy of Italian locative relations with lexical realizations.

4. EVENTS AND AKTIONSART

We assume an *event structure* along the lines of Pustejovsky (1995), which incorporates some revisions by Dini and Bertinetto (1995). An event structure is defined as a matrix of type *aktionsart* with at most two attributes, EVENT and STATE. The value of the attribute EVENT is a relation which is of type *dynamism* (for instance, a *motion* relation); the value of the attribute STATE is a relation which is of type *stative* (for instance, a *locative* relation). In turn, every relation has an attribute INDEX, whose value is either a plural index or a singular index. If both the attributes EVENT and STATE are well typed for a certain semantic representation, the feature structure has to be interpreted as *the event denoted by the relation in* EVENT *will prototypically result into a state, which is in the denotation of the relation in* STATE (see Dini, 1998 for a justification of this approach). Here we provide a full fledged skeleton of a generic event (as it will become immediately clear the attributes EV and STATE do not need to be both present):

---

[2] Locative prepositions can also be used to express the origin of the motion, but we do not consider such uses here.

$$(5) \quad \begin{bmatrix} \text{EV}_{dynamism} \begin{bmatrix} \text{IND} & plural \vee singular \end{bmatrix} \\ \text{STATE}_{stative} \begin{bmatrix} \text{IND} & plural \vee singular \end{bmatrix} \end{bmatrix}$$

The traditional vendlerian classes (Vendler, 1957) plus the class of punctual events, which has been identified by Moens and Steedmann (1988), are defined as subtypes of *aktionsart* with the following constraints:

- **process**: a subtype of *aktionsart* for which only the attribute EVENT is appropriate and the index of the relation in EVENT is plural;

- **punctual**: a subtype of *aktionsart* for which only the attribute EVENT is appropriate and the index of the relation in EVENT is singular;

- **accomplishment**: a subtype of *aktionsart* for which both EVENT and STATE are appropriate and the index of the relation in EVENT is plural;

- **achievement**: a subtype of *aktionsart* for which both EVENT and STATE are appropriate and the index of the relation in EVENT is singular;

- **state**: a subtype of *aktionsart* for which only STATE is appropriate.

The type *aktionsart* appears as the value of the standard HPSG attribute NUCLEUS; its subtypes are hierarchically represented as in Fig. 2. It is important to observe that telicity is obtained adding a resulting state to the basic structure of the predicate (technically, by using a multiple inheritance device).[3]

---

[3] In the hierarchy described in Fig. 5 the resulting state of telic predicates is an instantaneous state. Such a choice is due to the fact that the presence of a resulting state does not change the overall duration of the event. As for uses of *for*-adverbials over resulting states (as in *"John went home for two hours"*), a way to access the duration of the resulting state is nevertheless needed. In Dini (1998) this is obtained by associating *for* with two slightly different lexical entries. Cross-linguistic data, namely the fact that languages such as Spanish, French and German use two different prepositions, support this approach.

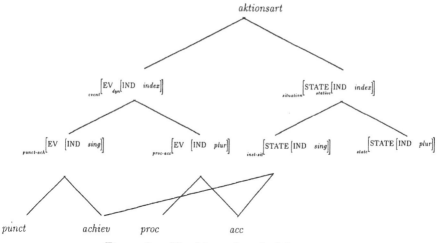

Figure 2. The hierarchy of *aktionsart*.

5. A Compositional Semantics for Motion Verbs

5.1. *Verbal Semantics*

On the basis of the theory of *aktionsart* defined above we identify three main classes of motion verbs:

- achievements (*"partire"*, 'to leave', *"arrivare"*, 'to arrive', *"uscire"*, 'to go out');
- accomplishments (*"attraversare"*, 'to cross', *"tornare"*, 'to come back'), *"andare"*, 'to go', ;
- processes (*"nuotare"*, 'to swim', *"galleggiare"*, 'to float');

We can compare this classification with the one proposed by Talmy (1985), which takes into account the lexicalization patterns, i.e. the incorporation of semantic components such as *Path* and *Manner* into the verbal root. According to the parameter of path/manner incorporation, we distinguish between:

- *path-motion verbs*, which incorporate the path (*"arrivare"*, 'to arrive', *"tornare"* , 'to come back'); this is supposed to be the most common case in Italian;
- *manner-motion verbs*, which incorporate the manner of motion (*"nuotare"*, 'to swim', *"galleggiare"*, 'to float', *"camminare"*, 'to walk').

Path motion verbs are syntactically distinguished from manner motion verbs in that only the former admit a goal PP introduced by a locative static preposition.[4] Since in our system the presence of these PPs is always associated with telicity (because they denote a stative relation which occurs as an attribute of STATE), the following constraints on the interaction between *aktionsart* and path/manner incorporation are predicted: [5]

$$
(6) \quad a. \quad \begin{bmatrix} \text{EV}_{path\text{-}motion}\begin{bmatrix} \text{IND} & index \end{bmatrix} \\ \text{STATE} \quad stative \end{bmatrix}
$$

$$
b. \quad _{proc}\begin{bmatrix} \text{EV}_{manner\text{-}motion}\begin{bmatrix} \text{IND} & plur \end{bmatrix} \end{bmatrix}
$$

Notice that these two classes are also distinguished by a different behavior with respect to the Unaccusative Hypothesis: path motion verbs are always unaccusative whereas manner motion verbs are unergative (Burzio, 1986; Levin and Rappaport Hovav, 1995; Pustejovsky, 1995; Pustejovsky and Busa, 1995). This fact is coherent with the linking theory we will provide in Sect. 5.2.

The validity of the generalization in (6) can be tested on a class of verbs which has been at the center of a long discussion in the *aktionsart* literature (cf. Dowty, 1979; Levin and Rappaport Hovav, 1995; Pustejovsky, 1995; Verkuyl, 1994): this class of variable behaviour verbs contains lexically underspecified verbs like *"correre"*, ('to run'), *"rotolare"*, ('to roll'), *"strisciare"*, ('to crawl'), *"volare"*, ('to fly'), which can be realized either as unergative processes or as unaccusative accomplishments, as the well known alternation of auxiliary selection in Italian shows. Verbs of this type select *"essere"* in presence of a goal PP (unaccusative telic reading), but they select *"avere"* otherwise (unergative atelic reading):

---

[4] The difference between prepositions like *"a"*, *"in"*... and complex prepositions like *"fino a"* ('to'), *"vicino a"* ('next to') is that the former are always syntactic arguments which fill an argument position in the semantics of the verb, whereas the latter are adjuncts which semantically modify the whole event. As a consequence, the former are used only if the predicate has a resulting state while the latter are used also with events lacking a resulting state.

[5] Although the first class can be further specified as path-motion achievements and path-motion accomplishments, depending on the plurality óf the index, there is no need to specify these possible completions in the sort resolved metalanguage we have adopted.

(7) a. Leo ha corso a Torino *in/per un'ora
Leo ran in Torino *in/for an hour

b. Leo è corso a Torino in/*per un'ora
Leo ran to Torino in/*for an hour

These verbs are basically *manner-motion* verbs, in that they specify the (agentive) *modality* of the change of place. However, they can also be used as telic predicates, and thus can have a static PP as goal. Since the information about the way in which the movement is performed should be preserved also when these verbs are used as accomplishments, a revision is necessary of Talmy's stipulation, according to which only one parameter is incorporated in the verbal root (either *Path* or *Manner*, not both). The hierarchy ruling path/motion incorporation is revised as in Fig. 3.

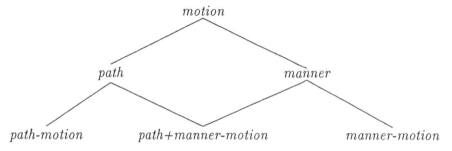

Figure 3.   Hierarchy of lexicalization types.

Variable behaviour verbs, such as *"correre"*, belong to the under-specified class of process/accomplishment (*proc-acc* in Fig. 2, and receive the following lexical entry:

(8) $_{proc\text{-}acc}\left[EV \ _{manner}\left[IND \ plur \right] \right]$

The hierarchy described in Fig. 5, together with constraints such as the ones described in (6) (where the type *path-motion* is replaced by *path*) guarantees that such a lexical entry is specified either as a telic path+manner-motion verb, or as an atelic manner-motion verb. The fragment of type hierarchy responsible for such an inference is repeated in Fig. 4.

In (9) we reproduce the semantic part of three lexical entries exemplifying pure *path-motion verbs*, pure *manner-motion verbs* and the

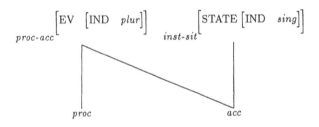

Figure 4. The fragment of type hierarchy responsible of variable behaviour verbs.

underspecified class we just considered (with the underspecified type *manner*).

(9) a. *andare* ≡

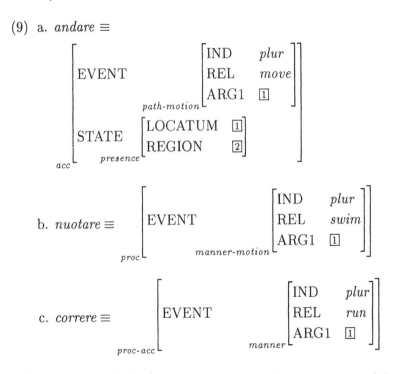

Notice that this approach is superior to the one proposed in Levin and Rappaport Hovav (1995): whereas Levin and Rappaport Hovav (1995) assume that variable behaviour verbs are exceptions, and as such need to be listed in the lexicon, we derive their behaviour from a single (underspecified) lexical entry and an independently needed type inference device.

The present theory, however is still incomplete. Consider for instance the lexical entry of a verb such as *"andare"* in (9a). Such a representation is incomplete in that it does not specify the mapping of the semantic structure into syntax. Moreover, the present theory does not justify why the ARG1 of the *move* relation is coindexed with the LOCATUM role of the spatial relation. In the next two sections both problems will be addressed.

5.2. Mapping the Event Structure into Syntax

Following the standard view, we consider linking theory the compositional mechanism which maps semantic structures onto syntactic realization. This section, in particular, focuses on the mapping of static PPs onto the STATE attribute of the NUCLEUS of the heading verb. We will follow the syntactic tradition (Chomsky, 1981; Grimshaw, 1990; Levin and Rappaport Hovav, 1995) according to which the alleged goal PPs are considered syntactic arguments. However, we refuse the strict HPSG (and GB) assumption that the only semantic contribution of the arguments of a relation is binding the participants' indices. This may be the case of elements which do not introduce any relation, such as NPs, but considering locative PPs as semantically 'inert' with respect to the verbal relation has the undesirable consequence of obscuring the compositional nature of the verbal complex. This view on the composition of locative arguments with the main predicate is defended, among others, by Jackendoff (1990; 1996). Informally, our linking theory is based on the following assumptions (we adopt the valence structuring of Pollard and Sag, 1994, Ch.9):

- The first argument of a relation in EVENT corresponds to the subject (the unique NP in SUBJ).
- The second argument of a relation in EVENT corresponds to the direct object (the first NP in COMPS).[6]
- The relation in STATE, corresponds to the content of the indirect object (the last PP in COMPS).
- Every syntactic argument has a semantic counterpart (i.e., every element in SUBJ or COMPS has either its index or its content structure shared with some value in NUCLEUS).

Contrary to the standard assumption, the semantic import of a subcategorized PP is not an *index*, but a whole relation, which becomes part of the semantics of the predicate through structure sharing. This

---

[6] For the sake of simplicity, we are not assuming here a syntactic representation of unaccusativity. For a more realistic account see Di Tomaso and Dini (in preparation).

explains why, in Romance languages like Italian, the same prepositions head stative modifiers and arguments of dynamic relations: it is not the semantic value of the preposition which changes, but its role, i.e. whether it is a predicate of a whole event or it is a part (STATE) of an event structure.[7]

More formally, linking theory is conceived, along the lines of Davis (1995) and Dini (1995), as a set of types which relates the attribute NUCLEUS of the lexical sign to its valence lists. These types are hierarchically organized as described in Fig. 5.

5.3. *Interactions with Control Theory*

In order to identify the participant which effectively undergoes a change of position in the motion event, an index of the dynamic relation (EVENT) has to be associated with the LOCATUM of the stative relation in STATE. Assuming a standard HPSG architecture, a module able to perform such an index identification is already available, i.e. Control Theory. Consider the following sentences:

(10) a. Leo è andato a comprare il latte
      Leo has gone to buy the milk

   b. Leo ha mandato Lia a comprare il latte
      Leo has sent Lia to buy the milk

The motion verbs in (10) head an infinitival clause, whose unexpressed subject is identified with the matrix subject in (10a) and with the matrix object in (10b). This behavior patterns with the one of control verbs which, in Pollard and Sag (1994), are semantically classified as either *orientation* or *influence*. For this reason, we assume that motion verbs fall within the domain of Control Theory. If this is the case, no additional machinery is needed to perform a correct coindexation in sentences such as the ones in (11).[8]

---

[7] It might be argued that two entries of the same preposition are needed anyway, in order to satisfy the HPSG Content Principle. However, it has been shown in Dini et al. (1995) that a less constrained version of the content principle is desirable in order to reduce the possible sources of ambiguities in the lexicon. Such a version has been adopted also in the Italian TDL grammar.

[8] For spatial PPs to fit the standard HPSG Control Theory we are forced to assume that they have a non empty SUBJ list. This assumption is independently supported by the fact that this PPs can appear in copular constructions.

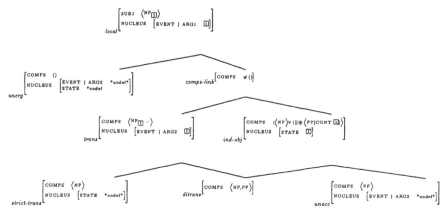

Figure 5. A fragment of a Linking Theory for Italian.

(11) a. Leo è andato a Torino
Leo has gone to Turin

b. Leo ha mandato Lia a Torino
Leo has sent Lia to Turin

The generalization is the following: whenever a static relation enters into the context of an *orientation* verb, such as *"andare"*, we predict that the locatum is coindexed with the EXPERIENCER role (*"Leo"* in (11a)); whenever it enters into the context of an *influence* verb such as *"mandare"*, we predict that the locatum is coindexed with the filler of the INFLUENCED role (*"Lia"* in (11b)). Thus, the fact that (11a) predicates the final position of *"Leo"*, whereas (11b) predicates the final position of *"Lia"* simply follows as a consequence of Control Theory.[9] The central role played by Control Theory in determining the binding of the indices explains why no verb can surface with a dynamic preposition (such as *"per"* and the polysyllabic prepositions such as *"verso"* and *"lungo"*) as an argument. Since motion verbs with an argumental PP fall under the Control Theory, we should expect either the subject or the object to control the unbounded index of such a PP. However, since *"per"* PPs are typed as containing an event filling the role of

---

[9] We predict that no transitive verb can exist, in italian, and, arguably, in any language, such that the goal phrase expresses the position of the subject rather than the object. Note that this is a perfectly logical possibility: there could be some verb like * *"puscerellare"* with the meaning *"I pushed something, and, as an effect of this act, I found myself in a certain place"*. However, as a matter of fact, no such a verb exists in Italian, the reason being that it would overtly violate the principles governing Control Theory.

their first argument (cf. Fig. 1), an index clash would be generated (an attempt to unify *ref-ind* with *ev-ind*), thus resulting in a semantically uninterpretable sentence (cf. Dini and Di Tomaso, 1995). This is the reason for the ungrammaticality of sentences such as the following, under the goal interpretation of the *per*-PP:

(12)   a.   * E' corso per Torino
         He has run to Turin

      b.   * Ha mandato un pacco per l'America
         He has sent a parcel to USA

      c.   * E' andato per l'America
         He has gone to USA

6. CONCLUSION

We have presented an analysis of motion verbs and spatial prepositions which eliminates the need to treat as a case of homonymy the use of the same prepositions in static and dynamic locative expressions. The semantics of the verbal complexes can be compositionally built using only the static sense of prepositions. This result has been obtained by exploiting the interaction of three modules of the grammar: *aktionsart*, linking theory and control theory. As far as motion verbs are concerned, the analysis has proven able to capture the well known influence of locative arguments on *aktionsart*.

ACKNOWLEDGEMENTS

We are grateful for discussions and comments to Pier Marco Bertinetto, Valentina Bianchi, Federica Busa, Ray Jackendoff, Diego Marconi, James Pustejovsky and the anonymous reviewers. A grant from the organization CELI (Centro per l'Elaborazione del Linguaggio e dell'Informazione) has partially supported this work.

REFERENCES

Asher, N. and Sablayrolles P. (1995) A typology and discourse semantics for motion verbs and spatial PPs in French. *Journal of Semantics* 12, 163–209.

Boons, J. (1987) La notion sémantique de déplacement dans une classification syntaxique des verbes locatifs. *Langue Française* 76, 5–40.

Burzio, L. (1987) *Italian Syntax.* Dordrecht: Reidel.

Carpenter, B. (1992) *The Logic of Typed Feature Structures.* Cambridge Tracts in Theoretical Computer Science 32. New York: Cambridge University Press.

Chomsky, N. (1981) *Lectures on Government and Binding.* Dordrecht: Foris.

Davis, A. (1995). *Linking Theory and the Hierarchical Lexicon.* Ph.D. thesis, Stanford University.

Dini, L. (1995) Unaccusative Behaviors. *Quaderni del Laboratorio di Linguistica* 7, 92-122. Scuola Normale Superiore. Also appeared in *Surface based Syntax of Romance Languages,* Reader of the 1996 European Summer School in Logic, Language and Information.

Dini, L. (1998) *Events and their Measures.* Ph.D. thesis, Scuola Normale Superiore.

Dini, L. and Bertinetto P.M. (1995) Punctual verbs and the linguistic ontology of events. *Quaderni del Laboratorio di Linguistica* 7, 123-160. Scuola Normale Superiore.

Dini, L. and Busa F. (1994) Generative operations in a constraint-based grammar. In H.Trost (1994) *KONVENS '94, Verarbeitung Natürlicher Sprache.* Informatik Xpress 6, Germany.

Dini, L. and Di Tomaso V. (1995) Events and individual in Italian dynamic locative expressions. In *Proceedings the 4th Conference on the Cognitive Science of Natural Language Processing.*

Dini, L., Mazzini G., Battista M., Pirrelli V. and Ruimy N. (1995) The italian core grammar. LRE Report 61029, Delivery E-D5-IT, CEC, Luxembourg.

Di Tomaso, V. (in preparation) On the Interaction between Motion Verbs and Spatial Prepositions. Scuola Normale Superiore, Pisa.

Di Tomaso, V. and Dini, L. (in preparation) Yet another explanation of the Unaccusative Hypothesis in Italian. Scuola Normale Superiore, Pisa.

Dowty, D. (1979) *Word Meaning and Montague Grammar: the Semantics of Verbs and Times in Generative Semantics and in Montague's PTQ.* Dordrecht: Reidel

Grimshaw, J. (1990) *Argument Structure.* Cambridge, Mass.: MIT Press.

Herskovits, A. (1986) *Language and Spatial Cognition.* Cambridge, Mass.: Cambridge University Press.

Higginbotham, J. (1995) *Sense and Syntax.* Oxford: Clarendon Press; New York: Oxford University Press; Cambridge, Mass.: Cambridge University Press.

Hobbs, J., Croft W., Davies T., Edwards D. and Kenneth Laws K. (1987) Commonsense metaphisics and lexical semantics. *Computational Linguistics* 13, 241–250.

Jackendoff, R. (1983) *Semantics and Cognition.* Cambridge, Mass.: MIT Press.

Jackendoff, R. (1990) *Semantic structures.* Cambridge, Mass.: MIT Press.

Jackendoff, R. (1996) The Proper treatment of measuring out, telicity, and perhaps even quantification in English. *Natural Language and Linguistic Theory* 14(2),305-354.

Kalita, J. and Lee, J. (1996) An informal semantic analysis of motion verbs based on physical primitives. Accepted for pubblication in *Computational Intelligence.*

Krieger, H.-U. and Schäfer U. (1994a) *TDL*—a type description language for constraint-based grammars. In *Proceedings of the 15th International Conference on Computational Linguistics, COLING-94, Kyoto, Japan.*

Krieger, H.-U. and Schäfer U. (1994b) *TDL*—a type description language for HPSG. part 1: Overview. Research Report RR-94-37, DFKI, Saarbrücken, Germany.

Krifka, M. (1992) Thematic relations as links between nominal reference and temporal constitution. In I. Sag and A. Szabolcsi (1992) *Lexical Matters.* Stanford: CSLI Lecture Notes 24, 29–53.

Lang, E. (1993) A two levels approach to projective prepositions. In C. Wibbelt (1993) *The Semantics of Prepositions: from Mental Models to Natural Language Processing.* Berlin: Mouton de Guyter.

Laur, D. (1991) *Semantique du déplacement et de la localization en francais.* Ph.D. thesis, Université Toulouse le Mirail.

Levin, B. and Rappaport Hovav M. (1995) *Unaccusativity.* Cambridge, Mass.: MIT Press.

Mc Kevitt, P. (1995) *Artificial Intelligence Review, 8, Special Volume on the Integration of Language and Vision Processing.*

Marconi, D. (1997) *Lexical Competence.* Cambridge, Mass.: MIT Press.

Moens, M. and Steedmann M. (1988) Temporal ontology and temporal reference. *Computational Linguistics* 14(2),15–28.

Neumann, G. (1993) Design principles of the DISCO system. In *Proceedings of TWLT 5,* Twente, Netherlands.

Olivier, P. and Gapp, K. (in press) *Representation and Processing of Spatial Expression.* Mahwah, New Jersey: Laurence Erlbaun.

Pollard, C. and Sag, I. (1994) *Head Driven Phrase Structure Grammar.* Chicago and Stanford: University of Chicago Press and CSLI Publications.

Pustejovsky, J. (1995) *The Generative Lexicon.* Cambridge, Mass.: MIT Press.

Pustejovsky, J. and Busa, F. (1995) Unaccusativity and Event Composition. In V. Bianchi, P. M. Bertinetto, J. Higgimbotham and M. Squartini, editors, *Temporal Reference, Aspect and Actionality: Syntactic and Semantic Perspectives.* Torino: Rosemberg & Sellier.

Sablayrolles, P. (1993) A two-level semantics for French expressions of motion. Technical report, DFKI Research Report.

Serianni, L. (1988) *Grammatica Italiana.* Torino: UTET.

Talmy, L. (1983) How language structures space. In H. Pich and L. Acreolo (1983) *Spatial Orientation: Theory, Reasearch and Application.* Plenum Press.

Talmy, L. (1985) Lexicalization patterns: Semantic structures in lexical form. In Shopen T. et al. (1985) *Language typology and syntactic description, vol. 3. Grammatical categories and the lexicon.* New York: Cambridge University Press.

Tenny, C. (1994) *Aspectual Roles and the Syntax-Semantics Interface.* Dordrecht: Kluwer Academic Publishers.

Tenny, C. (1995) How motion verbs are special. *Pragmatics and Cognition 3,* 31–73.

Vendler, Z. (1957) Verbs and Times. In *Linguistics in Philosophy.* Ithaca: Cornell University Press.

Verkuyl, H. (1993) *A Theory of Aspect.* Cambridge: Cambridge University Press.

Zingarelli, N. (1995) *Vocabolario della lingua italiana.* Bologna: Zanichelli.

SABINE REINHARD

A DISAMBIGUATION APPROACH FOR GERMAN COMPOUNDS WITH DEVERBAL HEAD

1. INTRODUCTION

Word formation, in particular compounding, is an extremely productive process in German as well as in many other languages. As a result, vast numbers of lexical entries have to be encoded by hand. This is true not only for monolingual lexica, but also in the context of machine translation, where for each compound a separate transfer rule has to be written. Also, if the application domain is not extremely restricted, natural language processing (NLP) systems will encounter unknown words, which is particularly true for systems with free spoken language input, such as Verbmobil.

This shows that mechanisms are needed which automatically determine the meaning of the compound in order to be able to assign a meaning to the entire sentence or turn. This in turn is necessary, among other things, to establish the correct translation correspondance.

The automatic determination of the semantic relation is a quite difficult task since compounds are highly ambiguous and mostly only become (if at all) unambiguous in context, cf. Downing (1977); Finin (1980) among many others. This chapter, however, deals with a class of compounds which seem to have natural preferred readings: N-N compounds with a deverbal head constituent. If the head constituent is a nominalization it is possible that the relation is determined by the argument structure of the underlying verb. I.e. an argument of the argument structure of the underlying predicate is satisfied by the first constituent. Otherwise, a more or less specifiable modifying relation holds between the two constituents. Compare the examples in (1). In a) and b) an argument position of the underlying verb *"besprechen"* ('to discuss') is satisfied: in a) it is the agent-role, thus the semantic relation between the constituents is unambiguous. The same holds for the theme-role in b), whereas in c) just a temporal modifier relation holds between the constituents.

H. Bunt and R. Muskens (eds.), Computing Meaning, Volume 1, 339–356.
© *1999 Kluwer Academic Publishers. Printed in the Netherlands.*

(1) a. [mitarbeiterbesprechung]   ⟶ [besprechen(agent: mitarbeiter,
         'team meeting'   theme: nil   )]

     b. [projektbesprechung]   ⟶ [besprechen(agent: nil,
         'project discussion/meeting'   theme: projekt   )]

     c. [nachmittagsbesprechung]   ⟶ [besprechen(agent: nil,
         'afternoon meeting'   theme: nil,
                                                     mod: nachmittag)]

Extensive corpus studies have been carried out in order to obtain a basis to implement the automatic disambiguation of the relation holding between the constituents. The aim of the empirical investigation was to find out just which verbs permit this kind of nominalization. Furthermore, it should reveal which arguments of these verb classes can be realized only internally (i.e. morphologically as first constituent), only externally (i.e. syntactically), and which can co-occur (i.e. one argument internally and another externally). The investigation presented here is restricted to German nominalizations on the suffix *"-ung"*. Since these formations are extremely frequent and show all the interesting characteristics of other nominalization forms they seem representative.

The goal is to predict, from the lexical semantic structure of the head constituent and certain restrictions on the non-head constituent, the relation holding between the two constituents. The automatic interpretation leads to an abstract representation of the meaning of this relation. The approach taken here assumes that the way internal and external argument inheritance is realized depends on the semantic class of the base verb. The compositional semantic interpretation is among other things supposed to simplify the translation task.

Since the work has been conducted within the Machine Translation project Verbmobil, the Verbmobil semantic classification will be briefly described in the next section. In section 3, the patterns of internal and external argument inheritance with respect to *"ung"*-nominalizations will be presented. In section 4, the description of the implementation of the compound disambiguation will follow.

2. THE VERBMOBIL SEMANTIC CLASSIFICATION

In Verbmobil, 'aktionsart' (state, activity, accomplishment, achievement; cf. Dowty, 1979) and thematic roles are assigned to verbal predicates and their arguments. For the thematic roles a kind of proto-role approach in the spirit of Dowty (1991) had been adopted: i.e. role assignment is graduable and there are arguments whose role semantic properties are subsumed under two different semantic roles in other approaches. But unlike Dowty, who just assumes Proto-Agent and Proto-Patient, in Verbmobil we added a third role with experiencer properties[1]. Thus, the following three roles exist: *arg1*, *arg2*, and *arg3*, where *arg1* corresponds more or less to an agent or stimulus, *arg2* to an experiencer or goal, and *arg3* to a theme or patient. Furthermore, sortal information, such as *communicat-sit*, *move-sit*, *mental-sit*, etc. is associated with every verb and sortal restrictions on the verbal arguments are encoded.

The information available in Verbmobil can be mapped onto various more theoretically oriented semantic classification schemata. For a semantic classification behind the findings of the investigation presented here cf. Rapp & Reinhard (1997), where a decomposed lexical semantic structure is assumed (as in e.g. Dowty, 1979; Jackendoff, 1990; Levin & Rappaport, 1988), from which the verb's thematic and event structure can be inferred.

3. ARGUMENT INHERITANCE PATTERNS

In this section I will present some empirical findings on argument inheritance with *"-ung"*-nominalizations. For a more detailed description cf. Rapp & Reinhard (1997) where not only patterns for internal and external argument inheritance are described but also the interpretation of the resulting formation (event nominalization, content nominalization, result nominalization) and a comparison with related work on nominalization (e.g. Grimshaw, 1990; Bierwisch, 1989). In Reinhard (to appear), in addition, a formalization in the HPSG-framework can be found.

One issue of the "Frankfurter Rundschau", from which all nouns (simplex and compounds) ending on suffix - *"ung"* had been extracted, served as the main corpus for the investigation. The numbers found – around 2,800 *"ung"*-nominalizations (types, not tokens) of which about 50% (i.e. 1,400) were compounds – show the high productivity of this kind of word formation and underline the motivation of the approach envisaged here. Moreover, the Verbmobil corpora have been studied.

---

[1] In Reinhard (to appear) this role is called 'Proto-Goal', and also the justification for this assumption is given.

Sortal restrictions were assigned to about 530 nouns, about 420 base verbs were classified and annotated with the necessary information outlined in the previous section.

The investigation showed that only certain types of verbs permit a derivation on the suffix *"-ung"*, and that their behaviour with respect to argument inheritance differ considerably. In general, semantically complex predicates are more subject to this kind of derivation than simple predicates, such as states and activities.

So far, seven classes could be determined with a particular internal/external argument inheritance pattern:
- Causative accomplishments
- Non-causative accomplishments
- Non-symmetrical causative 'communication' verbs
- Symmetrical causative 'communication' verbs
- Non-PSYCH 'effect' verbs
- PSYCH 'effect' verbs
- Locative-causative verbs

3.1. *Causative Accomplishments*

Causative accomplishments are characterized in the Verbmobil classification by the following features, which can be used to extract this particular class of verbs:

(2) roles: arg1 (=agent), arg3 (=theme)
    'aktionsart':acc(=accomplishment); (vorbereiten 'to prepare')

In most cases, the **first constituent** of a compound corresponds to the direct object, i.e. the theme (3). cases a modifier such as a temporal (4) is also possible. An interpretation of the first constituent as subject is impossible. A disambiguation (of whether an arg3- or a modifier relation holds) has to be brought about by sortal restrictions imposed on the direct object.

(3) Grundgesetzänderung, Terminverschiebung
    'constitution modification, 'appointment rescheduling'

(4) Zehnuhränderung
    'ten 'o clock modification'

A **postnominal NPgen** with a simplex *"-ung"* formation has to be interpreted as an arg3 direct object (5). If the arg3 direct object is already realized as first constituent of the compound, the postnominal NPgen can be analyzed as subject (6) or modifier:

(5) die Änderung des Grundgesetzes $\longrightarrow$ arg3-reading
'the modification of the constitution'

(6) die Änderung der Bundesregierung $\longrightarrow$ arg3-reading
'the modification of the federal government'

die Grundgesetzänderung der Bundesregierung $\longrightarrow$ arg1-reading
'the constitution modification by the federal government'

A **prenominal NPgen** only allows for proper names, which will get the arg1 subject reading (7) if the arg3-argument has been realized as first constituent or postnominal NPgen, otherwise an arg3-reading (8):

(7) Annas Konferenzvorbereitung $\longrightarrow$ arg1-reading
'Anna's conference preparation'

Kohls Änderung des Gesetzes $\longrightarrow$ arg1-reading
'Kohl's modification of the law'

(8) Kohls Änderung $\longrightarrow$ arg3-reading
'Kohl's modification'

It seems that two hierarchies are responsible for this behaviour: a thematic hierarchy for verbal predicates and a positional hierarchy for nouns (9).

(9) Verb: Agent > Experiencer > Theme

Noun: pren.NPgen > postn.NPgen > 1st const

Apparently, arguments lower in the verbal hierarchy have to be realized with priority. On the other hand, thematic hierarchy and positional hierarchy have to correspond. For the above examples this means that if a theme direct object is realized as first constituent, the agent subject can only be realized as postnominal NPgen (cf. solid lines). If, on the other hand, the theme is inherited as postnominal NPgen, a realization of the agent as first constituent is impossible, since thematic and positional hierarchies will cross (cf. dashed lines).

3.2. Non-Causative Accomplishments

Non-causative accomplishments – syntactically ergative verbs – are mostly the non-causative variants of causative/non-causative alternation pairs. They are characterized in Verbmobil by the following semantic features:

(10) role: arg3 (=theme), 'aktionsart': acc
     (sich beruhigen 'to stabilize', sich entzünden 'to become inflamed')

The arg3-subject can appear as first constituent (11):

(11) Wetterberuhigung, Herzmuskelentzündung
     'wheather stabilization', 'cardiac muscle inflammation'

If not internally realized, the theme subject can appear as **postnominal NPgen** (12) or **prenominal NPgen** (13):

(12) die Beruhigung des Wetters
     'the stabilization of the wheather'

(13) Susis Beruhigung
     'Susy's stabilization'

A modifier can only appear as postnominal NPgen if the subject is already realized internally:

(14) die Wetterberuhigung der letzten Tage
     'the wheather stabilization of the last days'

     ??die Beruhigung der letzten Tage
     'the stabilization of the last days'

3.3. Non-Symmetrical Causative 'Communication' Verbs

Causative attitude (i.e. PSYCH) verbs are devided here into 'communication' verbs (*"erklären"* 'to explain', *"mitteilen"* 'to inform', *"besprechen"* 'to discuss') which either denote a symmetrical or a non-symmetrical situation and causative psychological verbs (*"enttäuschen"* 'to deceive', *"begeistern"* 'to fill with enthusiasm'; cf. section 3.6).

Non-symmetrical communication verbs are characterized by the fact that the agent's activity makes the experiencer reach a certain psychological state. In Verbmobil, they have the following features:

(15) roles: arg1 (=agent), arg2 (=experiencer), arg3 (=theme)
'aktionsart': acc/ach; (mitteilen 'to inform', erklären 'to explain,
to declare')

The theme direct object (16) or a modifier (17) can be realized as **first constituent**. Disambiguation must be brought about by sortal restrictions. Strikingly, as opposed to causative accomplishments (cf. section 3.1), this verb class also allows for a realization of the agent subject (18). This argument inheritance behaviour, however, violates some constraints stipulated in the literature. For example, Selkirk (1982) states "a SUBJ argument of a lexical item may not be satisfied in compound structure", and similarly Lieber (1983) claims "only internal arguments can be linked by the non-head". An explanation for this inheritance behaviour might be seen in the fact that the theme argument denotes a mental content. Perhaps, it therefore does not have to be realized with priority.

(16) Terminmitteilung, Themenerklärung
'appointment information', 'topic explanation'

(17) Anfangsmitteilung, Schlußerklärung
'initial information' , 'final declaration'

(18) Politikermitteilung, Politikererklärung
'politician information', 'politician declaration'

Agent, theme, or modifier can be realized as **postnominal NPgen**. In analogy to the analysis of the first constituent, the disambiguation has to be accomplished by sortal restrictions:

(19) die Erklärung des Politikers/des Themas/des frühen Morgens
'the declaration of the politician/the topic/the early morning'

If the agent is realized as first constituent the theme cannot be realized externally, i.e. only a modifier is possible as postnominal NPgen then:

(20) die Politikererklärung *des Themas/des frühen Morgens
'the politician declaration of the topic/the early morning'

If on the other hand the theme is realized as first constituent, then modifier and subject are possible NPgen realizations:

(21) die Themenerklärung des Politikers/des frühen Morgens
'the topic declaration of the politician/the early morning'

Only a proper name subject can be realized as **prenominal NPgen**:

(22) Schmidts Themenerklärung
      'Schmidt's topic declaration'

The realization of the experiencer indirect object is only possible with
an external *an*-phrase:

(23) die Mitteilung an die Zuhörer
      'the communication to the public'

Thus, as compared to (9), the following behaviour holds for the two
hierarchies:

(24) Verb: Agent > Experiencer > Theme

      Noun: pren.NPgen > postn.NPgen > 1st const

3.4. *Symmetrical Causative 'Communication' Verbs*

Symmetrical causative communication verbs are characterized by the
fact that agent and experiencer correspond to each other. In other
words, in a certain communication situation, two or more agents can
be experiencer. Therefore they can be assigned the following roles:

(25) arg1/arg2, arg1/arg2, arg3

Syntactically, the agents are either realized as subject plus a *mit*-phrase
or both as a (then obligatory) plural subject.

(26) roles: arg1 and arg2 (=agent&experiencer), arg3 (=theme)
      'aktionsart': acc/ach; (absprechen 'to agree', sich einigen 'to agree
      on')

Here again, as with the non-symmetrical variant, the (plural) agent
subject (27) can be realized as **first constituent**. Theme direct object
(28) or a modifier (29) are also possible:

(27) Parteienübereinstimmung, Mitarbeiterbesprechung
      'parties agreement', 'team members meeting/discussion'

(28) Projektbesprechung
'project discussion'

(29) Nachmittagsbesprechung
'afternoon meeting/discussion'

Only plural subject proper names can appear as **prenominal NPgen**
also with internal theme realization:

(30) Peters und Pauls Besprechung
'Peter's and Paul's discussion/meeting'

Peters und Pauls Themenbesprechung
'Peter's and Paul's topic discussion'

3.5. Non-PSYCH 'Effect' Verbs

A specific type of causative verbs emerged which show a particular
behaviour in view of argument inheritance. This class of verbs denotes
an effect of a primary event which has been left implicit. This effect
can be psychological (see section 3.6) or non-psychological in nature
(16a, 16b) and can consist in a change of state or simply a state. They
will be called 'effect' verbs here (cf. Rapp & Reinhard, 1997) and can
be extracted via the following features:

(31)   a. roles: arg1 (=stimulus), arg3 (=theme)
         'aktionsart': acc/ach; (verschmutzen 'to pollute')
       b. roles: arg1 (=stimulus), arg3 (=theme)
         'aktionsart': state; (behindern 'to hinder')

Strikingly, also with these verbs, not only the theme direct object (32)
but also the stimulus subject (33)

(32) Umweltbelastung, Jugendgefährdung, Blutvergiftung
'environment stress', 'youth endangerment', 'blood poisoning'

(33) Dioxinbelastung, Lärmbelastung, Geruchsbelästigung, Alkoholge-
fährdung, Rauchvergiftung
'dioxines stress', 'noise stress', 'odour molestation', 'alcohol endangerment', 'smoke poisoning'

On the other hand, if the theme appears as first constituent the realization of the stimulus on a position higher in the hierarchy is impossible (34), whereas stimulus in first constituent position and external realization of the theme are possible (35):

(34) *die Umweltbelastung des Dioxins
     'the environment stress of the dioxines'

(35) die Dioxinbelastung der Umwelt
     'the dioxines stress of the environment'

As **prenominal NPgen** only the theme can occur.

Thus, with this class, the verbal and noun hierarchies show inverted behaviour as compared to (9):

(36) Verb: Agent/Stimulus > Experiencer > Theme

      Noun: pren.NPgen > postn.NPgen > 1st const

3.6. *PSYCH 'Effect' Verbs*

Psychological 'effect' verbs (in the literature also termed 'causative psychological verbs', cf. e.g. Grimshaw, 1990) as opposed to their non-psychological variants have an experiencer instead of a theme argument:

(37) roles: arg1 (=stimulus), arg2 (=experiencer)
     'aktionsart'=acc/ach/state; (begeistern 'to fill with enthusiasm',
     enttäuschen 'to deceive')

Both, stimulus and experiencer can be realized as **first constituent**:

(38) Kinobegeisterung
     'cinema enthusiasm'

     Zuschauerbegeisterung
     'public enthusiasm'

As with non-psychological effect verbs, only the experiencer can be realized as **postnominal NPgen** (39). The experiencer also can occur in this position if the stimulus argument is internally realized (40), whereas the other way round is impossible:

(39) die Enttäuschung der Zuschauer
'the deception of the public'

*die Enttäuschung des Films
'the deception of the film'

(40) die Kinobegeisterung der Zuschauer
'the cinema enthusiasm of the public'

*die Zuschauerbegeisterung des Kinos
'the public enthusiasm of the cinema'

As **prenominal NPgen** only the experiencer can occur.
Here the hierarchy behaviour in (41) holds:

(41) Verb: Agent/Stimulus > Experiencer > Theme

      Noun: pren.NPgen > postn.NPgen > 1st const

3.7. *Locative-Causative Verbs*

Syntactically, with this final verb class an agent is realized as subject,
a location as direct object, and an instrument theme as *mit*-phrase:

(42) Man isolierte das Kabel mit Gummi.
'They insulated the cable with rubber'

I regard a location argument as subsumed by the Proto-Goal arg2 and
the instrument phrase as an adjunct (if seen as subcategorized it would
receive an arg3). Hence the following semantic features hold:

(43) roles: arg1 (=agent), arg2 (=location)
'aktionsart': acc; (isolieren 'to insulate')

   The location argument (44) or the instrument (45) can appear as
first constituent of a compound, an arg1 subject is impossible. Disambiguation has to be brought about by sortal restrictions.

(44) die Kabelisolierung
'the cable insulation'

(45) die Gummiisolierung
     'the rubber insulation'

Only the arg2 location argument can be realized as **postnominal NPgen** (46), the instrument is impossible (47):

(46) die Isolierung des Kabels
     'the insulation of the cable'

(47) *die Isolierung des Gummis
     'the insulation of the rubber'

The agent subject can be realized as postnominal NPgen also, but in this case the location direct object argument has to be already satisfied (48). Otherwise, it will get an arg2 reading (49):

(48) die Kabelisolierung des Elektrikers $\longrightarrow$ arg1 reading
     'the cable insulation of the electrician'

(49) die Isolierung des Elektrikers $\longrightarrow$ arg2 reading
     'the insulation of the electrician'

     die Gummiisolierung des Elektrikers
     'the rubber insulation of the electrician'

Only a proper name can be realized as **prenominal NPgen**. It will be interpreted as subject only if the arg2 direct object is already realized (50). Otherwise it will get an arg2 reading (51):

(50) Peters Isolierung des Kabels $\longrightarrow$ arg1 reading
     'Peter's insulation of the cable'

     Peters Kabelisolierung
     'Peter's cable insulation'

(51) Peters Isolierung $\longrightarrow$ arg2 reading
     'Peter's insulation'

     Peters Gummiisolierung
     'Peter's rubber insulation'

For this class the following schema holds:

(52) Verb: Agent > Experiencer/Location > Theme

   Noun: pren.NPgen > postn.NPgen > 1st const

The main findings of the previous subsections are summarized in Table 1. Arguments in brackets may only occur in the positional sequences indicated, arguments without brackets can be realized on their own, without other arguments, at the positions indicated.

Although further investigations still have to be made – in particular reflexive or medial verbs seem to differ somewhat in their behaviour – and sortal restrictions on some arguments might be too loose to determine a unique interpretation, some generalizations emerged which can be used, at least by default, for an interpretation. Also, some interpretations can be excluded once and for all: e.g. a class1 compound can never get an arg1-relation reading.

4. IMPLEMENTATION

The constraints on the formation of deverbal noun compounds as outlined in the previous section, together with selectional restrictions on the verbal arguments, are used in an implementation to interpret the semantics of the compound. The necessary information is directly accessible in the Verbmobil system:

- thematic roles
- sortal information of the verbal predicate
- sortal restrictions on the verbs arguments
- sortal classification of nouns
- 'aktionsart'

Except for 'aktionsart', which is assigned in the tempus module, all other information is encoded in the Verbmobil lexical semantic database. Some example entries are repeated in (53) in a slightly abbreviated version.

(53) besprechen(L,I),arg1(L,I,I1),arg3(L,I,I2) I/communicat-sit
       I1/person I2/anything
      gehen(L,I),arg3(L,I,I1) I/move-sit I1/object
      meinen(L,I),arg2(L,I,I1),arg3(L,I,I2) I/mental-sit
       I1/person I2/anything
      mitarbeiter(L,I) I/human
      nachmittag(L,I) I/time

Table I.

class	argum. structure	'akt.art'/v.sort	prenom. NPgen	1st comp. const.	postnom. NPgen
1	a1,a3	acc	a3	a3	a3
			*a1	*a1	*a1
				*(a1	a3)
				(a3	a1)
			(a1	a3)	
			(a1		a3)
2	a3	acc	a3	a3	a3
3	a1,a2,a3	acc/ach communicat.	*a3	a3	a3
			a1	a1	a1
			*a2	*a2	*a2
				*(a1	a3)
				(a3	a1)
			(a1	a3)	
			(a1		a3)
4	a1/a2,a1/a2,a3	acc/ach communicat.	a1&a2	a1/a2	a1/a2
			*a3	a3	a3
				*(a1/a2	a3)
				(a3	a1/a2)
			(a1/a2	a3)	
			(a1/a2		a3)
5	a1,a3	acc/ach/ state	a3	a3	a3
			*a1	a1	*a1
				*(a3	a1)
				(a1	a3)
6	a1,a2	acc/ach/ state	a2	a2	a2
			*a1	a1	*a1
				(a1	a2)
				*(a2	a1)
7	a1,a2	acc (+ Instr)	*a2	a2	a2
			*a1	*a1	*a1
				(a2	a1)
			(a1	a2)	
			(a1		a2)

In Verbmobil, an event-based semantics with a neo-Davidsonian representation of semantic argument relations is used. All semantic entities are labeled (L being the label and I the event or instance variable). Each verbal entry consists of the predicate, it's argument(s), the sortal information of the verb, and the sortal restrictions on the first, second etc. argument. The noun entry is self-explanatory.

The implementation consists of two steps:

a. the decomposition of the compound into its constituents
b. the determination of the semantic relation holding between the constituents.

Step a) is necessary since there is no morphological component in Verbmobil. Morphologically complex formations are treated as unanalyzed units. Thus, the compound has to be broken up into its deverbal head and its modifying constituent (54)[2]:

(54) [mitarbeiterbesprechung(L,I))] —→
     [(besprechen(L,I),nom(L,I)),mitarbeiter(L1,I1)].

The actual disambiguation is performed by step b). (55) shows the pseudo-code for a part of the disambiguation algorithm for class 5 verbs (symmetrical communication verbs). If as in (54) the first constituent is the realization of the agent (arg1) argument of the underlying verb, the relation holding between head and non-head constituent will be called *arg1-relation*. If, on the other hand, a theme (arg3) argument is realized, the meaning will be represented as *arg3-relation*, for a modifier relation *temp-mod-relation*, *geo-mod-relation*, or *unspec-relation* are available.

(55) % class 5 (symmetrical causative communication verbs)
     % after decomposition of compound into head and non-head:

      a. check whether head has the argument structure
         'a1/a2,a3'
      b. check whether head is of sort 'communicat-sit'
      c. is sort of non-head subsumed by sort of agent argument
         (i.e. arg1) of head?
         if yes —→ arg1-relation
         if not continue with step d)
      d. is sort of non-head subsumed by sort of theme argument
         (i.e. arg3) of head?
         if yes —→ arg3-relation
         if not continue with step e)
      e. ...

The output for the examples in the introduction section is given in (56):

---

[2] A verbal predicate like besprechen(L,I) plus nom(L,I) is the convention for representing nominalizations.

(56) [mitarbeiterbesprechung(1,h)] →
     [besprechen(1,h),nom(1,h),mitarbeiter(110,h1),arg1(1,h,h1)]
     [projektbesprechung(1,h)] →
     [besprechen(1,h),nom(1,h),projekt(110,h1),arg3(1,h,h1)]
     [nachmittagssbesprechung(1,h)] →
     [besprechen(1,h),nom(1,h),nachmittag(110,h1), temp-mod(1,h,h1
     [besprechen(1,h),nom(1,h),nachmittag(110,h1),arg3(1,h,h1)]

For the third example in (56) there are two solutions. This is due to
the assumption that events of this sort are located in time and space,
i.e. take place at a certain time and at a certain place. Therefore, if
a noun specified as being of sort 'temporal' appears as a non-head
constituent, the relation between the two constituents will receive a
default interpretation as temp-mod-relation. Since *"Nachmittag"* also
can be interpeted as theme argument the second reading will result.

The output of step (b) is input to the Transfer module, where a
compositional translation of the compound is now possible without
stating any additional translation equivalences to the ones for the simplex nouns and verbs. The abstract semantic relation itself which has
been determined by step b) to be an arg1-relation, arg3-relation, temp-
mod-relation, and so on holding between the constituents will remain
implicit on the surface form (like in the German counterpart) or be
explicitly lexicalized depending on the language and situation. E.g. in
English, the arg1-relation determined for *"Mitarbeiterbesprechung"* in
(56) may be translated as the preposition *"of"*, as in *"meeting of the
team"*, or it may be left implicit, as in *"team meeting"*. By contrast, in
other languages such as French the same arg1-relation must be made
explicit on the surface by the preposition *"de"*, as in *"réunion du
personnel"*.

For the time being, only the interpretation of the internal inheritance
constraints has been implemented, i.e. the tests on possible external
NPgen constraints have been left out. The implemented algorithm has
been successfully tested on a small number of compounds so far, but
will have to be extended and applied to a larger test set.

5. CONCLUSIONS

The empirical investigation revealed a number of generalizations on
the argument inheritance behaviour of a subset of German deverbal
nouns. These can be used, at least by default, for an interpretation.

Also, some interpretations can be excluded once and for all. Further-more, on the theoretical side, the findings showed a violation of some stipulations on compound argument inheritance which were made in previous literature. The compositional approach described here, with the choice of an abstract semantic relation holding between the constituents, seems to be useful for several NLP applications. In a Machine Translation con-text, it allows on the one hand a reduction in the number of transfer rules, and on the other hand a modularity of the contrastive description. This also simplifies the extendability with respect to other languages.

ACKNOWLEDGEMENTS

This work was funded by the German Federal Ministry of Education, Science, Research, and Technology (BMBF) in the framework of the Verbmobil project under grant 01 IV 101 W9. I would also like to thank the anonymous reviewer for useful comments on an earlier version of this chapter.

REFERENCES

Bierwisch, M. (1989)   *Event Nominalizations: Proposals and Problems.* Linguistische Studien, Reihe A 194, 1–73.

Downing, P. (1977) On the Creation and Use of English Compound Nouns. In: *Language* 53(4), 810–84.

Dowty, D. (1979) *Word Meaning and Montague Grammar.* Dordrecht: Reidel.

Dowty, D. (1991)   Thematic Proto-Roles and Argument Selection.   In: *Language* 67, 547–619.

Finin, T. W. (1980) The Semantic Interpretation of Nominal Compounds. In: *Proceedings of the First Conference on AI,* 1980.

Grimshaw, J. (1990) *Argument Structure.* Cambridge, Mass.: MIT Press.

Jackendoff, R. (1990) *Semantic Structures.* Cambridge, Mass.: MIT Press.

Levin, B. & M. Rappaport (1988) What to Do with θ-Roles. In: Wilkins, W. (ed.): *Syntax and Semantics 21: Thematic Relations.* New York: Academic Press.

Lieber, R. (1983) Argument Linking and Compounds in English. In: *Linguistic Inquiry* 14 (2), p. 251–285.

Rapp, I. & S. Reinhard (1997) *ung*-Nominalisierungen: Interpretation, Bil-dungsrestriktionen und Argumentvererbung – Desambiguierung deverbaler Komposita. Verbmobil-Report 192, Universität Tübingen.

Reinhard, S. (to appear) *Deverbale Komposita an der Morphologie-Semantik-Schnittstelle: ein HPSG-Ansatz.* Doctoral dissertation, Universität Tübingen.

Selkirk, E. O. (1982) *The Syntax of Words.* Cambridge, Mass.: MIT Press.

INDEX

Studies in Linguistics and Philosophy

H. Hiż (ed.): *Questions*. 1978   ISBN 90-277-0813-4; Pb: 90-277-1035-X

W. S. Cooper: *Foundations of Logico-Linguistics*. A Unified Theory of Information, Language, and Logic. 1978   ISBN 90-277-0864-9; Pb: 90-277-0876-2

A. Margalit (ed.): *Meaning and Use*. 1979   ISBN 90-277-0888-6

F. Guenthner and S.J. Schmidt (eds.): *Formal Semantics and Pragmatics for Natural Languages*. 1979   ISBN 90-277-0778-2; Pb: 90-277-0930-0

E. Saarinen (ed.): *Game-Theoretical Semantics*. Essays on Semantics by Hintikka, Carlson, Peacocke, Rantala, and Saarinen. 1979   ISBN 90-277-0918-1

F.J. Pelletier (ed.): *Mass Terms: Some Philosophical Problems*. 1979

     ISBN 90-277-0931-9

D. R. Dowty: *Word Meaning and Montague Grammar*. The Semantics of Verbs and Times in Generative Semantics and in Montague's PTQ. 1979 ISBN 90-277-1008-2; Pb: 90-277-1009-0

A. F. Freed: *The Semantics of English Aspectual Complementation*. 1979

     ISBN 90-277-1010-4; Pb: 90-277-1011-2

J. McCloskey: *Transformational Syntax and Model Theoretic Semantics*. A Case Study in Modern Irish. 1979   ISBN 90-277-1025-2; Pb: 90-277-1026-0

J. R. Searle, F. Kiefer and M. Bierwisch (eds.): *Speech Act Theory and Pragmatics*. 1980

     ISBN 90-277-1043-0; Pb: 90-277-1045-7

D. R. Dowty, R. E. Wall and S. Peters: *Introduction to Montague Semantics*. 1981; 5th printing 1987   ISBN 90-277-1141-0; Pb: 90-277-1142-9

F. Heny (ed.): *Ambiguities in Intensional Contexts*. 1981

     ISBN 90-277-1167-4; Pb: 90-277-1168-2

W. Klein and W. Levelt (eds.): *Crossing the Boundaries in Linguistics*. Studies Presented to Manfred Bierwisch. 1981   ISBN 90-277-1259-X

Z. S. Harris: *Papers on Syntax*. Edited by H. Hiż. 1981

     ISBN 90-277-1266-0; Pb: 90-277-1267-0

P. Jacobson and G. K. Pullum (eds.): *The Nature of Syntactic Representation*. 1982

     ISBN 90-277-1289-1; Pb: 90-277-1290-5

S. Peters and E. Saarinen (eds.): *Processes, Beliefs, and Questions*. Essays on Formal Semantics of Natural Language and Natural Language Processing. 1982   ISBN 90-277-1314-6

L. Carlson: *Dialogue Games*. An Approach to Discourse Analysis. 1983; 2nd printing 1985

     ISBN 90-277-1455-X; Pb: 90-277-1951-9

L. Vaina and J. Hintikka (eds.): *Cognitive Constraints on Communication*. Representation and Processes. 1984; 2nd printing 1985   ISBN 90-277-1456-8; Pb: 90-277-1949-7

F. Heny and B. Richards (eds.): *Linguistic Categories: Auxiliaries and Related Puzzles*. Volume I: Categories. 1983   ISBN 90-277-1478-9

F. Heny and B. Richards (eds.): *Linguistic Categories: Auxiliaries and Related Puzzles*. Volume II: The Scope, Order, and Distribution of English Auxiliary Verbs. 1983 ISBN 90-277-1479-7

R. Cooper: *Quantification and Syntactic Theory*. 1983   ISBN 90-277-1484-3

J. Hintikka (in collaboration with J. Kulas): *The Game of Language*. Studies in Game-Theoretical Semantics and Its Applications. 1983; 2nd printing 1985

     ISBN 90-277-1687-0; Pb: 90-277-1950-0

E. L. Keenan and L. M. Faltz: *Boolean Semantics for Natural Language*. 1985

     ISBN 90-277-1768-0; Pb: 90-277-1842-3

V. Raskin: *Semantic Mechanisms of Humor*. 1985   ISBN 90-277-1821-0; Pb: 90-277-1891-1

…nes 1–26 formerly published under the Series Title: Synthese Language Library.

Studies in Linguistics and Philosophy

Studies in Linguistics and Philosophy

Further information about our publications on *Linguistics* is available on request.

Kluwer Academic Publishers – Dordrecht / Boston / London